INTRODUCTION TO COUNSELLING SURVIVORS OF INTERPERSONAL TRAUMA

by the same author

Counselling Survivors of Domestic Abuse
ISBN 978 1 84310 606 7

Counselling Adult Survivors of Child Sexual Abuse
3rd edition
ISBN 978 1 84310 335 6

The Seduction of Children
Empowering Parents and Teachers to Protect Children from Child Sexual Abuse
ISBN 978 1 84310 248 9

of related interest

Supporting Women after Domestic Violence
Loss, Trauma and Recovery
Hilary Abrahams
ISBN 978 1 84310 431 5

Understanding Adult Survivors of Domestic Violence in Childhood
Still Forgotten, Still Hurting
Gill Hague with Ann Harvey and Kathy Willis
ISBN 978 1 84905 096 8

Rebuilding Lives after Domestic Violence
Understanding Long-Term Outcomes
Hilary Abrahams
ISBN: 978 1 84310 961 7

Picking up the Pieces After Domestic Violence
A Practical Resource for Supporting Parenting Skills
Kate Iwi and Chris Newman
ISBN 978 1 84905 021 0

Working with Adult Abuse
A Training Manual for People Working With Vulnerable Adults
Jacki Pritchard
ISBN 978 1 84310 509 1

Disabled Women and Domestic Violence
Responding to the Experiences of Survivors
Ravi K. Thiara, Gill Hague, Ruth Bashall, Brenda Ellis and Audrey Mullender
Foreword by Nicola Harwin
ISBN 978 1 84905 008 1

INTRODUCTION TO

COUNSELLING SURVIVORS OF INTERPERSONAL TRAUMA

CHRISTIANE SANDERSON

Jessica Kingsley *Publishers*
London and Philadelphia

First published in 2010
by Jessica Kingsley Publishers
116 Pentonville Road
London N1 9JB, UK
and
400 Market Street, Suite 400
Philadelphia, PA 19106, US

www.jkp.com

Printed digitally since 2012

Library of Congress Cataloging in Publication Data

Sanderson, Christiane.
Introduction to counselling survivors of interpersonal trauma / Christiane Sanderson.
p. cm.
Includes bibliographical references and index.
ISBN 978-1-84310-962-4 (alk. paper)
1. Psychic trauma--Treatment. 2. Sexual abuse victims. 3. Victims of violent crimes. 4. Interpersonal relations--Psychological aspects. 5. Terror. 6. Post-traumatic stress disorder. I. Title.
RC552.T7S26 2010
616.85'210651--dc22

2009020881

British Library Cataloguing in Publication Data

A CIP catalogue record for this book is available from the British Library

ISBN 978 1 84310 962 4

MIX
Paper from responsible sources
FSC® C013604
FSC www.fsc.org

For James and Max and
In Memory of Didi Daftari 1962–2009

"Therapy is not about relieving suffering, it's about repairing one's relationship to reality" (Anonymous, 1994)

ACKNOWLEDGMENTS

There are many people that I wish to thank, most importantly all those survivors who have shared their stories and lives with me over many years. Their resilience and courage is a true inspiration. I would also like to thank Paul Glyn for his enduring support. There have been many colleagues and friends who have supported me throughout this writing process and a special thanks goes to Mary Trevillion and Paul Gilbert from Family Matters UK, Kylee Trevillion, Debbie Dallnock and Patricia Hynes at the NSPCC, Linda Dominguez, Lucy Kralj from the Helen Bamber Foundation, Andrew Smith, Mark Donnaruma, Didi Daftari, and Kathy Warriner. As always I would like to thank Jessica Kingsley for her patience and faith in me, along with all the staff at Jessica Kingsley Publishers especially Lisa Clark and Louise Massara for her expert direction. Finally this book would not have been written without the presence of Michael, James and Max – I thank you for your patience, support and love of life.

CONTENTS

Part III Professional Issues

List of Figures, Tables and Boxes

INTRODUCTION

In the last decade there has been a resurgence of interest in the impact of trauma on psychobiological functioning. To some extent this has been in response to providing support to those who have experienced trauma in the wake of acts of terrorism, such as 9/11 and the 7/7 bombings in London, mass genocide, war and natural disasters such as the Asian tsunami and earthquakes. This has stimulated vigorous research into the impact of trauma and the development of diagnostic and clinical techniques, along with specific protocols, to minimise the risk of developing long-term traumatic stress reactions.

Alongside this, increased awareness and reporting of child abuse, child sexual abuse, rape, domestic abuse and elderly abuse has prompted researchers and clinicians to investigate the impact of interpersonal trauma, especially multiple and repeated trauma committed by people known to the victim. Inherent to such interpersonal trauma is the repeated betrayal of trust by someone on whom the victim is dependent, and which they cannot escape. Such protracted interpersonal trauma can have lasting and pervasive effects which differ significantly from single event trauma.

Repeated acts of violence, abuse and humiliation within a relationship in which there is a power imbalance and in which the victim is, or has become, dependent on the perpetrator puts the individual at risk of developing a range of pervasive symptoms that colour their relationship to self, others and the world. A potent feature of interpersonal abuse is its paradoxical nature in which abuse masquerades as protection or affection. The overwhelming nature of interpersonal trauma in which there is no escape and which is suffused with contradiction, activates primitive survival strategies and psychobiological defences such as dissociation, alterations in perception and withdrawal. Under threat of physical and psychological annihilation, the individual has to disavow aspects of the self, basic human needs and any experience of vulnerability. In essence abusers dehumanise their victims through their shameless brutality. In turn the victim has no choice but to adapt to this by disallowing any human responses for fear of further abuse and trying to reconcile "Knowing what you are not supposed to know and feeling what you are not supposed to feel" (Bowlby, 1988).

The use of the term "interpersonal trauma" in this volume locates such trauma within attachment relationships and incorporates the central tenets of complex trauma of chronic, multiple and repeated traumatic events committed by someone who is in a position of trust, or to whom the individual is attached, or upon whom the individual is dependent. This allows for a deeper understanding of child abuse, child sexual abuse, rape within intimate relationships, domestic abuse, elderly abuse and abuse by professionals.

When abuse masquerades as affection, internal and external reality is compromised, and confusion reigns. In addition, the secrecy accompanying much interpersonal abuse prevents validation of the experience, rendering it inchoate and ineffable. It becomes an experience that cannot be named, or legitimised, cast into an abyss of silence. In the absence of words and sharing of the experience it becomes impossible to generate meaning, or make sense of the trauma, so that it becomes ossified as a nub of despair in which self, others and the world cannot be trusted. Thus, all relationships are seen as dangerous, suffused with terror, anxiety and anticipated retraumatisation, making it hard to trust and connect to others, including professionals.

The lack of legitimacy and pervasive fear of others makes it extremely difficult for survivors of interpersonal trauma to seek professional help for their abuse experiences. To risk connection only to have their trust betrayed again becomes a major concern in any professional or therapeutic encounter, rendering many survivors highly suspicious, hostile and resistant to any therapeutic engagement.

As interpersonal trauma within attachment relationships thrives on distortion of perception, falsification of reality, the betrayal of trust, disavowal of needs, and lack of relational authenticity, it is imperative that such dynamics are addressed and minimised in the therapeutic setting. What is critical is a genuine, sensitively attuned relationship which is predicated on honesty, authenticity and in relational warmth in which the survivor can become human again. Clinicians need to honour survivors of interpersonal trauma who despite repeated betrayals risk connection by engaging in a therapeutic relationship. This must be seen as a direct testament to hope that the essence of the self has not been annihilated and seeks relational connection.

In response to clinical evidence that prolonged and repeated exposure to violence and abuse in close relationships gives rise to complex post-traumatic stress (PTS) symptoms, counsellors will need to direct specific therapeutic attention and focus to such trauma. To undo the pervasive effects of interpersonal trauma, practitioners need to create a safe therapeutic environment in which to explore the abuse experiences without further traumatising the survivor. The secure base of the therapeutic relationships will enable the survivor to rebuild trust in self and others, and allow for reconnection to the disavowed aspects of the self.

The primary goal when counselling survivors of interpersonal trauma is not to hide behind protocols and prescriptive techniques to reduce the impact of trauma, but for clinicians to "know" their clients not just "understand" them (Bromberg, 1994) and create an authentic human relationship to undo the dehumanisation inherent in interpersonal abuse. This needs to be accompanied by rigorous assessment, establishing internal and external safety, integrating traumatic experiences, and grieving the numerous losses associated with interpersonal trauma. To accomplish this, practitioners need to contextualise the psychobiological effects and symptoms associated with interpersonal trauma as normal responses to trauma, and validate existing survival strategies and internal resources that have enabled the client to survive so far. These need to be honed and developed alongside a wider behavioural repertoire that the survivor can implement to restore the authentic self and self-agency.

It is only in the "human to human" relationship with the clinician that intersubjectivity can be restored and the survivor can relinquish the debasement of interpersonal abuse and permit deeply buried human experiences of joy, laughter, humour, aliveness, and vitality to blossom and flourish.

Interpersonal trauma impacts across myriad dimensions and clinicians must ensure that they have knowledge and understanding of the range of sociopsychobiological sequelae. To this effect, professionals working with survivors of interpersonal trauma will need to be mindful of the sociopolitical, cultural and economic factors that underpin and support interpersonal abuse. Interpersonal abuse is reflected not just in the micro-system of personal relationships but also in the prevailing sociopolitical macro-system especially in relation to falsification of perception, collusive secrecy and not wishing to speak the unspeakable. For this reason, socially constructed meaning around gender, race, power and control, domination and submission, and the hierarchical structure of families all need to be understood within the context of interpersonal abuse. This is particularly salient when working with survivors from marginalised or ethnic minority groups whose access to external resources may be more limited.

USE OF LANGUAGE

To legitimise the experience of interpersonal trauma, the terms "abuse", "violence" and "assault" will be used to include not just the use of physical force and assault but also the myriad forms of psychological, emotional, financial, or sexual coercion designed to entrap individuals and keep them in thrall to the abuser.

Counsellors may find the distinction between "victimisation" and "traumatisation" helpful when working with survivors of abuse as it enables survivors to acknowledge that while they were victims during the abuse, the pervasive effects have led to traumatisation rather than victimisation. This circumvents the pejorative effects of being labelled or identified as victims and its associated connotations. Counsellors also need to acknowledge that while the experience of interpersonal abuse is one of victimisation, survivors are rarely passive victims. Invariably they are active survivors who have developed strategies to manage the abuse. To emphasise these active responses, and to dispel the negative connotation associated with the term "victim", the term "survivor" or "victim/survivor" will be used.

Given that both genders experience interpersonal abuse, both the "she" and "he" pronoun will be used interchangeably throughout the book, unless specified as in case vignettes. The terms "black" and "ethnic minority" will be used to denote African, Caribbean and Asian individuals, unless specified. While the author acknowledges the differences and similarities between counsellor and therapist, these terms will be used synonymously, alongside the terms "clinician" and "practitioner".

USE OF CASE VIGNETTES

Real life clinical examples are used throughout the book. Clients kindly granted permission to use their material in the hope that this may be of help to others. However in order to ensure anonymity and maintain confidentiality, specific identifying features have been disguised and names have been changed. In some cases composite vignettes that encapsulate ubiquitous themes are used for illustration.

STRUCTURE OF THE BOOK

The book is divided into three parts. Part I aims to provide a solid understanding of the nature, dynamics, impact, and long-term effects of interpersonal trauma so that counsellors not only "understand" survivors of interpersonal trauma but come to "know" them (Bromberg, 1994). It also explores how to work with survivors of interpersonal trauma in the most effective way by emphasising the need for safety and a secure base in which to develop the therapeutic relationship. Part II consists of a range of interpersonal abuse experiences, which highlight unique features of each type of abuse, including prevalence data, nature and specific therapeutic considerations and challenges. To enable clinicians to acquire further knowledge, each of these chapters will be appended with a case vignette and a list of suggested reading. Part III considers the role of the professional working with survivors of interpersonal trauma and the impact such work can have on practitioners, and the importance of looking after oneself. Also included in this section is a list of resources that can be accessed by both counsellors and survivors. The book is designed as an adjunct to the counsellor's already existing therapeutic model, practice and techniques, and is organised in such a way that clinicians can "dip into" it to refresh or reacquaint themselves with specific features of interpersonal trauma, or types of abuse that they are unfamiliar with. Real life case examples will be used to illuminate the nature of interpersonal trauma and illustrate how to work with survivors of such trauma.

Chapter 1 aims to define interpersonal trauma, and investigate how it relates and differs from single event trauma. In Chapter 2, the nature and dynamics of interpersonal trauma is explored by examining the coercion, entrapment and control used by abusers to ensnare their victims, and hold them in thrall. Chapter 3 assesses the impact and long-term effects of interpersonal trauma on psychobiological functioning such as dissociation and hypervigilance as well as self-structures, and factors that render victims vulnerable to self-destructive behaviours including retraumatisation.

Chapter 4 looks at how to create a secure base and outlines the fundamental principles of safe trauma therapy with survivors of interpersonal trauma, in particular the importance of assessment, establishing safety, and creating a secure therapeutic base from which to explore and integrate the effects of interpersonal trauma. To counteract the annihilation and dehumanisation inherent in interpersonal trauma it is critical that the survivor is engaged in a human relationship in which to reconnect to dissociated parts of the self, develop trust and begin to connect to self and others. Chapter 5 examines common therapeutic themes and how to work with these most effectively

Chapter 6 addresses the particular nature of child abuse including child physical abuse, emotional abuse and neglect and how interpersonal abuse in the early years can result in pervasive neurobiological effects, and re-sculpt the brain. Child sexual abuse will be examined in Chapter 7 with particular emphasis on shame as a result of compromised body integrity, and concomitant distortion of perception.

With less than a 6% conviction rate for rape currently existing in the UK, Chapter 8 will look at rape and examine some of the factors that contribute to low disclosure rates and how rape may be hidden for many years. This is often related to being unable to legitimise the experience, and thus not able to name it, and fears of stigmatisation and retraumatisation through legal process and court procedures. While rape is often not a presenting problem, it can emerge during the course of the therapeutic process. In Chapter 9, the nature of sexual exploitation will be explored, especially through child and adult prostitution, and human trafficking into sexual slavery. The chapter will consider how children and adults are recruited, coerced and entrapped into sexual slavery and transported across borders, as well as the internal trafficking of children. The impact of cultural dislocation, fears of deportation and stigmatisation are considered, as exacerbating factors in traumatisation as ties with families and communities have to be severed so as not to bring dishonour on the family.

Chapter 10 will look at the complex nature of domestic abuse and the dynamics of traumatic bonding as an obstacle to leaving, as well as the increased risks faced in attempting to leave. The importance of safety planning and the role of support networks will be examined, along with the painstaking rebuilding of trust, autonomy and self-agency. The chapter will also investigate so-called "honour killings" and the pervasive intrusion and fears associated with stalking. In Chapter 11 the range of abuses, including physical, emotional, sexual, financial and neglect, committed against the elderly by family members or carers, will be explored, alongside difficulties around disclosure. Chapter 12 looks at institutional abuse in children's homes and care homes, and examines the multiple abuses that masquerade as care. The difficulties of breaking the mass collusion of silence and secrecy, stigmatisation, and not being believed, are considered and how these render survivors voiceless for decades. In Chapter 13 the betrayal of trust and abuse by professionals is considered, in particular by therapists. Psychological, financial and sexual abuse by health professionals is investigated, and the difficulties survivors of such abuse face when seeking therapeutic help and the myriad fears that may prevent engagement in any professional relationship. Counsellor reactions to disclosures of sexual abuse by therapists are also examined, especially disbelief and eroticisation.

In the last section, Chapter 14 looks at professional challenges and the impact of counselling survivors of interpersonal trauma, especially the need for thorough knowledge of the nature and impact of interpersonal trauma, awareness of own abuse or traumatic experiences, and how this can manifest when working with survivors. Issues around gender, sexual orientation and cultural diversity will also be explored along with ability to tolerate uncertainty. Finally, exposure and close proximity to the destructive nature of trauma can put huge stress on practitioners, giving rise to terror and revulsion, which can lead to a need to shut down and disengage. To prevent secondary traumatic stress and remain engaged it is imperative that clinicians prioritise self-care through regular supervision, balancing trauma work, and remaining connected to family, friends and life-sustaining activities.

Working with survivors of interpersonal trauma who despite repeated betrayals still risk connection is transformative. While working with trauma can be emotionally demanding and immensely distressing, it is often also the most rewarding work. It can enhance therapeutic skills and make for a more sentient practitioner who not only understands but comes to know their clients. Being in the presence of survivors' resilience and hope that has not been extinguished despite abuse, is testament to post-traumatic growth, and allows both survivor and clinician to access a deeper appreciation of what it is to be human and to be alive.

PART I

THE NATURE OF INTERPERSONAL TRAUMA AND CLINICAL PRACTICE

CHAPTER 1

WHAT IS INTERPERSONAL TRAUMA?

The term "trauma" conjures up different meanings and understanding not just between health professionals but also among those who have experienced trauma. As many survivors of interpersonal abuse do not conceptualise their experiences as trauma, they are often not able to legitimise their experience, or name it as trauma, and thus are prevented from seeking appropriate professional help. In order to work with survivors who present with a history of interpersonal abuse, counsellors need to be clear about what constitutes interpersonal trauma and how this knowledge can be used effectively to understand the range of trauma-related symptoms presented by clients.

This chapter looks at the essential components of trauma and how different types of traumatic experience have been conceptualised, in particular the differences between single event trauma and multiple and repeated trauma. Its main focus is on what constitutes interpersonal trauma experienced within the context of a relationship, or perpetrated by someone known to the survivor. It is hoped that by understanding what is meant by interpersonal trauma counsellors will be able to locate survivors' experiences and concomitant symptoms within a trauma framework.

COMPONENTS OF TRAUMA

Commonly trauma is either understood in very narrow terms such as major natural or manmade disasters, or generalised to mean any form of "stressful experience" (Sanderson, 2006). Dictionaries often define trauma as "distress" and "disturbance", whereas medical definitions emphathise "injury produced violently". Psychiatric conceptualisations refer to psycho injury, especially that caused by emotional shock, for which the memory may be repressed or persistent, and that has lasting psychic effect.

The American Psychiatric Association (APA)'s *Diagnostic and Statistical Manual of Mental Disorders IV-TR* (DSM-IV-TR) (American Psychiatric Association, 2000) criteria for trauma leading to post-traumatic stress disorder (PTSD) is largely derived from symptoms seen in survivors of combat, natural or national disasters, or what could be denoted as impersonal trauma (Allen, 2001). The diagnostic criteria incorporates both an objective event and subjective response in that it requires the presence of an actual and threatened serious injury to the physical self accompanied by intense fear, helplessness, or horror. This implies that it is not just the event that is critical but also the enduring adverse response to the experience, as distinct from horrific events that are not accompanied by enduring adverse effects.

The focus on physical injury or threat, however, is considered to be too narrow by many clinicians (Allen, 2001) as it fails to include threat to psychological integrity which threatens to undermine self-structures and related mental capacities. Although the APA have a diagnostic caveat in the case of children which states that "for children sexually traumatic events may include developmentally inappropriate sexual experiences without threatened or actual violence or injury" this is currently not extended to adults experiencing unwanted sexual experiences such as rape, or sexual slavery, or domestic abuse.

The criteria used in DSM-IV-TR are thought by some researchers to be further limited by neglecting to specify the impact of pervasive and habitual unpredictability and lack of control, which is considered by some to be a core aspect of trauma (Foa, Zinbarg and Rothbaum, 1992). Control and predictability is critical for individuals to feel safe and secure, monitor danger and take appropriate steps to avoid or minimise danger. In the absence of predictability, controllability is compromised leading to increased arousal, heightened conditioned fear responses, numbing and avoidance (Allen, 2001). In addition, as heightened arousal activates primitive survival strategies and diverts energy to subcortical functions, the individual is unable to make sense of the experience and generate meaning, making it harder to process the trauma.

SPECTRUM OF TRAUMA

A limitation in the DSM-IV-TR formulation of trauma is that it does not capture the broad range and types of traumatic experiences. For instance, it does not distinguish between different types of trauma such as those caused by natural disasters, accidents, or acts of terrorism and trauma which consists of physical or psychological assault on an individual within an attachment relationship. To account for these variations in traumatic experiences, some researchers have proposed a spectrum of trauma to enhance clinicians' understanding of impact and effects of trauma, symptomatology and potential treatment implications.

Allen (2001) proposes three main types of trauma: impersonal trauma, interpersonal trauma and attachment trauma. Impersonal trauma is characterised by manmade and natural disasters, interpersonal trauma by criminal assaults such as rape by a stranger, while attachment trauma refers to interfamilial abuse and child sexual abuse. Allen proposes that attachment trauma can have more pervasive effects compared with other types of trauma due to the presence of aversive dynamics such as the betrayal of trust, dependency needs, loss of bodily integrity, and inescapability.

In many respects, Allen's attachment trauma echoes Pamela Freyd's (1996) notion of "betrayal trauma" which is defined as trauma that occurs in relational contexts where a person violates role expectations of care and protection. The effect of such violations is the severing of human bonds and loss of important human connections.

While this continuum of trauma differentiates between different types of trauma, there may be overlap between each type such as car accidents (both impersonal and interpersonal) and acquaintance or date rape (interpersonal without a real established attachment). The main distinction used in this volume will be between impersonal trauma and interpersonal trauma.

A further crucial distinction that is not addressed in the DSM-IV-TR criteria for traumatic stressors is differentiating between single event trauma and multiple and repeated trauma. Impersonal trauma is usually associated with a single event, while interpersonal trauma commonly consists of a series of repeated traumatic experiences over prolonged periods of time. In addition, interpersonal trauma is characterised by multiple violations such as physical violence, sexual assault, emotional abuse and neglect.

To counterbalance these omissions in the classification criteria, Lenore Terr (1991) distinguishes between Type I trauma which is characterised by a single traumatic event, and Type II trauma which involves multiple, prolonged and repeated trauma. Commonly, Type II trauma is associated with much greater psychobiological disruption, including complex PTS reactions, denial, psychic numbing, self-hypnosis, dissociation, alternations between extreme passivity and outbursts of rage, and significant memory impairment.

Building upon these distinctions, Rothschild (2000) has further refined these categories to include Type IIA and Type IIB trauma, with Type IIB further subdivided into Type IIB (R) and Type IIB (nR). According to Rothschild (2000), Type IIA trauma consists of multiple traumas experienced by individuals who have benefited from relatively stable backgrounds, and thus have sufficient resources to separate individual traumatic events from one another. In Type IIB the multiple traumas are so overwhelming that the individual cannot separate one from another. The type of trauma most frequently associated with prolonged and repeated interpersonal trauma is Type IIB (R) in which the person had a stable upbringing but the complexity of traumatic experiences are so overwhelming that resilience is impaired, or Type IIB (nR) in which the individual has never developed resources for resilience. The latter is characteristic of those survivors of interpersonal abuse who have a history of childhood trauma such as physical or sexual abuse, and adult revictimisation.

COMPLEX TRAUMA

Perhaps the most field-tested revision of multiple and repeated trauma is Judith Herman's (1992b) complex post-traumatic stress disorder, which aims to elaborate on the current DSM-IV-TR criteria for traumatic events, by highlighting significant differences in terms of impact and symptomatology between single event trauma and multiple and repeated trauma. Complex post-traumatic stress disorder aims to expand the current diagnostic concept and truly capture the complex symptomatology that follows prolonged and repeated trauma. This more inclusive conceptualisation was submitted for inclusion in DSM-IV-TR in 2000 as a separate, stand-alone category. While not adopted as a separate classification, it was designated under "disorders of extreme stress not otherwise specified" (DESNOS). As the need for specific formulations of complex trauma has gained wider recognition, it is hoped that the APA will adopt this new category in DSM-V due in 2012.

The revised *ICD-10 Classification of Mental and Behavioural Disorders* (ICD-10) (World Health Organisation, 2007) has taken into account both prolonged trauma and the delay or protracted responses to it in their category of PTSD: "... a delayed or protracted response to a stressful event or situation (of either brief or long duration) of an exceptionally threatening or catastrophic nature, which is likely to cause pervasive distress in almost anyone...[that] may follow a chronic course over many years, with eventual transition to an enduring personality change."

While complex post-traumatic stress disorder was originally conceptualised to understand the impact and symptoms of childhood trauma, it has ecological validity in understanding the impact of abuse in adulthood. This formulation incorporates the impact of a series of "blows", or process of multiple, chronic and prolonged developmentally adverse traumatic events, such as sexual or physical abuse, war, or community violence committed in the absence of adequate emotional and social support. As it encompasses interpersonal, intrapersonal, biological and existential/spiritual consequences of repeated exposures to trauma, it is particularly apt in highlighting the symptoms seen in cases of habitual, repetitive and inescapable abuse in intimate relationships such as domestic abuse, elder abuse and sexual slavery, or those held in "captivity", or in thrall to their abuser. As Herman (1992b) argues, "Survivors of prolonged abuse develop characteristic personality changes, including deformations of relatedness and identity..." which are not accounted for in current formulations of PTS responses, and yet are manifest in survivors of interpersonal abuse.

DEVELOPMENTAL TRAUMA DISORDER

To further understand the impact of repeated interpersonal abuse across developmental stages in children, the Complex Trauma Task Force for the National Child Traumatic Stress Network have conceptualised a new diagnosis, provisionally called developmental trauma disorder (van der Kolk *et al.*, 2005). This formulation incorporates the features and impact of repeated and prolonged abuse through multiple or chronic exposure to one or more forms of interpersonal trauma such as abandonment, betrayal, physical and sexual assaults, threats to bodily integrity, coercive practices, emotional abuse and witnessing violence and death (van der Kolk *et al.*, 2005). Developmental trauma disorder is most likely to occur when exposure to such trauma is accompanied by the subjective experience of rage, betrayal, fear, resignation, defeat, and/or shame.

It is proposed that repeated, multiple acts of abuse and trauma across critical developmental stages can lead to developmental derailments, such as complex disruptions to affect regulation, disturbed attachment patterns, rapid behavioural regressions and shifts in emotional distress. This is commonly accompanied by a loss of autonomous strivings, aggression against self and others, failure to achieve developmental competencies, loss of bodily regulation such as sleep, food and self-care, and altered schemas of the world. Hyperarousal and hypervigilance can lead to altered perceptions, anticipatory behaviour and traumatic expectations, multiple somatic problems from gastrointestinal distress to headaches, apparent lack of awareness of danger resulting in self-endangering behaviour, self-hatred and self-blame, and chronic feelings of ineffectiveness (van der Kolk *et al.*, 2005).

INTERPERSONAL TRAUMA WITHIN ATTACHMENT RELATIONSHIPS

In response to clinical evidence, this book defines interpersonal trauma as prolonged and repeated exposure to chronic, multiple, and repeated abuse within relationships, which give rise to complex PTS symptoms. Such abuse is commonly committed by someone who is in a position of trust, or to whom the individual is attached, or upon whom the individual is dependent. Ubiquitous to interpersonal trauma is the abuse of power, use of coercion and control, the distortion of reality, and the dehumanisation of the victim. It is hoped that this definition will illuminate the impact of repeated violations, inescapable terror and inert surrender commonly seen in survivors of child abuse, child sexual abuse, and rape within intimate relationships, domestic abuse, elderly abuse, sexual slavery and abuse by professionals. Given the complex PTS symptoms, counsellors will need to direct specific therapeutic attention and focus to the dynamics of interpersonal trauma.

A significant characteristic of interpersonal trauma within relationships is that the violations are not always perceived as painful or life threatening, and frequently do not immediately evoke fear or helplessness. They may initially be experienced as confusing or distressing, rather than traumatic. The awareness of the betrayal and threat may come long after the experience has occurred as a result of later cognitive reappraisal of the event. This is commonly the case in child sexual abuse, sexual assault by partner or acquaintance, elder abuse and abuse by professionals. Usually it is only when the individual is in a place of safety, or when able to mentalise the experience, that the perception of betrayal of trust and relational bonds and the link to trauma can be made.

It is not until the person is able to understand the meaning of such violations that they can legitimise, and label it as abuse or trauma. This casts the survivor into an abyss of silence, where their subjective experience has to be hidden from self and others. Once cognitive reappraisal has occurred and there is recognition of the traumatising effects of such abuse, the individual may begin to manifest delayed complex PTS response, long after the events.

The repeated betrayal of trust within relationships accounts for such pervasive effects as fragmentation of self-structures, loss of self-agency and relational difficulties which are commonly found in survivors of interpersonal trauma. Research indicates that interpersonal trauma within attachment relationships is likely to have more devastating effects compared with other types of trauma as such experiences not only generate extreme distress but also undermine the mechanisms and capacity to regulate that distress (Allen, 2001; Fonagy, 1999; Fonagy and Target, 1997). Survivors of interpersonal abuse often lose the capacity for affect regulation to manage trauma symptoms and suffer a dual liability in not being able to seek comfort from their attachment figure, as (s)he is also the abuser. This reinforces the survivor's terror and sense of aloneness as the very person who can alleviate the terror is also the source of that fear.

The severity of interpersonal trauma within attachment relationships will vary in intensity and symptomatology depending on each individual's experience. In evaluating the extent of interpersonal trauma, and its impact, counsellors need to assess the level of dependency, the extent of coercion and control, intensity of traumatic bonding, the degree of violence experienced, the level of aggression and sadism encountered, and the frequency and duration of the abuse (Allen, 1997).

To fully understand the impact of interpersonal trauma and concomitant symptomatology, counsellors will need to familiarise themselves with the nature of interpersonal abuse, especially the use of deception, falsification of reality, and annihilation of the subjective self. The following chapter will look at the complex dynamics associated with interpersonal abuse that lead to traumatisation.

SUMMARY

- As definitions of trauma vary enormously it is critical to have a mutual understanding between clinicians and their clients of what is meant by trauma so that traumatic experiences can be legitimised, and named.
- The DSM-IV-TR (2000) definition of trauma derived from combat, natural or national disasters, or impersonal trauma, emphasises the presence of an objective event that entails physical injury and the subjective experience of fear, helplessness and horror.

- This criterion is limited in not distinguishing between the impact and effects of impersonal and interpersonal trauma. It also does not account for significant differences seen in single event traumas and those associated with multiple, repeated and prolonged trauma.

- A number of revisions have been proposed including Type I and Type II trauma (Terr, 1991), Type IIA and Type IIB trauma (Rothschild, 2000), complex traumatic stress disorder (Herman, 1992a; 2006) and developmental trauma disorder (van der Kolk *et al.*, 2005) to expand on current criteria.

- The 2007 revision of the *ICD-10 Classification of Mental and Behavioural Disorders* (World Health Organisation, 2007) in their classification of PTSD includes prolonged and repeated traumatic events, as well as delayed or protracted responses which can lead to enduring personality change.

- Any definition of interpersonal trauma has to take into account prolonged and repeated exposure to chronic, multiple, and repeated abuse in close relationships, which give rise to complex PTS symptoms.

- Interpersonal trauma is commonly committed by someone who is in a position of trust, or to whom the individual is attached, or upon whom the individual is dependent. Ubiquitous to interpersonal trauma is the abuse of power, coercion and control, distortion of perception, the distortion of reality, and the dehumanisation of the victim.

- It is only with such conceptualisation that the impact of repeated violations, inescapable terror and inert surrender commonly seen in survivors of child abuse, child sexual abuse, and rape within intimate relationships, domestic abuse, elderly abuse, sexual slavery and abuse by professionals can be fully illuminated.

CHAPTER 2

THE DYNAMICS OF INTERPERSONAL TRAUMA

Interpersonal trauma in relationships is rarely a single event. Invariably it is part of a process of habitual, repeated violations which the individual cannot escape either because they are held captive due to dependency needs, or because they are in thrall to the abuser. A central feature of interpersonal trauma is coercion and control which demands the inert surrender of the victim. This control is usually achieved through the distortion of perception, deception and concealment wherein abuse masquerades as protection. As a result interpersonal trauma is suffused with irreconcilable contradictions which are difficult to manage, leading to a collapse of psychological and physical integrity.

To understand the impact and long-term sequelae of interpersonal trauma, counsellors need to be apprised of the dynamics of interpersonal abuse. This chapter will examine how abusers dissemble their motives and behaviour in order to ensnare their victims through what is often called the "grooming" process. It will also look at how deception allows the abuser to become close to their chosen victim and, along with feigned affection and interest, to manipulate and ensure total surrender. This is accompanied by strategies to minimise risk of exposure, in which the abuser has to falsify and distort reality so that the survivor is uncertain as to what is really happening.

The chapter will also consider the process of dehumanisation of the victim and the annihilation of self-identity, which allows the abuser to insert a false or alien identity. When fused with the paradox of *knowing* and yet *not knowing*, silence and concealment is ensured, and traumatisation is complete.

ENTICEMENT AND ENTRAPMENT

To commit interpersonal abuse the abuser must first entice, ensnare and entrap the desired victim. This takes considerable deception, manipulation, coercion and control. Abusers often "groom" their victims over a prolonged period of time to ensure concealment and submission and thereby minimise the risk of exposure (Sanderson, 2004). To entrap their victims, abusers have to dissemble their true motives under the guise of affection, interest or protection. Through a potent fusion of charm, seduction and "love bombing", the abuser entrances the victim, and lures them into a masquerade.

To establish and develop trust the abuser feigns genuine interest and caring through a carefully constructed façade of charm and affection. Under this pretence, the abuser showers the chosen victim with love, attention and devotion to establish a special bond between them which creates dependency needs. This special bond is then used to coerce and subdue the victim into submission, and acceptance of abusive or exploitative behaviour. Once the special bond has been established, the abuser manipulates the victim's dependency needs by threatening to withdraw their love and affection if they fail to comply with their demands.

Alongside the flimsy façade of affection, or protection, the abuser begins to falsify the victim's reality and distorts their perception. Through the use of lies, deceit and distortion of reality, the abuser creates confusion in the victim so that they are unable to trust their own subjective perception of reality and inner experiencing. It is this dynamic that transforms what is abusive and traumatising into an illusion of loving, caring and nurturing behaviour. Abusers further exploit this "special relationship" by consistently over-riding the victim's felt experience by inserting false perceptions and untruths. The abuser may brainwash the victim to believe that they are the only ones who truly care for them and that others are deceitful in their motives. This strategy is designed to isolate the victim from others to consolidate the abuser's total power and control of the victim. Isolation from others thus increases dependency needs on the abuser, and minimises risk of disclosure. If trust in others is consistently undermined, the victim will be unable to risk disclosure for fear of not being believed or being blamed for the abuse. This tightens the bond and binds the victim to the abuser.

At the same time as enticing the victim, the abuser must also seduce other important figures in the victim's life such as parents, siblings, family members and friends. This is achieved through the application of precisely the same strategies of charm, seduction and dissembling. Once these important figures are in thrall to the abuser, risk of exposure is minimised. In addition, if a disclosure is made, it is less likely that the victim will be believed due to discrepancy between the abuser's charming persona and alleged abuse behaviour.

Many abusers are expert deceivers who are able to project a charming public façade while concealing their true motivation: to coerce, control and dominate. It is the ability to dissimulate that allows them to entice and ensnare not only their victim but also close and trusted others. As abusers need to be expert at manipulation in order to achieve their goal, they constantly refine and hone their craft. In addition, some abusers find their ability to deceive and dupe others arousing and an essential ingredient in the abuse process.

What counsellors need to be aware of is the impact the process of enticement and entrapment has on the victim in terms of distortion of perception and reality, and how the betrayal of trust impacts on relational dynamics. For some survivors of interpersonal trauma, the subtle and covert distortion of perception has a greater deleterious effect than the more overt abusive behaviour.

It must be remembered that abusers come from all socioeconomic, ethnic and religious backgrounds and share certain characteristics. They all have a desire to coerce and control, a need to subdue their victims into submission or inert surrender and to exercise complete domination. They are commonly charming and duplicitous while concealing their motivation, anger and hostility behind a mask of benign interest, care and concern. Some abusers, especially those who sexually abuse and engage in sexual exploitation, will use drugs or alcohol to induce substance dependency in the victim as a way of increasing their control. Alongside this, some abusers will coerce victims to engage in illegal activities to increase their culpability and minimise exposure.

DIFFERENT TYPES OF INTERPERSONAL ABUSE

There are many different types of abuses seen in interpersonal trauma. Some of them are overt such as physical violence, verbal abuse, sexual assault and sexual exploitation, while others are much more covert and subtle. Psychological abuse can consist of overt acts of humiliation designed to shame the victim, or strip any vestiges of self-esteem or self-worth. More subtle types of abuses come from failures in connection, failure in empathy and lack of recognition of needs. The distortion of reality and perception can be extremely subtle especially when it is suffused with contradiction. One such potent mixture is artificially enhancing the victim to feel better than others, creating feelings of grandiosity and entitlement, and then vilifying their very existence.

A central feature of interpersonal trauma in close relationships is the betrayal of trust which forces the victim to dissociate from the abuse, or compartmentalise it, whereby only positive aspects of the relationship can be accessed. This permits knowledge isolation, or "betrayal blindness", in which experiences are blocked and separated in the mind, preventing integration which aids survival and retains a semblance of functioning.

DEHUMANISATION AND THE ANNIHILATION OF THE SELF

In order to commit interpersonal abuse and unspeakable acts, the abuser has to dehumanise the victim. As the victim is stripped of any subjective sense of self and rendered into an "it", or "thing", the abuser is able to ensure total submission. All relational interactions become predicated on "I–it" (Buber, 1987) ways of relating, lacking any intersubjectivity. Over time the absence of any "I–Thou" relational dynamics, and the total coercion and control exerted by the abuser, leads to the annihilation of the self.

Through the erosion of all control, self-identity, self-agency and relational worth, the victim must either submit or die. And yet the victim does not die but is left "...at once dead yet left alive in the wake of her own destruction" (Grand, 2000). This is compounded by the annihilation of the victim's capacity to know either their internal or external reality. The victim has no choice but to adapt to and accommodate these distortions, and take on an "as if" existence (Shengold, 1989), a wordless and inauthentic self. As subjectivity is sequestered, the abuser is able to complete the desired "soul murder" (Shengold, 1989) by obliterating any vestige of authenticity.

Not content with the annihilation of the authentic self, many abusers go on to insert, or project, a fantasised identity onto the victim. In this the abused becomes whatever the abuser desires, be it sexual object, a container into which to evacuate unwanted feelings, or a plaything to be used and abused. This projective annihilation allows the abuser to impose a false identity (Mollon, 2005), or alien self (Fonagy *et al.*, 2002) which the victim is powerless to resist. Within this process of introjections, the victim often also absorbs the emotions that the abuser refuses to feel such as shame, guilt and responsibility for the abuse. These become internalised and serve to amplify the victim's already felt sense of shame and responsibility.

Once the abuser's projections and distortions are embedded, the victim begins to filter perceptions of self and the world through the abuser's eyes. This internalisation of distorted reality and imposed perception results in the victim viewing themselves as mere sexual objects, or shameful or all bad. The perpetrator's repudiated feelings may also be incorporated whereby the victim denies feelings and compassion for self and others. In some cases, this can lead to identification with the aggressor and re-enacting abuse experiences, objectifying others and becoming perpetrators themselves. This is often seen in survivors, who were sexually abused or exploited, procuring potential victims, or abusing those who are weaker and more vulnerable.

It is worth noting that once the survivor's authentic self has been sequestered and impregnated with the perpetrator's imposed identity, surrender is complete. At this point many abusers lose interest, because once victims have been "broken in" and rendered lifeless, there is nothing left to sequester. This is when the abuser will seek out future victims in order to start the cycle of victimisation and traumatisation.

DISSOCIATION AND COMPARTMENTALISATION

To manage the perpetrator's dehumanisation and repeated betrayal, the survivor has to conceal the vulnerable aspects of the self, in order to comply with the abuser's imposed identity. This activates further survival strategies and primitive defence mechanisms such as dissociation, or compartmentalisation. In this process the individual dissociates from their needs and feelings, which become imprisoned in an unassailable fortress. This fortress acts as a protective barrier for the core, or true self, to no longer experience painful emotions. As such the feeling, vulnerable part is separated from the false self that is exposed to abuse and betrayal. In this the person compartmentalises the hurt and the pain, and replaces it with an invulnerable, capable and highly resilient false self. This fractured self is most commonly associated with interpersonal trauma where the victim is highly dependent on the abuser and where protection and abuse co-exist.

IRRECONCILABLE PARADOXES

The paradoxical nature of such interpersonal relationships demands that the victim engage in "doublethink" (Orwell, 1949) by simultaneously accepting two mutually contradictory beliefs, "...to know and not to know..." (Orwell, 1949). Paradoxes promote dissociation from the abuse, often through compartmentalisation, which permits the survivor only to access the positive aspects of the relationship. As awareness of the betrayal threatens the attachment relationship, the survivor activates defence mechanisms, such as dissociation and compartmentalisation. This compels the survivor to banish knowledge of the abuse, as evanescent abuse experiences permit continued attachment to the abuser and focus on positive relational dynamics.

Dissociation allows traumatised individuals to develop an idealised attachment to the abuser by compartmentalising all terrifying interactions. It also serves as a mechanism for the abused to blame themselves, in order to retain an idealised image of the abuser. This promotes hope in that if the victim is obedient and complies with the abuser's demands then the abuse will stop and be replaced with love and care. In turn, this provides an illusion of control which prevents the victim from experiencing their unbearable sense of utter helplessness while shoring up the hope in a better future. In this "moral defence" (Fairbairn, 1952) however, attachment and identification with abuser is reinforced, which impacts on later relational dynamics, and self-destructive behaviours frequently associated with survivors of child abuse, child sexual abuse (CSA), domestic abuse, elderly abuse and institutional abuse.

The repudiated feelings of vulnerability, weakness, inadequacy and dependency are locked away into the core self, to be replaced by a façade of strength, invulnerability, omnipotence and compensatory grandiosity that characterises the false, or alien self. While the false self initially serves to protect the victim from experiencing the full emotional and psychological impact of the trauma, over time it can turn against the self by continuing to oppress the emotionally needy part, repudiating intimacy and sabotaging any future relational opportunities, including the therapeutic relationship.

In some cases the traumatisation and dissociation is so pervasive that the mind collapses and the trauma experiences are split off from conscious awareness. As the mind goes blank, the trauma is stored on a somato-sensory level, and the body transmits what can no longer be communicated (McDougall, 1989; Herman, 1992a; van der Kolk, McFarlane and Weisaeth, 1996). This fracture in conscious awareness and bodily experiencing gives rise to a variety of somatic complaints for which there is no organically based explanation as they are psychogenic in origin.

This is compounded in the case of sexual traumatisation wherein bodily integrity is compromised as the body responds to, and becomes aroused by, the sexual contact. Such arousal reduces the abuser's culpability as the victim (mis)perceives the arousal as indicative of wanting such sexual attention, making it hard to legitimise the experience as abuse. Many survivors experience this as their body colluding with the abuser and feel unable to trust their somatic responses, not realising that this represents the ultimate control, and triumph, the abuser has over the victim's body. In many cases of rape and child sexual abuse, abusers deliberately perform "pleasure"-inducing sexual acts to establish an abuse/pleasure dichotomy so as to co-opt the victim into their own abuse as a way to reduce legitimacy, minimise disclosure and ensure inert surrender.

The plethora of irreconcilable paradoxes which need to be heard and yet not being able to speak can create further confusions that become paralysing for the survivor. The human need to be visible is countered by the need to be invisible to avoid further abuse, and the need for intimacy and the dread of abuse, all pose insoluble dichotomies which promote further withdrawal from human contact, which reinforces the sense of dehumanisation. The striving for mastery of the experiences is further denied in the dissonance between the imperative to know what is seemingly impossible to know (Grand, 2000), and the absence of any confirmatory evidence, or sharing of experience.

THE DISTORTION OF PERCEPTION AND FALSIFICATION OF REALITY

It is evident from the already cited dynamics that much of interpersonal trauma is predicated on distortion and alterations in perception, in which the abuser falsifies and dissembles reality. This is not just confined to the external reality, but also includes the victim's internal reality and subjective experiencing. This is seen in the initial entrapment process and the omnipresent pretence of affection to conceal abuse, public charm to cover terrorisation and menacing violence. This embezzlement of the survivor's reality leads to a precarious sense of reality and a gnawing uncertainty about the world and their experiences. Moreover it interferes with continuity of self and ability to derive meaning, which is crucial in processing and integrating experiences (Krystal, 1988).

To manage these ruptures in knowing yet not knowing, and associated contradictions, the survivor has to relinquish own reality and adopt the delusory reality imposed by the abuser. As this is imbued with myriad lies and deceptions the survivor has little, if any, choice but to collude in the falsification of reality. In this the survivor is forced to collude in the occlusion of reality and abuse which further fuels the total power and control the abuser has to deceive others, and minimises risk of disclosure. These distortions in perception may become so embedded that it can take many years, even after the abuse has abated, to restore and trust subjective experiencing. Much of the therapeutic work will need to focus on repossessing own perceptions and own reality. In this survivors will be able to restore personal history, regain continuity of self and begin to derive meaning.

LEGITIMISING AND NAMING INTERPERSONAL TRAUMA

It is in the repossession of own perceptions and reality that the survivor is able to legitimise and name their experiences as abuse or trauma. While they are still in thrall to the abuser's delusory perceptions, they are unable to unscramble their own subjective experiences. A crucial component in reversing the subterfuge associated with interpersonal trauma is examining survivor's perceptions, evaluating distortions and restoring subjective reality. Until this is achieved, survivors will find it difficult to legitimise their experiences and name it as abuse, or trauma.

Many survivors of interpersonal trauma report the positive aspects of the relationship, naming it as "special" rather than traumatising, or abusive. Until survivors are able to name or legitimise their abuse they will not be able to access the full range of feelings and perceptions that have been concealed, or compartmentalised. In reclaiming banished feelings and perception the survivors can allow the vulnerable, sequestered self to return and begin to negotiate the world in a more authentic way.

One important aspect of legitimisation is to revoke the annihilation of truth, concealment and secrecy that the survivor was forced to collude in. Compulsory concealment and secrecy compromises integrity as the survivor has to deceive self and others, often through deliberate falsification and lies to ward off greater threats from the abuser. While this is a vital survival strategy it is experienced as colluding in own abuse, especially when opportunities for disclosure occur and yet the survivor is too terrified to expose the truth.

ENFORCED SILENCE AND SECRECY

Counsellors need to be aware of the power of enforced silence and secrecy as a factor in interpersonal trauma. The imperative to keep silent prevents the survivor from talking about the abuse which impedes processing of the experience. It is through the sharing of experiences that individuals are helped to make sense of them and to process their meaning, which is essential for integration. In addition, to ensure that the secret is not revealed the survivor becomes hypervigilant and avoids closeness with others to prevent inadvertent disclosure. This leads to withdrawal from others and reduced opportunities to reality check any confusing experiences or perceptions. This reinforces the survivor's sense of isolation and aloneness, while increasing the dependency on the abuser.

Silence is often further enforced through threat, and the conviction that the survivor won't be believed. Many survivors do not realise that at the same time as their reality is being falsified, the abuser is also dissembling and distorting the perceptions of those who are close to the victim. This is often done through lies and imputing doubts about the honesty and trustworthiness of the victim. This is all designed to minimise the risk of disclosure and exposure. Silence is also sometimes enforced through the shame associated with the abuse, fear of stigmatisation and fear of hurting others. Many survivors often protect significant others from the horror and terror of their abuse not wishing to bring dishonour and shame onto them. This is frequently seen in survivors of rape, sexual abuse and sexual exploitation. In protecting others the survivor sacrifices the potential for ending the abuse, resulting in deeper withdrawal into a "...sequestered, wordless self" (Langer, 1995).

A further factor in silence is the role of uncertainty as "What the tongue cannot speak and what reason cannot comprehend...what is absolutely certain and absolutely in doubt..." becomes impossible to articulate (Grand, 2000). When this is combined with the fear, apprehension and dread of exposure of the secret it is not surprising that the survivor is rendered speechless. This speechless terror often persists long after the abuse has ended, making it difficult for the survivor to recount their experiences, or construct a cohesive narrative. This often manifests in the therapeutic process where many survivors find it difficult to construct a continuous narrative of vague, distorted and fragmented experiences. Part of the therapeutic process thus becomes illuminating the silence and rendering it audible (Langer, 1995).

TRAUMATIC BONDING

Isolation of the victim from other sources of support acts as a powerful glue for traumatic bonding. To divide is to rule as it empowers the abuser in exerting total control and domination, which promotes submission and surrender. A common strategy used by abusers is to create a deliberate wedge between supportive others, such as family members, siblings, peers and friends. This strategy is part of the abuser's risk assessment in terms of exposure but also serves to strengthen the hold over the survivor. This is often achieved by distorting the perceptions others may have of the victim such as that they are inveterate liars, or dissemblers, that they are sly and wish to cause discord, and ultimately cannot be trusted. The abuser will frequently play the victim off against others to ensure a reign of confusion, uncertainty and distortion.

Traumatic bonding occurs when in the presence of inescapable life-threatening trauma which evokes fearful dependency and denial of rage in the victim. The core feature of traumatic bonding is that the abuser is both source of preserving life and destroying life. This activates primitive survival instincts such as flight, fight or freeze responses. As the victim invariably cannot fight or flee, the freeze response is the only option available. In this absence of any viable escape strategies the survivor cannot afford to access rage or anger as this will elicit further threat and danger, and so must be denied.

Pivotal to traumatic bonding is intermittent reinforcement in which threats and abuse co-exist with periods of love and affection (Dutton and Painter, 1981). This cyclical pattern of abusive and loving behaviour becomes the "superglue that bonds" (Allen, 2001) the relationship. It is important to note that the loving periods are characterised by extreme intensity which are misperceived as intimacy and love which serve to cancel out the intense fear associated with the abuse. While these biologically based survival instincts are mediated outside conscious awareness and beyond the survivor's control, they nevertheless result in perceptual changes. The survivor is compelled to change negative beliefs about the abuser, to humanise rather than demonise, to aid hope for survival. This invariably involves adopting the abuser's belief system and increased tolerance of the abuse through the process of dissociation, or compartmentalisation.

SELF-BLAME

To survive the process of dehumanisation, distortion of reality and traumatic bonding survivors frequently humanise the abuser while demonising the self. This is achieved through denial of reality and self-blame. Although blame is usually projected onto the survivor by the abuser, self-blame also serves a number of important functions to protect psychological integrity. It provides an illusion of power and control in which the survivor takes the blame for the abuse and traumatisation as a way to avert overwhelming feelings of utter helplessness. It is also a way of rekindling hope in that if only they were more obedient, compliant and like the abuser wants them to be, then the abuser would become more loving and caring. This results in increasingly compliant and submissive behaviour to elicit the longed for and much needed love. It is this hope that has not been extinguished that aids survival and the hope that one day things will improve and that the abuse will stop.

SHAME

Shame is ubiquitous to interpersonal trauma, not just in the nature of the abuses committed but in the helplessness and powerlessness in not being able to do anything about them. The repeated and inescapable nature of interpersonal abuse means that the survivor is in constant survival mode at a cost to higher cognitive processing, rendering escape strategies and opportunities for mastery impossible. This fuels any already existing shame which seeps like a virus to invade and infect the total being of the person. All pervasive shame activates a spiral of disconnection and inauthenticity, while mobilising feelings of worthlessness. In shame the individual will experience a need to conceal the true self and cover up vulnerability and dependency needs. This leads to retreat and withdrawal from others for fear of exposure.

The true self must be forever hidden, and any attempts to uncover shame will produce high levels of resistance, and further concealment. The survivor will often replace repudiated needs with a façade of invulnerability and self-sufficiency marked by an unapproachable exterior. This makes them difficult to engage but must be understood within the context of shame rather than obdurate resistance or hostility. In addition, there is a constant battle between wishing to be seen and wishing to hide which can be expressed in oscillation between reaching out for connection followed by rapid disconnection. Again these almost borderline features must be understood within the context of shame rather than a diagnosis of borderline personality disorder.

Clinicians need to remember that the origins of shame lie in a failure in connection, understanding, and empathy all of which are inherent in interpersonal abuse. Abusers deliberately ignore and deny the victims' needs and as such refuse to meet them. This is why adequate mirroring and acceptance of all aspects of the survivor is so critical in the therapeutic process, despite initial resistance.

SURVIVAL STRATEGIES

The terror states induced in interpersonal trauma need to be quelled in order to manage and survive repeated abuse. To soothe and regulate these terror states survivors activate a range of survival strategies. These include psychobiological mechanisms such as dissociation, avoidance and compartmentalisation as well as self-medication through substance misuse and self-harm. Survivors will also need to submit and surrender to the abuser which can become a strategy employed in all relationships. Such survivors will present as compliant, charming and seductive as a cover-up for the internalised rage. They will often employ similar tactics to the abuser to entice and entrap through compliments and charm to lure the clinician into liking and accepting them to the detriment of the concealed feelings.

In contrast some survivors will attempt to conceal their vulnerability and dependency through hostile and aggressive behaviour designed to push others away and avoid intimacy. Clinicians need to ensure that this is understood within the context of interpersonal trauma and not personalised. Some survivors will be so subdued and subjugated that they are unable to find any sense of self-agency and will surrender all responsibility for their recovery to the clinician, while others will activate protection and rescue strategies wherein they wish to protect the clinician from knowing the full horror of the interpersonal trauma.

Whatever survival strategies are used they need to be honoured for fulfilling their purpose which is to aid survival. Moreover, while they may now no longer be adaptive it will be hard for the survivor to relinquish them. Rather than jettison them, clinicians need to develop existing strategies and expand the survivor's behavioural repertoire so that the survivor has access to a broader range of strategies from which to choose. Through increased awareness of dynamics of interpersonal abuse, their origins and how these might manifest in the therapeutic setting, counsellors will be able to have a better understanding of the impact and long-term effects of interpersonal trauma and how best to structure the therapeutic focus.

SUMMARY

- Clinicians need to understand the dynamics associated with interpersonal trauma in order to have a better understanding of the impact and long-term effects. Ubiquitous to all interpersonal abuse is the use of coercion and control, which is used to entice and ensnare potential victims.
- Entrapment is achieved through grooming and deception wherein abuse masquerades as protection. The abuser feigns interest and affection in order to build a bond in which to terrorise the victim.
- Once the victim is caught in the web of deceit the abuse dehumanises the victim by repudiating all human needs and emotions which promotes the annihilation of the self. In the vacuum left by the annihilated self the abuser inserts a false or alien identity.
- The distortion of perception and falsification of reality of both the victim and any significant others minimises exposure and disclosure. It also serves to engender gnawing uncertainty and confusion in which the victim knows and yet does not know what is happening. This irreconcilable paradox makes it difficult to legitimise and name the experience as abuse, or trauma.
- Not being able to name the experience ensures concealment of the abuse through secrecy and silence. The fear of inadvertently revealing the secret leads to withdrawal from others and a retreat into isolation.
- This isolation serves as the glue for traumatic bonding in which the victim becomes even more dependent on the abuser. It is through the intermittent reinforcement of loving behaviour following episodes of abuse that the victim becomes ever more closely bound to the abuser.
- Ubiquitous to interpersonal trauma is self-blame and shame in which the survivor holds all responsibility for the abuse as a way of retaining an illusion of power and control, and the hope of a better future. Shame is often a combination of the shame that the abuser has denied in committing the abuse, the nature of the abuse and feelings of helplessness and powerlessness.

- To survive repeated abuse survivors adopt a myriad of survival strategies that aid survival. Rather than judging these, the therapist needs to honour and develop them alongside the introduction of a broader behavioural repertoire from which the survivor can choose.

CHAPTER 3

THE IMPACT AND LONG-TERM EFFECTS OF INTERPERSONAL TRAUMA

Interpersonal trauma overwhelms ordinary human adaptation to life as it threatens bodily and psychological integrity. It engenders helplessness, terror, powerlessness and produces intense feelings of fear, loss of control, and threat of annihilation. The threat to personal and environmental safety activates a cascade of neurobiological and psychological responses which can result in a range of physiological stress reaction and disconnection from self, others and the world. The repeated, persistent and unpredictable threat can disrupt psychobiological synchrony which causes ruptures in the stress response system and ultimately alters brain chemistry, locking the stress response system into overdrive.

The pervasive hyperarousal characteristic of interpersonal trauma impedes cognitive processing and mentalisation of the experiences and the full range of concomitant feelings, which become blocked from awareness. As the survivor becomes more out of contact with feelings and needs, tolerance of the abuse is increased while capacity to problem solve is reduced. This limits the capacity to process and integrate terror states into a coherent narrative, or to derive meaning from these experiences. Lack of meaning generates confusion and uncertainty, making it hard to legitimise interpersonal abuse.

Ubiquitous to interpersonal trauma is uncertainty and irreconcilable paradoxes which lead to distortions in perception, of self, others and the world. The paradox of *knowing* and yet *not knowing* ensures silence and continued concealment. To manage this, psychobiological mechanisms are activated that compromise psychological integrity allowing the survivor to tolerate the intolerable and survive unknowable and unbearable experiences. This is compounded by the betrayal of trust leading to withdrawal and social isolation. This reduces capacity to challenge the perpetrator's behaviour, reinforcing his or her power and control, and increasing the survivor's entrapment.

This chapter will examine the impact and long-term effects of interpersonal trauma including neurobiological effects, PTS responses, and dissociation all of which cause disruptions to identity, boundary awareness, and interpersonal relatedness, affect regulation, and reduced awareness of needs (Allen, 2001; Briere and Spinazzola, 2005). It will also assess impact and effects of prolonged and repeated trauma on physical health, and behavioural and cognitive changes alongside intrapersonal and relational difficulties. Awareness of the impact and range of effects will equip the practitioner with knowledge of the potential presenting symptoms and how best to work with these.

INTERPERSONAL TRAUMA AND MENTAL HEALTH

The impact of interpersonal abuse straddles a number of biological and psychological dimensions, and can have significant impact on mental health. Most commonly these cluster around PTS symptoms, altered states of consciousness, affect and behavioural regulation, and changes in cognitive and self-structures, including relational functioning. When interpersonal trauma is accompanied by sexual abuse or sexual exploitation there will also be some effect on sexual functioning and behaviour.

The complex dynamics of coercive control has considerable impact on survivors as the terror inherent in interpersonal trauma enthrals the survivor and reinforces her captivity. The total power and control of the abuser prevents the survivor from challenging or exposing the abuse. To manage this, the survivor must silence herself, become voiceless (Scarf, 2005), and withdraw from social contact. The annihilation of the self, imposed identity and psychological dependency on the abuser, endorse traumatic bonding and acceptance of the abuser's controlling and abusive behaviour.

Researchers have identified a number of psychiatric disorders associated with interpersonal trauma, in particular borderline personality disorder (Linehan, 1993), antisocial personality disorder, narcissistic personality disorder, body dysmorphic disorder, PTSD, dissociative disorders, depression, anxiety disorders, self-harm, eating disorders, substance dependency and schizophrenia (Read, 2008).

NEUROBIOLOGICAL IMPACT AND EFFECTS OF INTERPERSONAL TRAUMA

Trauma activates the autonomic arousal system releasing a cascade of neurochemicals and biochemicals that enable the individual to respond to danger. In the presence of threat, two structurally distinct biological defence systems are activated: the sympathetic and the parasympathetic nervous systems (Engel and Schmale, 1972). The sympathetic nervous system mobilises high-level energy necessary for fight (aggressive) and flight (fear) responses, while the parasympathetic nervous system decelerates heart and metabolic rate which precipitates the freeze (defeat) response most commonly seen in survivors of interpersonal trauma. In this state the individual becomes unresponsive and submissive with associated feelings of helplessness, emptiness, and hopelessness.

These neurobiological responses disrupt hippocampal and prefrontal cortex function, fuelling over-activation of the stress response system to the cost of higher cortical processing, limiting the capacity for problem solving and the organisation of mental states. The accompanying release of endogenous opioids induces somatic anaesthesia eliciting a state of apparent calm which allows for disengagement from reality. With prolonged and frequent activation the stress response system locks into overdrive, inculcating pervasive biologically mediated fear states outside conscious awareness, leading to disruptions to psychobiological synchrony, in particular dissociation and psychic numbing.

Repeated interpersonal trauma interferes with the capacity to integrate sensory, emotional and cognitive information into a cohesive whole leading to internal disorganisation and disruptions in attention, perception, and heightened irritability. Survivors often alternate between intrusive re-experiencing and numbing avoidance, "feeling 'overwhelmed' by traumatic memories and 'underwhelmed' by present day experiences" (Cantor, 2005, p.71). This results in oscillation between hypervigilance and hypovigilance which generalises to all encounters and perceived danger, even when in a place of safety. These neurobiological changes often manifest as PTS reactions and PTSD symptoms.

PTS REACTIONS

The intense fear, terror and helplessness inherent in interpersonal trauma activate PTS reactions. The predominate features of PTS reactions are hypervigilance, altered appraisal processes, lowered stress tolerance thresholds, increased irritability, elevated startle response and disruptions to arousal and affect modulation. These PTS reactions are implicated in the activation of PTSD symptoms such as flashbacks, hypervigilance, nightmares, amnesia, dissociation, emotional "frozenness", withdrawal, aloneness and being haunted by intrusive recollections of the trauma (Sanderson, 2008).

PTSD

The most common disorder associated with trauma is PTSD with one third of all trauma victims manifesting the full range of PTSD symptoms (Cantor, 2005). In the case of interpersonal trauma this may be considerably higher but may not be diagnosed as PTSD due to limitations in the current diagnostic criteria used by the DSM-IV-TR (America Psychiatric Association, 2000). While the current criteria is able to account for some of the symptoms seen in interpersonal trauma, it fails to capture the full impact and long-term effects of repeated and prolonged abuse, especially enduring changes to self-structures and personality. However it is worth noting that the ICD-10 produced by the World Health Organisation (2007) does include "enduring personality changes" as a result of repeated trauma and catastrophic experience (Brett, 1996; Cantor, 2005).

Lack of diagnosis of PTSD may also be due to the original trauma being sub-threshold for diagnosis with symptoms increasing over time (Cantor, 2005). This is due to survivors of interpersonal abuse not being able to name or legitimise their abuse experiences as trauma. Due to the myriad paradoxes inherent in interpersonal trauma in which abuse masquerades as affection, or love, many survivors are unable to name their experiences as abuse. The compartmentalisation of the abuse experiences outside conscious awareness means that the survivor is unable to link symptoms to trauma. This can result in delayed PTSD in which a period of numbing is followed by a gradual progression of evolving symptoms, or the onset of acute symptoms as a result of subsequent retraumatisation (Cantor 2005). PTSD may also emerge as a result of increased awareness or knowledge of abuse, and the reappraisal of experiences allowing for revised meaning and heightening perception of threat which compounds the original trauma.

When interpersonal trauma is compartmentalised and not linked to repeated abuse it makes it difficult for survivor and clinician to contextualise the array of presenting symptoms especially if they are sub-threshold. This has led some practitioners to focus on the co-morbid disorders such as depression, borderline personality disorder, self-harm and substance abuse rather than the framework of interpersonal trauma. This failure to connect symptoms to trauma can result in pathologising survivors leading to stigmatisation and retraumatisation (Sanderson, 2008).

PTSD is characterised by persistent re-experiencing of the trauma, active avoidance of trauma-related thoughts and feelings including numbing of emotional responsiveness, restricted range of affect and detachment, and persistent symptoms of increased arousal (Foa *et al.*, 1992; American Psychiatric Association, 2000). The trauma is re-experienced through recurrent and intrusive recollections, dreams, flashbacks, illusions and hallucinations and distress when exposed to stimuli that resemble or symbolise the trauma. To manage this, the survivor avoids any feelings or thoughts associated with the trauma, and any activities or situations that elicit recollections of the trauma. This is facilitated by psychic numbing, dissociation, detachment and psychogenic amnesia. Such primitive defence strategies lead to restricted range of affect, sense of foreshortened future and estrangement from others. The increased arousal seen in PTSD includes sleep disturbances, increased irritability, difficulty concentrating, hypervigilance, exaggerated startle response, and hyperarousal when exposed to external or internal stimuli that resemble or symbolise trauma.

While the criteria for PTSD accounts for many of the symptoms seen in trauma, they do not account for all the psychobiological symptoms associated with prolonged and repeated trauma. This has led a number of researchers to propose a separate, refined diagnostic category to incorporate the symptoms associated with pervasive interpersonal trauma (Herman, 1992b). Herman proposed a new category, complex post-traumatic stress disorder (CPTSD) which incorporates the consequences of prolonged and repeated exposure to violence and trauma. Field trials of DSM-IV indicated that childhood interpersonal trauma was a strong predictor of developing CPTSD and it was hoped to include this in future revision. Ultimately it was not included as a separate category but was subsumed under disorders of extreme stress not otherwise specified (DESNOS).

However, many researchers and clinicians feel that including prolonged interpersonal trauma under a miscellaneous collection of conditions is not specific enough to explain repeated trauma. This has led to a need for a new category to be included in DSM-V due in 2012 to account not only for the range of somatic, dissociative and affective sequelae but also loss of identity and changes in self and relational structures seen in repeated trauma.

CPTSD

Prolonged interpersonal trauma repudiates basic human needs for safety, protection, and belonging which not only dehumanises the individual but also threatens psychological integrity creating relational disturbances to self, others and the world. Herman (1992b) proposes that CPTSD is more able to account for the diffuse and pervasive symptoms associated with prolonged and repeated interpersonal trauma, including the myriad coping strategies necessary to preserve the illusion of goodness in the perpetrator.

To this effect, CPTSD incorporates additional criteria not included under the present PTSD categorisation. In acknowledging that interpersonal trauma impairs regulation of affect impulses, especially anger at self and others, CPTSD is able to account for the accompanying self-destructive behaviours such as self-mutilation, eating disorders, and substance misuse seen in survivors of interpersonal trauma. In addition, alterations in attention, perception and consciousness result in alterations in self-perception, characterised by a chronic sense of guilt, shame or inflated sense of responsibility. Negative self-perceptions in turn lead to impaired relational worth and relational disturbances, especially difficulties around trust and emotional intimacy. CPTSD is also more able to account for the range of diffuse psychogenic somatic complaints and alterations in systems of meaning, loss of faith in existing belief systems, and disconnection from the world and the value of life.

DEVELOPMENTAL TRAUMA DISORDER

One further revision which is being proposed for inclusion in DSM-V which is relevant to interpersonal trauma is developmental trauma disorder. As discussed in Chapter 1, this new diagnosis, based on the findings of the Complex Trauma Task Force for the National Child Traumatic Stress Network, aims to account for the impact of interpersonal trauma in childhood, and is provisionally called developmental trauma disorder (van der Kolk *et al.*, 2005). This new conceptualisation incorporates the features and impact of multiple, repeated and prolonged exposure to interpersonal abuse in childhood such as abandonment, betrayal, physical and sexual assaults and witnessing domestic abuse. It proposes that repeated, multiple traumas leads to developmental derailments such as disruptions to affect regulation, disturbed attachment patterns, rapid behavioural regressions and shifts in emotional states. This is accompanied by the loss of autonomous strivings, aggression against self and others, and failure to achieve developmental competencies. It is also associated with loss of bodily regulation such as sleep, food and self-care, multiple somatic complaints, altered schemas of the world, anticipatory behaviour and traumatic expectations. Most importantly it accounts for apparent lack of awareness of danger and resulting self-endangering behaviour, self-hatred and self-blame, and chronic feelings of ineffectiveness (van der Kolk *et al.*, 2005). Although the focus in this new diagnosis is on childhood interpersonal trauma, it can equally be applied to many of the symptoms associated with interpersonal trauma in adulthood.

DISSOCIATION

Dissociation is considered to be an adaptive survival strategy activated during overwhelming trauma in which there is no escape, which allows for "...mental flight when physical flight is not possible" (Kluft, 1992, p.2). As dissociation is present in a number of psychological phenomena, some researchers have argued for a continuum of dissociation (Figure 3.1) ranging from alert consciousness to severe detachment and accompanying mental states.

Alert consciousness	Mild detachment	Moderate detachment	Extreme detachment	Severe detachment
Internal and external awareness	Absorption in daydream and fantasy	Absorption in internal world, amnesia, PTSD, fugue	Unresponsive and disengaged "tuned out"	Dissociative identity disorder

Figure 3.1 Continuum of dissociation (adapted from Allen, 2001)

The BASK model of dissociation proposes that dissociation separates the links between **b**ehaviour, **a**ffect, **s**ensation and **k**nowledge (Braun, 1988) and so experiences are dismembered and rendered meaningless. This further impacts ruptures in perception, memory, and self-structures leading to a fragmented sense of self. Thus, repeated activation of dissociation and dissociative states disrupts integrated functions of consciousness, memory, identity and perception which can be sudden, gradual, transient or chronic (American Psychiatric Association, 2000). The most common dissociative disorders associated with survivors of interpersonal trauma are dissociative amnesia, dissociative fugue, and depersonalisation disorder. Dissociative disorders also have a high co-morbidity with other trauma-induced disorders such as PTSD, acute stress disorder, self-harm, eating disorders and substance misuse.

Some survivors of interpersonal trauma present as extremely high functioning and are often highly successful in many areas of their lives. This may be due to a form of dissociation, sometimes referred to as compartmentalisation in which the affective components of the trauma experiences are so deeply buried, or abstracted, that the survivor cannot attach any emotional responses to them, creating a split between the "observing self" and one's "experiencing self" (van der Kolk *et al.*, 1996). Such compartmentalisation is highly adaptive as it allows the individual to focus on cognitive skills of focusing attention on necessary survival tasks such as problem solving, planning and executing appropriate action without being overwhelmed by emotions.

Dissociation also gives rise to a number of somatic disturbances such as affect regulation, sleep disturbance, hypervigilance and hypovigilance. While hypervigilance allows for constant monitoring of the environment to ensure safety, hypovigilance endangers the individual as their detachment renders them unaware of any threats or danger. Dissociation is also a significant component in self-injury whereby survivors use self-mutilation either to induce dissociation, or to bring themselves out of dissociated states (Sutton, 2005).

DISTURBANCES IN AFFECT AND AFFECT REGULATION

Repeated activation of stress response systems impairs self-regulation and affect modulation and ruptures the survivor's capacity to tolerate or contain feelings appropriately. Traumatised individuals tend to vacillate between extremes of dissociation, or psychic numbing in which no feelings are experienced, and hyperarousal in which they are so overwhelmed by turbulent emotions that they fear disintegration. The propensity for avoidance and psychic numbing associated with affect dysregulation prevents traumatised individuals from knowing, or describing internal states and feelings, making it difficult to express needs, wishes or desires.

Lack of affect regulation means that the survivor is not able to self-soothe, leading to polarisation of feelings: either numb or overwhelmed. More significantly both states prevent mentalisation which means the survivor becomes embedded in feelings, believing them to be facts rather than signals, or healthy alerts to internal sensory states. There is no understanding that feelings can subside, be modulated or regulated, or that distress states can be made more tolerable. All emotions are feared and seen in tsunami-like proportions which are impossible to avert. This is complicated as intense, unmodulated feelings drown the capacity for thought. The lack of mental space to think further complicates the regulation of emotion as the survivor is unable to apply the brakes, which further impairs appraisal of reality.

Thus feelings become increasingly poor guides for appropriate action, resulting in habitual patterns of thinking, feeling, and doing.

Deficits in affect regulation also lead to disruptions in impulse control, including aggression against self and others. This can alienate others, reinforcing beliefs that other people are either sources of pleasure or terror, and causing uncertainty about reliability and predictability of others. In addition, all new situations are perceived as potentially threatening, while the familiar is generally perceived as safer, even if it is predictable as a source of terror (Streeck-Fischer and van der Kolk, 2000).

BEHAVIOURAL IMPACT AND EFFECTS

Impaired affect regulation leads to changes in behaviour, in particular behavioural control with impaired modulation of impulses resulting in being either over-controlled or under-controlled. Survivors who are over-controlled need to keep their emotions and behaviour in check so as not to attract the attention of the abuser for fear of punishment or reprisal. To manage interpersonal abuse, survivors compromise their behaviour by becoming submissive and compliant in all interactions with the abuser, modulating their moods and behaviours to what is expected of them in order to appease the abuser. In this survivors become hypervigilant, needing to walk on eggshells, and not ever being able to relax. In order to experience a semblance of control, some survivors resort to obsessive compulsive behaviours, such as compulsive "busyness", workaholism or ritualistic and addictive behaviours which leave no time for experiencing.

Being over-controlled and over-responsible may at times necessitate unleashing destructive or irresponsible behaviour either against self or others. Over-controlled survivors will usually direct these against the self through self-harm such as self-mutilation or substance misuse, or by engaging in risky behaviour. For many survivors self-harm is the only area in which they have control, or experience a sense of empowerment making this a valued resource. (Sanderson, 2006, 2008). It is also a way to avert suicidal ideation and suicidality. Thus, self-destructive behaviours revolve around anaesthetising unbearably intense feelings either through self-mutilation as a mechanism to induce or end dissociative states, or self-medication. Through intoxicating substances such as food, drink or drugs, survivors seek oblivion and refuge from a terrifying outer reality and excruciating inner world.

Some survivors will direct these aggressive impulses towards others not just for release of impulses but as a form of self-protection to keep others at bay by being hostile and prickly, thereby avoiding closeness and intimacy. Survivors of interpersonal abuse with poor impulse control may display high levels of reactivity and irritability whereby the merest perceived slight unleashes a torrent of aggression and hostile behaviours. The explosive rage or anger directed at others often mirrors the abuse directed at them by the perpetrator and as such represents a re-enactment of own traumatic experiences. This aggression and hostility towards others is often fuelled by anger at the perpetrator that cannot be expressed for fear of reprisal.

The shame, fear of exposure and subsequent stigmatisation associated with interpersonal trauma may result in social withdrawal and isolation making it difficult for survivors to develop close relationships and develop a support network. This may lead to agoraphobia or social phobia which reinforces the power and control of the abuse, and increased dependency needs. This in turn will limit their opportunities for reality testing and sources of protection. Such level of social isolation also reduces occupational and employment opportunities, and alternative sources for restoring self-esteem and self-agency. In combination, survivors will feel more trapped becoming resigned to the futility of escape, or rescue, and thus succumb to inert surrender.

IMPACT AND EFFECTS ON PHYSICAL HEALTH

If the interpersonal trauma includes physical violence and abuse then there will be a range of external and internal injuries. There may also be a number of old injuries that have failed to heal, or have not received medical attention. One common area of concern is damage to the brain as a result of repeated blows to the head. Survivors of interpersonal trauma may also present with a number of somatic complaints, including physical exhaustion and concomitant disruptions to the immune system as a result of hypervigilance, inability to relax and deprived sleep. Over-activation of the stress response system and chronic stress responses can also result in hypertension, circulatory disease, respiratory complications, nervous system and digestive system disorders, endocrine disorders, skin disorders, acute stress disorder, and chronic fatigue syndrome (Dobie *et al.*, 2004; Frayne *et al.*, 1999; Walker *et al.*, 2003).

Survivors of interpersonal trauma also often present with anxiety disorders and a range of somatoform disorders such as pain disorder, body dysmorphic disorder, hypochondria, conversion disorder and somatisation disorder (Allen, 2001; Sanderson, 2006). Clinicians need to be aware that such somatoform disorders represent symbolic communication about the abuse and need to be addressed accordingly. Some survivors shut down and become numb and unresponsive to their environment, with severe constriction of activity and paralysis.

Self-injury, self-mutilation and suicidality can give rise to a number of physical and health problems. Some survivors use food to exert control making them vulnerable to eating disorders such as anorexia nervosa, bulimia nervosa or obesity and concomitant health risks. Many survivors are also vulnerable to self-medication, especially excessive use of alcohol or drugs and especially those suffering domestic abuse (Sanderson, 2008). In the case of sexual abuse and sexual exploitation alcohol and drug misuse is used not only to manage the abuse but also because dependency is often induced as part of the entrapment process. Substance dependency will need specific therapeutic attention as it can give rise to a complex range of symptoms and clinicians must ensure that the multiple therapeutic needs are met. In the case of survivors who are sexually abused or sexually exploited, there may be sexual inhibition, reduction in libido and sexual difficulties. Some survivors may engage in risky sexual behaviour as a form of self-harm and an illusion of control.

COGNITIVE IMPACT AND EFFECTS

The distortion of perception and reality used by abusers in interpersonal trauma will have considerable impact on cognitive distortions such as self-blame, negative self-attributions and taking responsibility for the abuse. The paradoxical nature of interpersonal trauma necessitates cognitive shifts such as increased tolerance of cognitive inconsistency, or "doublethink", alterations in appraisal of reality, impaired judgment, self-doubt and inability to recognise the abuser's cruelty. To manage the contradictions and distortions survivors block conscious knowledge of their brutalisation through dissociation or compartmentalisation to obliterate the abuse. This allows survivors to disconnect from self, the full range of feelings, needs, desires and personal goals.

Repeated traumatisation also shatters assumptions about self, others and the world as a safe and benign place (Janoff-Bulman, 1985, 1992; McCann and Pearlman, 1990; Blackman, 1989; Goldberg, 1982) which impact on a sense of foreshortened future, loss of hope and loss of meaning. In the absence of meaning the survivor is prevented from constructing a coherent narrative of their experiences, leading to alexithymia (Krystal, 1988) or what Scarf (2005) calls "learned voicelessness". Alexithymia is a common reaction to unspeakable trauma as it acts as a defence against articulating feelings which are perceived as dangerous.

The impact of interpersonal trauma also disrupts mentalisation which impairs reflection of experiences or feelings (Fonagy *et al.*, 2002; Allen, Fonagy and Bateman, 2008). When in survival mode, energy is redirected away from operative thinking, reflection and articulation of emotions. This lack of mentalisation fractures internal resources and resilience leading to resignation and reinforcement of being trapped. A further shattered belief is in the beneficence of others leading to distortions in perception of the trustworthiness of others. Furthermore, distorted cognitive schemas about self and distortion of reality activate attributional errors, enhancing negative beliefs about self and others. Repeated activation of the stress response also impairs cognitive capacity to problem solve, decision making, attention and concentration which reduces opportunities for escape.

IMPACT AND EFFECTS ON MEMORY FUNCTIONING

Perhaps the biggest impact of interpersonal trauma is on memory and memory processing due to neurological disruptions in the limbic system, amygdala, and hippocampus (LeDoux, 1996; van der Kolk, 1994; Sapolsky, 2004). The neurobiological impact of high levels of stress and arousal interferes with memory on a number of levels, leading to fragmented memories. The area of greatest impact is memory formation, disruption to memory consolidation and retrieval, disruption in prefrontal cortex functioning, inhibition of neurogenesis, suppression of unwanted memories, and formation of new memories. While there are disruptions in explicit memory, there is often improvement of implicit memory. In combination these impairments are thought to account to some degree for PTSD symptoms such as flashbacks, intrusive memories and nightmares which are understood to be attempts to integrate experiences that were not fully encoded (Holmes *et al.*, 2001).

These neurological changes are compounded by dissociation which disrupts "...the usually integrated functions of consciousness, memory, identity, or perception of the environment" (APA, 2000). Many researchers and clinicians believe that trauma that threatens integrity of the personality is not processed in the same way as ordinary memories (Terr, 1994; van der Kolk, 1994) and are stored somatically outside conscious awareness as fragmented sensori-motor memories, physical sensation, or visual "flashbulb" images. It is these unprocessed visual flashbulb images that usually form the content of flashbacks, which are thought to be a way to integrated unprocessed experiences.

Lack of elaborate encoding is further implicated in disruptions to mentalisation and reflection leaving experiences and memories disorganised and incoherent. This means that experiences are laid down as affective mental representations, recorded in affective terms without further symbolic processing, and thus stored iconically or at somato-sensory/sensori-motor level rather than on a symbolic or linguistic level, As experiences are not processed, or modified, they are imbued with a timeless quality and intensity which can only be recalled through affect states, somatic sensation or visual images such as flashbacks, or fragmented snapshots with no coherent storyline or context.

As the formation and consolidation of memory is impaired, survivors of interpersonal trauma will experience a range of memory deficits, ranging from full memory recall, partial amnesia and total amnesia (Scheflin and Brown, 1996; Loftus *et al.*, 1994; Roe and Schwartz, 1996; Williams, 1995). Given the range of deficits and the fallibility of memory clinicians must be aware that some survivors will present a range of memories including continuous abuse memories, partial abuse memories, recovered abuse memories, inaccurate abuse memories and false abuse memories (Dale, 1999; Sanderson, 2006), partial or full amnesia.

IMPACT AND EFFECTS ON SELF-STRUCTURES

Repeated interpersonal trauma and persistent annihilation of the survivor's core identity and self-worth compromises the integrity of self-structures. Projective identification alongside persistent denigration and derogation of the survivor leads to the adoption of a false identity which is moulded to what is demanded by the abuser. The negative identity imposed upon them by the abuser leads the survivor to believe that they are worthless, shameful, inadequate and inherently flawed. Survivors have no choice but to adopt this imposed identity as they are unable to reality check such distortions as they are alienated from alternative sources of validation. As a result, the self-structures become identified with abuse, subjugation, and dehumanisation and infected with shame (Sanderson, 2008).

The lack of personal control and self-efficacy inherent in interpersonal trauma further corrodes self-worth and sense of self-agency. In addition, survivors begin to blame themselves for the abuse as this is safer than risking further abuse by challenging the abuser. Through self-blame survivors experience exaggerated feelings of responsibility for the abuse, and guilt for not managing it, which evoke increasingly more submissive and compliant behaviour to appease the abuser. This self-blame sequesters any vestiges of empathy and compassion for self, further reinforcing that they deserve the abuse and are not entitled to better treatment.

Interpersonal trauma is also closely linked to shame (Mollon, 2005), defilement, disgust and humiliation and concomitant self-loathing and self-hatred (Sanderson, 2006). Shame gives rise to a number of coping strategies to manage the conflict between the need to express and need to suppress, to be visible and yet remain invisible. This irreconcilable paradox endangers survivors as to be visible renders them vulnerable to more humiliation and abuse, while remaining invisible leads to dissociation from basic human needs. Excruciating shame leads to concealment and repudiation of needs and feelings, especially feelings of neediness, vulnerability, weakness and inadequacy. To cover up, survivors adopt a false self as a façade of strength, invincibility and self-sufficiency. While the oppression of needs increases the tolerance threshold for abuse, it paradoxically endangers the survivor through not being able to acknowledge the danger they face.

In the process of dehumanisation survivors have to neutralise the essence of self, or at the very least encapsulate it into a realm of inner retreat. This retreat into impenetrable loneliness is facilitated through dissociation, whereby the authentic self is concealed as a form of protection from shame, despair and harm from others. While the authentic self is imprisoned in an unassailable fortress, or "...put into cold storage" (Winnicott, 1965) it is replaced by a false self (Grand, 2000; Kalsched, 1996). This dissociated and disavowed self cannot be reflected upon, or mentalised and becomes sealed off from conscious awareness. This leads to an external locus of control and evaluation as the survivor is out of contact with inner needs and self-evaluation. In some cases such as infantile child abuse and CSA, the self is so shattered that there is no self (Sanderson, 2006) which necessitates particular therapeutic attention. This usually manifests as complete lack of vivacity, vitality, animation, and effervescence.

The false self develops to protect the dehumanised person whose heart and soul have been annihilated through trauma. To do this the false self grows up too fast and becomes precociously adapted to the outer world (Winnicott, 1960) in order to resist any unguarded spontaneous expressions of authentic self in the world. The chameleon-like nature of the false self enables the survivor to be whatever the abuser wants it to be. Most commonly this is manifest in fierce independence, self-sufficiency, invulnerability, and pseudomaturity. This false self often presents as a solid exterior which appears calm, contained, secure, and functional but is actually a veneer for the fragile, labile, insecure, helpless and developmentally immature true self. While this false self appears to be functional and acts a protection for authentic self, it is rigid and does not adapt to internal cues and as such is in constant conflict with the authentic self; this can lead to an identity crisis which can be the prompt to enter therapy.

Rather than focusing on inner needs the survivor looks outside and anticipates the needs of others, especially the abuser. One way to anticipate the needs of others is through mind reading, which is an adaptive survival strategy allowing survivors to adjust to the demands of the abuser, and subsume their own needs. This is often done in the futile hope that when the abuser's needs are satisfied their needs will be fulfilled. Living in the mind of others often results in becoming over-empathic towards others, to the detriment of self-empathy and self-compassion. The false self must ensure that the authentic self remains in exile and will do all in its power to protect concealment. This may lead to self-sabotaging behaviour in which the false self persecutes the true self, long after the abuse has stopped. The imperative is to protect the true self from others, and from itself in terms of keeping rage in check. While the false self can impede healing and recovery from trauma, it must be remembered that it was once adaptive in promoting survival and as such must be honoured not vilified. This needs to be addressed in the therapeutic process so that in the presence of external and internal safety the authentic self can re-emerge and the false self be gradually relinquished.

Alongside a false self, survivors of interpersonal trauma are also susceptible to developing what Orbach (2002) calls a "false body" or extra skin to protect and conceal the vulnerable self. This is often manifested in body armour or body rigidity to contain the seething mass of feelings and internal disintegration. Survivors who have been sexually abused or sexually exploited may adopt a false body of sexual availability by dressing in a sexually provocative way projecting an image of sexual allure which is in stark contrast to their frozen inner sexual feelings. This is an example of adopting the abuser's objectification as a sexual object. In contrast, some survivors repudiate all sexuality and conceal it beneath loose clothing, or obesity, to avoid any sexual attention.

IMPACT AND EFFECTS ON RELATIONAL FUNCTIONING

The betrayal of trust in interpersonal trauma significantly disrupts relational dynamics and affiliative functions, and causes consequent loss of trust in others, loss of relational worth, fear of intimacy, and social isolation. Interpersonal abuse in early childhood will have a profound impact on the development of relational models, especially internal working models (IWMs) of relational worth which act as a template for all future relationships (Bowlby, 1973). While the most profound impact is in early development, relational models are modified through later relational interactions thereby rendering adults who are being abused vulnerable to developing relational difficulties as interpersonal trauma "...destroys belief that one can be *oneself* in relation to others" (Herman, 1992a). Changes in relational worth result in distortions in relational schemas which allow for "traumatic bonding" (Dutton and Painter, 1981) to occur which acts as a "superglue" to bond the abuser and survivor. In the presence of danger the natural impulse is to run to the person closest for comfort and soothing, even if this is the very person who is causing the fear. This generates confusion and contradictions that cannot easily be resolved, and yet binds the survivor ever more to the abuser. This creates increased dependency on the abuser, increasing his power and control.

Traumatic bonding creates emotional attachments that are far stronger, more intense, and much more difficult to sever due to intermittent reinforcement. The alternating cycles of affection and care and psychological or physical punishment keep the survivor in a state of anxious anticipation and hope, and in thrall to the abuser. The power wielded by the abuser to annihilate or to preserve life evokes paradoxical gratitude, or pathological transference (Ochberg, 1988), which invokes positive feelings of love, compassion and empathy in the survivor.

The lack of relational trust and fear of intimacy precludes survivors from seeking support and closeness from others, which reinforces their social isolation. Many survivors prefer to seek refuge and solace in objects and things rather than people as these are more reliable. While some survivors do risk affiliation they are often disappointed and retreat from the threat of intimacy or fear revictimisation, oscillating between closeness and withdrawal. This will give rise to insecure attachment behaviours with survivors displaying either an insecure-dismissive, or insecure-fearful avoidant-unresolved attachment style (Sanderson, 2008). The one most commonly associated with interpersonal trauma is a disorganised-disoriented-dissociated attachment style which is characterised by dysregulated emotions, relational instability, under-developed self-capacities and approach-avoid behaviour pattern (Anderson and Alexander, 1996; Fonagy *et al.*, 1995; Liotti, 1992; Sanderson, 2008). Assessing survivors' attachment style is helpful in the therapeutic process as it is likely to manifest in the therapeutic relationship.

Survivors who have been sexually abused retreat from sexual intimacy as a further violation and so curb their sexual desires to avoid becoming involved. In contrast others may seek brief sexual encounters that are devoid of intimacy, in the belief that this will protect them from further hurt, while retaining a semblance of power and control. Fear of rejection, abandonment and future retraumatisation will lead some survivors to avoid engaging with professionals, including counsellors and therapists, making them highly resistant to any form of professional help such as health services, social or children's services. This is why it is critical for all professionals involved with survivors of interpersonal trauma to ensure the adoption of good practice models to minimise any perceived retraumatisation.

Survivors who have children and who are being abused, for example in domestic abuse situations, may not always be able to be emotionally available to children, or protect them from the abuse, or abuser (Hester, Pearson and Harwin, 2007; Calder, Harold and Howarth, 2006), due to the survivor's own psychological distress, depleted energy resources or self-medication. Any risk posed to children must be assessed within statutory guidelines, although professionals must remember that reduced parenting capacity may be the result of interpersonal trauma, and not deliberate harm, and that with appropriate support parenting skills can be restored.

The uncertainty and unpredictability of the abuser leads to distrust and suspicion of others. This makes it extremely difficult for survivors to enlist the help of others or to seek out allies. Some survivors will present as hostile or difficult as a way to ward others off and keep them at bay. This makes it extremely hard to get close to them, which, while a form of protection, also alienates them from others and reinforces a sense of utter aloneness. Those that are able to engage in close relationships may find it very difficult to set limits and boundaries, or express needs. This can lead to relational difficulties in which boundary violations become the norm and the survivor is unable to communicate basic needs. In this they may re-enact their abuse experiences by becoming compliant and submissive.

The disconnection from others catapults the survivor into an abyss of loneliness and enforced isolation which keeps the inner self safe and others from reaching in. The paradox of hope for protection and retreat helps the survivor to cope with the dread of annihilation in which others are seen as figures of hope and dread. In this, others offer the potential for making the survivor visible and yet they also threaten to eclipse the lack of self with an imposed identity. In the lack of connection with others and opportunities for "I–Thou" (Buber, 1987), survivors face psychological and relational death.

The relational distortions inherent in interpersonal trauma disrupt survivors' ability to distinguish between nurturing and non-nurturing caregivers. As their central organising relational principle is wanting to be taken care of and yet expecting to be retraumatised, they become frozen, especially in new relationships. As survivors have no concept or template of healthy relational dynamics they often end up seeking out and trusting those that manifest similar dynamics to the abuser and who may be harmful. Some survivors fear new relationships so much that they either stay, return to or renew links with the abuser "...because being mis-recognised feels so much more secure than being unrecognised and unknown" (Nachmani, 1995, p.430) making them vulnerable to revictimisation by the abuser.

IMPACT AND EFFECTS ON SEXUALITY

The impact and effects of repeated and prolonged sexual abuse commonly cluster around the personality being organised around sexual objectification which can generate confusions in sexual identity, and norms around sexual behaviour, and profound shame. Many survivors conflate sex with aggression and cannot conceive of sexual intimacy which is predicated on love and affection. Depending on the nature of the sexual abuse, sexual parts of the body may become fetishised leading to sexual aversions, or complete absence of sexual feelings. Some survivors become over-sexualised and become consumed with sexual preoccupations and compulsions, including compulsive masturbation. The inability to set sexual boundaries renders many survivors vulnerable to risky sexual behaviour, promiscuity and being lured into prostitution (Sanderson, 2006).

There are a number of sexual dysfunctions that are commonly associated with sexual abuse which will need to be assessed. These include impaired sexual motivation or sexual arousal, anorgasmia, vaginismus, dyspareunia, sexual anaesthesia and sexual anorexia (Sanderson, 2006). Many survivors of sexual trauma disconnect from their bodies during sexual contact activating conditioned or automatic sexual responses, outside any conscious experience of pleasure or release. The shame around any sexual feelings can be so paralysing that the survivor may freeze and dissociate to avoid any feelings. This can lead to avoidance of sexual intimacy and, in some cases, confusion around sexual orientation.

DISCONNECTION FROM LIFE

The dehumanisation and psychological death inherent in interpersonal trauma can lead to a total disconnection from self, others and life. Repeated and prolonged abuse sequesters the survivor's life energy force, resulting in loss of vitality, hope and spirituality, leaving the survivor "...at once dead and yet left alive in the wake of her own destruction" (Grand, 2000). All energy, no matter how meagre, is directed to survival and managing abuse symptoms. This prevents any expression of grief or mourning for the myriad losses associated with interpersonal trauma. It is only in the presence of internal and external safety that energy can be restored and that survivors can afford to grieve and restore hope to reconnect to life.

It is critical for counsellors to be aware of the impact and long-term effects of interpersonal trauma in order to make accurate assessment and to contextualise presenting symptoms within the context of trauma rather than pathologising survivors. Armed with this understanding of the impact, effective treatment interventions can be implemented.

SUMMARY

- The betrayal of trust, the distortion of perceptions and the paradox of *knowing* and yet *not knowing* ubiquitous to interpersonal trauma activates a number of psychobiological mechanisms which compromise psychological integrity yet aid survival.

- There are a range of responses, impacts and long-term effects that are unique to each individual. Most commonly these cluster around neurobiological effects in activating primitive survival mechanisms and stress responses. These release a cascade of neurobiochemicals and stress hormones, which, given the inescapable nature of interpersonal trauma, cannot be sufficiently discharged leading to post-traumatic stress symptoms and PTSD.

- Repeated activation of the stress response system can also lead to impairments in affect regulation which in turn can elicit dissociative states to manage unbearable feelings. This can invoke self-destructive behaviours such as self-injury, or self-medication through substance misuse or a variety of addictive behaviours.

- The distortion of perception leads to cognitive dissonance which necessitates cognitive restructuring, while prolonged neurobiological activation impacts on cognitive structures such as memory functioning. Interpersonal trauma impairs the encoding, consolidation and storage of memory which are stored on a somato-sensory level, outside of conscious awareness and coherent narrative.

- Interpersonal trauma also impacts on physical function and physical health. These can be either as a result of injury or prolonged stress response activation and hypervigilance which prevents sleep and relaxation putting the body in overdrive with no opportunity for recuperation.

- There are a number of behavioural difficulties associated with interpersonal trauma, not least over- or under-control of impulses and emotions. This can lead to irritability or rigid self-control and submissive and compliant behaviour.

- Interpersonal trauma has considerable impact on self-structures leading to the fragmentation of self, concealment of the authentic self and the adoption of a false self. While the authentic self is imprisoned in a fortress of protection, the false self often continues to persecute this sequestered self even long after the abuse has ceased.

- Lack of self-worth impacts on relational worth and relational schemas. Interpersonal abuse breeds insecure and disorganised attachment styles in which survivors vacillate between approach and avoid. The betrayal of trust leads to fear of intimacy and closeness with others which leads to social withdrawal and isolation, and reinforces traumatic bonding.

- In the case of sexual abuse survivors may experience a number of sexual difficulties including disconnection from sexual feelings, sexual aversions, preoccupations or compulsions. Lack of sexual boundaries can lead to risky sexual behaviours, while some survivors may avoid any sexual intimacy. Sexual trauma can also give rise to sexual dysfunctions ranging from impaired arousal, anorgasmia, vaginismus to dyspareunia. In some cases confusion around sexual orientation may manifest.

- Dehumanisation and the inescapable nature of interpersonal trauma leads many survivors to disconnect from self, others and life as they already experience psychological death. Depleted energy resources impact on vitality and spirituality, and prevent grieving the myriad losses and restoration of hope.

CHAPTER 4

CREATING A SECURE BASE

Fundamental Principles of Safe Trauma Therapy

The ubiquitous betrayal of trust in interpersonal trauma necessitates a safe therapeutic environment in which survivors can explore the full range of feelings and make sense of their experiences. To facilitate this, counsellors need to provide a secure base in which to restore safety and allow survivors to process traumatic material, and rebuild trust in self and others. The dehumanisation associated with interpersonal trauma can only be reversed in the presence of a warm, human and authentic relationship. To provide this clinicians must go beyond prescribed trauma protocols and ensure a sensitively attuned therapeutic relationship.

The emphasis needs to be not just symptom relief but also to promote growth, to gain mastery over and transform trauma through developing alternative ways of thinking about their experiences, acquiring new skills and abilities with which to overcome limitations of the past to create a positive future. This requires an integrative approach which is tailored to each individual's unique experience and which is flexible in adopting a range of interventions. Most crucially the therapeutic relationship is central to enable the survivor to reconnect to self, reclaim control, and develop self-efficacy and agency.

This chapter will look at the fundamental principles of safe trauma therapy and how to establish these when working with survivors of interpersonal trauma. It will examine how to create a safe and secure therapeutic setting which is well bounded and can act as a secure base from which to explore traumatic experiences. This is necessary before embarking on any therapeutic work as survivors must experience both external and internal safety to manage the return of dissociated feelings. In addition the chapter will look at the therapeutic process, managing sessions, and some of the challenges clinicians face when working with this client group. The role of the counsellor and the centrality of the therapeutic relationship will be explored in providing an opportunity to reconnect to self, others and the world.

FUNDAMENTAL PRINCIPLES OF WORKING WITH SURVIVORS OF INTERPERSONAL ABUSE

> Therapy is not about relieving suffering, it's about repairing one's relationship to reality. (Anonymous, 1994)

The complex nature of interpersonal trauma necessitates specific treatment focus. What is critical is for clinicians to not just "*understand*" survivors but to really "*know*" them (Bromberg, 1994). This can be achieved with thorough understanding of the impact and effects of interpersonal abuse. To implement effective treatment, counsellors must first conduct a comprehensive assessment to establish what the main areas of concern are for each individual survivor in order to devise a tailor-made care plan. Counsellors need to include an appreciation of already existing resources and acknowledge that these have aided survival. Rather than reject survival strategies they can be enhanced, cross-fertilised and developed alongside other alternative strategies to fully empower the survivor. A comprehensive assessment may identify a need for the involvement of other professionals and agencies. To ensure that all the needs of the survivor are met, counsellors must acquaint themselves, and form links, with the range of multi-agency resources available in the community in order to provide a comprehensive and holistic supportive network for survivors of interpersonal trauma.

The therapeutic process will not progress until safety has been established. This includes external safety in relation to the abuser and living arrangements, as well as internal safety in terms of managing psychobiological symptoms and turbulent internal affect states. Given the betrayal of trust in interpersonal trauma, survivors must also feel safe to trust the counsellor. To facilitate this, counsellors must create a safe and secure base not just in terms of clinical setting, but also in providing an authentic relationship in which honesty, clarity and explicitness are paramount. This reduces the risk of miscommunication, falsification of reality and distortion of perception characteristic of interpersonal trauma.

Counsellors also need to help survivors to reclaim control in order to restore autonomy, mastery and self-agency. This is initially facilitated by regaining mastery of the body and mind (van der Kolk, 2008) through affect regulation, distress tolerance and integrating dissociated aspects of the self. As the myriad psychobiological symptoms are often terrifying and confusing, counsellors need to provide a degree of psychoeducation to normalise them as traumatic reactions and link these to the abuse. Greater understanding of symptoms will instil a sense of control and help the survivor to manage them more effectively. This allows the survivor to feel more in charge and focused to master the impact and effects of traumatisation. Counsellors can also restore control to survivors by allowing them to set their own goals and manage the therapeutic sessions at their own pace. This is crucial given that during the interpersonal abuse they had to subsume their needs and desires to those of the abuser.

To further enhance safety counsellors need to establish a good working alliance and therapeutic relationship based on authenticity and honesty. The deception and subterfuge inherent in interpersonal abuse sensitises survivors to any verbal and non-verbal cues to monitor the authenticity of responses and reactions. Being frank and explicit in all communications enables the survivor to begin to trust the counsellor and risk connection. Survivors of interpersonal trauma must be honoured for risking connection despite repeated betrayals as it is a testament to hope that has not been extinguished. Pivotal to this is the therapeutic relationship in which "the therapist helps to heal by developing a genuine relationship with the patient" (Yalom, 1980, p.401). In the case of interpersonal trauma in early childhood in which the child has not had the opportunity to develop internal resources or resilience "...the relationship is the therapy" (Kahn, 1997, p.1).

In the safety of the therapeutic relationship the survivor can begin to explore the traumatic experiences, make sense of them and construct a more coherent narrative. Through this the trauma can be processed and integrated, and perceptual distortions challenged, allowing the return of the authentic self. In addition, as safety is established and consolidated, the survivor can come out of survival mode and begin to grieve and mourn the myriad losses associated with interpersonal trauma. The process of mourning will enable the survivor to begin to restore hope and start to reconnect to life. The renewed energy restores vitality and a zest for life in which survivors can move from surviving to finally feeling fully alive.

THERAPEUTIC AIMS

The central aims when working with interpersonal trauma are safety, stabilisation, mastery over neurobiological and psychological deficits, processing of trauma-related experiences and the integration of dissociated states (Streeck-Fischer and van der Kolk, 2000; de Zulueta, 2006; 2008). Herman (1992a) also emphasises the importance of grief and mourning to fully restore reconnection to self and others.

An integral part of working with interpersonal trauma is to enable survivors to name and legitimise their experiences as abuse. This is often very difficult if there has been considerable grooming, enticement and entrapment. Survivors of CSA, domestic abuse and elder abuse often believe that their relationship with the abuser is a "special" one which is predicated on love, nurturing and caring, not abuse. It is even harder to legitimise it as abuse if the survivor has dissociated from the abuse episodes, or has taken responsibility for the abuse and engages in self-blame. In addition, counsellors need to contextualise the range of presenting symptoms and convey that these are normal responses to brutalisation and traumatisation and not some failure or pathology in the survivor. Thus the therapeutic process must contain an element of psychoeducation in which the counsellor provides knowledge and information on the nature of trauma, its impact and effects. Such knowledge will enhance comprehensibility, increase the survivor's sense of control and allow for making sense of trauma experiences.

Restoring control and power will promote self-agency giving the survivor the confidence to find mastery over their symptoms and the effects of trauma. Counsellors need to validate how far the survivor has come and focus on resources and strengthen them. These can be co-opted to help the survivor to stabilise affect dysregulation. This can be facilitated through affect modulation and distress tolerance whereby the survivor is more able to manage emotions rather than resorting to the use of dissociation and dissociative states. This will allow for the integration of mind and body and restore the fractured self. By lifting the veil of betrayal and making the hidden visible the survivor can permit the annihilated, or buried, self to return. Counsellors need to exercise caution though, as integration and wholeness are initially experienced as unimaginably terrifying as fears of disintegration are evoked. This commonly signals the need for psychic numbing and dissociation and concomitant acting out or somatisation of self-destructive behaviours. This can lead to an increase in self-harm or self-medication. Rather than interpret this as resistance, counsellors must understand this as a form of protection for what was dissociated, or concealed. It is for this reason that the safe and secure base of the therapeutic setting is so pivotal so that the survivor can risk integration and reconnection to the authentic self.

Internal and external safety through the mastery of affect regulation and a safe therapeutic relationship will help to coax the hidden, vulnerable and needy self to emerge from its fortress and access the full range of feelings. Restoring fractured self-structures will also facilitate relational functioning. As the authentic self is able to risk connection it can begin to build trust in the self and others. This is most likely to flourish in an authentic, genuinely warm human relationship. Counsellors need to be human and authentic in their responses, to avoid any subterfuge, otherwise the survivor will retreat to the safety of their long-term prison. Improved relational functioning will permit survivors to identify and express their needs without fear of censure or humiliation. This will reduce the need for self-destructive behaviours as the survivor is more able to express and manage painful feelings without resorting to anaesthetisation.

As integration takes place the survivor can begin to mourn the losses incurred through traumatisation. As the concealed pain, hurt and unmet needs emerge, survivors can begin to grieve for the vulnerable, needy self that has been deeply buried. To this effect grief is an integral part of reuniting the dissociated parts. In the case of very early, prolonged traumatisation, grief becomes a central focus of the therapeutic work. Counsellors must remember that mourning is not a linear process and consists of many diversions. It is essential that counsellors are patient in allowing full grieving to take place so that the survivor can fully integrate and reconnect to self and the world, and live more authentically.

ASSESSMENT

In order to offer the most effective therapeutic intervention, counsellors need to perform a comprehensive assessment prior to commencing therapy. Given the complex nature of interpersonal trauma and its wide-ranging impact, it may be necessary to conduct the initial assessment over several sessions and to continuously monitor progress. The initial assessment needs to take into account the full range of current difficulties, and needs to identify any pre-existing problems that have been exacerbated or intensified by trauma, and those difficulties that specifically derive from traumatisation, or disclosure. It is also useful to ascertain the most troublesome aspects of the trauma for the client, and which cause the most distress.

Counsellors also need to assess the type of traumatisation that the survivor has been exposed to, such as whether it included sexual assault or physical assault, and the degree of cognitive distortion. Age of onset is also an important consideration as the earlier the onset the more primitive the psychobiological defences; earlier onset also means fewer opportunities to develop resilience or psychological resources. Later onset of interpersonal trauma is less likely to annihilate already acquired psychological resources, making it easier for them to be reinstated once in a place of safety. Another factor is the intensity, frequency and duration of the interpersonal trauma and how many developmental stages it straddles. Most researchers and clinicians believe that early trauma across a number of developmental stages, and of long duration, has the most severe psychobiological impact (Allen 2001, Sanderson, 2008).

Counsellors also need to consider genetic predisposition and temperament of each individual survivor to assess level of resilience not only to traumatisation but also in rebuilding or restoring psychological resources. Some survivors may not be able to restore or acquire the necessary resources and thus will need extra long-term support. This must not be interpreted as resistance or passivity but needs to derive from a frank and honest appraisal. There is huge variation between individuals in terms of access to psychological resources which are genetically or biologically based and not just due to learned helplessness or pathological dependency. Most survivors will have access to some resources, no matter how meagre, and these will have aided survival. Counsellors need to identify these and encourage survivors to honour these as they have helped them to survive. Once identified these resources need to be assessed, honed and built upon, as well as other supportive skills and resources being introduced to restore autonomy and self-agency to the survivor.

Part of the assessment needs to include evaluation of external safety and access to supportive others. This includes contact with abuser and degree of risk involved. It is also worth assessing if there is any risk to the survivor as a result of disclosure either from the abuser, or others who have been impacted by disclosure such as other family members or associates. This is especially the case in the case of associates involved in sexual exploitation, or families who feel dishonoured and advocate honour killing. Some survivors are also stigmatised by their community and may be ostracised or vilified, reducing access to social support. The presence of supportive others can have a powerful impact on recovery from trauma, and counsellors need to assess availability to a support network, and actively encourage survivors to access and develop a level of support.

THE THERAPEUTIC SETTING

Pivotal to establishing safety is a safe and secure therapeutic setting. The therapeutic space needs to be free from distractions such as loud noise, the ringing of telephones and interruptions. The therapy room needs to provide a calm oasis from any external clamour so that the survivor can begin to explore their inner state knowing that they have the counsellor's undivided attention. Given the distress associated with exploring trauma, survivors may need to have access to cloakroom facilities during the session. Terror states induce physiological needs for evacuation and survivors will need to access these with relative ease. In my experience, many survivors feel nauseous when exploring traumatic experiences and are often terrified of vomiting in session. Counsellors need to be prepared for this, and permit the survivor to break in session if necessary. Furthermore, some survivors when nervous and anxious may need frequent micturition but be too afraid to use the requisite facilities. Counsellors need to be explicit in discussing the use of such facilities during session.

While traditional therapeutic practice frowns upon offering refreshment to clients, counsellors may need to provide access to water for clients with elevated stress reactions such as respiratory difficulties, dry mouth and difficulty with swallowing due to the re-experiencing of trauma. At the very least, counsellors need to be clear and explicit around survivors bringing water or drinks into session, and whether they will offer water if the survivor is in distress. Similarly counsellors must be clear about providing tissues to clients and whether these are offered or left within easy reach of the client. These all need to be explicitly stated as survivors of interpersonal abuse are commonly terrified of expressing their needs for fear of rejection and many suffer in silence, become preoccupied by their unexpressed needs, and do not fully engage in the therapeutic process. A client who desperately needs to vomit or urinate or is gasping for water will not be able to focus on what is being explored until homeostasis is restored.

Counsellors also need to be aware of the seating arrangements. The captivity and inescapable nature of interpersonal trauma means that survivors will feel trapped if they cannot see an exit or escape route. To this effect counsellors need to allow survivors to sit within sight of, and with unimpeded access to, the door. Awareness of personal space is also important as the survivor may feel invaded by too close proximity, but may feel distanced and cut off if too far away. To maintain emotional warmth and human elements of the relationship it is preferable that counsellors do not create a barrier by taking notes. A further barrier to communication is if the sessions are taped as survivors may accede to this for fear of saying no. Knowing that they are being recorded will make survivors more self-conscious which could impede the trauma narrative. It may also invoke fears around confidentiality and the betrayal of trust.

CONTRACT

To avoid confusion and miscommunication, counsellors need to be explicit when drawing up the therapeutic contract. To minimise the unequal power balance between client and counsellors, counsellors must convey that the contract is a collaborative process which states rather than sets limits. The contract should contain areas of responsibility for both survivor and counsellor to enable clients to take control and charge of their recovery. Counsellors need to emphasise the collaborative nature of the therapeutic process, what they can and cannot offer, and any expectations they have of the client.

It is critical that counsellors do not offer or promise something that they cannot follow through on as this can have a devastating effect on the survivor in terms of betrayal of trust. Counsellors need to be clear about what they can offer such as flexibility in scheduling session, writing reports on behalf of survivors for court or other agencies, attendance at meetings or court attendance, out-of-hours contact, length of session, payment of fees, cancellations and holiday arrangements. While counsellors may need to be more flexible with this client group, they nevertheless need to be well bounded. It is often helpful if all this information is supported with a small printed leaflet that the survivor can refer to. Counsellors may also include information on this leaflet about their orientation, how therapy works, and what clients can expect from the therapeutic process.

Many survivors of interpersonal trauma, in particular those who have experienced domestic abuse, have concerns around confidentiality as they fear retaliation from their partner. Counsellors need to be absolutely explicit about areas of confidentiality and about the circumstances in which these would be broken. If counsellors have concerns about the survivor, or any dependent children, and need to share such information with other professionals, they must discuss these with the survivor before breaking confidentiality. In addition survivors need to be clear about taking of notes and who has ownership, and access to them.

BOUNDARIES

Boundaries in the therapeutic process act as an "envelope of trust" (Brown and Stobart, 2008) and are fundamental to safe trauma therapy. Counsellors need to be clear and explicit as to the nature of these boundaries so that the therapeutic space is safe for the survivor to express forbidden, concealed and shameful feelings and thoughts. Counsellors need to discuss the importance of boundaries with the client, emphasising that they keep both the survivor and the counsellor safe and should be negotiated collaboratively. Boundaries keep the survivor safe and provide a cushion for the counsellor as they act as psychological and physical containment for the therapist which in turn provides contained space for therapeutic work. Modelling healthy protective boundaries can also help survivors to reconstruct personal boundaries to replace historically rigid defences. They will also enable survivors to feel comfortable around expressing needs and being able to say no.

Given the unpredictability and uncertainty inherent in interpersonal trauma it is imperative that the therapeutic space is as predictable as possible through boundaries around time and length of sessions, predictable beginnings and endings of sessions, regularity and frequency of sessions. While counsellors may need to be flexible to accommodate clients rescheduling sessions when necessary, they must balance this with the potential danger of a collapse of boundaries. Throughout, counsellors must be explicit at all times so there is no doubt or confusion.

Counsellors must also be explicit around physical contact and touch. While this is not generally advocated, some counsellors do use touch in the therapeutic setting with good effect. Physical contact between client and therapist is hugely controversial and must only be considered after considerable thought and evaluation of the benefits and dangers of touch. A guiding principle is "if in doubt don't", and only ever if it is in the genuine interest of the client.

Other boundaries that need to be clearly stated are around dual relationships and how to manage chance meetings outside the therapeutic setting. Counsellors need to guide clients in terms of how to manage chance meetings: whether to say hello or just nod. This is critical so that survivors do not feel hurt or rejected if their greeting is not acknowledged. It is helpful when these boundaries are discussed if the counsellor provides a genuine rationale as to why they are in place so that the survivor can understand the reasons for them. Lastly counsellors need to be aware of boundaries around self-disclosure. While the use of self and self-disclosure can make for a very human therapeutic relationship (Woskett, 1999), counsellors need to monitor the level of disclosure. It is critical for counsellors to be authentic and transparent in the therapeutic relationship and this will necessitate some degree of disclosure. This may include immediate somatic reactions to the survivor's material but can also be around how the counsellor feels about the client. Frank and honest responses will be valued over fake responses that are made behind a façade of professional distance. Counsellors need to be mindful of to what degree they feel comfortable in responding to personal questions. If counsellors feel uncomfortable about disclosing personal information it is helpful to explain why they are reluctant to answer the question rather than be evasive. Whatever is disclosed must always be in the genuine interest of the survivor and must be succinct and pithy. Such self-disclosure is helpful when it aids the survivor's understanding or is used to normalise human responses. It should never be used to shift the focus away from the client, or contaminate the therapeutic process.

MANAGING SESSIONS

When working with survivors of interpersonal abuse, counsellors need to pay particular attention to length of sessions, pacing and managing therapeutic session. The intensity of traumatic experiences can be difficult to explore and regulate within the standard therapeutic hour. Some counsellors find that the "fifty-minute hour" is often not long enough for the survivor to settle, explore material and restore safety in preparation to leave. Counsellors may consider scheduling slightly longer sessions to ensure that the survivor is suitably contained when leaving to face the external world. In my experience a full sixty-minute hour is often more beneficial, although some advocate ninety-minute sessions. If counsellors do choose to schedule longer sessions this should be made clear at the beginning and be discussed as part of the contract. Counsellors need to be wary of adjusting length of sessions depending on material explored as this will feel chaotic and unpredictable to the survivor.

Whatever the length of session, counsellors need to manage and regulate the pace so that the survivor feels safe throughout. At the beginning of the session clients need time to settle in. Knowing the intensity of the traumatic material, some survivors need to "psyche" themselves up for the onslaught of turbulent feelings. This settling in can take many forms and is usually characterised by more general conversation. It is important that survivors are allowed to pace this until they are ready to look at more painful material. Survivors often fear that the therapist will forget about them in between sessions and they need to check that they have kept them "in mind". Thus the beginning of the session is a way to check that they have been kept "in mind", that trust and safety is still intact and that the counsellor is still present and engaged. This can be conveyed by ascertaining the survivor's current inner state, how they are feeling, what their immediate needs are, including thirst and hunger, and what is of particular concern to them at the moment.

Once survivors feel reassured that they still have control of the pace, and they have settled, they can move into exploring some of the traumatic material. Such exploration invariably unleashes turbulent and frightening feelings which need to be contained by the counsellor. During this phase, counsellors need to be aware of time so that they can regulate this exploration and restore safety in advance of the end of the session. Survivors will need at least ten to fifteen minutes to move from highly aroused emotional states to feel calm enough to leave and return to the outside world. It is essential that counsellors factor in time to restore safety so that the survivor feels contained enough to leave in order to minimise dissociative states or self-destructive behaviour to manage uncontained feelings. The regulation of sessions will also help the survivor to learn affect regulation which will promote greater internal safety and control.

To restore control to the survivor it is important for counsellors to allow them to pace the sessions. Survivors must not feel pressurised to explore traumatic experiences prematurely, or to feel they have to talk. They must be given the choice to go at a pace that is manageable for them, and if they do not wish to talk this must not be interpreted as resistance. Some survivors will be very reluctant to explore traumatic material, whereas others will rush through painful experiences with no mentalisation, very like rushing through the abuse episodes. While counsellors need to allow survivors to pace session, they can nevertheless help regulate them. Survivors who rush and evacuate can be slowed down through counsellor's tone of voice. If this is slowed down to become more rhythmic it can create a gentle ebb and flow which will soothe and regulate the survivor's internal state and pace. This is akin to the rhythmic tone used by a mother to soothe and regulate the infant's internal state.

In the case of silence, counsellors can gently prompt the client, not through asking questions but through paying attention to the non-verbal cues. Reflecting to the client that they can see how painful or difficult it is for them can regulate and encourage the survivor to communicate further. Breaking silence must be carefully managed. While silence is sometimes therapeutically necessary, silence can also be the loneliest, scariest place in the world, especially for survivors of interpersonal trauma who have been consistently silenced. Counsellors must find a balance between holding and breaking silence. When holding the silence, it is imperative that the counsellor remains embodied, engaged and present. If they become disengaged the survivor will disconnect further causing a rupture in the therapeutic relationship. To convey their presence, counsellors need to focus on the survivor by monitoring somatic changes and non-verbal cues such as skin tone, breathing, eye gaze and facial expression. These cues to the survivor's internal, unexpressed states can then be conveyed as a way to break the silence through reflections such as "I see that really touches you". This not only validates the survivor, but also reinforces the counsellor's presence and ability to make the hidden visible.

This tracking of the survivor's responses is critical in not just understanding survivors but in really knowing them. Survivors of interpersonal trauma were rendered invisible during the abuse and they had to conceal all feelings and thoughts. To have someone notice them and make them visible can be extremely restorative and healing. Counsellors can track affective cues through monitoring eye gaze, eye contact, body language, paralanguage, vocalisation, facial expressions, and tone of voice. Somatic cues such as changes in skin tone, breathing, holding breath, and "spacing out" are also a powerful way of tracking internal states. These cues can also alert the counsellor to disconnection and dissociative states. While all of these are potent ways of affirming and connecting with the survivor, counsellors need to ensure that this is not experienced as too intrusive as the survivor will feel scrutinised which can invoke discomfort as it mirrors the intrusiveness and scrutiny of the abuser.

THE THERAPEUTIC PROCESS

For survivors to enter therapy is a testament to hope and reflects the desire to connect despite repeated betrayal. It is a demonstration that the authentic self has not been obliterated and is still striving to be heard and made visible. Counsellors need to respect and honour the courage it takes to risk connection by providing an authentic therapeutic relationship based on total honesty, immediacy and transparency. The therapeutic process is highly complex and not linear, and requires patience in pacing the work to restore power and control to the survivor. There will be many diversions and distractions, not least practical aspects associated with interpersonal trauma such as environmental safety, outstanding court procedures, housing and establishing sources of support. Counsellors need to be patient, not rush the survivor but allow for diversions until the survivor can begin to direct the focus.

Phases of the therapeutic process

There are usually three main phases of the therapeutic process when working with survivors of interpersonal trauma (Herman, 1992a; Sanderson, 2008), although these are by no means sequential. Survivors commonly vacillate between phases as earlier material is revisited and integrated with new knowledge.

THE INITIAL PHASE

Following on from a comprehensive assessment, and negotiating the contract, the focus of the initial phase of the therapeutic process is on establishing safety. This is paramount as therapy cannot proceed without a reasonable level of safety (Herman, 1992a; Sanderson, 2006, 2008). It is during this phase that the working alliance is established through a mutual, collaborative relationship based on trust, respect, honesty and authenticity. A strong working alliance can facilitate the necessary containment, affect management, self-care and symptom control to name and explore traumatic experiences. The development of trust must be prioritised precisely because the survivor's trust has been consistently betrayed. This may be hard to do as lack of trust is so pervasive and omnipresent, despite being unformulated and unexpressed. Before trust can be established survivors often spend considerable time testing and challenging the clinician before being reassured. For this reason, trust should be seen as a process with fluctuating levels in engagement in which counsellors must remain constant and consistent no matter how much they are being tested. It is worth noting that some survivors entrust themselves too easily with huge expectations, only to feel let down.

To build trust, the counsellor must be reliable, and consistent in their responses, and maintain clear and safe boundaries. In addition, counsellors need to convey that they can manage the uncertainties, paradoxes and contradictions commonly associated with interpersonal trauma. With trust comes closeness and intimacy, and while survivors yearn for this, they are also terrified of such closeness. Counsellors must remember that closeness for many survivors is associated with danger, signalling invasion, violation, abuse. This terror will prompt them to retreat and get caught in a cycle of approach and avoid. Counsellors must link such behaviour to the trauma rather than interpret this as borderline personality disorder. In this phase counsellor interventions need to be sensitive, brief and mirror the survivor's emotional state, rather than being overly analytical.

Focus during the initial phase should also be directed to establishing internal safety through affect regulation, distress tolerance and developing containment strategies to manage post-traumatic stress reactions and fluctuating arousal states (see Chapter 6). This allows the survivor to feel more in control of their internal states and begin to identify needs. During this phase existing survival strategies can be identified, consolidated and employed to help stabilisation. The emphasis throughout this phase is on stabilising the survivor, restoring safety in preparation for the next phase in which traumatic material is explored in more depth.

THE MIDDLE PHASE

The focus in the middle phase is on metabolising trauma and exploring the traumatic experiences. Through this exploration survivors can begin to process and integrate the trauma, create meaning, and develop a more coherent narrative. Central to this is mourning the multiple losses associated with interpersonal trauma, not least loss of the authentic self, relational worth and lack of a secure base. The relationship between trauma and loss, the importance of mourning and the stages of grief are discussed in more depth in Chapter 5. When processing trauma counsellors need to consider using de-conditioning principles of controlled exposure to traumatic material, alongside the survivor's newly acquired skills of affect regulation. This can then be accompanied by a reconstruction of "shame and humiliation" to "dignity and virtue" (Mollica, 1988).

By mentalising emotions survivors can enhance self-awareness, understanding and control (Allen, 2006a; Fonagy *et al.*, 2002; Allen and Fonagy, 2006). Mentalising allows the individual to feel and think about emotions at the same time, rather than at a later point, and prevents them from becoming embedded feelings. It also allows the individual to identify, or become aware of emotion, modulate the intensity and duration of the emotion, and express the emotion in an appropriate way. Mentalising emotions also facilitates grieving which is pivotal in accepting the reality and full extent of trauma and abuse. It is through grieving that reconsolidation and restructuring can take place (Herman, 1992a) which are necessary ingredients in reclaiming power and control.

THE LATE PHASE

The focus in the late phase is on reconnection through the therapeutic relationship and consolidating new skills. This phase is about gaining greater mastery, developing new skills and enhancing self-esteem, self-confidence and self-efficacy. These skills will allow for reconnection to others and a reduction in social isolation. As survivors begin to relinquish primitive defences and establish healthy boundaries they begin to express needs and the full range of feelings. Most importantly they begin to say no without fear of punishment which reduces compliance and submissiveness, and permits more authentic interactions. The reconnection to self and others in this phase allows for reconnection to life in which survivors can make personally meaningful choices and are able to direct their lives and restore vitality. This is usually accompanied by a renewed zest for life, and capacity for pleasure, laughter and joy to live life more authentically.

ENDING

Although ending is implicit from the moment the therapeutic process begins, it can create anxieties for both survivors and counsellors which need to be explored. Counsellors and clients need to be clear which factors will indicate that ending is imminent. This may be because specific set goals have been achieved or because of more general improvement in self-esteem, self-efficacy, more cohesive self-structures or improved relational dynamics. Counsellors must collaborate with survivors in terms of how to work towards ending whether through goal setting, or reduction in frequency of sessions and opportunities for top-up sessions. Whichever route is chosen, endings must be carefully planned within a mutually agreed time frame. Counsellors also need to consider their position with regard to a survivor returning to therapy at a later point. Bearing in mind that personal growth is a dynamic, lifelong process, and that subsequent experiences can revive painful experiences, some survivors may wish to return for brief periods to address any concerns that may have been revived. Counsellors need to consider whether they can offer this through brief solution-focused contracts that focus on the specific difficulty.

THE ROLE OF COUNSELLOR

The role of the counsellor is critical when working with survivors of interpersonal trauma as they are the conduit for restoring trust and relational worth. To facilitate this, counsellors need to be fully present and authentic in all their interactions with clients. They also need to genuinely care about and value human experiences more than techniques, ideas and theories. That "Therapy should not be theory-driven but relationship-driven" (Yalom, 2008, p.204) is particularly so when working with survivors of interpersonal trauma who have been dehumanised and deprived of basic human needs of safety and connection.

Counsellors need to be able to listen to survivors on all levels and have an awareness of the concealed and hidden subtext, or latent content, and gently make this visible to the survivor. Deeply buried thoughts and feelings that have been ignored and remain outside conscious awareness need to be mentalised and integrated. Given the overwhelming nature of trauma, counsellors need to be calm and containing to instil confidence in the client that these turbulent feelings can be managed. Containment needs to be supported by an actively engaged stance rather than distance, or defensive dissociation. Given the subterfuge and deception inherent in interpersonal trauma it is imperative that counsellors are honest, frank and transparent to counteract the lies and falsification of reality experienced by survivors. Survivors are hypervigilant to non-verbal communication and will be acutely aware of any incongruence or mixed messages. They are also particularly skilled at reading non-verbal cues as this has been part of their survival repertoire, and will be able to sense when the counsellor is inauthentic or hiding behind a façade of professional caring.

To counter the judgment and repudiation of the authentic self by the abuser, counsellors must be genuinely non-judgmental, respectful and accepting of the survivor. Counsellors need to be able to connect to clients and possess a secure attachment style in which they are capable and not afraid of intimacy and be responsive and empathically attuned to the survivor. Through this connection they can convey that the survivor is not just understood but also known to the counsellor. While focusing on connection is critical, counsellors need to be mindful of the danger of enmeshment. This can be averted by counsellors encouraging validating the survivor's autonomy and resources, and acknowledging reciprocal influence. What is required is a synergy between empathic attunement and the setting of appropriate limits.

To manage the inexorable uncertainty associated with interpersonal trauma, counsellors need to be able to tolerate uncertainty, ambiguity and the unknown. They must be able to acknowledge that it is not possible to establish absolute truth or knowledge and may need to find a "good enough" certainty as a basis for the work. Alongside this counsellors need to be able to accept limits of what they can do, and not feel ashamed of their limitations. This circumvents self-aggrandisement and grandiosity as a cover for shame as well as modelling humility to the survivor. Counsellors who come across as too perfect, grandiose or charismatic may unwittingly display the very characteristics of the abuser which can evoke terror and fear in the survivor. It is for this reason that counsellors must be able to make mistakes, take risks and move out of their comfort zone and be prepared to challenge and be challenged. This can help survivors to face challenges, make mistakes and learn from such experiences.

THERAPEUTIC STANCE

When working with survivors of interpersonal abuse, counsellors must be authentic, emotionally present, visible, and actively engaged to track the full range of survivor feelings, consciously, subconsciously and somatically, and to reflect these accurately. While "[the client]...cannot heal in the absence of emotional visibility" (Salter, 1995, p.259), counsellors must guard against being too charismatic as this can be perceived as controlling and overpowering, while a distant, non-responsive therapeutic stance, with prolonged silences, can be experienced as rejecting, which reinforces abuse dynamics and alienates the survivor (Wilson and Lindy, 1994; Wilson and Thomas, 2004; Wilson, Friedman and Lindy, 2001; Wilson, 2003, 2004). Counsellors must also be careful not to be too charming or effusive as this will mirror the seductive qualities of the abuser used in the grooming process (Sanderson, 2008).

Counsellors must be reliable and consistent in providing a secure and containing therapeutic space predicated on empathic attunement and resonance to repair relational difficulties around trust, intimacy and attachment. Empathy and empathic attunement allow counsellors to connect, resonate and calibrate with the survivor's whole being, to track and match the client's internal and psychological state accurately with resonance and minimal distortion to minimise empathic strain or rupture (Wilson, 2003). If the counsellor is too detached, receptivity is blocked and matching impaired, leading to distortions in resonance. While there are variations among clinicians in empathic capacity, empathic resistance, empathic tolerance and empathic endurance (Wilson, 2002), these can be exacerbated by level of experience, knowledge of trauma work, psychological well-being and access to resources. If counsellors are to lift the veil of betrayal and make the hidden visible they need to adopt an engaged therapeutic stance to allow for the unfolding of the yearning for connection and longed-for relationship.

THE THERAPEUTIC RELATIONSHIP

Outcome research on the effectiveness of psychotherapy has consistently demonstrated the importance of the therapeutic relationship. Lambert (2003) found that 40% of the change in psychotherapy was dependent on client personal resources and resilience, 30% was due to the therapeutic relationship as represented by therapist warmth, understanding, trustworthiness, genuineness, validation, and acceptance, 15% was due to positive approach in instilling hope, and 15% was accounted for by techniques and strategies. This has led some clinicians to emphasise the centrality of the relationship with Yalom (2008) arguing that "...the relationship heals" (p.204) and Kahn (1997) asserting that "The relationship is the therapy" (p.1).

Clarkson (2003) proposes that there are five relationship sequences which are effective for change. The first of these is the *working alliance* which needs to be a collaborative endeavour to sustain the relationship even when ruptures occur. The *transferential/counter-transferential relationship* consists of unconscious wishes and fears transferred onto or into the therapeutic partnership such as a wish for a rescuer or fear of an abuser. In severe cases of interpersonal trauma the *reparative/developmentally needed relationship* is of particular importance as it provides a reparative, corrective and replenishing relationship to counteract the deficits in earlier, traumatising relationships, especially in childhood. In addition, counsellors also need to incorporate the real, here and now relationship, or the *person-to-person relationship* and the *transpersonal relationship* which represents the spiritual dimension of the therapeutic relationship.

The quality of the therapeutic relationship is of particular importance when working with survivors of interpersonal trauma as it offers a secure therapeutic space in which the hidden, vulnerable, authentic self, what Winnicott (1965) refers to as the "self in cold storage" and what Nijenhuis, Spinhoven and Vanderlinden (1998) call "the scared self", can emerge and be affirmed. The therapeutic relationship needs to be supportive and companionable (Heard and Lake, 1997) in order to build a "relational bridge" (Blizzard, 2003). It is through the felt security of the therapeutic relationship that survivors can increase external and internal relating so that dissociative defences can be relinquished, and allow for the development of alternative models of relationships.

In the therapeutic relationship "the therapist helps to heal by developing a genuine relationship with the patient" (Yalom, 1980, p.401) and provides the opportunity to learn secure autonomous attachment, restore relational worth and permit reconnection to self and others. In the case of early traumatisation before resilience and resources have been acquired, the relationship is the therapy (Rothschild, 2000). The therapeutic relationship however can elicit fear and terror, with the authentic self being too scared to come out of "cold storage", or fortress. Survivors will often peep out, and then retreat. This oscillation can cause considerable strain in the therapeutic relationship, but is necessary to build trust. The dehumanising aspect of interpersonal trauma along with the imperative to survive means that some survivors feel they have to neutralise others, including the therapist. This needs to be understood as a survival strategy to aid protection, rather than interpreted as hostility and rejection of the therapist. It is crucial that counsellors do not personalise such enactments and remain consistently connected and available to the survivor.

It is only when the client is visible and seen without fear of further traumatisation that they can begin to risk closeness and intimacy. For the client to feel truly met by the therapist and to feel that there is genuine caring, counsellors need to respond to the client authentically through the expression of genuine feelings and thoughts, and be prepared to reveal more of themselves. Thus natural human responses of sadness, tears, anger or laughter can allow survivors to access their own human, authentic responses, relinquish their armour and move from fierce self-sufficiency to interdependence. As survivors move towards authenticity they begin to renounce the false self and any concomitant defensive behaviours.

Many survivors of interpersonal trauma who have been stripped of autonomy and self-agency are often extremely compliant and submissive, and feel unable to take control of any aspect of their lives, including the therapeutic process. They are often consumed with rescue fantasies in which they surrender all responsibility for their recovery to the counsellor. This must be understood as part of the survivor's traumatisation and not pathological passivity. By making the therapeutic process a collaborative one survivors are encouraged to reclaim control and responsibility for their recovery. In contrast, some survivors fear merger and so present as dominant, hostile and critical as a way to avoid connection and closeness. Counsellors need to be mindful that by entering therapy the survivor's hope has not been extinguished no matter how rejecting and hostile the client may appear to be.

In many respects "...the therapist's role is analogous to that of a mother who provides a secure base from which to explore the world" (Bowlby, 1988, pp.138–9). This is pertinent as a significant consequence of interpersonal trauma is an insecure attachment style (Ainsworth *et al.*, 1978; Main, 1999). To provide a secure base and genuine therapeutic relationships, counsellors themselves must be in possession of a secure-autonomous attachment style in which they are able to connect to others, including their clients, and reflect on relational dynamics. They must feel secure enough in themselves to not feel threatened by either the powerful "developmental dependency" (Steele, van der Hart and Nijenhuis, 2001) or the extreme, dismissive self-sufficiency associated with survivors of abuse. Underlying both attachment styles is a striving for connection, and counsellors must be comfortable in responding to this.

Through being empathically attuned the counsellor can encourage survivors to become more aware of how hostile, dismissive and critical behaviour impacts on others, including the therapist. Knowing that their actions and behaviours do have an impact on others restores self-agency and self-efficacy. This can facilitate a greater awareness of reciprocal influence in relationships rather than the unidirectional flow associated with interpersonal trauma. A crucial aspect of the therapeutic relationship is that survivors may for the first time experience empathic understanding and attunement. This will allow them to develop empathy towards others, and recognise that empathy is bidirectional, not just from therapist to survivor. Recognition of the importance of reciprocal empathy will enable survivors to develop greater relational worth and relational skills which will enhance future relationships.

The therapeutic relationship is not an end itself, but the means to an end. Invariably, major internal shifts can occur when survivors form a genuine, trusting relationship in which they feel accepted and supported. It allows survivors to experience new parts of the self, and trust their own perceptions rather than overvaluing the perceptions of others. Survivors can transfer the counsellor's positive regard into personal positive self-regard. The therapeutic relationship promotes a new internal standard for the quality of genuine relationships and learnt secure attachment. Intimacy and closeness within the therapeutic relationship serves as an internal reference point and allows for the acquisition of new relational skills so that the survivor can develop confidence in and willingness to form other authentic relationships in the future.

Counsellors need to be aware, however, that the more engaged survivors become the more fearful they may become as they risk beginning to trust again. This will invoke the threat of decompensation leading to an increase in suicidal ideation and self-harming behaviour to restore the all too familiar pain and anguish which is being alleviated through the secure attachment and relational connection. For some survivors, the more trust is established the more fearful they become, anticipating and expecting to be betrayed again. The more secure survivors feel the more they will fear losing the secure attachment. This can lead to a resurgence of terrifying memories, thoughts and feelings, and activation of primitive defences that can sabotage the therapeutic bond. Counsellors need to be prepared for this and understand the terror and fear of secure attachment. One survivor used the example of the toxic shock experienced when coming out of the frozen cold into warmth. Initially this is experienced as excruciatingly painful as it takes some considerable time to acclimatise to the warmth. Some survivors may recoil from the pain by creating distance between themselves and the therapist, including terminating therapy. It is critical that these fears are addressed and integrated as the "...antidote to much anguish is sheer connectedness" (Yalom, 2008, p.205).

Counsellors need to take survivors' fears of security seriously and contextualise this within a trauma framework. While survivors yearn for security they are also terrified of it as they fear a repeat of the abuse experiences. Invariably the terror of abuse, abandonment and rejection outweighs the yearning for attachment. This will result in a number of barriers to avoid connecting such as hostile, aggressive behaviour, and avoidance and retreat. Those survivors who are compliant and submissive may also resist connection albeit in more subtle ways such as being inauthentic, overly charming, wanting to be rescued or rescuing counsellor by shifting the focus from self onto the counsellor. The overly compliant and charming client can be highly seductive as they cover up their anger and rage behind being the perfect client. Their charm may also be an indicator of internalised abuser dynamics whereby they charm others, including the therapist, to lure them into a subterfuge through compliments and adoration. Once entranced, survivors may then seek to control and manipulate the counsellor to make themselves feel more powerful.

Counsellors need to understand that barriers to building the therapeutic relationship represent myriad fears, not least fear of re-experiencing abuse, fear of retraumatisation, fear of losing control, fear of being judged, fear of not being believed, fear of not being able to provide coherent narrative due to fragmented memories, fear of disclosure and fear of the unknown and uncertainty. These reflect the multiple, contradictory and paradoxical aspect of the relationship experienced in interpersonal trauma.

TRANSFERENCE

These barriers underlie powerful transference dynamics which can have a profound effect on the counsellor. Commonly transference dynamics elicit "the three most common narcissistic snares in therapists...the aspirations to heal, know all and love all" (Maltsberger and Buie, 1974, p.627). Lack of self-agency compels some survivors of interpersonal trauma to surrender responsibility for recovery to the counsellor. In their hope for rescue, survivors will attempt to elicit the counsellor's "helper script". Survivors will often project their illimitable yearning for love, acceptance and nourishment onto the counsellors and, when these are not satisfied, they will vilify the counsellors and cast them in the role of persecutor. This then activates a re-enactment of the abuse relationship with the survivor becoming submissive, denying their needs, and suppressing their anger and rage. Some survivors feel compelled to protect the counsellor from any traumatic material either because they fear that the counsellor will not be able to manage the trauma, or to protect themselves from exploring traumatic experiences. Yet other survivors may displace their anger onto the counsellor as a test to see whether they will be punished, and to avoid connection. While most transference reactions are a replay of past relationships and represent re-enactments of abuse, they can also be in response to the here and now relationship between client and therapist.

COUNTER-TRANSFERENCE

"Counter" refers to the counsellor's counter feelings, or counter-transference to the client's transference. Survivors' projective identifications are a form of "psychic surgery" in which they evacuate unbearable intense emotional reactions onto the counsellor, thereby co-opting them to experience the feelings and impulses that are too painful or frightening to bear within themselves. This can elicit powerful emotional and cognitive counter-transferential reactions (CTR) in the counsellor (Wilson and Lindy, 1994). However, CTR may also represent the counsellor's own emotional experiences, including interpersonal abuse, and expectations of relationships. This would suggest that CTR are a complex interplay between client transference and projective identification, and the counsellor's own psychology, dissociation, projections and splitting. Counsellors need to consider whether feelings of guilt, anger and appeasement are truly a reflection of clients' own emotional experiences or whether they are indicative of their own expectations and experiences. Whatever the source of CTR, counsellors need to monitor, reflect and consistently assess CTR in order to put brakes on destructive re-enactments, and remain contained and containing (see Chapter 14).

Strong CTR, especially negative CTR, can lead to a range of feelings and thoughts in the counsellor that can rupture the therapeutic relationship. If counsellors feel vulnerable, or ashamed or embarrassed, they may themselves become narcissistic and retreat into an autistic state whereby they neutralise the survivor.

If there is a failure in compassion or trust in the survivor, counsellors may resort to appeasement behaviours as way of compensating for their negative CTR. This leads them to try too hard and become preoccupied with their own guilt, shame and inadequacy which render the survivor invisible. Alternatively the counsellor may relish the role of rescuer for narcissistic reasons of grandiosity, or in order to vicariously rescue themselves from their own abuse history. All of these need to be explored and understood prior to working with survivors of interpersonal trauma.

Somatic counter-transference is a rich source for understanding the therapeutic relationship, as somatic reactions can provide the clinician with a sense of the survivor's bodily state (Shaw, 2004). Somatic counter-transference, or embodied counter-transference (Field, 1989; Samuels, 1985), refers to bodily reactions or feelings experienced by clinicians when working with clients. However, like CTR, somatic counter-transference can represent both somatic resonance of the client's feelings or lack of embodiment, or the counsellor's own somatic reactions. While somatic reactions can give some indication, the counsellor cannot know this state fully, and must balance this with owning their own bodily reactions. What is critical is that counsellors working with traumatised, highly dissociative individuals may experience dissociative responses such as lapses of consciousness, numbing or depersonalisation. This may manifest as tiredness, lassitude, disruptions in attention and concentration. This will be noticed by the survivor, although not necessarily expressed, and counsellors must ensure that such somatic CTRs are discussed.

Despite repeated betrayals survivors who enter therapy have not extinguished hope and need for nurture and desire to live more authentically. In the safety of the therapeutic relationship this can flourish along with improved affect regulation, vitality and a stronger sense of self. Long-term, healthy interpersonal relationships can form new neuronal connections allowing survivors to move from disavowal of relationships to valuing them (Sanderson, 2006, 2008). They also provide continuity, constancy, and consistency which are critical in building trust. In combination, the therapeutic relationship allows for the emergence of more coherent internal relationship, and movement from "isolated subjectivity" (Chefetz and Bromberg, 2004) to intersubjectivity, and direct communication rather than communication through symptoms.

SUMMARY

- The therapeutic aims when working with survivors of interpersonal trauma are comprehensive assessment, establishing external and internal safety, processing and integrating traumatic experiences, and mourning the many losses.
- Comprehensive assessment is ongoing and needs to incorporate difficulties that preceded trauma, those that have been exacerbated by trauma, and

those that have resulted from the trauma, and disclosure. Clinicians also need to consider resilience, temperament, pre-existing resources, and current access to resources, including support network.

- To ensure safety, counsellors need to provide a safe and secure therapeutic setting which is well bounded yet flexible. They need to consider the safety of the therapeutic setting and the importance of boundaries, and be explicit in stating these. It is through the secure therapeutic space that survivors can begin to reconnect to self and develop self-trust and self-agency.
- Due to the complex nature of interpersonal trauma, counsellors need to be aware that the therapeutic process is not linear and counsellors need to tolerate diversions and distraction to remain constant and consistent in their responses.
- The role of the counsellor is critical when working with survivors as they need to be warm, engaged and sensitively attuned, and have a positive therapeutic stance. It is imperative that they are honest and authentic to counter the deception and subterfuge ubiquitous to interpersonal trauma.
- Outcome research on the effectiveness of psychotherapy has consistently provided evidence of the importance of the therapeutic relationship in promoting change. This is particularly pertinent to survivors of interpersonal trauma who need to counteract distorted and abusive relational dynamics. It is through the therapeutic relationship that survivors can begin to restore relational worth and begin to reconnect to others. They can learn and develop more effective relational skills and risk more authentic ways of relating. This in turn allows them to begin to relate to others without fear of abuse or abandonment, and gradually begin to reconnect to life.

CHAPTER 5

WORKING WITH SURVIVORS OF INTERPERSONAL TRAUMA

When survivors of interpersonal trauma enter therapy it is a testament to resilience in the face of trauma and repeated betrayal. It is critical that clinicians honour the survivor's courage to risk connection despite the betrayal of trust, and view this as direct evidence that hope has not been extinguished. In acknowledging and validating the survivor's strength, counsellors can begin the requisite therapeutic work to facilitate post-traumatic growth that will enable the survivor to reconnect to self, others and the world.

While each survivor will experience the interpersonal trauma differently depending upon the nature of the trauma, age, frequency and severity of abuse and degree or lack of support, there are a number of symptoms and long-term effects that are common to all types of interpersonal trauma. This chapter will examine the range of common effects and propose a number of therapeutic techniques that can ameliorate symptoms. As trauma impacts on psychobiological functioning it is critical to restore affect regulation and distress tolerance so that the survivor has greater control of turbulent emotions rather than resorting to the self-destructive and self-harming behaviours commonly associated with interpersonal trauma. Once a degree of control over such symptoms has been restored exploration of the trauma narrative can take place allowing the counsellor and survivor to challenge the legacies of the past. The chapter will also identify common defences which need to be understood and worked through so that work on shattered self-structures and relational difficulties, including sexual traumatisation, can begin. Finally the chapter will look at the role of loss and mourning in the integration of trauma and post-traumatic growth.

POWER DYNAMICS

A common feature of all interpersonal abuse is the imbalance of power and lack of informed consent on the part of the abused. Given the intrinsic unequal power dynamics in interpersonal abuse it is essential that counsellors minimise asymmetrical power relations by promoting a collaborative therapeutic encounter in which both parties share their unique expertise. This can be facilitated to some degree through the use of inclusive language to convey that the therapeutic process is a joint endeavour in which each individual has a crucial role. In essence, counsellors need to be mindful that the survivor is the expert in terms of self, and that the clinician is an experienced companion who brings professional expertise. This includes the need for counsellors to be culturally sensitive and aware. Interpersonal abuse occurs across all cultures albeit with considerable variation in definition and legitimisation. While counsellors need to contextualise trauma within a cultural framework, this needs to be counterbalanced with legitimising the survivor's abuse experience.

The imbalance of power allows for the inexorable dehumanisation seen in interpersonal trauma. To counteract this, counsellors need to strive for a genuinely human therapeutic relationship in which they are emotionally available and accessible, and do not hide between a professional mask of distance or detachment. To facilitate the survivor's reconnection to self and others, counsellors must be willing to connect with the client and allow for the expression of a full range of emotions including laughter and humour in a spontaneous, yet well-bounded relationship.

USE OF METAPHOR

A potent way to minimise power dynamics and utilise survivor's expertise is in the use of metaphor, especially if the metaphor is personally meaningful and highly relevant to the client. For example, survivors with an interest in gardening may respond to a gardening metaphor, while those interested in music will find a musical metaphor more accessible. This casts the survivor in the role of expert, as the counsellor cannot know all the subtle permutations of the client's interests and passions. It also involves the survivor more deeply in understanding and making sense of their experiences. Male survivors often respond extremely well to the use of metaphor as it allows them to construct their experience in a meaningful way while minimising use of language which reinforces victimisation. The use of metaphor also gives the survivor a sense of control in directing and pacing the therapeutic work. This allows for a sense of mastery and self-agency which is critical in restoring a sense of self-efficacy.

PSYCHOEDUCATION

Most survivors of interpersonal abuse have little or no understanding of the relationship between trauma and their symptoms, and often believe that they are losing their sanity. The terror of not knowing invariably heightens anxiety which only serves to increase hyper-reactivity. It is essential that counsellors normalise the range of psychobiological symptoms and contextualise them as reactions to trauma. As the survivor comes to understand their symptoms more they will feel less in thrall to them and more confident in being able to change them and restore equilibrium. This allows for a greater sense of control over their symptoms which will enhance their sense of internal safety and self-agency. In addition, gaining mastery over tumultuous affects decreases the survivor's sense of helplessness and powerlessness, and produces enhanced self-esteem.

Counsellors also need to provide psychoeducation on the therapeutic process to enable survivors to have a full understanding of what the counsellor can and cannot provide and what is expected of the client. Clarity on how the therapeutic process can impact on the survivor and what goals can and cannot be achieved allows for a degree of control in what can initially be a daunting process. Explicit clarification around the role of boundaries and confidentiality can enhance safety which is the foundation of a secure therapeutic base. Most importantly, equipping the survivor with such knowledge reduces the likelihood of boundary violations and sexual exploitation by the therapist. Psychoeducation can be employed throughout the therapeutic process, whenever questions arise that necessitate clarification. Counsellors must be mindful that deliberately withholding knowledge and information from the survivor is tantamount to abuse and an exploitation of the imbalance of power.

WORKING WITH AFFECT REGULATION

A common impact of interpersonal trauma is affect dysregulation in which the survivor is in thrall to tsunami-like feelings which threaten to overwhelm and enslave them. The unpredictability and uncontrollability of these powerful affects become so all consuming that the survivor is embedded in them. Given the pervasive heightened level of arousal any additional internal or external stimulation acts as a circuit breaker (Kalsched, 1996). In this the survivor's internal reality supersedes external reality, making it difficult to differentiate the source of the arousal. Being embedded in tumultuous affects makes it difficult for survivors to interpret their feelings, seeing them as facts rather than sensory experiences that are subject to interpretation. Furthermore, all somatic sensations, feelings and mental representations are felt to be reality rather than signals, or sources of information. Heightened arousal and the tsunami-like feelings drown out the ability for thought and compress the mental space to think and plan courses of action. This constricts the regulation of emotions, leaving them unmodulated, which further impairs appraisal of reality and capacity to respond implicitly to experience. Commonly survivors are propelled into a default position, or automatic pilot, which activates habitual patterns of thinking, feeling, and doing.

To restore affect regulation counsellors need to help the survivor to identify and label emotions, and any obstacles to processing these. Labelling and interpreting emotions more accurately promotes emotional literacy making it easier for the survivor to identify, name and interpret the origin of the emotion, enabling them to manage it more effectively. In order to reduce emotional reactivity counsellors need to encourage survivors to be more mindful of their emotions, to mentalise these and label them. In understanding the nature, function and origin of emotions survivors will feel more in control of these.

Psychoeducation on physiological arousal and sensory responses will enable the survivor to understand that affects are signals that need to be interpreted in order to adopt appropriate actions. It is also helpful for the survivor to understand that heightened affects are not indelibly engraved facts that exist in perpetuity, but that they will dissipate naturally, much like rhythmic waves in a constant ebb and flow. Such understanding can permit self-soothing which allows the survivor to feel more in control of her affects.

Once the survivor can conceptualise the nature of emotions, and accepts that they can be regulated and interpreted, the counsellor can introduce distress tolerance techniques (Linehan, 1993). Distress tolerance techniques provide the survivor with skills to tolerate emotions, both positive and negative, which are extremely helpful when they feel they are about to be engulfed by their affects. These techniques incorporate a range of cognitive behavioural techniques which include breathing exercises, relaxation techniques and awareness exercises, all of which enable the survivor to accept and manage reality rather than deny it. Linehan (1993) identifies four main techniques as being most helpful in acquiring skills for distress tolerance: *distracting, self-soothing, improving the moment* and *focusing on the pros and cons of tolerating distress* (Linehan, 1993).

Distracting reduces contact with emotional stimuli by distracting attention away from emotions through thoughts, images and sensations that counteract negative emotions. Self-soothing skills are achieved through comforting, nurturing and being kind and gentle towards the self through soothing each of the five senses. Improving the moment consists of replacing negative appraisals of oneself or the situation with more positive ones through imagery, relaxation or intense focus on one thing in the moment. Finally, thinking about the positive and negative aspects of distress tolerance allows the survivor to face and accept reality, rather than deny it, which permits more positive outcomes. In combination these skills enable the survivor to accept reality and life in the moment which allows them to process the feelings rather than avoid or deny them.

Discharging emotions is also critical in terms of affect regulation, especially deeply suppressed emotions such as anger and rage. Survivors can be encouraged to discharge these through a variety of physical releases such as punching or screaming into a pillow, going for a jog, riding a bike, playing tennis, tearing up paper, or vigorous dancing. Non-physical discharge of emotions can be achieved through writing letters, which are not sent, in which the survivor can express the full range of feelings without censorship.

To enhance the understanding of emotions and their impact, counsellors can encourage survivors to be more mindful of their internal state through mentalising (Fonagy, *et al.*, 2002). The central concept in mentalising is that internal states such as emotions or thoughts are opaque and can be understood through adopting an "inquisitive stance". To do so can promote a better understanding of self, others and relationships which allows for connection to self and others and a more engaged stance in the world. Mentalising also reduces the "mind blindness", or non-mentalising, seen in survivors of interpersonal trauma in mechanisms such as dissociation and compartmentalisation.

Mindfulness skills can promote mentalising in encouraging the survivor to concentrate the mind to observe, describe and participate in a non-judgmental way. Encouraging the survivor to focus on one thing at a time, and to focus on what works, can be extremely liberating and empowering. Mindfulness skills also increase awareness of cues and triggers to dissociation and detachment.

As the survivor is more able to manage overwhelming affects the need for defences such as dissociation are reduced. However, counsellors need to be aware of how and when survivors do dissociate in session and provide the survivor with appropriate skills to manage this. Cues to dissociation and detachment include somatic cues such as changes in breathing or skin colouration, eyes becoming unfocused, or changes in body tone either through rigidity, lassitude, or restlessness. Cognitive cues usually consist in change of content of the material being discussed and inhibited emotional expression.

Counsellor use of self can be a powerful way to track dissociative episodes in session. This is especially powerful through somatic counter-transference in which the counsellor may experience a number of somatic changes that resemble the dissociative process in the survivor. Counsellors commonly report feeling numb, heavy, or tired and compelled to close their eyes. This state of somnolence leads to a sense of disembodiment, restlessness and a desire to move away from the survivor, leave the room or avoid any engagement with the material under discussion. Some counsellors have experienced somatic sensations that resemble dissociative processes including leaving their body, losing track of time, and amnesia for what is being discussed. Such responses can be powerful indicators of dissociation in the client and need to be addressed in the session as this will provide an opportunity to come out of the dissociative state for both survivor and clinician.

Clinicians' use of somatic counter-transference can help make both counsellor and survivor aware of what is happening and allow for the implementation of grounding techniques to restore embodiment. Both parties need to focus on breathing to become embodied, which can be supported by sensory grounding techniques such as becoming aware of feet on the floor, touching and object, holding something or resuming eye contact. Alternatively focusing on a safe place, safe image or mantra can be effective to come out of a dissociative state. Cognitive grounding techniques such as focusing on the date, time, place or setting can enable both counsellors and survivor to become grounded in the present. In some instances it may be necessary to take a short break. Ideally counsellors need to introduce a variety of grounding techniques to find which are the most effective, both in and outside of session so that these can be easily integrated.

GROUNDING TECHNIQUES

Dissociative episodes, flashbacks, panic attacks and intrusive memories can make survivors highly anxious as they often feel that they are "going mad", or feel compelled to self-harm or self-injure. Grounding techniques can help survivors to reconnect through all five senses with present time, place and their body. Prior to working on grounding techniques, counsellors need to provide information on the function of flashbacks and how they impact physiologically and neurobiologically, and how grounding techniques can restore affect regulation and containment in the present. Counsellors need to identify triggers for flashbacks, intrusive memories and imagery and then explore a number of grounding techniques that the survivor can choose from. It is important that the survivor experiments to find which techniques work best for her, and then practises these daily so they become fully integrated and part of the behavioural repertoire. This will enable the survivor to activate effective grounding techniques automatically to subvert overwhelming internal stimuli.

Initially survivors need to practise self-talk that reminds them that they are having a flashback and that this is normal for someone who has been traumatised. Self-talk about how the flashback or memory is a past experience and that they are no longer in danger, can help the survivor to remain in the present rather than be catapulted back to an earlier experience. To aid this, survivors also need to choose from a number of techniques that have been shown to be effective (Sanderson, 2006). Ideally the survivor needs to ground themselves through as many sensory channels as possible. The most important technique is breathing as fear leads to a dysregulation in breathing as respiration becomes faster and increasingly shallow. As a result the body begins to panic due to lack of oxygen which causes dizziness, shakiness and more panic. Encouraging the survivor to regulate their breathing by breathing more slowly and deeply, all the way down to the diaphragm, increases the level of oxygen and reduces the panic. Counting to five as the survivor breathes in and out can help in holding the depth of breath.

Alongside breathing survivors might also consider stamping, or grinding their feet on the floor, or looking around the room, noticing colours, textures, shapes, people, and attending to sounds which are all effective ways of staying in the present. They may also name each object in the room as using and hearing their own voice can remind them of the present. Due to the paralysing effect of flashbacks or panic attacks, the survivor may find it useful to get up if they are sitting down, go into another room, switch lights on, open the windows, do some light exercise, or go for a walk outside to help reorient themselves. They might also reorient themselves by brushing their teeth, or taking a shower or bath. Listening to soothing music, especially when associated with pleasant experiences or memories can also help to soothe and relax, while invigorating music can counteract the pervasive sense of enervation. Survivors may also gain comfort from spraying their favourite scent, or smelling something that evokes pleasant memories, as smell is often the fastest of the sensory organs to evoke associated memories. To reaffirm the present the survivor can consult their diary, calendar, mobile phone, computer, or watch television.

To increase the connection with the physical world and restore embodiment, survivors can touch or hold (with care) something very hot or cold like a cup of tea or an ice cube. Eating or drinking something can also help, especially if it has a strong taste or texture such as chilli, lemon or crunchy apple. Heightened awareness of how the sensory experience of taste, chewing or sipping is experienced can further enhance embodiment. Survivors can also rub their skin, or use an elastic band to "ping" against the skin to remind them of their body. Focusing on the feel of clothes on the skin, or wrapping a blanket around themselves can help them to become more aware of the boundaries of the body. This can also be achieved by touching a favourite object, clothing or photograph, preferably one that did not exist in the past. If possible, survivors should access their support network by telephoning, or talking to someone who can help the survivor to reconnect to the present and remind them that they are safe and cared for.

The overwhelming power of flashbacks means that they can be exhausting and draining. It is essential that survivors make time for self-care and self-nurturing following such episodes by having a warm relaxing bath, lighting scented candles, having a warm drink, playing some soothing music or just relaxing, or sleeping. Cooking a favourite meal which includes foods the survivor associates with comfort and nurturing can also be a way of caring for the self. When the survivor feels ready it can be helpful to write down everything that she can remember about the flashback or intrusive memory and how she managed to get through it. This will help the survivor to remember the content of the flashback which can allow for increased processing and it will also be a reminder that she was not overwhelmed and can get through such terrifying reminders of trauma and abuse.

Grounding using all five senses can be adopted not just during flashbacks and intrusive memories, but can help survivors during moments of anxiety, panic attacks and depersonalisation (Sanderson, 2006). Essentially it enables the survivor to self-soothe and calm the self without resorting to dissociation, self-medication or self-injury. To facilitate this, survivors may need to make a list of trusted friends or family with whom they can connect by telephone, email or face to face. These individuals can reinforce positive messages and provide much-needed safe physical contact, reassurance and soothing hugs. When alone the survivor needs to be able to self-soothe by carrying a safe object around with them such as a pebble, crystal or favourite image. Touching or looking at the object keeps both the hands and brain occupied and helps with focus and control.

Focus and control can also be enhanced by writing poetry, prose or journal entries, making lists such as the ten most favourite books, films, music, sounds, smells, foods or paintings, or writing down positive messages. Reciting poetry, speeches or dialogue from plays, films or books, names of friends or relatives, favourite objects, or buildings can also help to restore focus and control as can engaging in creative art work, sculpting or pottery. Stroking a pet can also be soothing and calming as can rhythmically brushing hair, or gentle stroking of the arm or hands. To make this easier the survivor could use a pleasantly scented hand or body lotion so that two sensory channels are combined to enhance self-soothing.

With regard to self-injury there are a number of more specific grounding techniques, such as replacing the need to see blood with using a red marker pen, although this is counter indicated if the survivor then cuts lines. Survivors can replace the need to experience pain with a rubber band on either wrist or ankle and snap it whenever necessary. To alleviate numbing survivors could consider squeezing ice cubes, holding a refrigerated aluminium can, chewing strongly flavoured food stuff such as chilli, ginger root, raw onion, garlic or lemon, immersing hand or arm into a bowl filled with ice cubes, or putting an ice pack on their face (Sutton, 2005). It is critical in all grounding techniques to keep the eyes open, to focus on surroundings and to regulate breathing (Sanderson, 2006).

WORKING WITH SELF-HARM, SELF-INJURY AND SUICIDAL IDEATION

Lack of affect regulation and inability to self-soothe are commonly associated with self-harming behaviours such as self-injury, self-medication through drugs, alcohol or food, eating disorders, suicidal ideation and risky behaviours. When working with survivors who self-harm, counsellors need to identify and assess the range of self-harming behaviour and work towards enabling the survivor to find alternative ways of managing emotions and thereby exercise a greater choice of behaviours (Sanderson, 2006). Counsellors must also assess level of substance and alcohol dependency and whether the survivor needs to seek residential rehabilitation care prior to starting the therapeutic work. Some clinicians are reluctant to take on clients who are still self-medicating, while others will consider this albeit within a very well-bounded framework (Sanderson, 2006). If there are medical or psychiatric concerns, counsellors will need to liaise with appropriate clinicians. This is especially the case with survivors who have persistent suicidal ideation, and a history of parasuicide.

To ensure both survivor and counsellor safety, it is essential that a safety contract is drawn up and agreed by both parties. This is necessary to ensure that the survivor takes ownership of the self-harming behaviour and makes a clear commitment to reducing self-harm and keeping safe. It is often helpful to be explicit in the contract and to support this with a written copy that must be signed by both parties. Counsellors must be mindful that the contract may need to be revised and renegotiated as the therapeutic process evolves. The contract must be realistic, and rather than insisting cessation of all self-harming behaviour, it is more beneficial to specify achievable goals that will eventually lead to cessation. The goal must be to reduce the severity and frequency of self-injury, to take fewer risks by sterilising cutting implements, take better care of injuries, to reduce drinking and drug taking, and to replace these with more adaptive strategies (Sutton, 2005; Sanderson, 2006). The contract must also specify the need for honest disclosure, and the importance of verbalising the self-harm episode as well as a list of designated "safe" people that the survivor can contact during a self-harming episode. Counsellors must also be clear in how their own fears might impact on the survivor. To alleviate their own fears, counsellors might insist on total abstinence rather than facilitate a gradual reduction which may be more manageable for the survivor. In introducing alternative strategies it is hoped that survivors will exercise more choice and control over how to manage their emotions or dissociative episodes. In the case of actively suicidal survivors, counsellors need to encourage active commitment to staying safe by asking the survivor to call each day at a specified time rather than have the counsellor ring them to make sure that they are managing.

When working with survivors who self-injure, counsellors must help the client identify the function of self-injury and the triggers to dissociation and self-harming behaviour. Counsellors must enable survivors to make sense of self-injury, and to view it as a signal for unexpressed feelings which do not have to be acted upon (Sutton, 2004). It is also useful to make connections between self-injury and past experiences and to identify and challenge the self-talk that accompanies such behaviour. It is imperative to explore and identify alternative coping strategies and to gradually replace self-injury with more healthy affect regulation techniques (Sutton, 2005; Sanderson, 2006). These can be implemented by using an array of affect regulation and grounding techniques.

Counsellors must be careful to minimise secondary reinforcement of self-injury in focusing solely on the injurious behaviour. It is more helpful to focus on the antecedent to the self-injury and to reinforce positive behaviours. For example, rather than arranging out-of-session contact whenever an episode of self-injury has occurred, it is more helpful to have a regular mutually agreed time, such as three times a week, irrespective of whether self-injury has taken place or not. It is important to consistently offer alternatives to self-injury and to encourage the survivor to take ownership of the choices made. In addition, survivors must be urged to take ownership for their healing, and thereby take more control of it, and to take ownership of their wounds by tending to them which promotes self-care and self-regulation.

WORKING WITH TRAUMA NARRATIVE

Once affect regulation and grounding techniques have been integrated into the survivor's behavioural repertoire, exploration of the trauma narrative can begin. It is critical that this is not undertaken until the survivor has been able to restore a sense of control over their turbulent affects and physiological arousal. With this in place the survivor will be more able to manage any feelings that are aroused by exploring their traumatic experiences. It is important that the counsellor lets the trauma narrative unfold gradually and at a pace that is comfortable to the survivor, to minimise becoming enslaved by it.

One of the effects of interpersonal trauma is impaired and fragmented memory. This is partly due to neurobiological factors that prevent the encoding, storage and consolidation of traumatic memories (Sanderson, 2006) but is also due to avoidance of remembering the trauma. Thus one of the ameliorating effects of working through the trauma narrative is that it can facilitate the restoration of fragmented memories. Counsellors can employ a variety of techniques to facilitate memory recall such as the use of photographs, or recalling peripheral memories not just traumatic ones (Mollon, 2005; Sanderson, 2006), although they need to acknowledge the fallibility of memory and that some memories may not be preserved and thus not accessible to recall. In cases of severe trauma, and peri-traumatic dissociation, experiences may not be encoded and therefore not stored in a sequential way. Counsellors need to have accurate knowledge of memory processes and how memory can be transformed during processing and recall to understand that memory can be fallible, leading some memories to be accurate, some to be inaccurate and some a blend of both (Sanderson, 2006).

To avoid becoming enslaved to restoring full sequential memories, counsellors and survivors will need to acknowledge that not all memories will be accessible to recall and that this does not invalidate those memories that are intact. It is also worth noting that memories can be accessed in a variety of ways, and can be stimulated through all five senses, especially through olfaction which is one of the fastest routes for memory recall. In addition, recalled memories can manifest as sensory memories or visual images as well as sequential narrative and must be understood in relation to trauma. Being over-focused on memory recall can be counterproductive as it occludes many other important aspects of the interpersonal trauma, and counsellors may need to work with the survivor on an acceptable level of memory recall which is tolerable rather than be consumed with full restoration. Similarly the absence of full narrative memory does not necessarily confirm that no trauma occurred. Both counsellor and survivor will need to have considerable tolerance for uncertainty to avoid becoming entrapped in the search for full sequential memories.

While exploration is helpful to access memories, old pain and hurts, it is important not to become embedded in the trauma as this may prevent processing and integration. Exploration of the trauma narrative needs to be balanced with focusing on change and looking forward to create a future. To really transform trauma and abuse into a future zest for life, post-traumatic growth and empowerment, survivors must work on relinquishing the legacies of the past and take control of their future.

It is in the safety of the therapeutic relationship that survivors can learn to reconnect to themselves and others and experience opportunities for growth. Even temporary ruptures in the therapeutic relationship need not herald destruction and betrayal but can forge a deeper sense of connection based on honesty and mutuality which are more representative of non-professional relationships. Disconnections and reconnections can produce real growth and strengthen connections, provided the counsellor does not take them personally and can remain constant and available to listen and respond empathically to the disconnections.

CHALLENGING LEGACIES OF THE PAST AND COMMON DEFENCES

Survivors can be in thrall to the traumatic experiences and perpetuate the legacy of past abuse in their behaviour and interaction with others without realising it. This is often as a result of internalised distortions of perception or deeply embedded defence mechanisms. A good example of this is grandiosity or an inflated sense of self as a cover-up for shame and excruciating vulnerability. This can manifest in extreme narcissism and lack of empathy, whereby they see others as objects to be manipulated and controlled. This is often unconscious, and when confronted or challenged they are often horrified and devastated that they could behave like their own abuser. Alternatively, the individual may become over-identified with and embedded in a victim, or survivor, role, and believe that is the only way that they can relate to the world or others. Counsellors need to be aware that being in thrall to such self-constructions can be self-limiting as it can impede reality processing and post-traumatic growth. It is for this reason that counsellors need to encourage survivors to explore the legacies of the abuse and the compensatory structures and behaviours that are re-enacted. Rather than indulging the grandiosity, or re-shaming the survivor, counsellors need to focus on the underlying core issues of shame and vulnerability. Sensitive psychoeducation and exploration of the function of these defences, which were once highly adaptive, can enable survivors to relinquish these and find more appropriate and authentic ways of relating.

To support this, counsellors need to invite the survivor to challenge their beliefs around past experiences and their impact on the present. This involves identifying cognitive distortions, especially those imposed by the abuser, challenging them and replacing them with more accurate perceptions that reflect the reality of the abuse and trauma. In this survivors are able to reclaim disavowed perceptions and begin to trust themselves in their perceiving and experiencing. Survivors also need to entertain the new belief that the past doesn't have to predict the future, and that the power of the future is that it hasn't happened yet and so can be written by the survivor not the abuser(s) or trauma. A good metaphor here is to liken their life to a book, in which the early chapters have been completed, while the later chapters are yet to be written. This allows the survivor to be the author of her own life, in which she has control over how later chapters develop. In addition, survivors need to be aware that the best way of coming to terms with trauma is to create a great future in which they reconnect to life with vitality, self-agency and authenticity. It is for this reason that preoccupation and rumination on the past to the detriment of the future can become counterproductive as it can rehearse and stamp in failure, betrayal and hurt which become paralysing. Working through legacies of the past and integrating them is what is liberating and empowering rather than being consumed by them.

It is within the safety of the therapeutic relationship in which authenticity and honesty are paramount that the counsellor can help the survivor to confront the legacies and dysfunctions of the past, including defence mechanisms that are no longer adaptive. This has to be conducted in a sensitive, respectful manner as many survivors of interpersonal trauma have been labelled as difficult, chronic or failed clients by other professionals, as they have not been able to engage with them. This is often as a result of ingrained defence mechanisms that, while designed to protect the survivor from further harm, can be experienced as hostile, narcissistic or dismissive by others. Counsellors need to recognise that these defence mechanisms have served a valuable purpose in the past and may be hard to relinquish.

A good example of this is ambivalence in which the survivor yearns for closeness and yet fears engulfment, or retraumatisation. This irreconcilable double bind leads to oscillation between attachment and detachment, or approach and avoid, and idealisation and vilification of the therapist. Alternatively survivors may present as frozen to the point of paralysis as they retreat into their inner fortress, or become hostile, aggressive and dismissive to keep the counsellor at a distance to avoid impingement. Clinicians must identify the range of common defences and see them within the context of survival strategies and be empathic towards how hard it is to relinquish them.

Other common defences are submission and resignation wherein the survivor becomes overly compliant. Such survivors often present as "easy" clients as they are charming, pliable and malleable. They often display considerable appeasement behaviour through smiling, being complimentary, and making the counsellor feel good about himself. This is often highly seductive and manipulative, and reflects the "love bombing" used by many abusers in interpersonal trauma. This ability to charm and seduce is not conscious and is invariably a façade for suppressed anger and rage. It is also a way of appropriating an illusion of power as the counsellor is enticed and entranced by the client. Such survivors may also try to protect or rescue the counsellor in the hope that if the counsellor feels safe and protected they may then be able to rescue the survivor. In contrast some survivors may present as helpless and in need of rescuing, which in turn elicits rescuing behaviours in the clinician. Most of these defences are unconscious and they must be mentalised in a sensitive and a supportive way for survivors to be able to change them. Shaming or misinterpreting such defences will only force the survivor to retreat further and cause a collapse of the therapeutic relationship.

Clinicians must also guard against misinterpreting silence and withdrawal and be mindful that much of interpersonal trauma is unspeakable and that survivors are commonly rendered speechless and inchoate. Counsellors need to be mindful that "...what the tongue cannot speak and what reason cannot comprehend...what is absolutely certain and absolutely in doubt..." becomes impossible to articulate (Grand, 2000). This "learned voicelessness" (Scarf, 2005) rarely represents deliberate resistance or obdurateness but reflects the horror of interpersonal trauma in which meaning and language is obliterated. The role of the clinician is to help the survivor to "...graft speech onto silence" (Langer, 1995) and make the sequestered wordless self visible and audible. Similarly when survivors are withdrawn this represents a need to retreat to an inner fortress for protection from further hurt or pain rather than deliberate resistance. Humour and wit can also be a powerful defence in distracting from inner pain, and can be highly seductive. Survivors who are witty and are able to recount entertaining stories may use this as a form of self-soothing to minimise the impact and effect of the trauma.

Similarly, constant talk is a way to avoid terrifying silence which can resemble abuse episodes which were perpetrated in silence, or reflect the silent inner void that can never be filled. Talking becomes a way of filling that void and is also a way for the survivor to control the session so that the counsellor cannot impinge either through reflection, questions or interpretations. Streams of consciousness also prevent the survivor from mentalising, which in turn reduces the ability to process the trauma. Rushing through the trauma narrative often resembles the sense of urgency during the abuse to get through it as quickly as possible without mentalising or processing it, in order to restore control. Counsellors need to regulate such evacuations by modulating the survivor's narrative.

Due to the dehumanisation of interpersonal trauma, many survivors lack empathy and compassion for themselves. This can result in being over-empathic towards others, in the hope that they will then show empathy to them, or a total lack of empathy or compassion for anyone. The lack of empathy must be understood within the context of the abuse whereby no empathy or compassion is shown to the victim, making it difficult for them to empathise with self or others. A critical aspect of the therapeutic relationship is to nourish nascent empathy and compassion for the self, from which the survivor can then develop genuine, unconditional empathy for others. One way to achieve this is to challenge and transform negative attributions such as self-blame for being abused, not stopping the abuse, and not managing or tolerating the abuse (Miller and Porter, 1993). Counsellors also need to challenge other distorted perceptions that have been inserted by the abuser, to ensure that the survivor can re-evaluate these and reject them appropriately. In order to track changes in empathy, counsellors need to monitor the degree of empathy felt by the survivor and how this manifests in the therapeutic process as well as in relationships outside.

Until defence mechanisms are worked through, and survivors can embrace empathy, integration will be sabotaged by internal oppressors, through self-destructive behaviour and refusal to relinquish defences. Such sabotage is usually unconscious and not deliberate and needs to be handled sensitively to avoid further shaming the survivor. Counsellors may find it more helpful to focus on extending the survivor's behavioural repertoire through the incorporation of more healthy coping strategies rather than concentrating on demolishing defences so that the survivor can exercise more choice over which behaviours to adopt. Alongside this, counsellors need to honour and validate the defences as they were once highly adaptive and aided survival. Validating survivors' resources and coping strategies is a testament to their resilience and capacity to change, rather than an indication of their pathology.

WORKING WITH SELF-STRUCTURES

A crucial therapeutic goal when working with survivors of interpersonal trauma is to reverse the ubiquitous dehumanisation and restore self-structures. Given the deception and distortion of reality it is essential to enable survivors to trust their own perceptions, and to remain grounded enough in their own reality even when challenged by others or when others attempt to distort it. To retain and maintain contact with their own reality, inner experiencing and feelings rather than subverting or subsuming them, can be both liberating and empowering as it allows the disavowed authentic self to emerge. Gaining renewed confidence in internal locus of evaluation and control will also reduce the need for splitting, compartmentalisation, and the masquerade of the false self.

To fully understand the fragmented or repudiated self, counsellors will need to enter the survivor's inner frame of reference that has been disavowed, and rendered inchoate. To do this means entering a realm of contradictions where paradox reigns, which can be extremely challenging for counsellors. Initially the survivor will resist attempts to enter the rigid fortress that now encapsulates the self as this will be experienced as impingement. The rigid armour is there to protect the vulnerable self and to seal off seething emotions that cannot be expressed. The threat of fragmentation and internal collapse is so dangerous that the survivor will resist any attempts to connect to those self-structures, let alone allow the counsellor to do so. Counsellors need to be sensitive and patient in seeking contact with these self-aspects until the survivor is ready to open the door. Furthermore, counsellors need to understand and feel the emptiness, flatness, intense fear, and terrifying affects that cannot be controlled, or that have been split off in the inner self. These existential affects are rarely understood or ameliorated through the use of specific techniques or technical responses but are most responsive to a warm, genuine and shared empathic encounter.

It is also worth noting that survivors may deny the counsellor access to these disavowed parts due to "malignant contagion" (Grand, 2000) in which the survivor fears that if she were to access these brutalised aspects of the self the counsellor would become contaminated. Thus the fortress not only protects the vulnerable self-structures, but also protects others from the abuser's brutality and disavowed seething rage. Survivors will often open the door slightly, peep out and then retreat back in, until sufficient trust in self and the counsellor is established to venture out for longer periods of time. Once trust has been established the survivor can move from existing "as if" (Shengold, 1989) to be increasingly more authentic. In this the survivor will be able to relinquish the masquerade of the false self and facilitate a reduction in appeasement behaviours such as compliance and submission, or hostility, dominance and rage.

Some survivors genuinely feel unable to restore fragmented or disavowed self-structures. They are in thrall to powerful rescue fantasies due to the lack of any adult self-structures. They reside in a primitive, infantile state of utter helplessness. Due to the lack of self-structures they are totally dependent on someone else rescuing them. In such cases the emphasis of the therapeutic work becomes the therapeutic relationship in which the counsellor provides the secure base and mirroring necessary to erect and construct requisite self-structures (Sanderson, 2006). Counsellors need to guard against interpreting such helplessness as manipulative, and work in collaboration with the client on developing nascent self-aspects and enable them to organise these into a coherent whole (Sanderson, 2006). This can be challenging, painstaking and long-term work which can be highly rewarding as the survivor moves from inchoate self-structures and utter dependency to an individuated, integrated self that is enlivened and full of vitality.

WORKING WITH THE RELATIONAL SELF

A crucial function of the therapeutic relationship is to rebuild trust and connection to self and others which can enhance relational worth and relational identity. In combination with rebuilding self-structures it permits the survivor to relate more authentically to others rather than be compelled to comply and submit. An impact of interpersonal trauma is to undermine trust in self and others which elicits relational apprehensiveness necessitating withdrawal and a concomitant reduction in social support. This social isolation reinforces aloneness and lack of trust in others. The therapeutic relationship, in providing a secure base, allows the survivor to work through relational paradoxes such as the yearning for closeness and imperative to avoid, and the need to be visible and the need to conceal. The double bind of desire for intimacy and fear of engulfment, and the expectational effect of further betrayal or abuse, can be explored in the therapeutic relationship and worked through.

The therapeutic relationship is also an opportunity for the survivor to learn to distinguish between genuinely nurturing and nourishing relational dynamics and those that are coercive and controlling, leading to entrapment. This is achieved through the clinician's respect for the survivor's autonomy and self-agency and in encouraging the development of an internal locus of evaluation and control rather than being dependent on these from others. This can be usefully combined with reducing the survivor's inflated sense of responsibility for the feelings and thoughts of others. Such over-responsibility is often reflected in hypervigilance in relation to others, or second guessing and anticipating their needs, thoughts and feelings.

During interpersonal trauma, mentalisation is blocked or diverted to "mind reading" the abuser. This impedes space for reflection, especially self-reflection. When in survival mode, survivors are unable to mentalise unmet needs, emotions and thoughts, and these get blocked and pushed out of awareness permitting increased tolerance of abuse. Anticipating the needs, wants, and demands of the abuser is a crucial survival strategy as it enables the survivor to adjust to the demands of the abuser which could protect them from further abuse. However, it necessitates the survivor subsuming her needs under those of others and focusing on satisfying the abuser's needs first in the hope that they will then fulfil theirs. In addition, having others in mind can lead to being over-empathic towards others, while repudiating empathy for the self. In essence, mind reading represents a loss of self because anticipating the needs of others impedes being centred, or grounded in self-experiencing, thereby reducing trust in self-perceptions and intuition. While such "mind reading" was highly adaptive during the interpersonal trauma it can become mal-adaptive as every time the survivor "mind reads" she disconnects from her own sense of self.

In inhabiting the phenomenological world of "other" the survivor repudiates and disavows own needs, feelings and thoughts, and becomes whatever the abuser wants her to be. It is critical that counsellors enable the survivor to remain in her own frame of reference and not become lost in "other" to fully restore relational authenticity. As the survivor begins to stay connected to the self and is able to increase an internal locus of evaluation, she will be able to reduce malleability and the need to mind read. This in turn will lessen the need to enable others and allow the survivor to reduce the heightened sense of responsibility for the quality of relationships. In being able to relate more authentically the survivor can develop more reciprocal relationships based on mutual respect rather than coercion and control. In providing a healthy, respectful therapeutic relationship in which the survivor is visible and audible, the dread of psychic annihilation by others is modulated allowing for increased relational worth.

The coercive control and relational distortions in interpersonal abuse prevent the acquisition of effective interpersonal skills, and clinicians may need to consider ways of enhancing such skills. This can be facilitated through the connection and engagement in the therapeutic relationship, but may also need to be more explicitly addressed through psychoeducation. Counsellors can enable the survivor to become more mindful of interpersonal relationships in balancing priorities and demands, building mastery and self-respect, and by emphasising the importance of honesty, integrity and mutual respect. This will permit the survivor to identify and express needs, feelings, thoughts, fears, and beliefs more assertively. In combination developing relational skills and relational worth will reduce the need for defensive self-sufficiency in permitting connection to others without feeling shame or fear of abuse (Sanderson, 2006).

Counsellors must also be mindful when interpreting transference and counter-transference reactions. While these may indicate the transference of past relational experiences with significant others, they may also be lodged in the here and now experience in the therapeutic process. To ascribe them to classic transference reactions, and ignore the possibility that they reflect the current therapeutic relationship, risks invalidating the survivor's perception. This will be reminiscent of the abuser's distortion of the survivor's perception and will be perceived as further abuse which can lead to a collapse of the therapeutic relationship. To manage this, practitioners must be willing to reflect and monitor their own reactions to working with interpersonal trauma, their attachment style and how this informs their relational experiencing. This can be more easily achieved in the presence of an authentic relationship between counsellor and survivor rather than adopting a masquerade of clinical distance and detachment.

WORKING WITH SEXUAL TRAUMATISATION

In the case of survivors who have experienced sexual abuse, sexual violence, or sexual exploitation, counsellors will need to assess the impact this has had on relational apprehensiveness and fear of intimacy. This may necessitate a degree of psychoeducation around sexuality and how this can be compromised as a result of sexual violations. Traumatic sexualisation as result of sexual violation can lead to sex becoming the central organising principle of the individual in which they perceive themselves as primarily a sexual object to be used and abused by others (Sanderson, 2006). Despite this, survivors are often suffused with sexual fearfulness, sexual shame, and sexual anorexia which can impair motivation, arousal and orgasm. In addition the survivor may suffer from vaginismus and dyspareunia making sexual intercourse extremely painful. These in turn can either evoke sexual aversions and phobias in which the person avoids any sexual relationships or over-sexualisation such as satyriasis in males, or nymphomania in females. In over-sexualisation the survivor may engage in risky sexual behaviour through indiscriminate sexual promiscuity, unsafe sexual practices or serial concurrent relationships which are characterised by lack of relational intimacy all of which render the survivor vulnerable to retraumatisation (Sanderson, 2006).

To counteract the impact and effects of sexual traumatisation, counsellors need to help the survivor to differentiate between sexual activity and sexual desire, and to understand that sexual responsiveness during sexual violence is a response to the sexual act rather than the violator. It is crucial to normalise sexual responses in the presence of sexual acts through psychoeducation on the sexual arousal cycle and concomitant physiological response. In addition, survivors need to be mindful that sexual and physiological responses such as flashbacks, or fantasies that incorporate sexual traumatisation, are prompted by fear, not desire, anxiety, not pleasure, and represent unprocessed aspects of the trauma that need to be integrated.

Counsellors must also emphasise that sexual traumatisation does not mean that sexuality has been compromised and ensure that they do not avoid exploring the sexual violation(s). Throughout it is imperative that counsellors impress upon the survivor that it is not sexuality that is objectionable but the lack of consent that is objectionable and abusive.

Counsellors may also need to challenge negative beliefs and attitudes to sexuality as a result of sexual traumatisation. It is critical that survivors are able to distinguish between sexual arousal and sexual desire, in that the two are quite separate things whereby a person may not desire a sexual experience even though they may be aroused by it. Counsellors must be explicit in emphasising that it is the sexual activity, such as oral sex, and not the person that the victim responds to, a factor that many sexual abusers and rapists capitalise on. They often perform sexual acts that are highly arousing in order for the victim to feel complicit in the sexual violation. For instance rapists may elicit sexual responses by performing cunnilingus or fellatio on the victim to increase arousal and lubrication and induce orgasm. Male survivors may need to become aware that they can experience involuntary erections, ejaculation and orgasm in the presence of fear, or when under stress. These physiological responses can occur involuntarily even when unaccompanied by any sexually arousing state and can occur during passion as well as in the absence of passion or desire.

There are a number of useful techniques that can help the survivor to reclaim their sexuality such as self-exploration and increased sexual awareness, relaxation and embodiment, desensitisation, breaking old associations and sensate focus (Sanderson, 2006). These can be employed alongside discussion of sex and sexuality in a sensitive, non-shaming way. To facilitate this, and to contain any anxieties the counsellor may have, it is critical that counsellors have a good knowledge and understanding of sex and sexuality and feel comfortable in discussing such matters. To this effect counsellors need to be aware of their own attitudes and beliefs around sex and sexuality, comfort around sexuality, and sexual orientation. They also need to be aware of their own experiences of sexual violations as well as any sexual inhibitions or shame. Moreover, counsellors need to be able to talk in a meaningful way about sex without embarrassment or recoiling from some of the sexual violations that the survivor may have experienced. Finally, counsellors will need to ensure that the exploration of sexual traumatisation is conducted without being voyeuristic or intrusive, and to minimise and contain any concomitant sexual arousal (Sanderson, 2006).

LOSS, GRIEF AND MOURNING

Interpersonal abuse and trauma is inexorably linked to loss, and yet survivors often do not feel entitled to grieve due to self-blame, and negative self-beliefs. The losses sustained in interpersonal abuse occur across all dimensions including physical and psychological losses, material losses, as well as spiritual losses (Sanderson, 2008). In order to fully recover from interpersonal abuse survivors need to identify the full range of losses and begin to mourn these. Common examples of losses due to interpersonal trauma include actual and symbolic losses such as loss of self, loss of autonomy and self-agency, loss of esteem, loss of status and loss of trust in self, others and the world as a benign place. Material losses can include loss of home, employment, or possessions as well as family, friends, pets and a sense of belongingness. In addition survivors face loss of health and well-being, loss of continuity and belief in a future, as well as spiritual losses such as loss of faith and hope.

Obstacles to grieving such as shame, self-blame and lack of legitimacy must also be identified and worked through before the grieving process can begin. Counsellors must be mindful of the stages of the grief process and the fact that these stages will not necessarily manifest in a linear or sequential way. The impact of interpersonal trauma is such that the survivor may face myriad challenges such as housing, legal processes or financial crisis that will need focus and attention and over-ride the therapeutic process. Counsellors will need to be patient and sensitive to detours and diversions, and not interpret these as resistance and avoidance but contextualise these. This necessitates an element of flexibility in the therapeutic process in which psychological support becomes just as important as therapeutic interventions (Sanderson, 2008).

Counsellors can use a variety of techniques that have been shown to be helpful in the bereavement process (Kübler-Ross, 1969; Parkes, 2001; Worden, 2003) although acknowledging the many losses is the beginning of self-compassion and empathy which is necessary for healing to occur. It is only through mourning these losses that the survivor can begin to reconnect to the authentic self, others and the world (Sanderson, 2008). This allows for post-traumatic growth in which the survivor is enlivened and is able to restore vitality to fully engage in the world in an authentic way without being consumed by fear and terror. In living life the survivor is no longer just surviving but thriving, and has managed to truly transform the interpersonal trauma.

POST-TRAUMATIC GROWTH

In working with survivors of interpersonal trauma, counsellors need to be mindful of the possibility of post-traumatic growth and focus on the positive outcomes when healing from trauma. A genuine belief in positive growth rather than paying lip service, or merely replacing negative experiences with positive ones, is a powerful way to healing and recovery. Integrating positive and negative experiences underpins post-traumatic growth in which a positive approach is balanced with realism, and assessed in relation to each individual survivor. The presence of hope is evident from the moment the survivor enters therapy and shows a willingness to trust again despite past betrayals. It is a testament to the tremendous courage to risk again which needs to be validated from the outset, not just in words but in deep recognition and understanding of how difficult and costly this is. This clear indicator that the survivor has not abandoned hope and that the self has not been totally annihilated, allows for the restoration of vitality and life energy to allow for further growth.

As the therapeutic relationship is critical for reconnection, counsellors need to constantly monitor the quality of the therapeutic relationship, as it is only in the presence of a safe and secure therapeutic environment that self-structures can be rebuilt and the survivor can reconnect to self, others and life. It is in the presence of a genuine human relationship that the person can counteract the dehumanisation of the interpersonal abuse, and allow the repudiated self to re-emerge. It is through immediacy and spontaneity, and the human qualities of humour and laughter, that the survivor can begin to reconnect. The un-extinguished hope must be honoured and nourished through the therapeutic relationship alongside a heightened appreciation of life, resilience and reconnection to disavowed spirituality. It is when the survivor can relinquish her fear of living that she can begin to embrace life and take control of her future in which needs, feelings, thoughts and actions can be celebrated rather than repudiated.

Working with survivors of interpersonal trauma can also be life changing for clinicians in that they may also experience post-traumatic growth. Such work can be emotionally demanding and immensely distressing and yet is often extremely rewarding. Being in the presence of those who have been betrayed and still risk connection can be, and often is, transformative as it can enhance therapeutic skills and make for a more sentient practitioner. The resilience and hope that has not been extinguished despite betrayal is testament to post-traumatic growth, and allows both survivor and clinician to access a deeper appreciation of what it is to be human and to be alive.

SUMMARY

- Interpersonal trauma impacts differently depending on the type of abuse or violation, the age of the victim and the extent, severity and duration of the abuse. Despite this, there are a number of commonalities that clinicians need to be aware of that apply across most interpersonal abuse.
- The misuse of power and control in interpersonal trauma demands that counsellors are aware of power dynamics in the therapeutic process and endeavour to minimise these by being transparent, authentic and explicit in their work, especially around boundaries.
- Before commencing any therapeutic work, counsellors must ensure external and internal safety. Stabilisation of tumultuous feelings and PTSD symptoms

can be facilitated through affect regulation, distress tolerance, mentalising, and mindfulness skills.

- These skills will restore internal control and promote a reduction in dissociation and self-destructive behaviours such as self-harm, self-injury, self-medication, and risky behaviours that render the survivor vulnerable to retraumatisation.
- With increased control over internal arousal and regulation skills, survivors can begin to work through the trauma narrative and begin to challenge the legacies of the past including negative attributions and distorted perceptions. It will also facilitate the restoration of fragmented memories and allow for a sense of continuity.
- Such skills also allow for exploration of common defences, which, while adaptive during the interpersonal trauma, may have become mal-adaptive in keeping the survivor in thrall to the interpersonal abuse.
- Interpersonal trauma impacts on both self-structures and relational worth and counsellors need to ensure that therapeutic focus includes restoration of fragmented self-structures and the disavowed vulnerable self. In promoting reconnection to the authentic self the survivor can begin to reconnect to others in a more authentic way.
- Relational apprehension and difficulties must also be worked through the therapeutic relationship which is predicated on genuine human connection, to offset the dehumanisation associated with interpersonal trauma. This promotes relational worth and the skills for mutuality, respect and reciprocity.
- In the case of sexual traumatisation, counsellors need to work with how this has impacted on the survivor to reclaim sexuality and sexual pleasure without feeling shame or guilt.
- Interpersonal trauma engenders myriad losses that survivors find hard to legitimise. To fully integrate the trauma, survivors need to overcome the obstacles to grieving and mourn the range of losses to ensure self-compassion and allow for post-traumatic growth.
- Working with survivors of interpersonal trauma not only promotes post-traumatic growth in the survivor but also in the clinician in appreciating the human qualities of hope and resilience and a renewed appreciation of life, making them more sentient practitioners.

PART II

SPECTRUM OF INTERPERSONAL ABUSE

CHAPTER 6

CHILD ABUSE AS INTERPERSONAL TRAUMA

Every decade a high-profile child death due to abuse highlights the plight of vulnerable children in their own homes. The tragic deaths of Victoria Climbié in 2000 and most recently "Baby Peter" in (2007) bring to public attention the extent of child abuse and the suffering such children endure. Such cases inexorably lead to questions around how such abuse can occur. Sadly, in the UK approximately one child a week is murdered either by a parent, family member or carer. Research has shown that up to 80% of children murdered are not on any child protection register (Brandon *et al.*, 2008). More disturbingly, for every child that dies there are many more who are seriously injured, many of whom also go undetected by social services or other agencies responsible for safeguarding children.

Given the hidden nature of child abuse it is impossible to ascertain how many children are being abused at any one time, as statistical data may merely reflect the tip of the iceberg. This suggests that many children do not come to the attention of professionals and are unlikely to have received therapeutic intervention as children or young adults. As a result they can become vulnerable to entering either the criminal justice system, or the mental health system.

Clinicians frequently report that clients who enter therapy with a variety of presenting symptoms may also have a history of child abuse. This is particularly the case with clients who have a history of substance abuse, alcohol addiction, and self-harming behaviour. In such cases it is imperative that clinicians address not only the addictive or self-harming behaviours, but also explore the factors that underlie the need to self-medicate. This chapter will look at the various types of child abuse, how it impacts on the child and later adult. It will highlight some common and recurring themes and how these can be addressed in the therapeutic process.

RANGE OF CHILD ABUSE

The Children Act 1989 and 2004 defines a child as anyone under 18, whether living independently or not, and identifies a number of categories of child abuse: physical abuse, emotional abuse, sexual abuse and neglect. It also includes the abuse of children through prostitution, fabricated or induced illness, organised or multiple abuse, female genital mutilation, and forced marriage, which can lead to honour crime.

These categories are thought to cause "significant harm" (Children Act, 1989) if such ill treatment causes the impairment of health or development, including, for example, impairment suffered from seeing or hearing the ill treatment of another, as in the case of domestic abuse, or the abuse of a sibling.

While these broad categories of abuse are often overt, there are myriad subtle abuses that are more covert and yet can cause significant harm, and frequently underpin more overt abuse. These include failures in connection to the child, deficits in adequate mirroring, the inability to recognise or accept psychological needs, or refusal to satisfy these. These often arise either due to lack of knowledge, or due to the narcissistic needs of the parent, or carer, who sees the child as an object to satisfy unmet needs, or as an extension of the self. Such dynamics can be enacted consciously, unconsciously or through default, wherein the primary caregiver's mental health is compromised, such as in severe depression, suicidal ideation or substance misuse. In combination these can lead to complex dysfunctional family dynamics in which the child is lured into a "folies à deux" wherein it sacrifices its own needs and focuses on satisfying the parent's need.

DEFINITION OF CHILD ABUSE

In order to clarify the various categories of child abuse, the document *Working Together to Safeguard Children* (Department of Health, 2006) aims to define each of the major abuses.

Physical abuse

This is the Department of Health's definition: "Physical abuse may involve hitting, shaking, throwing, poisoning, burning or scalding, drowning, suffocating, or otherwise causing physical harm to a child. Physical harm may also be caused when a parent or carer fabricates the symptoms of, or deliberately induces, illness in a child".

Emotional abuse

Emotional abuse is defined as:

> ...the persistent emotional maltreatment of a child such as to cause severe and persistent adverse effects on the child's emotional development. It may involve conveying to children that they are worthless or unloved, inadequate, or valued only insofar as they meet the needs of another person. It may feature age or developmentally inappropriate expectations being imposed on children. These may include interactions

> that are beyond the child's developmental capability, as well as overprotection and limitation of exploration and learning, or preventing the child participating in normal social interaction. It may involve seeing or hearing the ill treatment of another. It may involve serious bullying causing children frequently to feel frightened or in danger, or the exploitation or corruption of children. Some level of emotional abuse is involved in all types of maltreatment of a child though it may occur alone.

Neglect

The definition of neglect is:

> ...the persistent failure to meet a child's basic physical and/or psychological needs; likely to result in the serious impairment of the child's health or development. Neglect may occur during pregnancy as a result of maternal substance abuse. Once a child is born, neglect may involve a parent or carer failing to:
>
> - Provide adequate food, clothing and shelter (including exclusion from home or abandonment)
> - Protect the child from physical and emotional harm or danger
> - Ensure adequate supervision (including the use of inadequate caregivers)
> - Ensure access to appropriate medical care or treatment
>
> It may also include neglect of, or unresponsiveness to, a child's emotional needs.

Neglect activates a number of emotional responses such as intense terror of being left alone, an agonising sense of isolation and desolation, and fervid concern for siblings or primary caregiver.

Sexual abuse

Working Together to Safeguard Children defines sexual abuse as:

> ...forcing or enticing a child or young person to take part in sexual activities, including prostitution, whether or not the child is aware of what is happening. The activities may involve physical contact, including penetrative (e.g. rape, buggery, or oral sex) or non-penetrative acts. They may include non-contact activities, such as involving children in looking at, or in the production of, sexual online images, watching sexual activities, or encouraging children to behave in sexually inappropriate ways. (Department of Health, 2006) (See Chapter 7).

PREVALENCE

The hidden nature of child abuse makes it extremely difficult to get accurate data on incidence and prevalence rates. Statistics show that in the UK on average one child a week dies at the hands of a parent or carer and it is thought for every death, at least ten children are injured (Brandon *et al.*, 2008). The most common causes of death are injuries to the head and neck including fatal fractures of the skull or facial bones, and injuries to the thorax or multiple body regions, while some die due to asphyxiation or a foreign body entering through a natural orifice, or a foreign body in the respiratory tract. Invariably child deaths come to professional or public attention, and are recorded statistically. This is, however, less likely to be the case in children who are suffering physical abuse below the level of medical intervention, emotional abuse, sexual abuse, or neglect.

Most professionals involved in safeguarding children believe that prevalence and incidence data are merely the tip of the iceberg, and that much child abuse remains undetected by professionals. This is reflected in high-profile cases such as Victoria Climbié, or the father who sexually abused his two daughters for 25 years, impregnating them 19 times and fathering seven surviving children. Research has also shown that of the number of children killed or seriously injured between 2003 and 2005, 45% were not on the child protection register (Brandon *et al.*, 2008), and of the 189 cases of death or serious injury due to abuse or neglect which were subject to a serious case review between 2006 and 2007, 80% were not known to social or children's services. This would suggest that the number of children at risk of significant harm is considerably higher than the 29,200 children currently on the Child Protection Register (Boseley, 2008). This may be particularly the case where children are suffering emotional abuse, or neglect, which may never be discerned or brought to professional attention.

In terms of category of abuse, the most common appears to be neglect. Of those children subject to a Child Protection Plan (CPP), 45% are at significant risk due to neglect, 25% are at risk of emotional abuse, 15% at risk of physical abuse and 7% at risk of sexual abuse, while around 8% of children are at risk of multiple abuse. Boys appear to have a slightly elevated risk of abuse at 51% while 49% of children deemed at risk are female.

Recent estimates of prevalence of child abuse suggest that one in ten children in the UK suffers from physical, emotional or sexual abuse, or neglect, and that fewer than one in ten cases of maltreatment are investigated or substantiated by child protection services. Gilbert *et al.* estimate that 4–16% of children in the UK suffer physical abuse, 15% suffer from neglect, 10% experience emotional abuse, and 15% of girls and 5% of boys experience CSA (Gilbert *et al.*, 2009a; 2009b).

WHO IS AT RISK?

All children are at risk and every child matters. Research has shown that some children may be more at risk than others. This is especially the case of children with physical or mental disability, and children already in care, and those living in families in which there is domestic abuse, substance abuse, or mental illness. There also appears to be gender differences with child mortality rates elevated in boys at 84% compared to 64% of girls dying at the hands of caregivers in 2006 (Boseley,

2008). Age is also a risk factor, with Brandon *et al.* (2008) suggesting that there are two peaks of vulnerability: babies and older teenagers.

Between 2005 and 2007 the majority of serious cases of child deaths were in children below the age of one, with most of those under six months. A quarter of all cases were children over the age of 11, with a minority between 16 and 18. It is worth noting that some of the deaths in the 16–18-year-old group were suicides, some of them due to a history of abuse. The smallest number appears to be children aged between six and ten (Brandon *et al.* 2008).

PERPETRATORS

The perpetrators of child abuse can be anyone who cares for children and has parental authority over them. This includes biological parents, step-parents, "guesting parents", adoptive parents, foster carers, carers in children's homes, institutions, or special needs schools. Some research has shown that there is an elevation of child abuse from step-parents and "guesting fathers". Some of these carers may inflict abuse on children, unwittingly believing them to be legitimate child-rearing practices. This may be due to different cultural practices, or through lack of knowledge of the impact of such practices on children. Arguably, child abuse through "omission" is significantly different from child abuse through "commission", in which the carer deliberately and intentionally harms the child, although the child may not be able to differentiate between the two. Carers who commit deliberate harm on children are often extremely deceptive in covering up the abuse by misleading others, especially professionals, in falsifying how injuries were sustained, covering bruising with make-up, or, as in Baby Peter's case, chocolate and medicated cream.

DYNAMICS OF CHILD ABUSE

This level of deception and subterfuge underlies much of child abuse in which abuse masquerades as protection and reality is consistently distorted. Child abuse is characterised by the falsification of reality in which surface interactions appear normal and serve to occlude the hidden violence. This robs the child of her reality, distorting self-perceptions and invalidating subjective experience. Such distortion can be "crazy making" as the child strives for meaning and comprehension. The space between knowing and not knowing leads to unremitting uncertainty, while the deception and lies serve to annihilate the truth. As the child cannot know reality she enters an "as if" existence (Shengold, 1989), in which she normalises her experiences in order to accommodate the abuse.

To manage this falsification of reality the child either physically withdraws into frozen watchfulness, or into psychic withdrawal through dissociation. Dissociation allows the child to develop an idealised attachment to the abuser by splitting off, or compartmentalising, all terrifying interactions with the abuser in order to retain an idealised image of the carer. The cost of idealising the abuser is self-blame, in which the child takes full responsibility for their abuse. This also allows for a false illusion of control over the abuse, as they believe if they were better behaved, or not so inherently flawed, their carer would not hurt them and would provide them with the love and care so desperately needed. Dissociation also allows traumatic experiences to be dismembered, and anaesthetised so that they can no longer be felt, leaving the child disembodied.

Alongside such traumatic bonding, there is a danger of contamination of the abuser's brutality. The dehumanisation and objectification of the child can lead to identification with the aggressor in which the abuser's brutality is incorporated by the child, and re-enacted with others, especially more vulnerable children, including younger siblings. Alternatively the child identifies with the idealised image of the carer in becoming a protector of younger siblings, or the non-abusing parent, whereby they sacrifice their own vulnerability, fear, pain and grief. The unremitting confusion and need for hypervigilance in anticipation of further abuse, can lead to a range of attention deficits such as distractibility, impulsivity, hyperarousal, and poor concentration, which in turn lead to behavioural and cognitive deficits.

IMPACT OF CHILD ABUSE

> Our brains are sculpted by our early experiences. Maltreatment is a chisel that shapes a brain to contend with strife, but at the cost of deep enduring wounds. (Teicher, 2000)

The most pervasive impact of child abuse is during the first ten years of life, especially the first two, becoming more circumscribed with age (van der Kolk *et al.*, 2005). If the abuse straddles a number of critical developmental stages, more complex emotional, behavioural and neurobiological sequelae ensue. Physical abuse not only leads to physical injury, neurological damage, disability and death, but has also been linked to aggression and violence, educational difficulties, and emotional and behavioural problems, including self-harm and later substance abuse.

Emotional abuse in early infancy impacts on developing mental health, behaviour and self-esteem. Emotional abuse typically includes a degree of humiliation, or shaming, emotional abandonment or the rejection of the child's striving for connection, love or shared emotionality. Instead of getting comfort and mirroring from the caregiver, the child has to be the comforter and mirror for the caregiver. In becoming the caretaker, the child identifies with adult caretaking that it is deprived of but cannot apply to the self. To manage this the child is catapulted into pseudomaturity and learns that it is unable to depend on anyone, including the therapist when entering therapy. The suffering experienced through emotional abuse promotes an over-developed sense of empathy for others, and lack of compassion or empathy for the self. As the child's needs are ignored, or rebuffed, the child becomes ashamed of any basic needs it may have and is compelled to banish these to an inner fortress to protect them from a dangerous, rejecting outer world.

Emotionally abused children, and later adults, often present as compliant and overly responsible, with a facade of self-sufficiency, invulnerability and fierce independence. As adults they make good caretakers and may enter the helping professions such as counselling, social work, or nursing in which their underlying unmet needs are split off, or compartmentalised, as they continue to direct their care and protection towards others. As the emotionally abused child is continually shamed for having or expressing emotions, they may separate from all feelings and felt experiences, including positive feelings such as joy, excitement and vitality. This helps to protect the shame-based identity at the cost of self-expression as all feelings are associated with pain and misery. For many such adult children the only way to discharge any feelings is through self-destructive behaviour such as self-harm, or self-medication through alcohol, drugs and a range of addictive behaviours.

Early childhood neglect impacts on the child's, and later adult's, ability to form attachments, which impairs relational and social functioning. Accompanying distorted beliefs about being unloved and unlovable lead to a heightened sense of isolation and need for withdrawal. Nutritional deficiencies due to neglect can lead to impaired growth and intellectual development which impede educational progress resulting in lowered self-esteem, reinforcing the sense of inadequacy and lack of worth. Children who have been sexually abused will also experience a reduction in self-worth other than as a sexual object. This over-valuation as a sexual object promotes inappropriate sexualised behaviour in which the child and later adult can only relate, or communicate with others, in a sexually seductive or sexualised way (see Chapter 7).

To manage abuse in childhood, the authentic self has to retreat to protect itself from further pain and humiliation. This self is replaced by a false self which is precociously adapted to the outer world (Winnicott, 1960). The false self repudiates the needy and dependent part of the child in order to become self-sufficient and avoid the shame of acknowledging and expressing needs, or displaying unguarded and spontaneous expressions of self. This external façade of toughness and self-sufficiency conceals a profound, secret dependency, which is so shameful that it can never be revealed, even to the clinician. While this allows the vulnerable self to be encapsulated and sealed off from further violation, it can also lead to separation and disconnection from the authentic self. In this cocoon the child cannot mobilise effective self-assertion to defend itself to individuate or permit spontaneous expressions of self.

In such a rigid psychological defence system (Kalsched, 1996) the vulnerable self is concealed at considerable cost. In entering a form of psychological cold storage it retreats from the vivacity of life and ossifies. Deprived of oxygen, and the life blood of connection, it becomes imprisoned in a seemingly impenetrable, self-destructive fortress preventing any further growth or development, forever trapped in a limbo, or zombie-like existence. Over time, even in the presence of safety, inner persecutory voices serve to prevent re-entering the world, further imprisoning the vulnerable self. In this the child, and adult survivor, will oscillate between retreating for protection, and self-persecution to prevent reconnection to self, others and the world to prolong the psychological death of the vulnerable self.

Such imprisonment is further reinforced by self-blame in which the child feels that the abuse is fundamentally their fault, because that was what the child was told either explicitly or implicitly. Self-blame is also a way to maintain a false illusion of control to combat the pervasive sense of helplessness. Thus if the child believes it is to blame it can endeavour to be better and can become good enough, and thereby obtain the much-needed love. In addition, it is too risky for a dependent child to blame their parent, for fear of ever more severe consequences. This leads to the idealisation of the parent and concomitant vilification, or psychological annihilation of the self. This toxic cocktail of false beliefs and disavowal of the self leads to anger turned inwards and severely compromised mental health, and associated problems such as anxiety, depression, substance abuse, eating disorders and self-destructive behaviours, including suicidal ideation.

The DSM-IV Field Trial into the impact of repeated and multiple trauma in early childhood has found that childhood abuse leads to complex developmental derailments including disruptions to affect regulation, disturbed attachment patterns, rapid behavioural regressions and shifts in emotional states, and educational deficits (van der Kolk *et al.*, 2005). As a result the Complex Trauma Task Force for the National Child Traumatic Stress Network and Bessel van der Kolk have conceptualised a new diagnostic category to understand repeated and prolonged abuse and exposure to interpersonal trauma such as abandonment, betrayal, physical and sexual assaults and witnessing domestic abuse, provisionally called developmental trauma disorder (van der Kolk *et al.*, 2005). As mentioned earlier, this is being considered for inclusion by the American Psychiatric Association in DSM-V due to be published in 2012.

Childhood abuse engenders intense and uncontrollable internal affects such as rage, betrayal, fear, resignation, defeat and shame. To ward off and manage the recurrence of these emotions children will either avoid experiences that precipitate them, or engage in behaviours that will promote a subjective semblance of control in the face of potential threats. This will manifest in either frozen avoidance, or as re-enactments of the trauma. Abused children commonly react in a fearful, enraged or avoidant emotional way to relatively minor stimuli that would have no significant effect on secure children. In addition, they have difficulty restoring homeostasis and returning to baseline. This is accompanied by reduced insight or understanding of reactions, and an inability to connect these to the abuse. Such children, and later adults, anticipate and expect trauma to recur and respond with hyperactivity, aggression, defeat or freeze responses to minor stress. They are invariably confused, dissociated and disorientated when faced with stress, consistently interpret events in the direction of return of trauma, and their pervasive sense of helplessness necessitates hypervigilance and being constantly on guard, leading them to over-react even to non-threatening situations, or minor threat.

The repeated and prolonged cascade of neurochemical changes that enable the child to cope with a dangerous and malevolent world, can become wired and stamped in to predispose the child to pervasive biologically mediated fear states outside of conscious awareness. While this is highly adaptive in the trauma-inducing environment in order to survive, these responses can generalise to all subjectively perceived danger, whether external or internal, with no rational mind, even if in a place of safety. Such defensive adaptation enhances survival in a world of constant danger and yet can result in highly irritable, impulsive, and suspicious behaviour characterised by explosive violence. As the individual is swamped by intense flight/fight reactions that the mind cannot control, they become even more hypervigilant to the point of paranoia, leading to decreased judgment, verbal ability and decision making, and a diminished recognition of own pain through dissociation (Teicher, 2000). This can lead to attack as the best form of defence as an automatic response throughout life for any minor infringement on the individual's personal space, safety or status.

Negative self-attributions, loss of trust in caretakers, loss of belief that someone has them in mind and will look after them and make them feel safe, can make it very difficult to form stable attachment relationships so desperately needed. In addition, expectations of being revictimised, abused, or abandoned, can reinforce distrust making it difficult to connect to others. Alternatively, such fears may result in insecure attachments where the child and later adult becomes excessively clingy, compliant and submissive. The disconnection and dissociation can in turn lead to a high tolerance threshold for pain, both self-inflicted and that inflicted by others (Teicher, 2000) and a preoccupation with revenge and retribution.

A further impact of repeated and prolonged abuse is that the child is deprived of all autonomous strivings, resulting in aggression towards self and others, while failure to achieve developmental competencies, and altered schemas of the world, serve to reinforce anticipatory behaviour and traumatic expectations. Developmental trauma activates a cascade of neurobiological changes accompanying somatic problems from gastrointestinal distress to headaches and self-regulatory impairments in appetitive behaviours. Hypovigilance can lead to lack of awareness of danger and failure to moderate self-endangering behaviour, which when combined with self-hatred and self-blame, chronic feelings of ineffectiveness, and lack of assertion, increases vulnerability to further victimisation and traumatisation.

There is considerable evidence that trauma interferes with neurobiological development and capacity to integrate sensory, emotional and cognitive information into a cohesive whole due to the breakdown in ability to process, integrate and categorise what is happening (Sanderson, 2006). Traumatic experiences become dissociated into incomprehensible sensory fragments which cannot be mobilised to execute appropriate pans of action (van der Kolk and Fisler, 1995) resulting in re-enactments rather than considered responses. This leads individuals to express fundamental needs implicitly, through behaviour, in the form of interpersonal enactments, play or fantasy, rather than explicit requests.

As abused children are unable to rely on significant others, and fear the expression of needs, they are not able to regulate their emotional states leading to uncontainable hyperarousal. As hyperaroused children learn to ignore what they feel and what they perceive (van der Kolk 2008) they cannot achieve a sense of control or stability over their internal states. As a result children and survivors of interpersonal trauma commonly experience intense fear responses, without being able to mentalise their experience, and react as though they are being traumatised all over again (Streeck-Fischer and van der Kolk, 2000). This activates a cascade of behavioural responses in an effort to minimise threat and regulate emotional distress. Such children cannot master their experiences and differentiate, or "decentre" them from being one's reflexes, movements and sensations and merely experiencing them (Piaget, 1952). In addition, traumatised children organise their behaviour around keeping the secret, and deal with helplessness with either compliance or defiance, and will attempt to acclimatise in any way they can to their entrapment (Piaget, 1952). Thus concomitant behaviours must be viewed within the context of interpersonal trauma rather than being labelled as "oppositional", "rebellious", "antisocial" or "unmotivated".

Clinicians need to be mindful that deficits in emotional self-regulation lead to lack of continuous sense of self, and poorly modulated affect and impulse control, especially aggression directed against self and others. Abused children see other people as either a source of pleasure or terror and will submit to them accordingly. This is exacerbated by uncertainty around the reliability and predictability of others, which is invariably expressed as distrust, suspiciousness and fear of intimacy. Anything new, including people, is perceived as potentially threatening, while the familiar is perceived as safer, even if it is a predictable source of terror (Streeck-Fischer and van der Kolk, 2000). Ultimately deficits in emotional regulation contribute to the aetiology of affective disorders such as depression, self-harm, eating disorders; dissociative and somatoform disorders; metabolic and immunological disorders such as chronic fatigue syndrome; and personality disorders, in particular borderline personality disorder, antisocial personality disorder and narcissistic personality disorder which are characterised by a lack of insight and connection to their origin in trauma.

LONG-TERM EFFECTS OF CHILDHOOD ABUSE

The long-term effects of childhood abuse cluster around affect dysregulation, ranging from dissociation and numbness through to high levels of anxiety and arousal. The need to be in control is also a prominent feature, which is often manifest in rigid, over-controlled behaviour or poor impulse control and acting out, with many survivors oscillating between the two. Childhood abuse also promotes myriad cognitive changes, in particular negative automatic thoughts and self-attributions in which survivors believe that they are inherently flawed and are to blame for the abuse. Such cognitive distortions enable the survivor to rationalise and normalise the abuse. One area of particular difficulty for survivors of childhood abuse is in interpersonal relationships. Many survivors still fear punishment and are thus compliant and submissive, with extremely high tolerance thresholds for further abuse. They often feel over responsible and cannot express their needs, or alternatively become consumed with their own needs leading to narcissism whereby their needs obscure the needs of others such as partners, or children.

Box 6.1 Core clinical symptoms of child abuse

- Affect dysregulation – volatility
- Need for control – over or under-controlled, fear of losing control
- Hypervigilance
- Inauthentic self
- Fierce independence, self-sufficiency, difficulty asking for help
- Belief that they are flawed and deserved abuse
- Lack of trust
- Relational difficulties – fear of intimacy, approach and avoidance
- High tolerance threshold for abuse
- Compliance – submissive, "good client", taking care of therapist
- Hostile – dominant, resistant, rejecting of help
- Fear of dependency
- Dissociation from body
- Expectation to be hurt or abused again
- Inability to mentalise
- Perfectionism
- Lack of compassion for self and abused child
- Profound loneliness
- Shame

The relational difficulties are predicated on fear of dependency and shameful neediness which is concealed by self-reliance and managed by vacillation between approach and avoidance. The lack of trust can also lead to withdrawal and isolation and a chasm of loneliness in which people and relationships are avoided and all needs disavowed. To fill the inner void many survivors resort to self-medication through a variety of addictions, in particular alcohol and drug misuse, or to a variety of self-harming behaviours.

CORE THERAPEUTIC GOALS

The core therapeutic goals are to establish safety and restore control to the survivor, especially control over chaotic internal states. The focus needs to be on integrating the traumatic experiences and gaining mastery of the body and mind (van der Kolk, 2008) through affect regulation and cognitive restructuring. By challenging negative self-attributions and automatic thoughts, the survivor can begin to reduce self-blame and develop compassion for the traumatised child. This in turn reduces perfectionism and moderates excoriating self-punishment in the face of perceived failure.

Box 6.2 Core therapeutic goals

- Establish safety
- Restore control
- Establish trust
- Affect regulation
- Mastery of body and mind
- Cognitive restructuring
- Reconnect to authentic self
- Express needs without shame
- Reconnect to others through the therapeutic relationship
- Reduce perfectionism and self-punishment
- Reduce self-harming behaviours by offering alternative coping strategies
- Reconnect to world

To overcome relational difficulties it is imperative to establish trust through the therapeutic relationship so that the survivor can begin to reconnect to self and others. This allows the survivor to move from primate defences necessary to survive, to connect to others without fear of further abuse or hurt. As the survivor emerges from a primary survival mode, energy and vitality is restored permitting a renewed sense of aliveness and engagement with the world. The pervasive and crippling fears can finally be relinquished freeing the survivor to embrace life and enhanced spirituality.

THERAPEUTIC CHALLENGES

Working with survivors of childhood trauma can be demanding and challenging at times due to their fear of dependency and expectation of being abused again. Fears around visibility and invisibility can lead to oscillation between wanting to be close and needing to retreat. Counsellors need to be patient and accepting of such volatility and remain steadfast and consistent. In anticipating rejection, punishment or abuse, survivors will test the clinician's investment and constancy through volatile behaviour and boundary violations to see whether they can be truly accepted, rather than punished or rejected. Counsellors must ensure that they do not personalise hostile or volatile behaviour but view them within the context of trauma and as a re-enactment of abuse dynamics.

Some survivors are highly compliant and present as good clients in being submissive and biddable. This represents a need to protect and take care of the counsellor which needs to be addressed and worked through. While such clients are often less challenging on the surface, it is imperative that counsellors do not collude and perpetuate such over-protective behaviour. Clinicians need to ensure that the survivor feels safe enough to explore and express the full range of feelings and not censor them through compliance, or fear of punishment or rejection. The task is to encourage more authentic ways to relate to others, including the counsellor. Not to facilitate this is tantamount to reinforcing abuse dynamics.

Survivors of abuse often expect to be punished and will feel fearful and uncertain when this does not occur. Counsellors must understand this and ensure that they do not act out or become punitive, especially when the client is behaving in a volatile or hostile manner. Counsellors must also be mindful that the therapeutic process is not linear, and that the many digressions and regressions are an essential and necessary feature of working through interpersonal trauma. Counsellors must be able to tolerate impulsive, often narcissistic behaviours and see these within the context of abuse rather than pathologising the client, or allowing them to impede the therapeutic work, and allow post-traumatic growth.

Case vignette: Sandra

Sandra entered therapy in her early thirties at the behest of her partner. She was a successful business woman with a substantial addiction to cocaine which was causing considerable conflicts in her relationship. The initial stage of therapy was focused on assessment and finding an addiction treatment programme to reduce the substance misuse.

During these early stages a picture of early childhood abuse emerged that had given rise to a number of symptoms. Sandra was the oldest of four siblings and was often the primary focus for her father's and stepmother's frustration. Her biological mother had had a drug-induced psychotic breakdown when Sandra was four and disappeared from her life literally overnight. Her father refused to talk about her mother, or to pass on any communication from her such as letters, cards or presents. Sandra's father quickly replaced his ex-wife with a newer, younger model, who was an alcoholic. Ill equipped at a young age to manage four very needy children she frequently physically abused the children, concealing bruises with make-up. Sandra's father, who was often away on business, would upon his return beat all four children into submission for not behaving in his absence. In this chaotic household, Sandra had to restore order through being responsible for her siblings as well as household chores. At no time was there any attempt to soothe or regulate the children's fears and emotions.

By the time Sandra was 15 she was seeking solace through self-medication, consuming copious amounts of alcohol and cannabis, and engaging in sexually risky behaviour. She was terrified of becoming attached, concealing her unmet needs behind a relational façade of self-sufficiency and self-reliance. This pattern continued throughout Sandra's adult life whereby she would shower her partners with expensive gifts, holidays and treats, seemingly not expecting anything in return. Her neediness, over-controlling and obsessive compulsive behaviour would initially be hidden behind grand gestures of generosity but could not be quelled long term. After a few months these would emerge turning Sandra into a demanding, controlling, obsessive and possessive partner with impulsive outbursts of anger and rage, usually leading to the end of the relationship. Sandra could not see her part in the breakdown of these relationships, believing she had behaved impeccably and that she was being punished by others unfairly. Sandra found it very difficult to connect present behaviour to past experiences and had little or no understanding of her behaviour.

Sandra needed to make links between her childhood abuse, which she had normalised, and her current behaviour. This proved to be very difficult as she oscillated between taking no responsibility and being overly responsible for all the problems encountered. She would often exercise her need for control during the therapeutic sessions by being rejecting and being dismissive of any help, followed by uncontainable dependency needs by demanding out-of-hours phone contact whenever she felt out of control. Much of Sandra's recovery was facilitated through affect regulation and reconnecting to the small child who felt abandoned and rejected. In reconnecting to her disavowed dependency needs and making sense of her early experiences she was gradually able to permit the expression of needs in a more assertive explicit manner, rather than volatile re-enactments. In addition, once she was able to quell her overpowering internal states, she was able to mentalise and move from primate dichotomous thinking to more adaptive thinking in which she could tolerate more nuances. Sandra was also able to move from a punishment orientation to a more accepting way of relating. In being less judgmental and demanding of self she was able to be less judgmental and demanding of others, and was able to begin to express her needs without fear of shame or humiliation, allowing her to relate to others more authentically.

SUMMARY

- Child abuse often goes undetected by agencies tasked with safeguarding children to such an extent it is not known how many abused children there are. Many adults who were abused in childhood have not received therapeutic intervention and may thus be vulnerable to a range of mental health difficulties, or enter the criminal justice system.
- There are a range of abuses that are perpetrated on children including physical abuse, emotional abuse, sexual abuse and neglect, with emotional abuse underlying all of the abuse. While all children are at risk of child abuse by primary caregivers, the most vulnerable to abuse are the very youngest.
- Interpersonal trauma in early childhood can have lifelong effects as research has shown that early childhood stress can resculpt the brain resulting in heightened arousal states and hypersensitivity to danger.
- These changes underpin what is provisionally called developmental trauma disorder which aims to describe and understand not only the range of neurobiological changes, but also cognitive changes such as negative self-attributions and cognitive distortions, as well as impaired relational dynamics.
- The focus of the therapeutic process is to restore safety and control over internal states and establish trust. It is through the therapeutic relationship that the survivor can begin to reconnect to the banished vulnerable self and begin to reconnect to others, and live more authentically without fear of further abuse, or punishment.

SUGGESTED READING

Allen, J.G. (2001) *Traumatic Relationships and Serious Mental Disorders.* Chichester, UK: Wiley.

Allen, J.G. (2006) *Coping with Trauma: Hope through Understanding.* Second edition. Washington, DC: American Psychiatric Publishing.

Briere, J. and Scott, C. (2006) *Principles of Trauma Therapy: A Guide to Symptoms. Evaluation and Treatment.* Thousand Oaks, CA: Sage.

de Zulueta, F. (2006) *From Pain to Violence: The Traumatic Roots of Destructiveness.* Second edition. Chichester, UK: Wiley.

Gerhardt, S. (2004) *Why Love Matters: How Affection Shapes the Brain.* London: Routledge.

Herman, J.L. (2001) *Trauma and Recovery.* Second edition. New York: Basic Books.

Levine, P.A. (1997) *Waking the Tiger.* Berkeley, CA: North Atlantic Books.

Mollon, P. (2002) *Remembering Trauma: A Psychotherapist's Guide to Memory and Illusion.* Second edition. London: Whurr.

Rothschild, B. (2002) *The Body Remembers.* New York: Norton.

Sapolsky, R.M. (2004) *Why Zebras Don't Get Ulcers.* Third edition. New York: Henry Holt.

Sinason, V. (ed.) (2002) *Attachment, Trauma and Multiplicity: Working with Dissociative Identity Disorder.* Hove, UK: Brunner/Routledge.

Teicher, M. (2002) 'Scars that won't heal: the neurobiology of child abuse. *Scientific American 286,* 3, 68–75.

CHAPTER 7

CHILD SEXUAL ABUSE AS INTERPERSONAL TRAUMA

The complex dynamics inherent in child sexual abuse (CSA) makes this type of abuse particularly traumatic. While some CSA is accompanied by physical violence, the majority is conducted by stealth in a complex masquerade of caring and loving behaviour. Perpetrators of CSA expend a considerable amount of time and energy on grooming both the child and any significant adults in the child's life in order to gain their trust and to minimise the risk of disclosure. During this lengthy process the child perceives and normalises the CSA within the context of a special, loving relationship, making it hard to legitimise and name it as abuse. Thus CSA is not easily categorised as "traumatic" in conventional terms, although the degree of distortion of reality, betrayal of trust and manipulation can have traumatising effects.

What is critical when working with survivors of CSA is to legitimise and name the abuse and to dispel and dissemble myriad layers of cognitive distortion and restore a semblance of reality. To this effect, counsellors need to be aware of the complex and protracted grooming process, the impact this has on the child, and the range of cognitive distortions. This chapter will explore the myriad strategies that perpetrators of CSA employ, how these impact on the child and how these manifest in adult survivors in the therapeutic process. The systematic and repeated betrayal inherent in CSA erodes the child's and survivor's trust in self and others and much of the therapeutic relationship will need to focus on the restoration of trust. To achieve this, counsellors need to be aware of the centrality of the therapeutic relationship in restoring trust and control to the survivor so that they can begin to reconnect to the self and others and begin to live more authentically, and allow for post-traumatic growth.

DEFINITION OF CHILD SEXUAL ABUSE

The definition of CSA focuses primarily on the sexual components of abuse in which the child is used as a sexual object for sexual gratification through a variety of physical contact and non-contact activities. In *Working Together to Safeguard Children* (Department of Health, 2006) CSA is defined as:

> ... forcing or enticing a child or young person to take part in sexual activities, including prostitution, whether or not the child is aware of what is happening. The activities may involve physical contact, including penetrative (e.g. rape, buggery, or oral sex) or non-penetrative acts. They may include non-contact activities, such as involving children in looking at, or in the production of, sexual online images, watching sexual activities, or encouraging children to behave in sexually inappropriate ways.

This definition highlights that CSA incorporates both contact and non-contact activities. Clinicians need to be aware of the spectrum of sexual activities to fully understand the nature of CSA to ensure appropriate assessment and enable survivors to name their experiences. Table 7.1 outlines the range of contact and non-contact sexually abusive activities that have been identified and commonly seen in CSA.

Table 7.1 Spectrum of child sexual abuse activities

Non-contact activities	Contact activities
• Grooming of adult – parent, primary caregiver, other adults	• Open-mouthed kissing
• Grooming of child – online and offline	• Sexual fondling for abuser's gratification
• Sexually motivated invasion of personal space	• Coercing the child to touch own or others' genitals
• Insisting on sexually seductive behaviour, or dress	• Forcing child to engage in sexual games
• Nudity, disrobing	• Masturbation – of the child, abuser, or mutual
• Verbal comments	• Oral sex (rape) – to child, abuser, or animal
• Forced sleeping, bed sharing	• Ejaculating over child
• Deliberate genital exposure	• Inserting objects, sweets, small toys into vagina, anus
• Voyeurism	• Penetrating child's vagina, or anus, with objects, or adult sex aids
• Forcing child to watch, listen to or read about sexual acts – pornography	• Digital (fingers) or penile penetration
• Use of drugs – drugging child, using drugs or alcohol to desensitise	• Dry intercourse
• Overt sexual behaviour	• Forced sexual activity with others – children, adults, ring members
• Photographing, or filming child in sexual poses – child abuse images	• Forced sexual activity with animals (bestiality)
• Getting child to recruit other children	

Child sexual abusers often engage in non-contact and contact activities when sexually abusing children. Initially there may be little physical or sexual contact to gain the child's trust, which over time escalates into actual sexual contact. In addition, not all abusers seek penetration, instead seeking satisfaction through masturbation. Irrespective of non-contact or contact activities, the impact of coercion, distortion of reality and sexualised behaviour can nevertheless impact on the child and later adult.

A crucial factor in non-contact behaviours is that the coercion and distortion of reality makes it harder for the child to legitimise it as abuse because penetrative sex was not a feature. In the case of contact behaviours, the child is manipulated into believing that sexual activity between adults and children is normal in such "special" relationships and just another way of demonstrating love and affection. Such distortion must be taken into consideration when working with children and adult survivors of CSA, as they have not been able to give informed consent due to naïvety, or the imbalance of power (Sanderson, 2006). In addition, if the sexual contact behaviours were gentle and experienced as pleasurable, children are further impeded in identifying and naming their experiences as abusive. Clinicians need to be mindful that abusers often deliberately engage in sexually arousing activities which are experienced as pleasurable to ensure that the child feels complicit in the sexual abuse, thereby reducing the risk of disclosure. Such distortions of perception and reality exert considerable impact on the child, and will need to be explored and challenged in the therapeutic process.

THE DYNAMICS OF CHILD SEXUAL ABUSE

One of the characteristics of CSA is that it may not necessarily be experienced as traumatic, making it harder to identify as interpersonal trauma. CSA rarely starts as an act of rape but is committed over considerable time in which the abuser entraps the child into a relationship in which they come to care for the abuser and see him or her as someone who genuinely cares for them and who would never hurt them. Most abusers present themselves as loving and caring individuals who only have the child's interests at heart. In befriending the child, the abuser lures and ensnares the child into a relationship in which any unmet needs are met before embarking on any sexual contact. As the "special" relationship becomes established the child fears losing the abuser's love and attention and will submit to any demands, including sexual, that the abuser may make. To avoid rejection or abandonment the child will go to any lengths to prove the love they have for each other and keep the abuser happy, including engaging in sexual activity. In this dynamic the child believes that (s)he is a willing participant in the sexual relationship rather than identifying it as abuse or trauma.

THE GROOMING PROCESS

To fully appreciate the dynamics of CSA, practitioners must have clear understanding of the psychological impact of the grooming process and how this distorts the child's, and later adult's, perception. It is critical that the distortions of reality are identified and challenged during the therapeutic process so that the survivor can legitimise the abuse.

In order to gain access to children, many abusers groom significant adults in the child's life, including the parent(s), primary carer, and other adults (Sanderson, 2004). Through high levels of deception the abuser gains their trust to ensure access to the child and minimise risk of exposure. This process, which can take several months, or indeed years, consists of complex risk assessment strategies to ensure that the true purpose remains undetected. In gaining the adults' trust, the abuser will be able to gain the child's trust. In addition, if the abuser has befriended the significant adults in the child's life it is less likely to be believed that abuse has taken place. While grooming the adult(s) the abuser will show little or no interest in the child and focus all attention on the adult relationship. This is an opportunity to assess the quality of the attachment in the child's relationships with other adults and the likelihood of disclosure. In addition, the abuser will gather information about the child such as particular interests, hobbies and passions to facilitate the grooming of the child.

Once trust has been established, the abuser will turn his or her attention to the child. Through being helpful to the primary carer by offering free child care or taking the child out to the park, cinema or sporting activities, the abuser begins to gain unsupervised access to the child. Initially the abuser may test the child's ability to keep secrets by allowing the child to do things that are not usually permitted such as staying up late, eating or drinking forbidden things, or watching inappropriate television programmes or films. If the child reveals these innocuous secrets the abuser may disengage as the risk of disclosure is too great. However, if the child does not reveal the secret, the abuser will begin to increase physical contact with the child.

Initially the physical contact consists primarily of affectionate, non-sexual touching such as tickling, rough and tumble play, stroking, hugging, or providing soothing comfort when the child is upset. Over time the physical contact will become increasingly sexualised. If the child resists the abuser may implement a number of strategies such as reminding the child how much (s)he loves the child and that such contact represents proof of that love, pointing out that they have never objected before, or threatening the child with withdrawal of love. The fear of losing the special relationship commonly ensures compliance. Once the child's resistance is overcome, the abuser will establish sexual contact by performing sexual acts that are highly arousing and experienced as pleasurable. This renders the child complicit in the abuse in thinking that "If I like it then I must have wanted it". When this distorted perception is accompanied by statements such as "You like this", or

"Look how much you are enjoying it" the child believes that they wanted, or indeed initiated the sexual contact.

As the sexual contact escalates the child may begin to resist or threaten to disclose. The abuser will then either remind the child that they have not resisted so far, or that they will not be believed. As extra insurance the abuser will undermine the child's credibility by inserting doubts into the carer's mind with regard to the child's honesty. Abusers frequently create a divide between the child and significant adult to isolate the child from the carer, or non-abusing carer, to minimise the child's credibility. Similarly, the abuser will tell the child that they will not be believed, or that they will be blamed and punished for telling wicked lies as the carer does not really care about the child.

With older children the abuser may use pornography to arouse and desensitise the child to sex between adults and children as a way of normalising CSA. In addition, alcohol or drugs may be used to dis-inhibit the child to make them compliant in the abuse, and to ensure silence. Some abusers may drug the child in order to break down any potential resistance and impede memory recall. In imbibing illegal drugs, smoking or drinking alcohol, the child is lured into criminal activity and will fear prosecution if they disclose. This fear of being perceived as criminal is also present when the child has been coerced into posing for photographs or child abuse images. In this process the child is involved in producing and, if sent by mobile phone or internet, distributing child abuse images. Counsellors need to be aware of the impact the indelibility of such images might have on the survivor and that other paedophiles will be able to access them, long after the sexual abuse has stopped.

In combination, the above strategies alongside coercion and the deliberate distortion of reality will make the child feel complicit in the abuse and therefore reduce the risk of exposure of the abuse. It is essential that practitioners address the method and form of grooming in the therapeutic process to challenge distorted perceptions and restore a semblance of reality.

PREVALENCE

Due to the hidden nature of CSA, lack of universally agreed definition and research complexities, it is difficult to obtain accurate data on the incidence and prevalence of CSA. Those data that are available merely represent the tip of the iceberg. Many children do not disclose or come to the attention of authorities either during childhood or in adulthood, and fall outside any meaningful statistical recording. There have been a number of examples of these such as Josef Fritzl, who held his daughter captive for 24 years and fathered seven children; the British man who sexually abused his two daughters for 27 years impregnating them 19 times, resulting in seven surviving children, and the Scottish man who sexually abused his three daughters over a 19-year period, fathering two children. These cases attest to the power abusers wield over victims and family members to ensure silence, and how they are able to manipulate and deceive others, including professionals, in order to continue to abuse. It also highlights that CSA rarely exists in isolation of other abuse such as physical and psychological abuse, and domestic abuse.

According to the Department of Children, Schools and Families, the number of children subject to Child Protection Plans for CSA is 7% in the year ending March 31, 2008 (Department for Children, Schools and Families, 2008a) although this is generally considered to be the tip of the iceberg as CSA is still largely undetected due to secrecy and silence surrounding such abuse. It is worth noting that fewer than one in ten maltreated children are investigated and substantiated by child protection services, partly due to the degree of deception that abusers engage in to avoid detection and minimise risk of exposure, normalisation of abuse by the survivor, fear of consequences if abuse is exposed, and profound sense of shame or stigmatisation especially in cases of incest.

Estimates of CSA vary enormously with some studies suggesting that in the UK approximately 15% of girls and 5% of boys experience CSA when employing a broad definition, and that between 5–10% of girls and 1–5% of boys experience penetrative sex (Gilbert *et al.*, 2009b). The Survivors Trust argue that the generally accepted UK prevalence rate of CSA for girls is 21% of the total adult population which represents 4.1 million females, while for boys it is 11% of total adult population which represents around 2.5 million males (Survivors Trust, 2008). This is nearer to the figure of one in four females and one in six males that has been found in a number of studies (Sanderson, 2004, 2006) with some researchers suggesting it is as high as one in three females (Salter, 2003). Whatever the prevalence rate, it is clear that much of CSA is hidden and that survivors fear the consequences of disclosure which accounts for some of the complex dynamics in the therapeutic process including uncertainty of abuse, denial, retraction and minimisation of the CSA.

WHO IS AT RISK?

All children are at risk, with girls at higher risk than boys, with estimates of 73% of victims of CSA being girls, and 27% boys (ChildLine, 2003). Incidence and prevalence consistently indicate that girls have slightly higher risk than boys although this may be accounted for to some degree by lower reporting rates among males. Males may find it much harder to disclose a history of CSA due to cultural norms around gender, especially masculinity, acknowledgment of vulnerability and males seeking help. Girls seem to be more at risk of intrafamilial CSA, a disparity that is only somewhat evened out in CSA outside the family (Sanderson, 2004).

In terms of age, there is evidence that the sexual abuse of children can begin at any age including babies (Sanderson, 2004), with some abusers deliberately targeting pre-verbal children to minimise the risk of disclosure. It is thought that 33% are below the age of six, 33% between 6 and 12, and a further 33% are between 12 and 18 years old (Sanderson, 2004), although increasingly younger children are being used in the production of child abuse images. Practitioners need to be mindful that although CSA may start in early childhood it can continue over many years including into adulthood. In such cases the survivor, despite an adult chronological age, may be suspended in an earlier developmental age.

There has been considerable research that indicates that children with disabilities, especially developmental disabilities, have higher risk of CSA (Valenti-Heim and Schwartz, 1995) with estimates ranging between 39% and 68% of girls and between 16% and 30% boys with disabilities at risk. It is also argued that some disabilities, especially learning disabilities, may be due to abuse. Children with high dependency needs through chronic illness may also be at risk given the negative consequences of disclosure especially if the abuser is a carer. Children who are socially excluded, in care or have a history of previous abuse, are also considered to be at an increased risk of CSA. Abusers will prey upon pre-existing vulnerabilities and the fact that there will be fewer trusted adults in the child's life, thereby minimising disclosure. Refugee and trafficked children are also at risk as they risk deportation if they disclose.

Generally abusers tend to target timid, unconfident, lonely and vulnerable children who are easy to groom and manipulate, while minimising the risk of exposure. This is put to particularly good effect in a recently identified trend of "internal trafficking", whereby young teenage girls are lured into a relationship by slightly older, often very attractive, teenage boys for the purposes of prostitution. The girl initially will have sex with a "relative" of the boyfriend to prevent him from getting into further trouble, and once "broken in" will be coerced into having sex with other men (see Chapter 9).

PERPETRATORS OF CHILD SEXUAL ABUSE

In the same way any child is at risk, perpetrators of CSA come from all types of socioeconomic and ethnic backgrounds. Most abusers look and act within what are considered as "normal" parameters, making them difficult to identify. The majority of paedophiles present themselves as extremely kind, caring "pillars of the community". In reality they are wolves in sheep's clothing whose disguise allows them to manipulate not only children, but also significant adults in the child's life. In the words of sex-crime expert Ray Wyre, they are not monsters because "...monsters do not get close to children, nice men do" (Wyre, 2002). Paedophiles may adopt a variety of disguises including actual or faked vulnerabilities to avoid detection. One paedophile used his disability to groom the parents of his victims knowing that most people would not suspect a disabled person of being a child molester.

Research and statistical data indicate that between 80 and 95% of child sexual abusers are male (Sanderson, 2004), and between 10 and 15% are female, although CSA by females may be under-reported and largely unrecognised. The impact of sexual abuse by females can give rise to additional traumatisation which practitioners need to address in the therapeutic process (Sanderson, 2006). It is thought that two thirds of abusers target girls, one quarter target boys, and one in ten target both genders. The most significant finding is that most CSA is perpetrated within the family. Current research shows that in approximately 87% of cases the abuser is known, and trusted. The children's charity ChildLine found that 57% of their callers reported CSA by someone in the family, while 30% were known to the child, were not a family member but were a neighbour, family friend or involved in the child's life in some capacity, with only 13% of CSA perpetrated by a stranger (ChildLine, 2003).

Perpetrators of CSA range in age from pre-teens to the elderly, with an increase in reports of young adolescents sexually abusing younger children including siblings. Researchers and clinicians working with adult perpetrators have found that many paedophiles start sexually offending against children while teenagers, with the average age of onset as young as 14, although some children as young as nine have been identified as sexually abusive (Sanderson, 2004; Skuse *et al.*, 2003; Skuse, quoted in *The Guardian*, 2003). Many of these child perpetrators have been sexually abused themselves and as such are both victims and abusers, with as many as one in eight boys going on to sexually abuse in adolescence thus providing compelling evidence for the intergenerational transmission of sexually abusive behaviour.

While there are some commonalities among perpetrators of CSA, they are not a homogenous group but have a diverse range of motivations and *modus operandi*. Practitioners need to be aware of the range of paedophilic behaviour, how this manifests and the impact each experience has on the child and later adult survivor, without generalising or stereotyping.

IMPACT OF CHILD SEXUAL ABUSE

There are a number of factors that will determine the impact of CSA which clinicians must take into consideration when working with survivors of CSA. One significant factor is the chronological and developmental age of the child when the abuse first started, and the concomitant cognitive stage, as this will impact on the child's vulnerability to abuse, ability to make sense of it, and degree of self-blame and normalisation. The younger the child the less likely the child can make sense of the abuse and the more likely it will be normalised. In addition a pre-verbal child will not be able to disclose. Clinicians also need to be mindful of the impact of CSA which occurs over a number of cognitive stages to track the course of the child's and later adult's perception and understanding of the CSA.

Other factors that influence the impact of CSA are the nature of the abuse experiences, the severity, duration, and frequency of the abuse, and whether the CSA involved multiple abuses, or abusers, and the degree of sadistic and ritualistic elements. The presence of other types of abuse such as physical, or emotional abuse, and general domestic abuse will also influence degree of impact. Research has also identified that the nature of the relationship to the abuser is critical in terms of impact whereby the closer the relationship between the child and the abuser, either biologically or emotionally, the greater the sense of betrayal of trust (Sanderson, 2006). A further critical factor is the child's temperament, degree of resilience to trauma, and quality of other attachment relationships. Children who have at least one secure attachment relationship may be inoculated to some degree and can develop a level of resilience to the CSA, whereas those children who have never experienced any secure attachment will not be able to build up resilience, rendering them more vulnerable to long-term negative sequelae.

The most pervasive impact of CSA is the annihilation of truth and the survivor's capacity to know reality. This leads inexorably to a collapse of authenticity akin to what Shengold (1989) has designated as "soul murder". To cope with this total obliteration of reality, the child and later survivor has to surrender their subjectivity, relinquish the authentic self and submit to the falsified and distorted reality imposed by the abuser. To achieve this the child has to disconnect from the vulnerable self and replace it with an alien, or false self, imposed by the abuser (Sanderson, 2006; Mollon, 2005). Many abusers endeavour to obliterate the authentic self through dehumanising the child, so that they can impregnate the child with the perpetrator's projections, which usually consist of either a compliant sexual being, or an object of defilement that has invoked the depraved lust of the abuser.

Once the child has been dehumanised, or "broken in", the abuser loses interest in the now psychologically lifeless child due to their lack of vitality and despoiled innocence. To manage the systematic cognitive and sexual assaults, the child must repudiate all feelings and spontaneity and replace these with a false self which is organised around the demands and desires of the abuser. To oxygenate and give birth to the false self, the child has to imprison the essence of the true yet vulnerable self into an impregnable inner fortress. While this is designed to protect the child from the trauma of the CSA, it also allows for high tolerance levels for trauma and abuse, and the distortion of reality. The more deeply the core self has been imprisoned, the more difficult it will be for it to re-merge. Counsellors need to be mindful of this as the reconnection to the authentic self can be a treacherous process in which the survivor's fears of further abuse will lead to repeated vacillation between wishing to reconnect and needing to retreat for protection.

A corollary to the distortion of reality is the imperative to keep the CSA secret. The compulsory annihilation and concealment of the truth requires the child to compromise any sense of integrity as he is forced to tell lies to both self and others. The child cannot afford to allow the secret to be exposed and so has to withdraw from and disconnect from others to minimise the risk of the secret being revealed through an incautious comment. Effectively the child is sequestered into a wordless silence and isolated from the comfort of others in order to continue to occlude the truth. Alongside the child has to cope with two conflicting realities whereby he has to behave normally during the day, and as a sexual object at night. This can lead to role confusion with the child in a perpetual state of uncertainty of how to behave. The space of "knowing" yet "not knowing" promotes an "as if" existence where the child is in constant doubt about what is reality and what is not (Shengold, 1989).

In addition to compromised cognitive integrity, the child also experiences compromised bodily integrity as the body responds with pleasure to the sexual abuse, including orgasm. This can evoke a potent cocktail of feelings in which the child tries to reconcile pleasure and arousal to abuse with shame, self-loathing and guilt. Many survivors feel, in losing control over their body, that their body has betrayed them, and that they no longer have any self-agency. Often the survivor does not realise that their body had responded normally in the presence of arousing touch, and that abusers deliberately create such pleasurable responses in order to make the child feel complicit in the abuse and to induce shame and guilt. The shame and guilt diffuses the abuser's culpability and renders the child a willing participant in the sexual abuse. It is often this false belief that impedes the survivor's ability for self-compassion and being able to legitimise the trauma of CSA. Counsellors must be mindful of this and ensure that the survivor dissembles and restructures such false beliefs in order to restore full accountability for the abuse to the abuser and accept and acknowledge their vulnerability in such abuse. This is often hard for many survivors, as they cling to the belief that they are responsible for the CSA to ward off unbearable feelings of helplessness and powerlessness.

LONG-TERM EFFECTS OF CHILD SEXUAL ABUSE

Although each survivor will be impacted differently by CSA there are a number of long-term effects commonly associated with CSA (see Box 7.1 below) all of which need to be addressed in the therapeutic process. Counsellors need to ensure accurate assessment of which core symptoms predominate and which are of most concern to the survivor rather than generalise therapeutic interventions. A clear focus on what has impacted the most on the survivor and how this still manifests is crucial in providing the appropriate therapeutic framework and intervention. The repetitive nature of systematic sexual abuse impacts on a range of psychobiological functions, including fragmented memories. Many survivors are unable to access coherent memories of the abuse either due to dissociation or as a way to manage knowing yet not knowing. This leads to considerable uncertainty and a desire to restore full narrative memory. Counsellors need to be mindful that this may not be possible and that the emphasis must be on restoring mental health rather than full memory recall (Sanderson, 2006).

There are also a number of psychiatric disorders commonly associated with CSA, in particular a variety of dissociative disorders, schizophrenia (Read, Hammersley and Mullen, 2005), body dysmorphic disorder, and a range of personality disorders such as borderline personality disorder, antisocial personality disorder, and

Box 7.1 Core clinical symptoms of child sexual abuse

- Range of post-traumatic stress symptoms – flashback, intrusive memories, impaired affect regulation
- Dissociation and dissociative states
- Fragmented memory
- Distorted perception and distorted reality
- Impaired mentalisation
- Denial of needs
- Difficulties around trust, power and control
- Disconnection from vulnerable self and presence of false self – shattered or fragmented self
- Disintegration anxiety
- Body armour – disconnection from self
- Relational difficulties
- Shame and guilt
- Self-harm – self-medication
- Shattered assumptions about self, others and the world
- Compromised sexuality

narcissistic personality disorder (Sanderson, 2006). Many survivors may also suffer from depression, a range of anxiety disorders, especially PTSD, self-harm, suicidal ideation, eating disorders, self-medication and substance dependency. To ensure that survivors of CSA are provided with the appropriate treatment, it may be necessary for counsellors to build links with psychiatric services in order to make any necessary referrals for those conditions that the counsellor is ill equipped to treat. It may also be useful to forge links with local general practitioners as there are a number of physical symptoms that may necessitate medical treatment in particular irritable bowel syndrome, chronic fatigue syndrome, and chronic pelvic pain. If the survivor has sexual difficulties counsellors may also need to consider referring the client to a psychosexual therapist.

WORKING WITH SURVIVORS OF CHILD SEXUAL ABUSE

When working with survivors of CSA counsellors need to be mindful of a number of recurrent themes that will emerge during the therapeutic process. It is imperative that counsellors acknowledge that CSA is not always experienced as traumatic but is embedded in what the survivor believes to be a "special" loving relationship. This false belief attests to the power of the distortion of reality imposed by the abuser making it difficult for the survivor to identify and name the abuse. Counsellors will need to spend considerable time exploring such cognitive distortions in order to enable the survivor to legitimise the abuse and trauma. This can be further hindered by the survivor who has normalised the abuse and thus may be resistant to exploring the true nature of the CSA experiences. Counsellors need to be sensitive in understanding such resistance as a defence against challenging long-held cognitive distortions and the uncertainty inherent in knowing and yet not knowing.

Survivors may also be fearful of the consequences of breaking the compulsory silence by disclosing the secret of CSA. Having kept the secret for so long, the survivor may be rendered speechless when given the opportunity to disclose. Survivors of CSA may also fear naming the abuse as it would mean having to acknowledge the reality of their experiences which can feel like retraumatisation as the full horror of the abuse is explored. Such exploration will revive myriad emotions, especially shame, guilt and self-loathing which the survivor will understandably wish to avoid. Counsellors need to be sensitive in understanding these very real fears and pace working through the abuse at a rate that is comfortable for the survivor.

A common obstacle to exploring the CSA experiences is when the abuse experience generated sexual arousal in the child. Survivors often feel deeply ashamed if they experienced sexual pleasure, erections or orgasm during the abuse. This often leads to self-blame and the false belief that they must have wanted, or encouraged, the CSA. When working with survivors who experienced sexual arousal and pleasure during the sexual abuse, counsellors need to provide a degree of psychoeducation to enable the survivor to have a clearer understanding of the sexual arousal cycle and how the body responds to certain touch. Counsellors need to normalise the sexual responses as normal reactions in the presence of certain sexual activity and touch, and help the survivor to differentiate between sexual activity and sexual desire by emphasising that the survivor responded to the sexual activity, *not* the rapist.

Counsellors also need to emphasise that the sexual arousal does not mean that sexuality has been compromised and that it is not the sexual response and sexuality that is objectionable, but the lack of consent and abuse. It is essential that counsellors do not avoid processing the sexual arousal aspects of the CSA as they need to understand fully the physiological reactions to the abuse and the meaning the survivor has derived from these. In addition counsellors must help the survivor to make sense of any sexual flashbacks, fantasies or dreams. Many survivors believe that any dreams or fantasies about the CSA is evidence of their arousal and therefore desire for such sexual encounters. In reality these are prompted by fear and anxiety around the CSA and is a way for the body and mind to process confusing experiences and gain mastery over them.

Providing information on CSA in terms of somatic responses and cognitive distortions is one of the core therapeutic goals when working with survivors of CSA (see Box 7.2). As in all forms of interpersonal trauma, counsellors need to establish clear therapeutic goals based on in-depth assessment of the survivor's experiences.

Box 7.2 Core therapeutic goals

- Establish safety
- Establish trust
- Restore control over bodily integrity
- Restore perception
- Restore mental health rather than focus on full memory recall
- Develop a more coherent narrative of CSA
- Legitimise sexual nature of abuse
- Provide information on CSA, sexual arousal and symptoms through psychoeducation
- Reduce fear of intimacy and impaired relational dynamics through the therapeutic relationship
- Allow grief and mourning of losses associated with CSA
- Restore compromised sexuality
- Restore connection to self, others and the world

It is only when safety and trust have been established, and the survivor has been able to restore control over bodily integrity, that a full exploration of the CSA can begin. This process will allow for restructuring of cognitive distortions and enable the survivor to begin to trust their own perceptions again. Counsellors must ensure that they do not contaminate the survivor's perception but allow the survivor to reconnect to the self and the full range of their experiencing. The therapeutic relationship is critical to this process in reducing fear of intimacy and discovering new ways of relating to others more authentically without fear of abuse. Part of the therapeutic process will involve an element of mourning the myriad losses associated with CSA in order to allow for post-traumatic growth.

CHALLENGES IN THE THERAPEUTIC PROCESS

Working with survivors can be challenging for clinicians especially when working with cognitive distortions and fragmented memories. The degree of uncertainty inherent in CSA can be difficult for counsellors and they must be able to tolerate the "not knowing" as well as the "knowing". Counsellors must also feel comfortable talking about and exploring the sexual components of CSA without recoiling in horror, disgust or embarrassment. It is critical that they show the survivor that they can hear the abuse narrative, not be overwhelmed or disgusted by it. To facilitate this, counsellors need to have a high degree of self-awareness of their own attitudes and beliefs about sex and sexuality, and a good knowledge of sexuality. They must also be aware that survivors of CSA often present as highly seductive and that this needs to be understood within the context of CSA in which the survivor's central organising principle is to be sexual. Many survivors of CSA believe that this is the only way to relate to others and are often unaware of how seductive they are. It is critical that counsellors address this and enable the survivor to relate in non-seductive ways. Given the sexual components of CSA the therapeutic process may give rise to powerful erotic transference and erotic counter-transference which the counsellor needs to manage in a sensitive way within the context of the abuse experiences.

In contrast, some survivors will re-enact the abusive experiences by identifying with the abuser and attempt to control and dominate the counsellor through hostile and sadistic attacks. Clinicians need to understand this as a reaction to being abused and as a way of acting out aspects of the experience that they were not able to express, and not personalise it. Whatever type of transference, erotic or hostile, counsellors need to utilise it as a rich source for understanding the impact the CSA has had on the survivor and strive to make sense of it (Sanderson, 2006).

Working with survivors of CSA is not a linear process and survivors will often oscillate between wishing to be visible and needing to retreat into invisibility. Counsellors need to contain any frustration and be constant in tolerating approach and avoidance behaviours, and understand them within the context of CSA rather than pathologising them. Many survivors use the therapeutic relationship to test boundaries or re-enact suppressed behaviours in order to find new, more healthy ways of relating. This can make for testing and turbulent sessions which the counsellor needs to contain in order for the survivor to work through their experiences. It is critical that counsellors separate their own sensitivities from the client's process, and access their own professional and personal support network to avoid secondary traumatisation and ensure that they do not succumb to "burnout" (see Chapter 14). With appropriate support in place the counsellor can "hold" the survivor's traumatic experiences and enable the process of post-traumatic growth to unfold.

Case vignette: Miranda

Miranda was sexually abused by a family member within a few months of birth until the age of eight. As this was all she had ever known, Miranda normalised sexual contact between adults and young children and could not understand why her sexual advances to other members of the family were frowned upon and discouraged. Miranda's abuser made a point of emphasising how "special" their relationship was and that the sexual activity was proof of how much he loved her. What bothered Miranda was that her mother never touched her sexually and she believed this was evidence that she did not love her, a false belief on which the abuser capitalised. The abuser would consistently remind Miranda that her mother did not care for or love her by criticising her for working and leaving Miranda with the abuser. At the same time the abuser would tell Miranda's mother what a scheming, manipulative child she was who could not be trusted. Unaware of this, neither Miranda nor her mother could see that such untruths were designed to drive a wedge between mother and daughter to minimise exposure.

When the abuse was discovered through medical examination for recurring cystitis, the mother severed all contact with the abuser and contacted child protection services. Rather than relief that the secret was out, Miranda was furious with her mother that she had banished the only person who loved her. This further damaged the already tenuous relationship between mother and daughter with the child withdrawing and retreating into a spiral of resentment, anger and self-harm. She refused to talk to child protection workers and was not able to engage with a number of child psychologists and therapists. She believed that they were attempting to poison her mind against the abuser, and that he was the only one who really cared. Although the abuser was charged and sentenced, Miranda would not accept that the "special" relationship was predicated on abuse.

By the time Miranda reached her teens, her relationship with her mother had disintegrated and they lived almost separate lives albeit under the same roof. Miranda refused to attend school and spent her days cutting her arms, binge eating and contemplating suicide. By the time she entered therapy she was grossly overweight, severely scarred through years of self-mutilation, and hoping to renew contact with her abuser who was due to be released from prison. Miranda still could not see what the abuser had done as sexually abusive, although she was able to acknowledge that when he asked her to have sex with other men these men were child sexual abusers.

Miranda was very defensive and ambivalent about therapy, frequently not turning up for her appointments. She was hypervigilant and paranoid that our work was being recorded by her mother and that it would be used against her to stop her from seeing her abuser. It was clear that she was unable to trust anyone, including her therapist. She would constantly test boundaries around trust and safety, and interrogate her therapist as to her motivation in the therapeutic work. Over many months of vacillation and painstaking exploration of the "specialness" of her relationship with the abuser, Miranda began to question why her abuser had insisted she have sex with other men, especially as the things they did to her was the same as her abuser did, and yet did not feel like love. As she began to question her abuser's motivation in exchanging her for money she began to question how "special" this relationship really was. This led to an increase in Miranda's self-harm and suicidal ideation as she oscillated between seeing her abuser as loving and caring and as a paedophile.

Once Miranda was able to dissemble the distortion of reality and layers of cognitive distortion she was able to see that not only was she a victim of CSA but that her mother had also been groomed by the abuser. Gradually Miranda was able to acknowledge that her mother did care for her in severing all contact with the abuser and involving the authorities once the abuse was discovered. This recognition enabled Miranda to see the level of cognitive distortion that both she and her mother had been exposed to and how this had prevented them from ever being able to relate to or care for each other. This became a critical turning point in the therapeutic process allowing Miranda to reclaim and trust her own perceptions and begin to rebuild a much-needed relationship with her mother.

SUMMARY

- The distortion of reality and subterfuge inherent in CSA can make it difficult to identify and legitimise it as trauma and abuse which has significant impact on how survivors construe the CSA experience.
- To date there is no universally agreed definition of CSA, which makes it difficult to understand research findings and statistical data on incidence and prevalence rates. What is clear is that CSA is under-reported, with only one in ten cases coming to the attention of child protection services. This is further hampered by the spectrum of CSA behaviours which includes both contact and non-contact behaviours.
- CSA rarely starts with an act of rape and children, and significant adults, are commonly groomed by the abuser over a period of time to establish trust and build a "special" relationship, in order to minimise exposure and disclosure. Much of the abuse in CSA is in the distortion of reality and distortion of perception necessary for the betrayal of trust.
- CSA impacts on emotional, cognitive, physical, sexual, and relational functioning all of which need to be explored in the therapeutic process. Particular focus needs to be on any sexual arousal, including orgasm, that accompanied the sexual abuse. Counsellors need to explore this and provide psychoeducation on the nature of the arousal cycle and differentiate between arousal due to pleasurable sexual activity and arousal elicited in abusive sexual activity which is predicated on lack of consent and coercion.
- The goal of the therapeutic work is to establish safety and trust to explore the full impact of CSA on the survivor. Emphasis needs to be on restoring

control to the survivor and to restore the survivor's perception of reality by repudiating the contaminating effects of the abuser's cognitive distortions.

- It is through the safety of the therapeutic relationship that the survivor can begin to reconnect to the hidden, vulnerable self, and allow for reconnection to others and the world. Through this process the survivor will be able to relate more authentically without the pervasive fear of betrayal and abuse.
- In order to work with survivors of CSA, clinicians need to ensure that they have access to professional and personal support in order to avoid burnout or secondary traumatic stress. Support will allow them to fully engage with the traumatic aspects of CSA without recoiling in horror or disgust, and facilitate post-traumatic growth.

SUGGESTED READING

Allen, J.G. (2001) *Traumatic Relationships and Serious Mental Disorders.* Chichester, UK: Wiley.

Allen, J.G. (2006) *Coping with Trauma: Hope through Understanding.* Second edition. Washington, DC: American Psychiatric Publishing.

Briere, J. and Scott, C. (2006) *Principles of Trauma Therapy: A Guide to Symptoms. Evaluation and Treatment.* Thousand Oaks, CA: Sage.

De Zulueta, F. (2006) *From Pain to Violence: The Traumatic Roots of Destructiveness.* Second edition. Chichester, UK: Wiley.

Fonagy, P., Gergely, G., Jurist, E.L. and Target, M. (2002) *Affect Regulation, Mentalisation and the Development of the Self.* New York: Other Press.

Herman, J.L. (2001) *Trauma and Recovery.* Second edition. New York: Basic Books.

Levine, P.A. (1997) *Waking the Tiger.* Berkeley, CA: North Atlantic Books.

Mollon, P. (2002) *Remembering Trauma: A Psychotherapist's Guide to Memory and Illusion.* Second edition. London: Whurr.

Rothschild, B. (2002) *The Body Remembers.* New York: Norton.

Sanderson, C. (2004) *The Seduction of Children: Empowering Parents and Teachers to Protect Children from Child Sexual Abuse.* London: Jessica Kingsley Publishers.

Sanderson, C. (2006) *Counselling Adult Survivors of Child Sexual Abuse.* Third edition. London: Jessica Kingsley Publishers.

Sinason, V. (ed.) (2002) *Attachment, Trauma and Multiplicity: Working with Dissociative Identity Disorder.* Hove, UK: Brunner/Routledge.

Walker, M. (2003) *Abuse: Questions and Answers for Counsellors and Therapists.* London: Whurr.

CHAPTER 8

RAPE AS INTERPERSONAL TRAUMA

As the sexual violence in rape is often experienced as a threat to life, bodily and psychological integrity, which overwhelms human adaptation to life, it needs to be understood within the context of interpersonal trauma. The traumatic nature of rape activates a cascade of psychobiological responses to aid survival which in turn give rise to a range of psychological and emotional responses such as terror, loss of control, threat of annihilation, loss of agency, dehumanisation, objectification, shame and self-blame. Although these responses will vary depending on the context of the rape and individual experiences, there are a number of commonalities.

As the immediate responses to rape are not homogenous, ranging from numbness to uncontrollable emotional reactions, counsellors need to be mindful that there is no unitary response to rape to ensure that survivors' responses are not contaminated by the practitioner's anticipated stereotypical reactions. While some survivors of rape will seek counselling immediately after the assault, many do not. Survivors may fear retraumatisation when talking about rape, or believe falsely that the best way to move on is to "put it behind" them. In addition, the felt sense of shame invariably makes it difficult to talk about rape to partners, family or friends, let alone professionals. To this effect, some rape survivors will enter therapy with a variety of presenting symptoms other than rape. As trust is established they may begin to reveal their rape experience. Counsellors who have not been trained in, or lack experience of, working with sexual violence may find it difficult to know how to respond to disclosure of rape.

This chapter aims to increase awareness of rape, the contexts in which rape occurs, incidence and prevalence rates, and highlight those who are most vulnerable to rape and who the perpetrators are. It will also explore the nature and dynamics of rape and how this impacts on survivors. To enable clinicians to have a full understanding of rape, the chapter will explore the long-term effects of rape, especially the role of sexual arousal and fear of compromised sexuality. A significant component of working with survivors of sexual violence, and especially rape, is the recognition that although rape is about power and control, survivors often conflate this with compromised sexuality. Practitioners need to be aware of, and be able to provide accurate information on, the function of rape, how some rapists manipulate sexual arousal to establish control and power, and how this impacts on the survivor. Through the safety of the therapeutic process the survivor will be able to explore the rape experience, make sense of their responses, and reclaim their sexuality. It will also allow for the restoration of control over psychobiological symptoms and enable the survivor to begin to trust self and others again.

DEFINITION OF RAPE

When defining rape it is essential to highlight the role of power and control, domination and anger, rather than an expression of sexuality. Many survivors fear compromised sexuality as a result of rape, and professionals need to emphasise that rape is an act of violence and domination through the use of sexual assault. To this effect, Rape Crisis England and Wales define rape as "... an act of violence and domination and anger. It uses sexual acts including penetration as weapons." (Rape Crisis England and Wales, 2008). To emphasise the lack of consent they further define sexual assault as:

> ...an act of physical, psychological and emotional violation, in the form of a sexual act, which is inflicted on someone without consent. It can involve forcing or manipulating someone to witness or participate in any sexual acts, apart from penetration of the mouth with the penis, the penetration of anus or vagina (however slight) with any object or the penis, which is rape. (Rape Crisis England and Wales, 2008)

The legal definition of rape is encapsulated in the Sexual Offences Act (Home Office 2003) whereby rape is when "A intentionally penetrates the vagina, anus, or mouth of another person B with penis and B does not consent. A does not reasonably believe that B consents". Sexual assault by penetration is when "A intentionally penetrates the vagina or anus of B with a part of his body or anything else. B does not consent. A does not reasonably believe that B consents". Both of these acts of sexual violence have a maximum sentence of life imprisonment attached to them. Sexual assault is when "A intentionally touches B. The touching is sexual. B does not consent to the touching and A does not reasonably believe that B consents". Sexual assault carries a maximum sentence of ten years imprisonment.

As can be seen from these legal definitions the issue of consent is a critical component. The word "consent" in the context of the offence of rape is now defined in the Sexual Offences Act 2003 (Home Office 2003): "A person consents if he or she agrees by choice, and has the freedom and capacity to make that choice." The essence of this definition is the agreement by choice. The law does not require the victim to have resisted physically in order to prove a lack of consent. The question of whether the victim consented is a matter for the jury to decide, although the Crown Prosecution Service (CPS) considers this issue very carefully throughout the life of the case.

There is some controversy around the notion of "reasonable belief" in consent. The Act specifies that for a belief to be reasonable, A has to ascertain whether B consents and has to consider such attributes as disability or extreme youth. This is a major change in the law as A has the responsibility to ensure that B consents to the sexual activity at the time in question, and has to provide evidence that B consented. Arguably a victim who is intoxicated either through alcohol or drugs is unable to consent, although the degree of intoxication is often a factor under consideration during prosecution proceedings.

The 2003 Act fails to consider more complex dynamics in which rape occurs, for example in domestic abuse, or when an individual is unable to give "informed" consent due to lack of knowledge, or where there is no genuine choice because of fear of worse consequences. This is often the case for teenagers who may agree to sexual activity with an older person even though it is against the law, or detrimental to them in the long term. Or in the case of young girls who "consent" to sexual activity with gang members in order to obtain protection for themselves, or their family. To this effect, the current Act is not able to fully appreciate the spectrum of rape contexts and how this reduces consent.

THE SPECTRUM OF RAPE CONTEXTS

To fully understand rape necessitates an awareness that rape can occur in many contexts (see Box 8.1) and that the context in which it occurs will influence not only likelihood of disclosure, and reporting to police, but also impact and long-term effects. The context in which rape occurs will also impact on the ability of the survivor to legitimise and name their experience as rape. Most people assume that the most common form of rape is stranger rape, and this type of rape is probably the easiest to legitimise. However, the majority of rapes and sexual assaults (82%) are committed by someone known to the victim, and over 50% of these are committed by partners, or former partners of the victim (Walby and Allen, 2004), making it much harder to legitimise such assaults as rape. This is especially the case in acquaintance or date rape where an initial attraction and engagement renders the victim complicit, or rape by a partner in a long-term relationship.

Rape by those in authority, or who have been invested with trust, such as professionals or carers, may also be hard to legitimise as the survivor fears the consequences of resistance. In the case of drug or alcohol-induced rape the victim may have little or no recollection of the rape, and thus may fear being disbelieved as they are unable to provide a coherent account. If the rape has occurred abroad, language barriers, fear of being disbelieved, or fear of reprisal may impede disclosure or seeking help.

Rape as a display of power, domination and humiliation is most overtly seen in rape in prisons; in the military and during war, ethnic cleansing, or mass genocide; in prostitution and sex trafficking (see Chapter 9); and in homophobic rape, all of

Box 8.1 Spectrum of rape contexts

- Predatory rape by stranger
- Acquaintance rape, or date rape
- Drug or alcohol-assisted rape
- Domestic rape – used to control and dominate intimate partner, or former partner
- Rape by family member – CSA
- Elder rape
- Homophobic rape
- Rape of those with disabilities – physical or mental
- Institutional rape – in children's homes, care homes
- Rape by professionals – GP, therapist, tutor, mentor, carers
- Group or gang rape
- Rape within gang culture
- Rape abroad
- Prostitution, sex workers
- Human trafficking – sexual slavery
- Prison rape
- Military rape – armed forces
- Rape in war, ethnic cleansing, or mass genocide
- Rape of refugees, displaced persons, asylum seekers
- Rape as "sexual correction" of homosexuals and lesbians

which are difficult to report due to humiliation, stigmatisation or fear of retaliation. In areas of the world facing political destabilisation, such as Haiti, groups of men maraud females and subject them to gang rape, while in South Africa it is not uncommon for males to gang rape lesbians as a form of sexual correction (Kelly, 2009). It is also manifest during rape within gang culture, which is a growing phenomenon of great concern among teenagers. Some gangs demand rape as an initiation rite, or will gang rape the girlfriends of other gangs as a display of power. Gang rape is also commonly used to assert power and control, to punish or humiliate, especially in response to any perceived slights (Batmanghelidjh, quoted in Cohen, 2009). Overall it is a display of power which sends out a strong message to the community that the perpetrators are a force to be reckoned with and to be feared. This has led to some girls complying with being raped in order to gain protection for themselves, or extended family members. The majority of such rapes are never disclosed for fear of retaliation.

INCIDENCE AND PREVALENCE OF RAPE

Due to difficulties around legitimising rape and low reporting rates, the incidence and prevalence of rape remains largely hidden. It is estimated that one in four females experience some form of sexual assault in their lifetime, and that 20% of females in the UK experience sexual assault in adulthood (Kershaw *et al.*, 2001). For males it is estimated that between 1.5% and 3% of males in the UK experience sexual assault (Kershaw *et al.*, 2001), while one in four males will experience some form of sexual abuse before reaching 18 (Bevan, 2008). Reporting rates of rape are extremely low with only 13% of victims informing the police, and less than 6% of reported rapes resulting in a conviction in the UK.

The majority of rapists are known to the victim (Kelly *et al.*, 2005), a finding supported by Rape Crisis England and Wales who found that 97% of their callers identified their rapist as someone known to them. Walby and Allen (2004) in analysing British Crime Survey figures, concluded that only 18% of reported rapes were by strangers. This would indicate that the biggest risk of rape is from someone known to the victim, which may account for the low reporting rates.

There are a number of barriers to disclosure, not least lack of legitimacy and guilt around perceived complicity. This makes it difficult to name the rape and access appropriate sources of help. This is compounded when the rape is accompanied by sexual arousal, as the survivor believes, falsely, that such arousal is evidence that they are complicit. The concomitant shame and self-blame further silences the survivor. Survivors may also fear not being believed, or being stigmatised, especially in the case of homosexual, or homophobic rape, prostitutes or trafficked sex workers. The very real threat and fear of retaliation can be a strong incentive to minimise disclosure, as can fear of retraumatisation. Many survivors fear being retraumatised through the process of disclosure, prosecution and court proceedings, and feel it is not worth it, especially with such extremely low conviction rates. If they feel let down by professionals during disclosure or by those in the criminal justice system, they may lose trust in professionals making it hard to seek further help such as counselling and psychotherapy.

It is interesting to note that barriers are not just around disclosure, but also around seeking medical help, with only 29% of female rape victims seeking medical help. Of those that did seek medical help, the majority (65%) did so by seeing their GP, while 35% went to accident and emergency departments. In terms of the cost of rape, it is estimated that the overall cost of sexual offences in 2003–2004 was £8.5 billion with each case incurring a health-related cost of £73,437 (Walby and Allen, 2004).

WHO IS AT RISK OF RAPE?

As with all interpersonal trauma, anyone is at risk of rape. While the majority of rape is committed by males on females, rape also occurs in same sex and transgendered relationships, and some women are known to rape men. Rape also occurs across all cultures and all ethnic groups. A large proportion of rape is perpetrated in intimate relationships where it is used to control and dominate a partner and ensure total surrender and submission. Rape is also ubiquitous in controlling prostitutes and those who have been trafficked into sexual slavery, where it is used to "break in" new recruits and as a form of punishment and humiliation. It is a way of asserting power, control and domination over the sex worker to ensure absolute compliance and to prevent escape. This is especially potent with trafficked women whose shame and humiliation at being raped prevent disclosure as they do not want to bring dishonour on to their families, and fear deportation in case their families further reject them.

Children, those in care, the elderly and those with physical or mental disabilities are also at risk of rape, especially as the risk of disclosure is minimised. Prisoners, those living in institutions, those in the military or individuals living in war zones, are also at risk of rape with little opportunity for disclosure due to fear of retaliation. Individuals with a previous history of forced sex are at particular risk of revictimisation and sexual assault (Kreiter *et al.*, 1999), and there is a strong link between CSA and adult rape (Sanderson, 2006). Prisoners are especially vulnerable as it is estimated that some 80% of the prison population has a history of CSA (Bevan, 2008).

The British Crime Survey found that 17% were unable to give consent due to high levels of alcohol, while 6% of victims were drugged in some way (Walby and Allen, 2004), usually through Rohypnol or sleeping tablets. In addition 8% of victims were unconscious or asleep, while 29% were subjected to force or intimidation (Walby and Allen, 2004). The use of force and intimidation is a potent characteristic of the rape of adolescent females, some as young as 13, by gangs, or gang members. Rape within gang culture is of huge concern as gang members use rape as a display of power and control not only over the victim, but also over rival gangs and the larger community. Rape is meted out as punishment and humiliation, especially on girls who are involved with rival gang members, or for perceived insults, lack of respect, or rejection of a gang member. The punishment usually consists of gang rape which the victim cannot disclose for fear of reprisals towards self, or their extended family (Batmanghelidjh, quoted in Cohen 2009) or other members of the community. Alongside gun and knife crime, rape is another potent way of asserting power, control and domination over individuals and the community.

PERPETRATORS OF RAPE

As rape occurs in many different contexts, rapists come from a diverse range of backgrounds, both socioeconomically and ethnically. Male rapists come from all age groups, although there is considerable concern that increasingly younger males (some as young as 13) use rape as a display of power and control within gang culture, and, due to fear of reprisal, remain undetected. In addition, there is heightened awareness that more and more young children resort to sexual assault and rape of other children as a way of asserting power. The majority of rapists are male and they generally assault females, although rape also occurs between males. The rape of males by males occurs in same sex relationships, as well as in homophobic assaults, prison, the military and CSA.

Females are also known to rape, not just males but also other females, and account for 1% of all incarcerated rapists. Estimates indicate that as much as 6% to 24% of rape and sexual assault is perpetrated by females (Coxell, King, Mezey and Kell, 2000), and they are thought to account for 48% of male sexual assault in adulthood. Research has shown that females enforce a range of sexual assaults such as forced cunnilingus (38%), forced fellatio (63%) and vaginal intercourse (44%).

A critical finding in the research on rape, is that rape is rarely sexually motivated but is about asserting power and control. Groth and Birnbaum (1979) in their study of male rapists found that there are four types of rapists: the *power-assertive rapist,* the *anger-retaliation rapist,* the *power-reassurance rapist* and the *anger-excitation* rapist, and that between 60% and 70% were motivated by power, 20% to 40% were motivated by anger, and between 2% and 5% were sadistic in nature. Thus rape must be seen as an act of violence, domination and humiliation that is channelled through sexual acts. Rape not only asserts power over the victim, but also displays power and control over others in the victim's life and community. It shows other men that their wives, girlfriends, daughters, sisters or mothers, are not safe and can be violated. This is frequently seen in rape in war or mass genocide, and is a form of both punishment and humiliation. The use of rape as control, domination and punishment is also frequently seen in rape by partners, or ex-partners in domestic abuse. Rape is also a potent form of retaliation for perceived slights or rejection as seen in gang culture, or with ex-partners, and is a way of demanding respect. Counsellors need to be aware of the motivation of rapists, and the function of rape, to fully understand the impact of rape. It is only with such understanding that counsellors can enable survivors to see rape in terms of power, control, domination and humiliation, rather than sex or sexuality.

NATURE AND DYNAMICS OF RAPE

Counsellors need to be mindful that rape is a serious crime using power and control and is not about sex or a sexual relationship, and convey this to the survivor. Rapists can be highly manipulative and resort to a variety of strategies to gain total submission. While the predatory rapist uses sheer physical force and strength to overcome resistance, such as in stranger, prisoner, or gang rape, many of the other types of rapist will resort to a variety of strategies to minimise the risk of disclosure. Some rapists will use persuasion to gain initial access to the victim. To entice the victim they may use manipulation, deception, entrapment or coaxing, such as is seen in acquaintance or date rape, CSA, sex trafficking and sexual exploitation, and rape by professionals. Some rapists will use coercion to compel the victim to submit either through verbal threats, intimidation, use of authority or status, or through incapacitation such as drugs like Rohypnol, or alcohol.

One powerful strategy used by some rapists, is to perform acts that are sexually arousing. This strategy serves several functions for both rapist and victim. Sexual arousal in the victim serves to make the rapist feel even more powerful and in control as he is able to elicit sexual responses from the victim and has more control over the victim's body than the victim has. In addition, the rapist misinterprets the sexual arousal to shore up the distorted belief that it is not rape but consensual sex, which the victim wanted and is enjoying. For the survivor, sexual arousal is misperceived as evidence of consent, or a consensual act, making it easier for the rapist to coerce the victim into continuing sexual involvement. If the survivor feels complicit in the rape, they are less likely to disclose or report the rape due to shame, or fear that they will not be believed or are less credible.

It is critical that counsellors understand the dynamics and nature of sexual arousal during rape and that they explore this with the survivor to challenge any distorted perceptions. Counsellors will need to use psychoeducation to facilitate a better understanding of the sexual arousal cycle and enable the survivor to differentiate between sexual arousal and sexual desire, and see these as two separate things. It is essential that survivors understand that even though they may be aroused by a sexual experience this does not mean that they desire it. In addition, survivors need to be aware that it is sexual activity, such as oral sex, not the person, the rapist, that they are responding to. To elicit sexual arousal in females, and increase lubrication and dilation, the rapist may perform cunnilingus or rhythmic masturbation, leading to orgasm. In the case of male victims, counsellors need to remind survivors that males can experience involuntary erections, ejaculation and orgasm in the presence of fear or while under stress, and that these are physiological responses unaccompanied by any sexually arousing state. Ejaculation and orgasm are physiological responses that can occur involuntarily as a result of genital manipulation and stimulation, and can occur in passion and outside passion and desire. Some rapists deliberately manipulate this to try to elicit sexual arousal through performing fellatio or rhythmic masturbation.

Sexual arousal during rape engenders a profound sense of shame and confusion in survivors. One way to reconcile perceived complicity and the concomitant shame is self-blame. Self-blame also serves to minimise the fact that the survivor was overwhelmed, coerced or manipulated by the rapist. This is especially the case in male rape victims who feel that they should be capable of defending themselves against assaults, especially sexual assault. It is essential that counsellors recognise, and convey to the survivor, that sexual arousal or co-operation does not mean consent. Both are psychobiological defence mechanisms that are activated in the presence of fear and danger and are necessary for survival. It is only with such understanding that the survivor can clarify and attach accurate and objective meaning to their responses and begin to relinquish distorted perceptions such as complicity and self-blame.

The net result of employing strategies and eliciting sexual responses is to minimise the risk of disclosure and prevent the victim from being able to legitimise such experiences as rape. If the survivor cannot name the experience as rape, it is less likely to be reported and detected. Such survivors may also not feel able to access other sources of help such as counselling and this reinforces their isolation and shame. In the absence of being able to process their experience, they are less able to integrate and are more likely to live in fear and shame.

THE IMPACT OF RAPE

The impact of rape varies from individual to individual and is dependent on the context of the rape, relationship to the rapist, the level of coercion and control, and degree of fear of retaliation. Survivors of rape will vary in their reactions from numbness through to heightened and uncontrollable emotional reactions. It is critical that counsellors understand that reactions will vary from person to person and do not expect or anticipate stereotypical responses. Despite the variation, there are some common responses that characterise the impact of rape (see Box 8.2).

Box 8.2 Common reactions to rape

- **Emotional shock:** I feel numb. How can I be so calm? Why can't I cry?
- **Disbelief and/or denial:** Did it really happen? Why me? Maybe I just imagined it. It wasn't really rape.
- **Embarrassment:** What will people think? I can't tell my family or friends.
- **Shame:** I feel completely filthy, like there's something wrong with me. I can't get clean.
- **Guilt:** I feel as if it's my fault, or I should've been able to stop it. If only I had...
- **Depression:** How am I gonna get through the day? I'm so tired! I feel so hopeless. Maybe I'd be better off dead.
- **Powerlessness:** Will I ever feel in control again?

- **Disorientation:** I don't even know what day it is, or where I'm supposed to be. I keep forgetting things.
- **Flashbacks:** I'm still reliving the assault. I keep seeing that face and feeling like it's happening all over again.
- **Fear:** I'm scared of everything. What if I have STDs or AIDS? I can't sleep because I'll have nightmares. I'm afraid to go out. I'm afraid to be alone.
- **Anxiety:** I'm having panic attacks. I can't breathe. I can't stop shaking. I feel overwhelmed.
- **Anger:** I feel like killing the person who attacked me!
- **Physical stress:** My stomach (or head or back) aches all the time. I feel jittery and don't feel like eating.

The most common responses to rape are emotional shock, numbness, disbelief and denial that the rape happened. This is often accompanied by embarrassment, shame and guilt, and fear that the rape was their fault. Survivors of rape will often feel a total loss of control and powerlessness and a sense of disorientation. Fear and anxiety predominate especially around somatic and psychobiological reactions, as well as everyday encounters.

Box 8.3 Common fears associated with rape

- Fear of being alone
- Fear of the dark
- Fear of abandonment, rejection
- Fear of being touched, hugged
- Fear of something bad happening
- Fear and avoidance of places, people, situations, e.g. public loos, parks (male survivors may fear urinals and only feel safe in cubicles)
- Fear of expressing anger or being angry
- Fear of being out of control (need to be in control)
- Fear of sleeping and nightmares
- Fear of intimacy – avoiding others, running away from others

- Fear of compromised sexuality or sexual dysfunction – being asexual, non-sexual, or overly sexual, sexual acting out to prove sexuality
- Fear of men and women – fear of gender of professionals they may need to work with, e.g. police officer, counsellor, doctor
- Fear of speaking out
- Fear of relaxing
- Fear of feeling, frozen emotions or disconnection from feelings
- Fear of making poor choice of partner
- Fear of hugging children
- Fear of being inadequate
- Fear of accepting compliments
- Fear of feeling constricted
- Fear of not being able to say no
- Fear of people's motives, that they will be raped again
- Fear of intrusive thoughts

Many of the psychobiological responses to the trauma of rape, such as post-traumatic stress symptoms, are experienced as involuntary reactions outside the victim's control and as such mirror the lack of control during the rape which evokes further anxiety and fear of "going crazy". Impaired recall of the rape can lead to fears of not being believed and can hinder the survivor from legitimising rape. In addition, barriers to reporting and working through rape experience due to fear of stigmatisation, or retraumatisation, may result in isolation and withdrawal from others. This is often compounded by shattered assumptions about the self, others and the world as no longer a safe place.

The physical impact of rape is not just confined to physical injuries but include the risk of sexually transmitted infection, and also risk of pregnancy. It is essential that survivors of rape have access to medical services and testing facilities to respond to the physical effects of rape. In the case of pregnancy, the survivor may need access to counselling in order to explore feelings and consider all the available options.

To manage the trauma of rape survivors may resort to alcohol or drug abuse to obliterate the horror and terror of their experience. Some survivors may use self-harm and suicidal ideation as a way of managing the impact of rape, while others may no longer wish to live, and attempt suicide. Counsellors need to ensure that they conduct a full assessment on all levels of functioning, and ensure that predominant concerns are addressed and worked through.

To understand the impact of rape within a post-traumatic stress disorder framework, Burgess and Holmstrom (1974) have formulated rape trauma syndrome which consists of three stages: the Acute Stage; the Outward Adjustment Stage and the Resolutions Stage (see Figure 8.1).

While the impact varies from person to person, it is clear that recovery takes time and occurs in stages. These stages are not linear and survivors will vacillate between stages, and differ in how long they remain in each stage, with some survivors locked into the Acute Stage for years, and in some cases a lifetime. Counsellors need to understand that each survivor processes the rape experience differently and remain constant in their support of the survivor throughout the various stages.

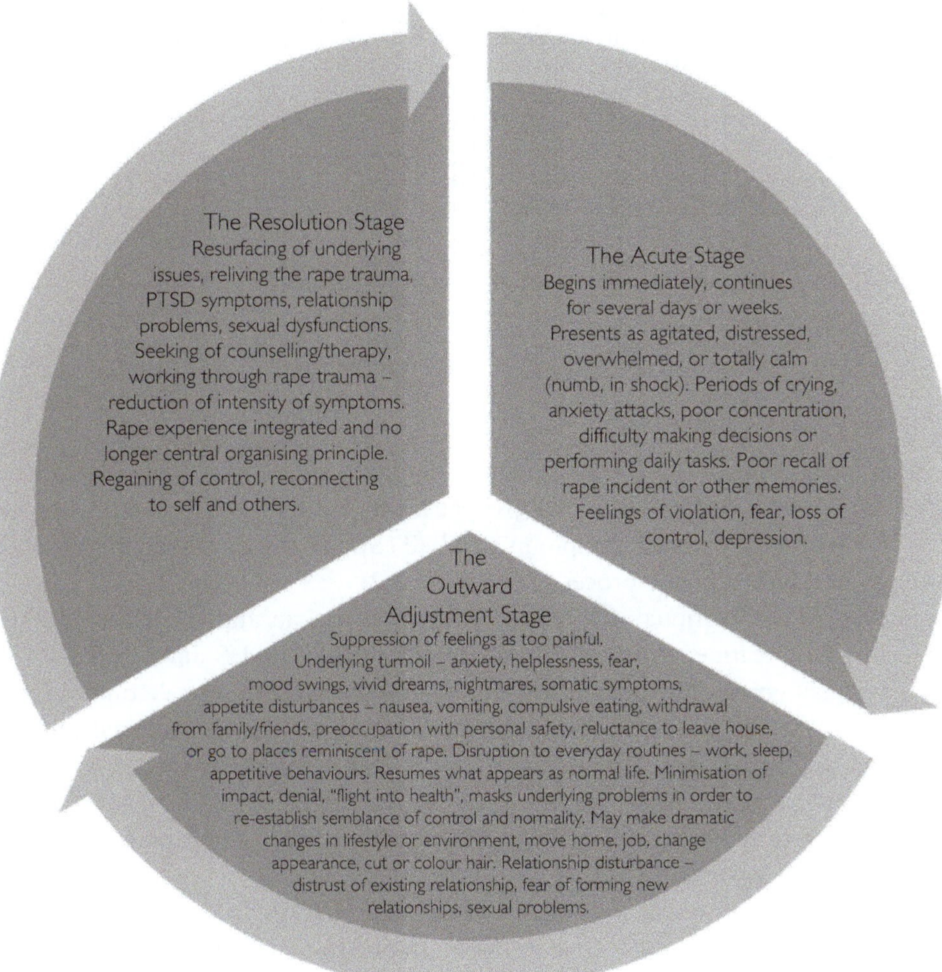

Figure 8.1 Rape trauma syndrome (adapted from Burgess and Holmstrom, 1974)

The Resolution Stage	The Acute Stage	Avoidance behaviors and actions	Increased physiological arousal characteristics
Uncontrollable intrusive thoughts about the rape, constantly remembering the incident. Recurring and realistic dreams about rape. Flashbacks of the rape, it is experienced as though it is happening in the here and now. Heightened anxiety and distress when in the presence of any event that symbolises or resembles the rape. Avoidance of talking about the rape, or any stimuli or situations which act as reminders of the rape.	Social withdrawal is a form of psychic numbing, denial and a sense of emotional or psychological death in which no feelings are experienced. This is often manifest in living. While not necessarily suicidal, there is dramatically reduced interest in their children, partner, friends, family or job. Any feelings that do emerge are greatly restricted in range, be it joy or pain. Impaired memory and amnesia impedes recall of the details of the rape.	Through avoidance behaviours survivors will avoid any thoughts, feelings, or cues which could bring up the overwhelming and most traumatic aspects of the rape. This is often characterised by avoiding areas associated with the rape such as parks, woods or urban areas where the rape occurred.	These consist of exaggerated startle responses, hyperalertness and hyper-vigilance. Impaired sleep and poor sleep patterns, such as difficulties in falling or staying asleep. Memory impairments can lead to poor concentration, which impacts on the performance of even mundane, everyday tasks. There may also be elevated levels of irritability, hostility, rage and anger, which further isolates and alienates the survivor.

Figure 8.2 Four symptom categories in rape-related post-traumatic stress disorder (adapted from National Center for Victims of Crime, 1992)

LONG-TERM EFFECTS

Research has shown that many survivors of rape suffer from rape-related post-traumatic stress disorder (RR-PTSD) (Kilpatrick, Amstadter, Resnick and Ruggiero, 2007). There are four major symptoms of RR-PTSD all of which need to be worked through in the therapeutic process (see Figure 8.2).

According to the National Center for Victims of Crime and the Crime Victims Research and Treatment Center, 31% of rape victims in the US develop RR-PTSD, with over half going on to develop depression (National Center for Victims of Crime and Crime Victims Research and Treatment Center, 1992), and suicidal ideation. Research has shown that rape victims are 4.1 times more likely to attempt suicide, with 13% of all rape victims making serious attempts on their life. There is also a strong link between rape and alcohol and drug dependency (Kilpatrick, Amstadter, Resnick and Ruggiero, 2007).

In line with other research on the long-term effects of interpersonal trauma, some of the physiological changes in the brain due to the traumatic impact of rape may be highly resistant to any form of therapeutic or pharmacological interventions. One change that is associated with trauma is reduced ability to accurately gauge the passage of time which impedes the keeping of appointments, including therapeutic sessions. In addition, the activation of survival mechanisms such as flight or fight may be reset as a result of rape, which leads survivors to become over-aroused to any environmental cues and interpret these as danger. This makes it virtually impossible to differentiate between degrees of danger, whereby any environmental, or internal cue, no matter how benign, can activate a full stress response.

Counsellors need to address the range of RR-PTSD symptoms, but also work through all the other core clinical symptoms that may present, or emerge during the therapeutic process. As these symptoms will vary from survivor to survivor, counsellors need to ensure that they conduct detailed assessment throughout the therapeutic process to ensure that all long-term effects and symptoms are worked through.

Box 8.4 Core clinical symptoms of rape

- Child conceived through rape
- Sexual health problems
- Risky sexual behaviour – sexual acting out
- Serious long-term injury and organ damage
- Rape-related PTSD
- Withdrawal
- Impaired relationships
- Sexual dysfunctions, compromised sexuality
- Phobias – social phobias
- Depression
- Panic attacks
- Loss of trust
- Self-harm and self-mutilation
- Substance abuse
- Eating disorders, obesity
- Suicide and suicidal ideation
- Sense of foreshortened future – hopelessness
- Increased risk of repeat assault, correlated with severity of initial assault

WORKING WITH SURVIVORS OF RAPE

Ideally, the sooner survivors are able to talk about the rape experience the sooner they can begin to process their experience and start their recovery. However, many survivors of rape find it extremely difficult to talk about their rape, and may remain silent for many years. Thus counsellors who do not specialise in working with survivors of rape need to be aware that a proportion of clients who enter therapy may not initially disclose rape, and that such disclosure may not occur until trust has been established. The counselling process is an opportunity for survivors to receive the much-needed support and comfort that was not available immediately following the rape. The therapeutic space is also a secure base in which to make sense of the rape experience (Allen, 2001), and to work on the concomitant symptoms. In order to effect this, counsellors need to work on two parallel levels, one which focuses on the past as in the actual rape experience, and the other which focuses on the present to alleviate current stress and symptoms (Allen, 2001).

Some survivors may be so traumatised by rape that pharmacological intervention may be indicated, and counsellors my need to establish links with local medical and psychiatric services that can offer such options. In addition survivors may also benefit from talking to other survivors of rape, and may benefit from any local agencies that specialise in running support groups for rape victims. In order to ascertain the best form of intervention, counsellors need to conduct an in-depth assessment on how the rape has impacted on the survivor, both at the time of the rape and subsequently. It is critical to establish those symptoms that are a result of rape, and those that pre-existed and have been reactivated by the rape, as well as assessing the survivor's level of resilience. It may also be necessary to have some awareness about how the rape has impacted indirectly on the survivor's family, especially if they have children.

There are a number of interventions that have been found to be effective when working with survivors of rape such as cognitive behavioural therapy, prolonged exposure therapy (Foa and Rothbaum, 1998; Foa *et al.*, 1991) cognitive processing therapy (Resick and Schnicke, 1992; Resick *et al.*, 2002), dialectical behavioural therapy (Linehan, 1993), trauma-focused cognitive behavioural therapy (TF-CBT) (Cohen, Mannarino and Deblinger, 2006), eye movement desensitisation and reprocessing (EMDR) (Shapiro, 1995), anxiety management training and psychoeducation (Kilpatrick, Amstadter, Resnick and Ruggiero, 2007). Irrespective of the preferred therapeutic model used, counsellors need to ensure that there are clear therapeutic goals in place (see Box 8.5) and that the therapy is conducted in a safe and secure base.

A prerequisite to working with survivors of sexual violence and rape is to provide information about sex and sexuality to undo the distortions resulting from the rape experience. To achieve this counsellors themselves need to have a good knowledge and understanding of sex, sexual arousal and sexuality, alongside an awareness of how sexual arousal during rape impacts on survivors.

Box 8.5 Core therapeutic goals when working with rape

- Assessment
- Crisis intervention
- Establish safety and trust
- Restore control – external and internal through affect regulation and distress tolerance
- Legitimise rape and enable the survivor to name it
- Restore control over trauma-related symptoms
- Reduce intensity of symptoms
- Normalise responses within context of interpersonal trauma
- Facilitate understanding of impact of rape on range of dimensions – emotional, psychological, cognitive, behavioural, relational and sexual
- Process sexual components of rape such as flashbacks which are prompted by fear and anxiety, not desire or pleasure; normalise sexual responses; and emphasise that sexuality is not objectionable but lack of consent is and that sexuality does not have to be compromised
- Reduce shame and self-blame
- Rebuild self-respect and trust
- Rebuild shattered assumptions and altered perceptions of self, others and the world
- Reconnect to self, others and the world
- Integrate rape experience and accept it has happened
- Work with consequences of rape
- Psychoeducation on sex and sexuality
- Reclaim sexuality

Through psychoeducation the counsellor needs to help the survivor to differentiate between sexual activity and sexual desire, and understand that any sexual arousal is a response to the sexual activity and *not* the rapist. It is also crucial that the survivor is able to understand that intrusive thoughts, flashbacks, dreams and fantasies about rape are prompted by fear not desire. Such flashbacks represent anxiety and not pleasure and are the body's way of processing trauma in order to integrate the experience. Counsellors also need to normalise the survivor's sexual responses and explain that these are normal in the presence of certain sexual activity. Most importantly, survivors need to be reassured that their sexuality has not been compromised, and that it is not sexuality that is objectionable but the lack of consent as in rape that is objectionable and abusive. It is imperative that counsellors do not avoid exploring the sexual components of the rape experience so that survivors can fully understand their reactions and regain mastery over them.

Such exploration must be accompanied by a warm, compassionate, empathic attunement through authentic connection and the ability to hear the trauma of rape without blaming, recoiling, distancing or hiding behind a clinical mask and protocols. It is only through a human connection that the brutalisation, dehumanisation and objectification inherent in rape can be undone. Counsellors need to provide a calm, containing environment, in which the focus is on the survivor *not* the rape. As the therapeutic process is not linear, there is a need for flexibility and the capacity for the counsellor to restore control to the victim to pace the therapeutic process, to talk, or not talk. Counsellors need to be mindful that even in silence the survivor is conveying a wealth of information through non-verbal communication. It is also important that counsellors consistently identify the survivor's strengths and existing resources and work towards augmenting these, be honest about what can and cannot be done, and ensure that they do not make assurance, or promises that they cannot fulfil.

THERAPEUTIC CHALLENGES WHEN WORKING WITH SURVIVORS OF RAPE

There are a number of therapeutic challenges that counsellors face when working with survivors of rape. A significant challenge is to be able to bear the pain of being able to hear the trauma of rape without being overwhelmed, or disconnecting from the survivor. Counsellors need to ensure that they can mange their own responses to rape and that they are able to contain any fears that may emerge. Listening to the details of rape can be highly distressing and can also be arousing, and counsellors need to be prepared for the range of responses that may be elicited. Some counsellors may feel that they may be perceived as too intrusive or voyeuristic when exploring the rape and feel uncomfortable in witnessing such horror. This may invoke witness guilt, which, while normal, is nevertheless deeply uncomfortable. It is essential that counsellors are able to differentiate between normal counter-transference reactions, and reactions that impede the therapeutic process. Whatever the range of responses, it is critical that counsellors have solid professional and personal support networks to access to explore their reactions.

Counsellors also need to have an awareness of cross-cultural attitudes and beliefs around rape so that they are able to be more culturally sensitive when working with diversity. The role of honour, and the responsibility for loss of honour, plays a crucial role in some cultures. Many cultures believe that the protection of honour lies with the victim, and if rape occurs that the victim is to some degree responsible for that. This will impact on the survivor's understanding and feelings around rape, and how it is perceived in their culture. Counsellors must respect the origins of such values and be culturally sensitive to the survivor to avoid alienating or shaming them further. To this effect counsellors need to be respectful, accepting and engaged at all times despite differences in cultural values and beliefs.

To avoid the negative impact of working with survivors of rape, such as burnout or secondary traumatic stress (STS), counsellors need to ensure they have comprehensive professional support through regular supervision, and consultation. They also need to balance trauma work with other professional work and make sure that they look after themselves. It is only when professionals are adequately supported that they will be able to sit alongside survivors of rape, hear their trauma, and be able to support them on their journey to recovery.

Case vignette: Cynthia

Cynthia, a 30-year-old Middle Eastern woman, entered therapy due to chronic marital problems. As a mother of two young children, she felt depressed and dissatisfied with her husband, especially in their sex life. After several months of exploring the root of her dissatisfaction and depression, Cynthia revealed that some years prior to her marriage she had been raped by a more senior work colleague who had asked her out on a date to which she eagerly agreed. Her restricted upbringing in the Middle East had rendered Cynthia somewhat naïve and not very knowledgeable about sexuality, a fact that the rapist exploited. After a pleasant dinner and copious amounts of alcohol, the rapist took her back to his flat and raped her.

Cynthia knew that what had happened was inappropriate, but felt that by having agreed to go out on a date with him, she was complicit and could therefore not denote it as rape. Her shame and humiliation prevented her from disclosing the rape to anyone, while her insecure immigration status prevented her from informing the police. Cynthia was also unable to tell her family as she feared that this would bring dishonour on them. Thus she remained silent for many years, not able to talk to friends or even her husband about the rape. Her husband-to-be felt safe as he had an extremely low libido, and seemed uninterested in sex. It was the birth of her second child, a boy, that reactivated the rape experience by putting her in touch with her feelings of powerlessness and lack of control. As she explored the rape she became aroused by the memories of the experience and began to fantasise about engaging in risky sexual behaviour, and wanting to go to clubs and bars where she could meet men. Cynthia was bewildered by her fear and attraction to rape stimuli and felt she was "going crazy", especially as she felt that the sexual arousal she felt with the rapist was infinitely more stimulating and arousing than what she felt with her husband.

Through exploring her experiences and fantasies, and through receiving psychoeducation to clarify the role of sexual arousal in rape, Cynthia was able to gain some understanding of her contradictory reactions, and normalise her responses. As Cynthia became more aware of the impact of rape she was able to make sense of what had happened to her and link this to her current symptoms. This enabled her to regain more control over her symptoms and challenge the distorted beliefs and perceptions associated with rape. Through the therapeutic process she was able to reduce the intensity of her reactions, and reclaim her sexuality without the contamination of the rape. This enabled Cynthia to stop re-enacting the rape experience in fantasy, reduce the risky sexual behaviour and begin to resume intimacy with her husband.

SUMMARY

- The impact of rape will vary depending on the context of the rape, although there are a number of common responses. Rape needs to be understood within the context of interpersonal trauma as it threatens life, bodily and psychological integrity, and overwhelms human adaptation to life.
- The traumatic nature of rape activates a cascade of psychobiological reactions to aid survival, which in turn give rise to a range of psychological and emotional responses such as terror, loss of control, threat of annihilation, loss of agency, shame and self-blame.
- The spectrum of responses to rape can range from numbness to uncontrollable emotional reactions, fear of retraumatisation or retaliation, avoidance, fear of stigmatisation, impaired trust, and fear of compromised sexuality.
- Many of the psychobiological responses are experienced as involuntary reactions outside the victim's control such as those underpinning RR-PTSD which mirror the lack of control during the rape. The uncontrollable nature of symptoms evokes further anxiety and fear of "going crazy".
- Sexual arousal during the rape can lead to shame and the false belief that the survivor is complicit in the rape and are to blame, while impaired recall of the rape can lead to fears of not being believed which in combination can hinder the victim from legitimising the rape.
- Barriers to reporting and working through the rape experience such as fear of re-experiencing the trauma and disconnection from self, can impede survivors from seeking appropriate help, leading them to further isolation and withdrawal from what they perceive as a hostile world.
- Counsellors need to enable survivors to legitimise rape, restore safety, restore control over trauma-related symptoms, reduce the intensity of symptoms, and normalise these within the context of interpersonal trauma. In addition they need to facilitate understanding of the impact of rape on a range of dimensions – emotional, psychological, cognitive, behavioural, relational and sexual.

- It is important that counsellors do not avoid exploring the sexual components of rape so that survivors are able to understand that flashbacks are prompted by fear and anxiety, not desire or pleasure, and that sexual responses are normal. It is also important to emphasise that sexuality is not objectionable but lack of consent is and that sexuality does not have to be compromised. This will help to reduce shame and self-blame, rebuild self-respect, and rebuild shattered assumptions and altered perceptions of self, others and the world.

- Knowledge and understanding of the impact of rape will enable counsellors to assess individual needs and urgent concerns, identify pre-existing issues reactivated by the rape, and those that have emerged as a result of rape. A warm, compassionate empathic attunement through authentic connection, and ability to hear trauma of rape without blaming, recoiling or distancing will enable the survivor to begin the journey of recovery. Counsellors need to be mindful that the therapeutic process is not linear but demands flexibility and the ability to restore control to the victim. Counsellors also need to identify strengths and existing resources and augment these.

- Counsellors need to ensure that they have access to professional and personal support to minimise being overwhelmed by working with rape, and avoid STS. With this in place they will be able to provide a secure therapeutic space in which the survivor can process and integrate the rape and begin the journey of recovery.

SUGGESTED READING

Anderson, I. and Doherty, K. (2008) *Accounting for Rape: Psychology, Feminism and Discourse Analysis in the Study of Sexual Violence.* London: Routledge.

Bourke, J. (2007) *Rape: A History from 1860 to the Present.* London: Virago Press.

Dimeff, L.A. and Koerner, K. (2007) *Dialectical Behaviour Therapy in Clinical Practice: Applications Across Disorders and Settings.* New York: Guilford Press.

Foa, E. and Rothbaum, B.O. (2002) *Treating the Trauma of Rape: Cognitive Behavioural Therapy for PTSD.* New York: Guilford Press.

Groth, A.N and Birnbaum, H.J. (1979) *Men Who Rape: The Psychology of the Offender.* Cambridge, MA: Perseus Publishing.

Linehan, M.A. (1993) *Skills Training Manual for Treating Borderline Personality Disorder.* New York: Guilford Press.

Matsakis, A. (2003) *The Rape Recovery Handbook: Step by Step Help for Survivors of Sexual Assault.* Oakland, CA: Harbinger Press.

Preble, J.M. and Groth, A.N. (2002) *Male Victims of Same Sex Abuse: Addressing their Sexual Responses.* Baltimore, MD: Sidran Press.

Resick, P. and Schnicke, M. (1993) *Cognitive Processing Therapy for Rape Victims.* London: Sage.

Stark, E. (2007) *Coercive Control: How Men Entrap Women in Personal Life.* New York, Oxford University Press.

Thornhill, R. and Palmer, C.T. (2000) *A Natural History of Rape: Biological Bases of Sexual Coercion.* Cambridge, MA: MIT Press.

CHAPTER 9

SEXUAL EXPLOITATION

Child and Adult Prostitution, Human Trafficking and Sexual Slavery

Sexual exploitation takes many forms but is primarily seen in child and adult prostitution, international and domestic trafficking of individuals for sexual purposes, and sexual slavery. Whatever the form of sexual exploitation, it is inexorably linked to violence, control and domination through the use of force, coercion, abduction, fraud or deception. In essence sexual exploitation is predicated on the abuse of power and control over someone who is vulnerable and unable to give informed consent. The complex interplay of physical and psychological violence, entrapment and imprisonment omnipresent in sexual exploitation can lead to severe repetitive traumatisation which often remains hidden and outside public awareness. This makes sexual exploitation one of the most pernicious forms of interpersonal trauma.

Children, young people and adults, in particular females, are all vulnerable to sexual exploitation either through forced prostitution or sexual trafficking across international borders, and national borders as in internal trafficking. In sexual trafficking individuals are transported from location to location, and repeatedly sold to "recruiters", "couriers" and pimps for the purpose of sexual exploitation in either private houses, or flats, brothels, saunas or massage parlours. This is often conducted within highly organised criminal networks alongside drugs and guns, in which females become a lucrative, low-risk, high-profit commodity. As trafficked and sexually exploited girls and women are usually enslaved in off-street locations it is very difficult to ascertain the full extent of precisely how many are in sexual servitude.

The level of brutality, and physical and sexual violence, alongside fear of reprisals to self or family members, and fear of criminalisation as sex worker or drug addict, prevents the enslaved from escaping, rendering them powerless to resist their fate. Unless freed through police raids or turned out onto the streets either through illness, sexually transmitted infections or age, many sexually exploited women do not come to the attention of the authorities. This is especially the case of young girls subjected to internal trafficking as they are forced to endure years of abuse and sexual exploitation. As authorities become more aware of the complex nature and dynamics of sexual exploitation and are able to liberate those who have been enslaved, clinicians may well encounter survivors of such abuses in their clinical practice. It is crucial that they have a full understanding of the complexity and impact of sexual exploitation and enslavement.

To this effect, this chapter will look at the range of sexual exploitation with particular emphasis on child and adult prostitution, human trafficking, both international and domestic, and sexual slavery. It will identify those most at risk and those involved in recruiting and exploiting them, as well as dissecting the complex nature and dynamics of sexual exploitation and how it impacts on individuals. Clinicians need to be aware of the long-term effects of sexual enslavement and brutality and how this manifests in the therapeutic setting. To facilitate recovery from years of abuse, counsellors need to provide a secure base in order for the survivor to explore the range of effects, restore their faith in humanity, begin to trust again and re-establish a life outside of sexual exploitation.

THE SPECTRUM OF SEXUAL EXPLOITATION

The spectrum of sexual exploitation includes a number of activities each of which share commonalities such as power, control and coercion, as well as some significant differences. The most common form of sexual exploitation are highlighted in Figure 9.1.

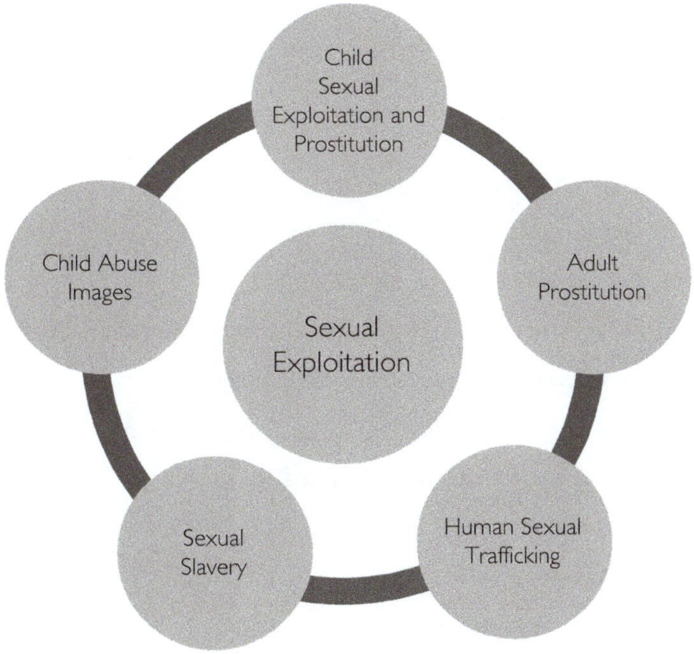

Figure 9.1 The spectrum of sexual exploitation

According to the *Safeguarding Children and Young People from Sexual Exploitation* consultation draft, the sexual exploitation of children and young people under 18

> ... involves exploitative situations, context and relationships where young people (or a third person or persons) receive "something" (e.g. food, accommodation, drugs, alcohol, cigarettes, affection, gifts, money) as a result of them performing, and/or another or other performing on them, sexual activities. Child sexual exploitation can occur through the use of technology without the child's immediate recognition: for example being persuaded to post sexual images on the internet/mobile phones without immediate payment or gain. In all cases, those exploiting the child/young person have power over them by virtue of their age, gender, intellect, physical strength and/or economic or other resources. Violence, coercion and intimidation are common, involvement in exploitative relationships being characterised in the main by the child or young person's limited availability or choice resulting from their social/economic and/or emotional vulnerability. (Department for Children, Schools and Families, 2008b)

Sexual exploitation is not an isolated activity and is frequently associated with other types of crime, especially highly organised crime such as human trafficking, drug trafficking and the illegal gun trade (see Box 9.1).

Box 9.1 Links between sexual exploitation and other crimes

- Human trafficking (both into, out of and within the UK)
- Prostitution – off and on the street
- Sex tourism
- Child sexual abuse
- Domestic abuse
- Forced marriage – forced child marriage
- Female genital mutilation
- Grooming of children (both on and offline)
- Pornography – manufacture, distribution and downloading child abuse images
- Organised sexual abuse – paedophile and sex rings
- Drug-related crime – cultivating, trafficking, dealing, possession
- Organised crime – international and national
- Immigration-related offences
- Domestic slavery
- Gun trafficking

The link between sexual exploitation and highly organised crime attests to the lucrative nature of prostitution and human sexual trafficking and the power that all those involved wield over the individual sex worker, and significant others in their life, making escape nigh on impossible.

PROSTITUTION

It is estimated that there are around 80,000 prostitutes in the UK, 70% of whom entered the sex industry before the age of 18, with an average entry age of 15 (Home Office, 2004), although children as young as 11 have been known to be enslaved. This indicates that child prostitution is a common entry route into the sex industry. Counsellors working with prostitutes, or ex-sex workers, need to be aware of this link in order to assess and work through pre-existing vulnerabilities, not just the sexually exploitative experiences.

Child prostitution

Due to the hidden nature of child prostitution, it is not known how many children are enticed into sexual exploitation, or are currently working as child prostitutes in the UK. The generally acknowledged figure is estimated to be around 5000 children with a female to male ratio of 4:1 (Home Office, 2004). Entry into child prostitution consists of a notoriously complex interplay between emotional, psychological and economic factors (see Figure 9.2). Many children become vulnerable

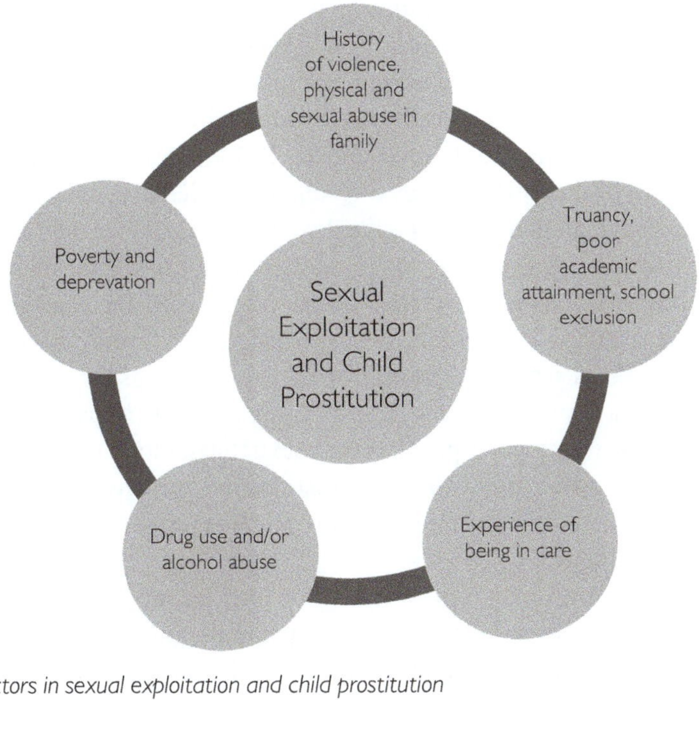

Figure 9.2 Risk factors in sexual exploitation and child prostitution

to child prostitution through poverty, or as a survival strategy. Frequently such children come from chaotic backgrounds with a history of familial physical and sexual violence.

The Home Office report *Paying the Price* (Home Office, 2004) found that 85% of prostitutes experienced physical violence while 45% experienced familial sexual abuse prior to being ensnared by the sex industry. To escape such abuse, children often run away from home, become homeless and thus become vulnerable to sexual predators or criminal elements, such as those involved in theft, drugs and prostitution, in order to survive. Some children escape familial abuse by being taken into care for their own protection. However, there is a high correlation (70%) between child prostitution and experience of being in care, with many sexual predators and pimps recruiting children in residential care. Abused children and those in care are extremely vulnerable to sexual predators as they have been deprived of love, affection and attention, making them highly susceptible to anyone offering to satisfy these basic needs. Such children often confuse desire with love and are more likely to be entrapped and ensnared.

Children from deprived and chaotic families often feel empowered by prostitution especially if the pimp and the clients make them feel special or provide much-needed "love" and attention. Empowerment may also come from having an income whereby the child may come to measure their value by the amount of money they earn. Increased spending power may also become a measure of success, especially in relation to peers, which can enhance chronically low self-esteem and the pervasive sense of worthlessness. Abused and neglected children may seek empowerment in any way possible including prostitution as a way to attach value to their lives, and to gain a sense of control, no matter how illusory (Lenihan and Dean, 2000).

Drugs play a pivotal role in sexual exploitation and prostitution, with between 80% and 95% of both child and adult prostitutes addicted to drugs, most commonly heroin and/or crack cocaine (Home Office, 2004). Research suggests that 25% of children enter child prostitution as a result of problematic drug use, either due to exposure to criminal elements associated with drugs, or as a way to earn sufficient money to maintain a pre-existing drug addiction, not just their own but sometimes that of a boyfriend (Home Office, 2004). While 25% have a pre-existing drug problem, the majority of children develop drug addiction after entering prostitution. This can be as a result of being forced to take drugs by their pimp to induce addiction, or as a result of self-medication to manage the impact of sexual exploitation, and cope with repeated physical and sexual assaults. Drug addiction can be a primary factor in preventing exit from prostitution for financial reasons, and lack of access to specialist addiction treatment programmes makes it very difficult to deal with the drug addiction.

Children can be lured into prostitution in a variety of ways. Some children are entrapped or sold into prostitution by family members, especially mothers or "aunties" on the fringes of prostitution, or by male relatives who have been sexually abusing them for some time. Some children may be specifically targeted and groomed, both on and offline, by sexual predators or pimps, who may operate individually, or as part of an organised crime network or syndicate. Child abusers and pimps are known to frequent crack houses and clubs with a high level of drug dealing, where they deliberately target young and vulnerable drug users. In providing free access to drugs they begin to control the young person, and demand payment through sexual favours for themselves and others.

There is increasing evidence that some vulnerable young girls between 12 and 14 are befriended by older boys or young men, usually between 18 and 25, who "love bomb" them by showering them with attention, affection and gifts, to obtain an emotional hold over them. Once the girl is in thrall to this "boyfriend" and dependent on this special friendship, the boyfriend begins to control and dominate all aspects of her life. He may also ply her with drugs and alcohol to make her more malleable. Through the use of domination and control the "boyfriend" begins to demand she perform sexual favours for his friends or relatives to which she complies for fear of losing his love. Once ensnared the girl is forced to sell sex under the threat of physical and sexual violence, and is then passed around a number of males. At this point the girl is considered to have been "broken in", as evidenced by total submission and surrender, and can then be sold on to another pimp, leaving the "boyfriend" free to hunt down and groom his next victim.

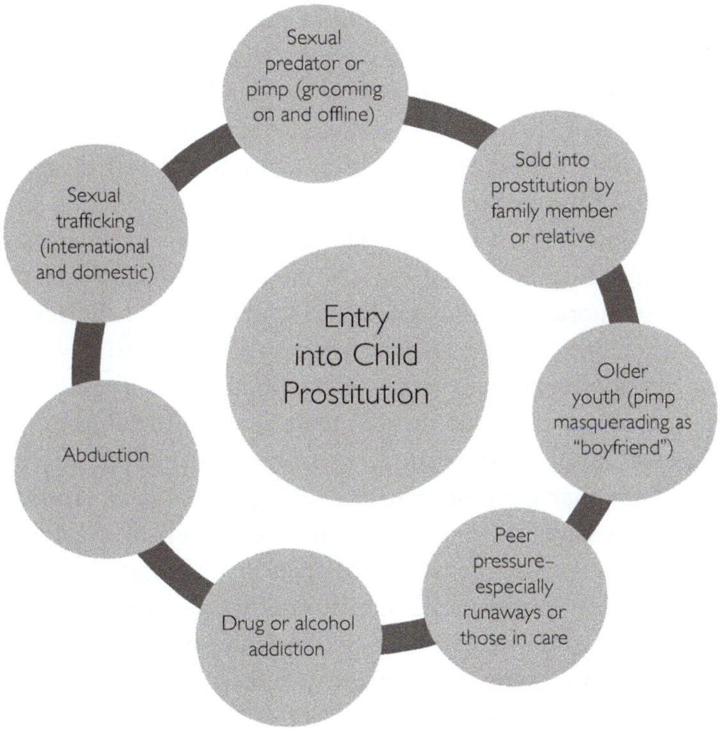

Figure 9.3 Entry into child prostitution

Runaways or young people in care may also be recruited into prostitution through peer introduction, or peer pressure. Runaways may be introduced to prostitution by other children who are already in forced prostitution or by their pimp, or as a survival strategy on the streets, or as a way of supporting a drug or alcohol addiction. Children in care or exclusion units may be recruited by their peers who are already involved in prostitution, or if resistant may be bullied into such activity through the threat of violence. High-profile cases of abuse by staff in residential children's homes indicate that some staff may be a source of recruiting children into prostitution whereby the child is offered or sold to interested parties, or members of an organised sex ring. If the child is already being abused they may see prostitution as empowerment as at least they are being paid for their services, giving them a semblance of control, rather than it being taken from them.

Some sexual predators may deliberately loiter around residential children's homes, or exclusion units, in the hope of grooming a vulnerable child, or in some cases abducting a child. Given that many young people in care frequently abscond, their abduction may be falsely attributed to running away, and less likely to draw full attention from the police. The abduction of children for sexual exploitation from orphanages and children's homes in other countries is by no means unusual and supplies innumerable children for international sexual trafficking. Staff in children's residential care homes may feel powerless and helpless in preventing the recruitment of children into prostitution, as was seen in the case of Aliyah Ismail in 1998 who died at the age of 13 while in the care of Harrow Council from a methadone overdose, and was found to have contracted six sexually transmitted infections through prostitution. It is worth noting that her behaviour was deemed by the agencies involved in her care to be sexually promiscuous rather than evidence of child prostitution. It is thus essential for practitioners to guard against conflating sexual promiscuity, child exploitation and prostitution.

While the majority of child prostitutes are females, males are also at risk of being enticed into sexual exploitation. The number of male child prostitutes, or rent boys, may be more hidden as males are more reluctant to seek help through street and outreach projects due to fear of homophobic and stigmatising responses. Many young males are entrapped into the sex industry as a result of poverty and deprivation, drug abuse or to supplement their income if having to support family members. Research by Barnardo's suggest that boys are enticed into prostitution at a much younger age than girls, often below the age of ten (Barnardo's, 2002). Some rent boys are heterosexual in orientation and feel ashamed of the sexual services they offer, making it even harder to access specialist support services. In addition, child male prostitution is generally less visible although some rent boys do operate on the street, or are employed in massage parlours, or saunas. While some may be controlled by pimps, some operate independently rendering them even more isolated from their community.

In order for them to exit prostitution it is crucial that child prostitutes be given access to specialist support services and refuges rather than be criminalised. It is only within a safe haven that they can begin to recover from the impact of sexual exploitation, become free of drug addiction and begin to rebuild their shattered lives.

It is worth noting that child sexual exploitation is highly organised with sexual predators and pimps operating in war zones across the globe, especially those countries subject to mass genocide, or struck by natural disasters such as the Asian tsunami, or earthquakes. In the ensuing chaos many children are orphaned, lost, or homeless with no access to food, making them vulnerable to any help offered by "kindly" adults, or already recruited children. Evidence has also emerged that some sexual exploitation is perpetrated by aid workers and peacekeepers who exploit the very children they are tasked to protect, compounding their sense of powerlessness and betrayal (Csaky, 2008).

Adult prostitution

The hidden nature of adult prostitution makes it difficult to obtain any accurate statistical data on prevalence and incidence rates, although it is commonly accepted that there are around 80,000 male and female prostitutes in the UK (Home Office, 2004) working in a variety of settings ranging from street prostitution, to massage parlours, saunas, brothels or as escorts, or call girls or rent boys. While some prostitutes believe they entered prostitution of their own choosing, the majority, around 90%, of adult prostitutes were forced or coerced into prostitution (Kelly and Regan, 2000) often while they were still children. Research has shown that 70% of forced prostitutes were enticed before the age of 18, or below the age of consent (Home Office, 2004). According to Melrose, Barrett and Brodie (1999) around 50% of these had a history of child sexual abuse, and/or chaotic and violent family backgrounds. While some 25% entered prostitution through pre-existing drug use, the majority became addicted either through the entrapment process, or to manage the brutality of sex work by means of self-medication.

Very few forced prostitutes operate independently, with 80% to 95% controlled by pimps who hold them in captivity through verbal, physical and sexual abuse, or through controlling their access to drugs. Every area of their life is controlled by the pimp, and they are closely monitored and dominated to ensure that they do not escape. Those adult prostitutes held captive in brothels are not allowed to venture outside without a minder or chaperone to minimise the risk of escape.

Humiliation, and physical and sexual violence are commonly used by both clients and pimps to control the prostitute. In some extreme cases this has resulted in death, with over 90 women involved in prostitution being murdered either by their pimp or client (Kinnell, 2006; 2008). Alongside the constant threat of violence, there is the use of alcohol or drugs to further control prostitutes and ensure compliance. An addicted sex worker is more malleable and more dependent on their pimp and therefore more likely to submit.

HUMAN SEXUAL TRAFFICKING

The Palermo Protocol to the UN Convention against Transnational Crime 2000 (United Nations, 2004) aims to prevent, suppress and punish international and domestic trafficking in persons, especially women and children. The definition used by the Palermo Protocol states that trafficking in persons shall mean

> ...the recruitment, transportation, transfer, harbouring or receipt of a person, by means of the threat or use of force or other forms of coercion, of abduction, of fraud, of deception, of the abuse of power or a position of vulnerability or of giving or receiving of payments or benefits to achieve consent of a person having control over another person, for the purposes of exploitation. Exploitation shall include...the exploitation of the prostitution of the others or other forms of exploitation.

In the UK, the Sexual Offences Act 2003 makes it an offence to intentionally arrange or facilitate the movement of a person either across international borders or within the UK for the purposes of committing an offence by:

- paying for the sexual services of a child
- causing or inciting child prostitution or pornography
- controlling a child prostitute or child involved in pornography
- arranging or facilitating child prostitution or pornography.

Furthermore, trafficking within the UK for sexual exploitation is punishable with a custodial sentence of up to 14 years. The sheer scale of sexual trafficking and sexual exploitation has led some commentators to argue for a need to create a separate offence of sexual exploitation (Kelly and Regan, 2000).

International or cross-border trafficking for the purpose of sexual exploitation and sexual slavery is highly organised and frequently runs alongside drug and gun smuggling. Its scale is such that the UN Office on Drugs and Crime considers it to be the fastest-growing international organised crime, with estimates ranging between 700,000 to two million women and children trafficked across international borders every year with estimated annual profits of between $12 billion and $17 billion (cited in Moorhead, 2007). There have been several waves of human trafficking with the original wave emanating from Asia, then Africa, and currently Eastern Europe. Currently the UN estimates that there are some 127 "source countries" and 137 "destination countries" involved in human trafficking for sexual purposes. Typically, vulnerable children and young adults, in particular females from war-torn or politically or economically destabilised countries are either abducted, or lured with false promises of better lives in another country, into what is effectively sexual slavery. Ubiquitous to this process is the use of deception, coercion, physical and emotional violence, rape and forced drug or alcohol dependency to ensure total surrender and submission.

A number of ways of recruiting have been identified ranging from abduction to the use of "introducers" to dupe victims into accepting respectable and lucrative putative job opportunities in another country. Some of these "introducers" pose as respectable businessmen, "uncles" or "aunties", or as "boyfriends" in order to gain the victim's trust. In some cases parents are implicated in the transaction out of economic desperation. Increasingly, many "recruiters" are female, some of them former prostitutes or ex-trafficked women, who lull the victim into a false sense of security by acting as a "chaperone" on the initial part of the journey into sexual slavery. During the long, often circuitous journey across countless international borders, the girls are sold from owner to owner of diverse nationalities. A typical example is provided by Glenny (2008) in which a young girl is passed through the hands of Moldovans, Ukrainians, Russians, Egyptians and the Bedouin, before reaching the destination country of Israel.

As the girl is passed between "couriers", pimps and handlers to crime syndicates, each new owner will ruthlessly ensure submission though isolation, physical and sexual violence, and humiliation to "break them in" for their sexual enslavement. Those that are resistant are gang raped, or subjected to the most humiliating sexual activities until they finally submit. In some instances, the rapists are disguised as police officers to condition a fear of authority and minimise the risk of disclosing their ordeal to the police. In addition, non-compliance will be punished with beatings and threats of reprisals against their families. This is all designed to prepare the victims for their fate upon arrival in the destination country where they are sold into debt bondage to a brothel, or pimp.

Human trafficking is not confined to international borders but can also occur within national borders across counties or states, usually known as internal, or domestic, trafficking. Recruitment in internal trafficking commonly consists of attractive young males targeting vulnerable teenage girls who may be less attractive and suffer from low self-esteem. The boy will befriend and "love bomb" the girl with the express purpose of becoming her boyfriend. During this process the "boyfriend" will groom the girl by creating a divide between her and her family and friends, and by providing access to alcohol or drugs. Once the girl has fallen in love, the "boyfriend" will manipulate her to have sex with his friends, or extended family as proof of her love for him. Once she has complied with such requests she is considered to be "broken in" and is passed or sold on to a brothel, or into street prostitution. This process is often facilitated by deliberately inducing drug or alcohol dependency. Once the girl has been sold on, the "boyfriend" will go on to repeat the process with a new vulnerable young girl.

SEXUAL SLAVERY

A further form of sexual slavery is seen in cases where females are incarcerated and held captive, both physically and psychologically, sometimes for many years. The most recent example is seen in the case of Josef Fritzl who imprisoned his daughter Elisabeth at age 18 for over 24 years in the cellar under the family home, repeatedly raped her and fathered seven children, three of whom remained in the cellar with their mother, while three were brought up by Fritzl and his wife above ground, and one who died shortly after birth. Concurrent to Elisabeth Fritzl's imprisonment, Wolfgang Priklopil abducted a ten-year-old girl, Natascha Kampusch, and held her captive in a converted cellar underneath his house for over eight years, while in America Phillip Garrido abducted 11-year-old Jaycee Lee Dugard, held her captive for 18 years and fathered two daughters. What is not clear is whether Priklopil actually sexually abused Natascha as she has been reluctant to discuss this aspect of her captivity.

While these three cases involved actual physical imprisonment, there have been a number of cases where children have been held in thrall to their abusers and used as sexual slaves. Most recently a 56-year-old British man from Sheffield was discovered to have used his two daughters from the age of eight and ten as sexual slaves, raping them in three-day rotations throughout their adult lives, impregnating them a total of 19 times and fathering seven surviving children. This case shares similar dynamics to that of the 72-year-old Dundee man who used his three daughters from the age of 8 and 12 until their late twenties as sexual slaves and fathered two children. While such cases are considered to be rare, they may represent the tip of the iceberg of incest and sexual slavery perpetrated by some fathers. What links all the above cases is the level of deception, control and domination exercised by the perpetrators to conceal their activities for so many years.

A further form of sexual slavery is seen in cases of forced child marriage commonly seen in parts of India, Nepal, Bangladesh and sub-Saharan Africa, especially Mali, Niger, Nigeria and Uganda. Under the auspices of ancient traditions, parents consent for money, protection from sexual assault or pregnancy outside marriage, to sell their children from as young as eight into marriage. In the UK, according to the British Foreign and Commonwealth Office reports, there are around 250–300 cases a year of children as young as 13 sent to South Asia and forced to marry. In north Africa and the Middle East, forced marriage is used to coerce young girls into sexual abuse and forced labour, whereby the groom becomes the owner of the child bride, who may be raped by both the husband and other male relatives (Save The Children UK, 2008).

CHILD ABUSE IMAGES AS SEXUAL EXPLOITATION

A further danger for trafficked children is being coerced or sold into the production of child abuse images, or for online web streaming sex shows. It is worth noting that a considerable proportion of child abuse images are of south-east Asian and Oriental children, and more recently, what appear to be children from Eastern Europe. The lucrative nature of producing and distributing child abuse images and the links between crime and pornography make such sexual exploitation an easy target for national and international organised crime.

The addictive nature of viewing and collecting child abuse images, with some collections as large as 500,000 to a million images, means there is a constant demand for new children (Sanderson, 2004). This has led some paedophiles to target and groom children, often over the internet, to engage in sexually provocative poses that are then uploaded or put into a live stream. This co-opts the child into being not only a producer but also a distributor of their own child abuse image (Sanderson, 2004). Children are also traded by family members and paedophile rings for the express purpose of producing sexual images of them.

While many individuals who look at child abuse images claim that they merely "look" and would never engage in actual "hands on" child sexual abuse, they are nevertheless implicated in CSA by supporting the demand for such images (Sanderson, 2004). More importantly, the children used in the making of such images are left with the knowledge that such images will continue to exist in perpetuity for future paedophiles to access and misuse. Such a legacy makes it very difficult for the survivor to recover from CSA as there is a constant threat that those images are being accessed by someone and that they might be identified and confronted with their abuse. In some cases such images can be used to threaten the child and later adult for the purposes of blackmail or to ensure silence and reduce the risk of disclosure.

PREVALENCE OF SEXUAL EXPLOITATION

Prevalence rates of sexual exploitation are difficult to quantify given the hidden nature of such abuse, much of which is conducted behind closed doors on private premises such as massage parlours, sauna, brothels or private homes rather than on the streets. Research in 2002 collating data from 111 areas of Child Protection Committee districts in the UK found that an average of 19 girls and 3 boys in each area were subject to sexual exploitation (Department for Children, Schools and Families, 2008). Research by the children's charity Barnardo's reported that there were 507 separate cases of child sexual exploitation, with cases identified in every borough (Harper and Scott, 2005), while research by the Coalition for the Removal of Pimping (CROP) in their report *Parents, Children and Pimps: Families Speak Out About Sexual Exploitation* (2005) found that 107 families between August 2002 and June 2005 had been affected by sexual exploitation, in most areas in the county.

In the absence of robust statistics, the Home Office (2004) estimate that there are around 5000 child prostitutes working in the UK either as street prostitutes, in massage parlours or saunas, or in brothels, with a ratio of four females to each male.

It is further estimated that there are around 80,000 adult prostitutes, 70% of whom are recruited before age 18, with an average entry age of 15 (Home Office, 2004, Kinnell, 2008). Alongside this, most sex workers have a history of physical abuse (85%), 45% a history of CSA, while 70% have spent time in care, and between 80% and 85% of street prostitutes have a history of drug misuse, in particular heroin and/or crack cocaine.

According to the charity Save the Children UK (2008) at any one time 1.8 million children are being sexually exploited across the world and forced into prostitution, pornography or sex tourism, with an estimated 1.2 million children trafficked each year. In the case of cross-border trafficked women accessing services in seven European countries, the majority (92%) have been found to have been enslaved into sex work and 4% into domestic labour, with 80% exploited for at least one month, and 20% for over one year. Most of these women had a pre-existing vulnerability with 50% reporting a history of physical abuse, 32% sexual abuse and 22% reporting both. Most were sexually abused before the age of 15 by either a father or stepfather, with a quarter reporting abuse by more than one perpetrator.

WHO IS AT RISK OF SEXUAL EXPLOITATION?

While all children are potentially at risk of sexual exploitation, research data indicates that the main risk factors for sexual exploitation are a history of physical and/or sexual violence in childhood, abandonment and neglect as well as domestic abuse. Vulnerability to sexual exploitation is also increased in those children who are placed in care, especially in children's homes or institutions, and those children who run away from home and are homeless. These are often the easiest to entice and coerce, as they are most vulnerable and will arouse the least suspicion. There is also considerable evidence that problematic drug and alcohol misuse is a major risk factor in sexual exploitation, as is financial debt (Home Office, 2004).

Children with poor educational attainment, a history of truancy, disrupted schooling or educational exclusion, and those with a range of disabilities, including learning disabilities, are also at significant risk from sexual exploitation. Such children also often suffer from low self-esteem, isolation and loneliness which make them more susceptible to the attention of sexual predators. Other risk factors include social exclusion, poverty and deprivation, prevalence of informal economies, familial and community offending patterns, risky sexual behaviour, contact with vulnerable peers, experience of violence, intimidation and fear, contact with known perpetrators, congregating in places of concern and prevalence of undiagnosed mental health problems.

While such children are most at risk, sexual exploitation can also occur in less obviously vulnerable children, and they can become vulnerable as a result of the sexual exploitation. Such children may be groomed both on and offline, or may become involved with a boyfriend with a drug habit, and sell sex in order to fund drug use. Often the child or young adult is not aware that they are being groomed for the purposes of sexual exploitation by their "friend" or "boyfriend", and are unaware of the potent use of emotional manipulation, power and control used to isolate the victim from family to increase dependency on the exploiter.

Cultural practices may also play a significant role in ritual sexual exploitation as seen in India and Ghana through religious traditions such as *devadasi* and *trokosi* in which children are offered to priests, then confined and controlled in the temple for further sexual exploitation (Nair, 2004; Bales, 2004).

PERPETRATORS OF SEXUAL EXPLOITATION

Sexual exploiters target girls and young women, as well as boys and young men, from all backgrounds and ethnic groups including UK nationals and migrant children. As sexual exploitation is predicated on an imbalance of power within the relationship, the perpetrator always has some sort of power over the victim which increases as the exploitative relationship develops. This power imbalance is combined with the use of coercion, deception, isolation, intimidation and threats of reprisal to inculcate fear and submission. Commonly, males sexually exploit girls, whereas males and females exploit boys and young men. While the majority of sexual exploiters are male, increasingly females are being used during the initial enticement to minimise suspicion. Most sexual exploiters are non-relatives, but may be known to the victim or consist of someone they have recently met. In some cases the exploiter may be a parent, carer, or other relative who offers the child to a sexual exploiter or uses the child within organised familial abuse, or closed community abuse. This usually involves producing and distributing child abuse images, national and international trafficking, or selling the child into sexual slavery to organised crime syndicates. Increased access to technology opens up more opportunities for strangers to sexually exploit especially online.

Due to the lucrative nature of sexual exploitation, whereby the exploiter can earn up to £7000 per week per sex worker (Home Office, 2004), many perpetrators are part of, or affiliated with, organised crime syndicates which use highly sophisticated tactics. Procurers commonly target areas where children and young people congregate without adult supervision such as shopping centres, cafes, takeaways, pubs, sports centres, cinemas, bus or train stations, local parks, playgrounds, taxi ranks, or internet sites. In some cases they use younger men or boys, or females, to build initial relationships and introduce children to others in the perpetrator network. Some procurers focus on children in care and loiter near children's homes in order to "befriend" specific children, or haunt crack houses frequented by vulnerable children. Once recruited, the victims may be pressurised to entice friends and peers to accompany them to locations where they are raped and coerced into sex work. Many of those involved in sexual exploitation are affiliated with organised crime syndicates that are primarily involved in drug and gun trafficking and thereby see the child or adult merely as a commodity to exploit. If they are unable to purchase or entice victims they may resort to abduction especially those most vulnerable and least likely to arouse suspicion.

THE NATURE AND DYNAMICS OF SEXUAL EXPLOITATION

Sexual exploitation is predicated on coercion, deception, enticement and the use of violence, predominantly sexual, physical or psychological. The initial enticement is often highly seductive and potent making it hard to resist, and is designed to lull the victim into a false sense of security. The aim of deception and enticement is to occlude betrayal, abuse and exploitation. Sexual violence such as rape, gang rape and degrading sexual acts are commonly used to "break in" and force the victim to submit, and ensure total control. In trafficked children and women 90% of the violence is sexual, and 76% physical, with 95% of women subjected to both. Physical violence commonly consists of severe, debilitating beatings, whippings, cigarette burns, and torture tactics such as immersing the head in water or holding a gun to the head. Threats are also a common control tactic with 89% of trafficked women reporting being threatened, and 36% reporting that their families are threatened. Such threats are palpable on a daily basis and can represent a real reason not to attempt escape. Escape is further hindered through constant monitoring and supervision by minders, with 80% reporting that they are never out of sight of a minder, and only 10% reporting that they were seldom free from supervision (Zimmerman *et al.*, 2006).

Systematic rape and violence further induces numbness, apathy and resignation in the victim leaving them lifeless and drained of all vitality, initiative and self-agency and preventing them from escaping. Once the victim has been "broken in", lost their freshness and virginity, they become lifeless and lose their value. This heralds the advent of a downward spiral into increasingly degrading sex work including street prostitution.

In addition, enslaved women have no control over who does what to their bodies, and when unable to seek help for physical injuries, pain or infection, they have no choice but to surrender to the sheer force of the debilitating effects of their abuse. Once compliance has been enforced, the victim is further controlled though the continued use of violence, humiliation or drugs and alcohol. Initial enticement is facilitated through deception and grooming processes to gain trust and lure the victim into a false sense of security.

Drugs and alcohol also play a crucial role throughout sexual exploitation, from the enticement stage through to managing the impact of sex work. Drugs or alcohol are used as an entry into sexual exploitation either to lower resistance, lower inhibitions or to elicit substance dependency. Once dependency is created, the sex worker becomes more malleable and easier to control through withholding or providing access to drugs in a punishment/reward cycle which reinforces dependency and traumatic bonding. Furthermore, many sex workers become dependent on drugs or alcohol as a form of self-medication to block out the brutality of sexual exploitation and the constant threat of sexual and physical violence.

Clinicians working with survivors of sexual exploitation need to be mindful of the function and dynamics associated with substance misuse and contextualise it as part of the abuse and exploitation. This is critical in provision of services as many agencies and counsellors feel unable to work with survivors who are still self-medicating. Yet survivors of sexual exploitation may find it difficult to access drug and alcohol services due to shame and stigmatisation. Clinicians may need to be more flexible in providing supportive therapy within a well-bounded contract which aims to reduce substance harm within a safe secure therapeutic environment in which to explore alternatives to affect regulation and promote internal safety.

Systematic and repetitive rape and violence not only elicits submission and surrender, but also induces shame, making it harder for the survivor to report their assaults and seek help if they do escape. This is especially the case in trafficked women who may be reluctant to return to their country for fear of bringing shame and dishonour onto their families. The shame, "loss of honour" and sense of being "damaged goods" as a result of rape and sexual exploitation will promote the need for withdrawal from others and reinforce isolation and alienation. In addition, unsafe immigration status, fear of deportation and fear of punishment can prevent reporting of the sexual exploitation, forcing victims to go underground where they may be vulnerable to further exploitation.

In the case of internal trafficking where the enticement is perpetrated by a putative "boyfriend" the victim may not be able see their partner as an abuser but may see the relationship as a voluntary, consensual one. This prevents them from identifying their experience as sexual exploitation which can prevent them from seeking help. This is particularly the case for those children who have been neglected, abandoned or in care, who tend to confuse or conflate sexual desire with genuine love and care.

THE IMPACT OF SEXUAL EXPLOITATION

The ubiquitous brutality and torture in sexual exploitation often conducted and repeated over may months or years leads to a range of neurological and psychobiological changes including dissociation and disruptions to memory. These are further exacerbated by long-term alcohol or drug use as self-medication. Repetitive dissociation necessary to manage the daily sexual and physical assault from either clients or their owner, results in the survivor presenting as vague, disoriented, tentative and unclear. The repeated activation of neurobiological changes leads to impairment in cognitive functioning, especially disruption to memory processing. According to Zimmerman *et al.* (2006), up to 63% of trafficked women report significant memory impairment that prevents them from providing a coherent and cohesive narrative of their experiences, or recalling details. This lack of coherent memory makes survivors reluctant to report their sexual exploitation to the police or authorities, and impedes accessing services such as counselling as they fear not being believed in the absence of being able to give a clear account of numerous experiences of rapes and sexual exploitation.

Due to repeated traumatisation the survivor may develop a range of physiological and psychological problems including PTSD. Repeated trauma in which there is no escape prevents the individual from regulating basic biological and safety alarm mechanisms which can lead to dichotomous physical and emotional responses to negative stimuli in which they are either numb or overwhelmed with intense emotional reactions. The inability to escape and accompanying helplessness exacerbates disorganisation of cognitive processes, and disables the instinctive ability to respond appropriately to danger resulting in hypervigilance, hyperarousal, and elevated startle response in which hypersensitivity becomes the body's only defence.

Zimmerman *et al.* (2006) also found high levels of poor physical health in trafficked women with 81% suffering from headaches, 71% reporting dizzy spells, 60–70% experiencing various sexual and reproductive health problems such as pelvic pain, 69% suffering back pain, while 82% present with chronic fatigue. In addition there may be long-term sexual and reproductive health problems as a result of untreated sexually transmitted infections, unwanted pregnancies and repeated terminations. When combined with mental health problems it may be necessary to conduct a full physical and psychiatric assessment to ensure that all the survivor's trauma symptoms are adequately addressed.

Many survivors of sexual exploitation will encounter difficulties in forming relationships with others due to their experience of betrayal leading to impaired trust, lack of confidence, and lowered self-esteem. This may include social withdrawal and isolation from their families and friends due to a profound sense of shame. Sexual exploitation can also impact on the survivor's family in eroding family cohesion and eliciting guilt for not protecting the child or young adult from being groomed and not being able to prevent the subsequent sexual exploitation. Family members may also be subjected to verbal and physical aggression from the exploited child or adult, and threats of violence from the perpetrator. This can put considerable strain on family relationships, which can render siblings vulnerable to being bullied, groomed and exploited. Siblings may consequently feel alienated, powerless and helpless as the instability in the family takes its toll and fears for the exploited sibling increases.

LONG-TERM EFFECTS

The multiplicity of symptoms seen in survivors of sexual exploitation and the cumulative effects of systematic sexual, physical and psychological abuse resemble those seen in torture victims, even after escape and when in a place of safety. Survivors may suffer from a range of untreated injuries as result of systematic physical and sexual violence which impede on physical well-being. In addition, PTS symptoms reduce responsiveness resulting in survivors presenting as apathetic, numb and disoriented. They may also appear hostile and hypersensitive, and highly resistant to any offers of help. Clinicians must understand this as a fear response due to their multiple betrayals and real concern for themselves and family members who may face reprisals.

Alongside fear, survivors will be suffused with anxiety, intrusive memories, flashbacks and recurring nightmares. Fragmented memories lead to a lack of coherent narrative about their experiences and lack of a cohesive sense of self. Zimmerman *et al.* (2006) found that 95% of sexually trafficked women in their study suffered depression, with 38% experiencing suicidal ideation. Alcohol and drug dependency is one of the major long-term effects of sexual exploitation. Initially used to self-medicate, or as an entry into prostitution, prolonged misuse impacts significantly on physical and mental well-being. Clinicians will need to address the effects of substance misuse and ensure that these are addressed alongside the therapeutic work and that appropriate alcohol and drug services are accessed, including residential detoxification and rehabilitation.

Clinicians must guard against making assumptions, especially that sexually exploited survivors will eschew their sexuality or present as asexual, puritanical or embrace celibacy. There is evidence that sexually exploited survivors often engage in greater sexual risk taking (Zimmerman *et al.*, 2006), and display overtly sexual behaviour as a result of their objectification. It is also a way to seek validation to compensate for low self-esteem, to obtain acceptance, and as a way of maintaining a sense of control. All of these are underpinned by a distorted sense of self as primarily a sexual commodity and conditioned belief that their only value is sexual, and that that is what people expect. As a result they are only able to relate to others in a sexual way. This may manifest in the therapeutic setting, and must be understood as part of the conditioning process of systematic sexual abuse.

Years of sexual exploitation and being held captive and isolated from the world will have considerable effects on psychosocial functioning. Many trafficked women and sex workers are deprived of everyday social interaction and will find social encounters awkward and embarrassing. This is compounded by fear of being identified and stigmatised as a sex worker, and a constant fear of meeting an ex-client as they negotiate their way around the local community. Limited language skills other than those required for sexual interactions may create further barriers of social discourse. Guilt around being forced to entice and entrap others into sexual exploiting will further exacerbate a deep sense of shame. The dehumanisation and betrayal of trust inherent in sexual exploitation will make it hard to reconnect to others. As a result survivors may avoid forming close, intimate relationships. The shame surrounding sex work may make it hard to engage in personal relationships for fear of rejection. This may be exacerbated by fears and guilt around damaged reproductive health, any terminations, ability to have children, and capacity for parenting all of which may prevent the survivor from connecting to others.

Box 9.2 Core clinical symptoms associated with sexual exploitation

- Sexual and reproductive health risks – STIs, HIV, pregnancy, multiple terminations
- Physical injuries from repeated physical and sexual violence left untreated
- Poor physical health
- Drug and alcohol dependency
- Somatic problems – hypersensitivity, headaches, recurring nightmares, sleep disturbances
- Anxiety
- Depression
- PTSD symptoms
- Neurobiological effects – dissociation, compartmentalisation, derealisation, depersonalisation
- Impaired cognitive functioning especially fragmented memories
- Fragmented sense of self (no coherent self-narrative)
- Shame
- Stigmatisation and isolation from social world
- Sexual risk taking, compromised sexuality
- Suicidal ideation, and suicide attempts
- Guilt about having procured or enticed others into sexual exploitation
- Retraumatisation by police, immigration interrogation
- Fear of detention or deportation, or being exposed as an illegal immigrant
- Fear of close, intimate relationships

Cross-border trafficked women will fear returning to their home countries because of shame and stigma, and as a result will feel disenfranchised. This will evoke a further sense of alienation and isolation and damage their sense of safety. If they fear deportation they may enter the world of illegal immigrants making them susceptible to further abuse and exploitation. Sexually exploited children will also have fears about returning to their families and friends and may find it hard to re-enter the world. This is often compounded by years of missed schooling which makes it more difficult to find employment.

WORKING WITH SURVIVORS OF SEXUAL EXPLOITATION

As throughout the sexual exploitation the survivor will have had no control over her body or freedom of movement, the primary goal of working with survivors of sexual exploitation is to restore control and ensure that she knows that she is a free agent, has the right to make choices, and is permitted to say "No" as well as "Yes". To enhance safety and control it is critical to reduce unpredictability by explaining and informing the survivor about the process of counselling, boundaries and expectations. Most importantly the counsellor must be clear about confidentiality as the survivor may fear information being made available to authorities or the sexual exploiter.

From the outset, counsellors need to assess the survivor's level of physical pain, and general sexual and reproductive health. In the case of physical pain and health concerns it will be crucial to ensure that the survivor has access to medical attention and pain medication. This may be as a result of chronic pain associated with tissue or organ damage incurred during the sexual exploitation, or as a result of withdrawal symptoms from drug or alcohol dependency. If the survivor is highly anxious or depressed it may be necessary to consider medication to stabilise any negative effects.

It is paramount that counsellors avoid reinforcing negative self-beliefs such as being naïve or gullible to have been enticed into sexual exploitation. Counsellors must be clear in conveying the power of sexual exploiters and the range of potent strategies that they use to entrap victims. To counteract dehumanisation and restore faith in humanity it is imperative to communicate and check that the survivor knows that the clinician is genuinely interested in her, and cares for her well-being. To achieve this, counsellors must be human and ensure that basic human needs are met throughout the therapeutic encounter. Concern for basic physiological needs such as pain relief, thirst, hunger, temperature and energy level must be combined with identifying what the survivor's needs are and how these can be satisfied to restore well-being. It is helpful to allow the survivor to control the pace and content of sessions by asking about any urgent or immediate concerns and what she would like to discuss, rather than making assumptions or asking lots of questions. The goal is to encourage exploration of feelings associated with the experience rather than to enquire about what she did. For example it is more helpful to ask "How were you hurt?" than "How did you get here?" or "Did you feel free to go where you wanted?" rather than "Did you ever try to escape?"

Clinicians also need to identify pre-existing risk factors and vulnerabilities such as a history of childhood physical or sexual abuse, abandonment, experience of being in care, extreme poverty or deprivation, or any other trauma such as war, natural disasters, war or genocide. These vulnerability factors will need to be addressed alongside symptoms specifically associated with the sexual exploitation, physical and sexual brutality, and substance misuse. Counsellors will also need to assess the risk of retraumatisation due to criminal proceedings, or deportation

Box 9.3 Core therapeutic goals

- Reinstate control to the survivor and establish trust
- Ensure safety – internal and external
- Psychoeducation to normalise responses
- Physical, sexual and reproductive health problems and medical problems assessed and addressed
- Harm minimisation and reduction of drug or alcohol dependency, access to detoxification and rehabilitation services
- Reduction of PTSD symptoms
- Integration of fragmented memories into a coherent narrative
- Reduction in fear and anxieties
- Multi-agency liaison
- Restoration of self-esteem
- Reconnection to self, others and the world
- Assess and explore pre-existing risk factors with a view to integrating these
- Work through fears around deportation or living as an illegal immigrant
- Mourn the myriad losses

proceedings as a result of sexual exploitation or sexual trafficking. Counsellors must be mindful of the consequences of exiting sexual exploitation and assess external safety factors such as fear of reprisals if deported, or being ostracised by the family or community. Those survivors who have gone underground in order to remain in the UK as an illegal immigrant will live in constant fear of exposure and this may increase their vulnerability to further exploitation. The immediate concerns will be unique to each survivor and must be addressed accordingly.

Survivors of sexual exploitation will have encountered a number of losses through their experience which need to be mourned. These cluster around loss of safety during their captivity, loss of freedom, loss of trust in others, loss of childhood and access to schooling, loss of family and friends. In the case of those who were trafficked, loss of their country and cultural traditions become particularly acute and to some extent will mirror the losses associated with refugees. This is aptly described by Elizabeth Colson (1991) in her unpublished paper is "Coping in adversity", which highlights the reality of working with refugees:

> People who are expelled from their country have to cope with the violation of their homelands; grief for those who died *en-route* or on arrival; fear of continuing harassment from those who oppressed them, and fear of the unknown. They often find that familiar coping techniques no longer work, so have to develop new modes of behaviour – while coping with rage, and loss of trust in human beings. Sometimes they begin to see themselves as inhabitants of an immoral universe, where it is pointless to expect justice or decent treatment, except perhaps from the closest kin – and even these may fail in crisis. Cynicism and opportunism are not unlikely outcomes.

Thus counsellors need to work with survivors in healing a fragmented and haunted inner world and help rebuild a shattered and frightening social world in which they are no longer able to trust others and fear connection. This work can only be achieved if clinicians take a holistic and comprehensive view of the complex issues associated with sexual exploitation and adopt innovative and creative solutions to these, including working in a multidisciplinary context. Pivotal to this is to create a safe and secure base through the therapeutic relationship in which the brutality of sexual exploitation can be explored and the survivor can be empowered to recover from the myriad violations and losses. With this the survivor will be able to reconnect to self, others and the world free from the trauma of sexual exploitation.

THERAPEUTIC CHALLENGES

The range of complex effects of sexual exploitation necessitates flexibility on the part of the counsellors and a thorough understanding of the problems survivors might face. Non-attendance needs to be contextualised rather than seen as resistance, as does the struggle to manage alcohol and drug dependency. While some clinicians feel unable to work with clients who are still substance dependent, this can delay the healing process. Counsellors may consider working alongside drug and alcohol services and agree to engage in therapeutic work providing the survivor does not attend sessions while intoxicated.

Counsellors also need to be culturally sensitive and truly understand cultural differences in attitudes, especially around the centrality of loss of honour and shame, rather than dismissing these as cognitive distortions or irrational fears. Practitioners also need to challenge their assumptions of how survivors of sexual exploitation ought to present. Many survivors behave in a counter-intuitive way in not being distraught or relieved to have escaped their exploitation, and present as numb, distanced or shut down. In many cases, they may be so suffused with fears and anxieties about the future that the traumatic experiences of the past are overshadowed. It is important to work with the survivor's immediate concerns rather than adopt a linear or prescribed approach. Counsellors also need to contextualise any risky behaviour, such as risky sexual encounters or alcohol or drug misuse rather than appear judgmental.

There are a number of factors that become a significant barrier to talking about sexual exploitation, not least the shame of enslavement into sex work and the range of humiliating sexual acts survivors are forced to perform. Many survivors feel guilty for allowing themselves to be enticed and fear that they will be perceived as being complicit in their enslavement which creates a further barrier to disclosure. In addition, survivors may be reluctant to talk about their experiences due to memory impairment, lack of coherent narrative, poor recall for the specific details or sequence of events and fear of not being believed. In addition, mistrust of authority, including the clinician, may impede exploration of experiences, as will fear of retaliation for having escaped. Some survivors will feel guilt for having participated in illegal or criminal activities such as crossing borders, taking money for sex work, taking drugs or not fighting hard enough to escape. Other survivors may also wish to forget their period of enslavement and move on from their traumatisation by not thinking about or processing it as they genuinely believe that this will help them to move on. Whatever the reason for the reluctance to talk, counsellors must not categorise this as evasive or resistance to engage, but understand the reasons for this and be patient and sensitive in pacing the work.

In the case of trafficked survivors with limited language skills counsellors may need to avail themselves of an interpreter. In such instances they need to obtain evidence of their credentials, their integrity, and assurance of confidentiality. It has been known that some interpreters have translated inaccurately, have come from the same village or region as the trafficked woman, or been in the pay of sexual exploiters and informed on her. If an interpreter is necessary the survivor must be permitted to choose the gender of the interpreter and given an opportunity to assess how safe they feel in their presence. Alongside this, if possible the survivor also needs to be given a choice of gender of counsellor in a culturally sensitive way. This is particularly the case for women from cultures that have strict sanctions around male and female interaction. Some survivors of sexual exploitation may initially prefer a female counsellor, but may wish to see a male counsellor towards the end of their recovery to experience that males can be trusted and do not relate to her in a sexual manner.

A final therapeutic challenge is the pervasive uncertainty when working with survivors of sexual exploitation and the counsellor's ability to tolerate this. Common areas of uncertainty are restoring coherent memories, managing the trauma and being able to integrate it, ability to recover from substance abuse, the consequences of deportation or living as an illegal immigrant and the constant fear of being found out, finding employment outside the sex industry, and being able to reintegrate into their social world. Counsellors must also be mindful of their risk of vicarious traumatisation when working with survivors of sexual exploitation, and ensure that they look after their own physical and mental well-being (see Chapter 14) to ensure that they continue to provide a secure base in which to explore the survivor's experiences and enable them to reconnect to others and form healthy relationships free from the terror and shame of sexual exploitation.

Case vignette: Anya

Anya had been sexually abused by her stepfather since the she was eight years old. She was lonely, socially isolated, and suffered from excruciatingly low self-esteem. When Anya was 14 she met an older, very good-looking young man who showered her with attention and affection. Before too long they began a romantic relationship and Anya felt that she would finally find some happiness in her life. A few months into the relationship, Anya's boyfriend suggested that they run away together so that she would never have to suffer her stepfather's unwanted sexual assaults. Anya readily agreed and they made plans to move to a big city in the Midlands. As they did not have enough money to rent their own flat, they planned initially to stay with the boyfriend's relatives.

Once settled into their new home, Anya began to relax and enjoy spending time with her boyfriend, drinking and smoking cannabis. Unfortunately as neither of them were working they were unable to pay rent to the relative, who insisted that they contribute to their keep. Anya's boyfriend suggested that one way to solve this would be for Anya to sleep with his relative so that they would not be thrown out. Anya readily agreed as she did not want to go back to her stepfather.

Sleeping with her boyfriend's relative became a regular occurrence but put a strain on Anya's relationship with her boyfriend who became less interested in her. Anya tried everything to regain his affection, including sleeping with some of his other relatives. One night, several relatives turned up at the house and Anya was gang raped. Unbeknownst to Anya she was being groomed and lured into prostitution. Once broken in by the relatives and the gang rape she was sold into a local brothel where she was forced to service up to 20 clients per day. To manage the repeated sexual assaults Anya sought refuge in alcohol and increasingly harder drugs, which the brothel owner would provide instead of payment. When Anya contracted a serious STI which was highly resistant to treatment and continually flared up she was sold on to a pimp and forced into street prostitution. This led to an increase in drug use with a full-blown addiction to crack cocaine. Meanwhile Anya's boyfriend returned to their home town to start the grooming process all over again with another vulnerable young girl.

After several years of street prostitution, Anya was encouraged by an outreach worker to enter a drug rehabilitation programme. After several relapses, Anya finally managed to relinquish her addiction to crack cocaine and entered therapy. Initially Anya found it hard to engage in the therapeutic process as she found it difficult to trust anyone. Her sense of shame was palpable as was her sense of complicity in her sexual exploitation as she felt that she was consensual in agreeing to her boyfriend's requests. It was not until she could acknowledge how she had been ensnared and entrapped into sexual exploitation that she could find compassion for herself. This allowed her to grieve for the child whose vulnerability had been exploited initially by her stepfather and then her so-called boyfriend. The therapeutic process was not linear as issues of drug addiction and the sexual abuse by her stepfather alternated with working on the betrayal of her boyfriend and the degrading nature of the sex acts she was forced to perform.

Towards the end of therapy Anya decided to resume her interrupted schooling by taking an access course with the hope of entering a degree programme to read criminology. She hopes this will enable her to help vulnerable children and young adults avoid being entrapped into sexual exploitation.

SUMMARY

- The range of sexual exploitation includes child and adult prostitution, producing and distributing child abuse images, and human trafficking, both national (internal) and international.
- While all children and young adults are at risk, the most vulnerable to sexual exploitation are females, those with a history of childhood abuse, those who are or have been in care and who have been socially excluded, and those with learning disabilities. In terms of human trafficking the most at risk are also those from economically or politically destabilised countries, or those that are war torn or subjected to mass genocide.
- Sexual exploitation and human sex trafficking are highly lucrative and are often part of large organised crime syndicates who also profit from trafficking drugs and guns. Although individuals such as family members or relatives may sexually exploit children, they are often affiliated to some degree with the organised sex industry. Recruiters, handlers and chaperones are the individuals who establish the initial contact in order to sell them on to owners of massage parlours, saunas, brothels or pimps.
- Physical and sexual violence such as systematic rape is ubiquitous to sexual exploitation as is emotional and psychological coercion, the use of grooming and drugs and alcohol misuse.
- The impact of sexual exploitation is sexual enslavement, dehumanisation, objectification, social isolation and a variety of psychobiological effects such as PTSD and impaired physical, and sexual and reproductive health.
- The long-term effects of the brutality of sexual exploitation is compromised physical and psychological health including drug and alcohol dependency, memory impairment and suicidal ideation and attempts. There is also the danger of being forced to procure and entice others into sex work.
- When working with survivors of sexual exploitation it is critical to assess pre-existing risk factors such as a history of abuse, identify those associated with sexual exploitation and to be mindful of the potential for retraumatisation by criminal proceedings, and the consequences of deportation, the risks of returning home, or living as an illegal immigrant.
- The pervasive and pernicious uncertainty in working with survivors of sexual exploitation can be overwhelming and impact on the well-being of the counsellor or clinician rendering them helpless and vulnerable to vicarious traumatisation. Counsellors need to make sure that they take care of

themselves in order to provide a secure base to explore the range of effects and enable the survivor to begin to trust again and return to a life outside of the systematic brutalisation of sexual exploitation.

SUGGESTED READING

Barrett, D. with Barret, E. and Mullenger, N. (2000) (eds) *Youth Prostitution in the New Europe: The Growth of Sex Work.* Lyme Regis: Russell House Publishing.

Child Exploitation and Online Protection (CEOP) Centre (2007) *A Scoping Project on Child Trafficking in the UK.* London: Child Exploitation and Online Protection Centre.

Coalition for the Removal of Pimping (CROP) (2005) *Parents, Children and Pimps: Families Speak Out About Sexual Exploitation.* Leeds: Coalition for the Removal of Pimping.

Csaky, C. (2008) *No One to Turn To: The Under Reporting of Child Sexual Exploitation and Abuse by Aid Workers and Peace Keepers.* London: Save the Children UK.

Hester, M. and Westmarland, N. (2004) *Tackling Street Prostitution: A Holistic Approach.* London: Home Office.

Home Office (2004) *Paying the Price: A Consultation Paper on Prostitution.* London: Home Office.

Kelly, L. and Regan, L. (2000) *Stopping Traffic: Exploring the Extent of, and Responses to, Trafficking of Women for Sexual Exploitation in the UK.* London: Home Office.

Kinnell, H. (2008) *Violence and Sex Work in Britain.* Cullompton, Devon: Willan Publishing.

Melrose, M., Barrett, D. and Brodie, I. (1999) *One Way Street.* London: The Children's Society.

Save the Children UK (2008) *The Small Hands of Slavery: Modern Day Child Slavery: A Report by Save the Children UK.* London: Save the Children UK.

Van de Glind, H. and Kooijman, J. (2008) 'Modern-day child slavery.' *Children and Society 22,* 3, 150–166.

Zimmerman, C., Hossain, M., Yun, K., Roche, B., Morison, L. and Watts, C. (2006) 'Stolen smiles: the physical and psychological health consequences of women and adolescents trafficked in Europe.' Presentation on the health consequences among women who have been trafficked and the implications for services and policy. London School of Hygiene and Tropical Medicine. (Full report available at www.lshtm.ac.uk/genderviolence.)

CHAPTER 10

DOMESTIC ABUSE AS INTERPERSONAL TRAUMA

To fully understand domestic abuse (DA) as interpersonal trauma practitioners need to be aware of the psychobiological impact of repeated exposure to coercive control and terror, and how to facilitate recovery from DA within a secure, supportive therapeutic relationship. It is critical that mental health professionals routinely screen for DA, are cognisant of the complex relationship between DA and trauma symptoms, and implement appropriate therapeutic interventions without pathologising survivors. Counsellors must guard against medicalising or stigmatising survivors by ensuring that they contextualise the psychobiological effects of DA as symptoms of abuse and normal responses to trauma, rather than evidence of personality disturbance. This is critical in order to avoid victim blaming or replicating the abuse experience by labelling survivors as mentally unstable, reinforcing the abuser's accusations that the survivor is "crazy", and therefore culpable in the DA.

When working with survivors of DA counsellors must ensure that they do not collude with abuse dynamics in allowing their perceptions of the survivor to be corrupted or distorted, and be mindful of the wider social, political and economic factors that underpin and support DA. To this effect, counsellors need to be aware of how socially constructed meaning around gender, race, power and control, domination and submission, and the hierarchical structure of families shape and define personal relationships.

The focus of the therapeutic work needs to be on creating a secure base in which the survivor can restore safety, control and self-agency and enabling the survivor to make informed choices in their relationships and inoculating them against further abuse. It is crucial that therapeutic interventions are tailored to each individual's needs, ranging from supportive counselling during, or when leaving, an abusive relationship, to in-depth trauma therapy. The emphasis needs to be on exploring all available options in how to work through the impact of DA, including access to a range of services, in order to offer a holistic approach, and enabling survivors to make informed choices about which services to access. Inviting survivors to take control of their recovery is often the first step in rebuilding autonomy and self-efficacy to make personally meaningful choices.

This chapter looks at the range of DA experiences, who is most at risk and who the perpetrators are. In order to understand the impact of DA counsellors need to have good understanding of the nature and complex dynamics inherent in DA including the cycle of abuse and traumatic bonding. Exploring these will enable counsellors to have a greater awareness of the obstacles to leaving abusive relationships and the myriad losses associated with DA. Counsellors will also need to ensure that they provide the optimal support needed by the survivor, rather than their own agenda, and facilitate appropriate safety planning. The emphasis is on providing a secure therapeutic base in which the survivor can make sense of the DA, create a coherent narrative out of chaos, and begin the painstaking work of rebuilding a sense of self and re-establishing trust in self, others and the world.

DEFINITION OF DOMESTIC ABUSE

There is no universally agreed definition of DA and considerable variation in terminology. Historically the term "domestic violence" has been the preferred nomenclature and one that is still used by statutory and non-statutory organisations and agencies involved in DA. The current definition of domestic violence employed by the Home Office (2006) is "any incident of threatening behaviour, violence or abuse (psychological, physical, sexual, financial or emotional) between adults who are or have been intimate partners or family members, regardless of gender or sexuality." While this definition acknowledges the range of DA behaviour it does not reflect the use of coercive control in DA and the pattern of abusive or controlling behaviour perpetrated over time. Practitioners need to be mindful that DA rarely starts with an act of violence or physical attack, but is characterised by controlling behaviour that escalates over time, and reflects the perpetrator's need for dominance and the survivor's submission.

The Women's Aid Federation (2005) also use the term "domestic violence" and define domestic violence as

> … a pattern of controlling behaviour against an intimate partner or ex-partner, that includes but is not limited to physical assaults, sexual assaults, emotional abuse, isolation, economic abuse, threats, stalking and intimidation. Although only some forms of domestic violence are illegal and attract criminal sanctions (physical and sexual assault, stalking, threats to kill), other forms of violence can also have very serious and lasting effects on a person's sense of self, well-being and autonomy. Violent and abusive behaviour is used in an effort to control the partner based on the perpetrator's sense of entitlement. This behaviour may be directed at others – especially children – with the intention of controlling the intimate partner. Social and institutional power structures support some groups using abuse and violence in order to control other groups in our society e.g. institutional racism, heterosexist, and parents' violence to children. The unequal power relations between men and women account for the fact that the vast majority of domestic violence is perpetrated by men against women rather than vice versa.

The British Medical Association (2007) and Sanderson (2008), in incorporating these definitions, use the term "domestic abuse", and go on to highlight that DA can be passive or active and includes covert expressions of anger such as emotional neglect and failure to protect, as well as overt expressions of anger such as physical assault and rape.

SPECTRUM OF DOMESTIC ABUSE

To fully understand the nature of DA it is helpful to be aware of the spectrum of DA. As can be seen from the above definitions, it is generally accepted that DA includes physical, psychological, sexual and emotional abuse as well as neglect, economic or financial abuse, spiritual abuse and stalking, or cyberstalking. In cultural groups that practise female genital mutilation, forced marriage and honour killing as a form of power and control over females, these would also be subsumed under the spectrum of DA.

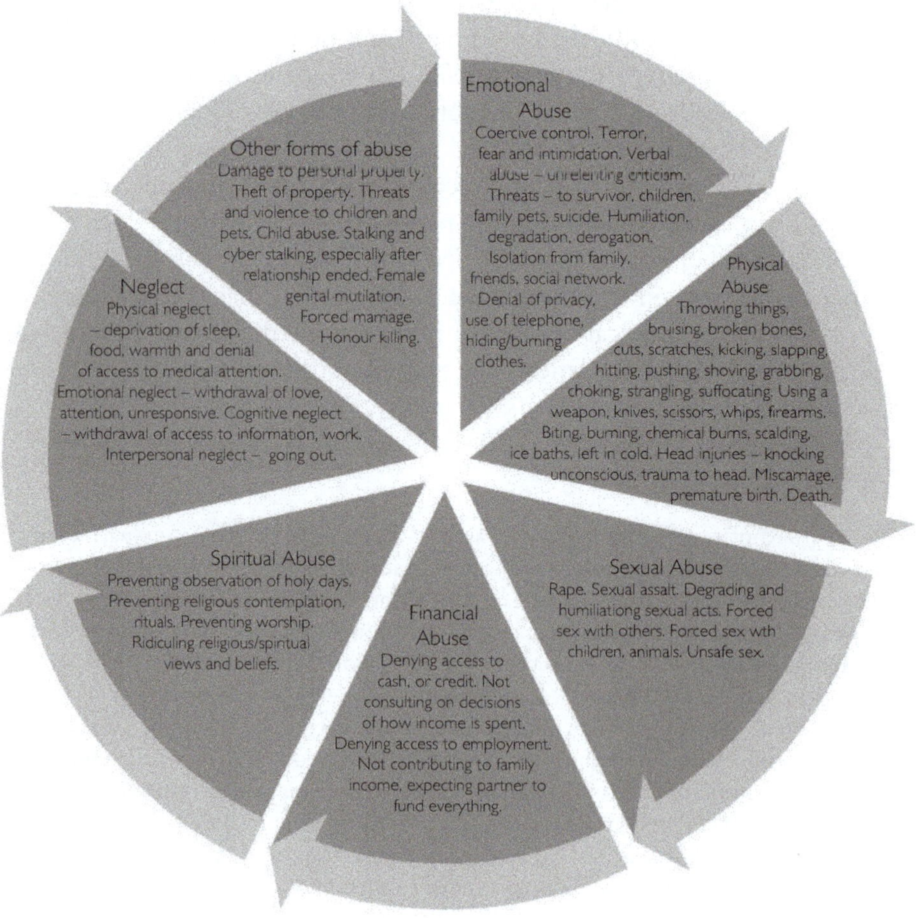

Figure 10.1 Spectum of domestic abuse (Sanderson, 2008)

INCIDENCE AND PREVALENCE OF DOMESTIC ABUSE

As in other forms of interpersonal trauma and abuse, incidents of DA are notoriously under-reported, and although the police receive on average one DA phone call every minute in the UK, it is thought that less than half of all DA incidents come to the attention of authorities. This indicates that any statistical data that is available represents the tip of the iceberg. Current research suggests that one in four females between 16 and 59 are at risk of DA, while one in five males are at risk. The British Crime Survey 2005–2006 found that one in 20 of all reported crimes in England and Wales were DA, with 29% of females and 18% of males reporting DA (Coleman, Jansson and Kaisa, 2007). On average two women are murdered every week in England and Wales by their partner or ex-partner (Women's Aid, 2007; Flood-Page and Taylor, 2003). Furthermore, DA accounts for almost a third of all violent crime against women, with one third of all emergency medical care administered to women experiencing DA (British Medical Association, 2007), and is the biggest killer of unborn children (Sanderson, 2008). In 90% of DA cases children are in the same or next room during the abuse episode, and 69% of DA incidents cause injury to the victim. Domestic abuse has one of the highest rates of repeated victimisation and on average a woman will be assaulted by her partner or ex-partner 35 times before reporting DA to the police.

WHO IS AT RISK OF DOMESTIC ABUSE?

Both males and females are at risk of DA as it occurs across all age groups, to people of any sexuality, ethnicity, culture, socioeconomic status and class. Some groups may be more vulnerable due to cultural norms of male and female power differences, impaired mental health or disabilities, access to resources, difficulties around disclosure or fear of further stigmatisation. Counsellors need to be aware that women are most at risk of being murdered when leaving an abusive relationship, and must ensure that appropriate safety assessment and planning is in place before embarking on such a course of action.

While both males and females are at risk, by far the most common abuse is that of females abused by males with 80% of survivors of DA identified as females (British Medical Association, 2007), with an increased risk during pregnancy (CEMACH, 2004; Sanderson, 2008). Research shows that one in five males are at risk of DA by females, with the majority experiencing emotional humiliation rather than physical violence. In lesbian, gay, bisexual and transgendered relationships research estimates indicate a similar pattern as in male to female abuse with 29% of gay men and 22% of lesbians experiencing DA at some point in their lives (Broken Rainbow, 2005) although it is generally accepted that this is grossly under-reported for fear of further stigmatisation.

According to the British Crime Survey the age group with the highest risk is 20–24-year-olds, with 16–19-year-olds a close second (Coleman, Jansson and

Kaisa, 2007) while the Women's Aid Federation reports that 26–35-year-old females are most at risk, necessitating refuge accommodation (Williamson, 2006). Children are also a high-risk group of being impacted by DA, with DA the highest killer of unborn children in the UK (British Medical Association, 2007; Sanderson, 2008).

It is argued that black and minority ethnic (BME) groups are more at risk of DA for longer because of fear of speaking out or violating cultural norms such as family honour ("izzat") and shame ("sharam") especially in Asian and Muslim women, and fear of consequences such as "honour killing" (Sanderson, 2008). This is exacerbated by lack of specific service provision, fears around racism, and in the case of refugee, or trafficked, women, fear of deportation or endangering their immigration status along with language barriers will increase the rsik of prolonged DA (Sanderson, 2008; Pryke and Thomas, 1998).

The British Crime Survey 2004–2005 found that females with disabilities were three times more at risk of DA, with males facing twice the risk. This risk is compounded with fears around disclosure due to isolation, dependency on abuser, lack of access to resources or cognitive impairments in terms of identifying their experience as abuse. Males and females with mental health problems, including substance abuse, may also be at an increased risk in that abusers invalidate the reality of DA by highlighting the survivor's mental impairments and "craziness" to undermine any allegations made. Women with children may also be at higher risk for fear of losing their children to child protection services, a fear that the abuser may regularly reinforce. Finally, stereotypes around class, socioeconomic status and age may increase the risk of not being believed among middle-class, higher socio-economic status groups and the elderly experiencing DA, thus reducing reporting and disclosure rates (Sanderson, 2008).

PERPETRATORS OF DOMESTIC ABUSE

Perpetrators of DA are not homogenous and come from all types of backgrounds and all ages, ethnicities, and social groups. Given that both males and females perpetrate DA it is important to understand DA in a gender neutral framework (Merrill, 1996). The most common characteristic in perpetrators of DA, irrespective of gender, ethnicity and social background, is the need to control their partner, and a belief that the intimidation and physical violence is an acceptable way to resolve conflict, release frustration and gain power over others (Sanderson, 2008). Alongside a need for control, many abusers display pathological jealousy predicated on relational and attachment insecurities, in particular fear of abandonment and rejection (Sanderson, 2008; Dutton, 2007). Abusers often oscillate between yearning for connection and closeness, yet fearing intimacy, a dynamic reflected in the abuse cycle (see Figure 10.2).

A further commonality is that many abusers hide behind a disarming façade of charm and as such behave differently in public than in private, making it difficult for others to really appreciate the level of abuse and coercion they are capable of. Counsellors need to be mindful that abusers can be extremely deceptive and will attempt to manipulate anyone, including professionals, in order to continue their masquerade (Sanderson, 2008). Many abusers invariable deny any abuse when confronted by either their victim or others, and commonly blame the victim or factors "outside" their control as a way of denying responsibility (Dutton, 2007; Sanderson, 2008).

NATURE AND DYNAMICS OF DOMESTIC ABUSE

Domestic abuse rarely starts with an act of violence. Many abusers initially present as extremely charming people who tend to "love bomb" their partner by showering them with affection and attention. Once the partner is in thrall to the abuser and entrapped into the relationship, the abuser will begin to wield coercion and control as a way of dominating the partner. This is usually effected through a complex and progressive cycle of abuse (Walker, 1979). While the cycle of abuse varies from couple to couple, and can vary in terms of duration from minutes, hours, days, months, or even years, the phases follow the same pattern: the tension-building phase, the assault phase and the conciliation, or honeymoon, phase (see Figure 10.2).

As the cycle is repeated, the assaults and violence usually increase in frequency and severity. In addition the more times the cycle is completed the less time it takes to complete. During the abuse cycle abusers usually engage in a number of dynamics and cognitive processes to support their justification to abuse and allow the cycle of abuse to be repeated (see Figure 10.3).

A critical element in the abuse cycle is that the conciliation phase instils hope in the survivor that the abuser can change and that the assault was a mere aberration. This leads to a reluctance to discuss the assault episode in any meaningful way and a return to normal behaviour which indirectly normalises the abuse, and permits future assaults. A critical aspect of the cycle of abuse is the process of intermittent reinforcement which leads to traumatic bonding, or Domestic Stockholm Syndrome (Dutton and Painter, 1981).

TRAUMATIC BONDING

Traumatic bonding occurs in the presence of life-threatening fear with no means of escape, evoking fearful dependency and denial of rage in the victim as the abuser has the power to preserve or destroy life. DA activates primitive instincts for survival, in particular the freeze response, rather than fight or flight, or escape strategies as the survivor cannot afford to access rage or anger as this will elicit further threat and danger. Pivotal to traumatic bonding is intermittent reinforcement in which the abuser alternates between threatening, abusive behaviour and loving, caretaking

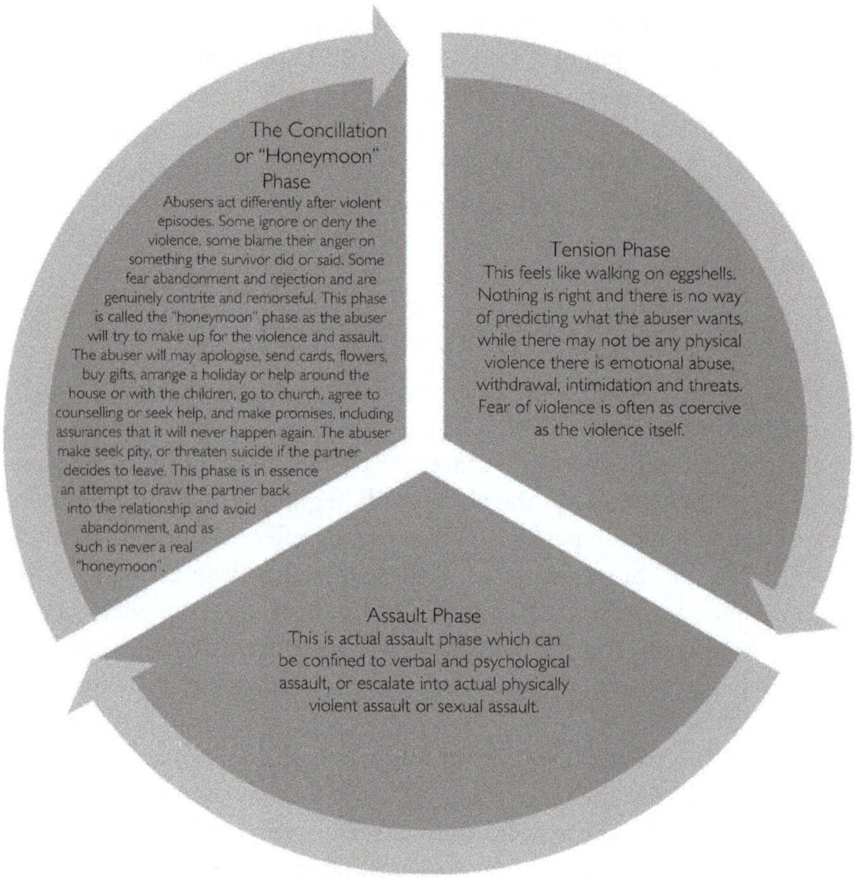

Figure 10.2 The abuse cycle (adapted from Walker, 1979)

behaviour (Dutton and Painter, 1981). Such oscillation and the unpredictable nature of DA results in an extremely strong emotional attachment that acts as a superglue to bond the relationship (Allen, 2001). The cycle of abuse engenders heightened intensity of fear and love which is often misinterpreted as evidence for depth of passion.

As traumatic bonding is biologically mediated it invariably occurs outside conscious awareness and the survivor's control. In order to ensure survival, survivors are compelled to change their beliefs about the abuser, to humanise rather than demonise, allowing them to adopt the abuser's belief system and thereby increase tolerance of the abuse (Sanderson, 2008). Traumatic bonding also accounts for the helplessness experienced by survivors which impedes self-agency rendering them powerless, with no means of escape as they remain in thrall to the abuser. It also underpins the myriad symptoms associated with DA such as PTSD, low self-esteem and cognitive distortions, which threaten psychological integrity (Dutton and Painter, 1981).

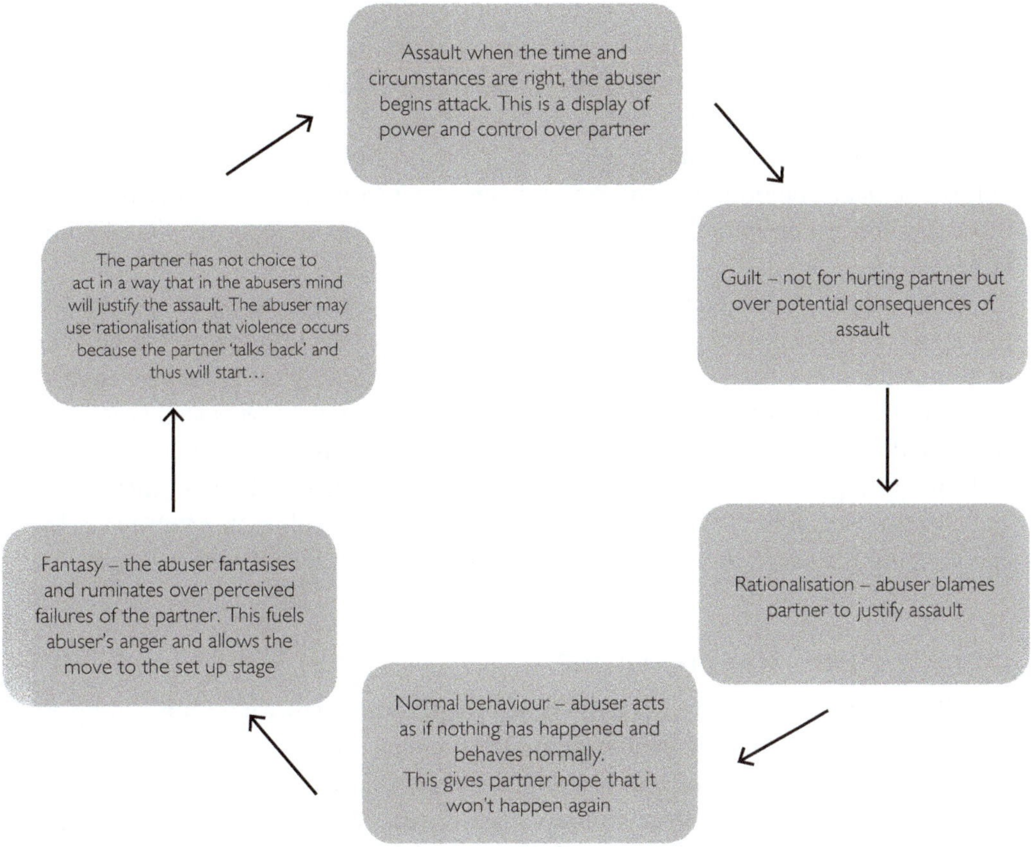

Figure 10.3 Abuser dynamics and cognitive processes that support cycle of abuse

Many survivors dissociate during the abuse episodes which permits them to access only the positive aspects of the relationship while compartmentalising the betrayal and abuse. This enhances survival through knowledge isolation, or "betrayal blindness" in which experiences are blocked and separated in the mind, allowing for a semblance of functioning. To revoke traumatic bonding, survivors need to explore cognitive disruptions, reduce knowledge isolation and integrate the abuse experiences.

OBSTACLES TO LEAVING

Compartmentalising the abuse experiences is only one of many obstacles to leaving an abusive relationship, and counsellors need to be mindful of the range of obstacles and be empathic in understanding how these reduce the survivor's self-agency rather than dismiss them. The most potent obstacle to leaving is the very real fear of being killed. Research has consistently shown than women are most at risk of being murdered by their partner, or ex-partner, when they leave an abuse relationship (Sanderson, 2008). The long-term effects of coercion and control, traumatic bonding and changed cognitions about ability to manage alone are also real obstacles to leaving. For some survivors the fear of not being believed, shame and stigmatisation reduce the ability to leave especially when access to resources such as housing, finances and support are limited. Those survivors with children will often make compromises and stay for the sake of the children rather than put them through the turmoil of leaving, especially if the partner is generally a loving father.

Counsellors need to be mindful of the many reasons that a survivor might wish to stay such as love or compassion for the partner, hope that things can change, fear of being alone or a deep sense of failure that the relationship is no longer tenable. Some survivors may not be able to challenge or infringe the myriad social pressures, values and religious beliefs that entrap them in DA and thus find ways of managing and minimising the abuse. Many survivors are also trapped by lack of knowledge and access to resources. Counsellors can help survivors to explore these obstacles by encouraging the survivor to draw up a list of reasons to stay and explore these.

IMPACT OF DOMESTIC ABUSE

To fully understand the impact of DA it is helpful to contextualise it within a complex trauma framework. This will enable counsellors to view the presenting symptoms as normal responses to complex and prolonged traumatisation rather than pathologise the survivor. Many of the core symptoms share features of PTSD and cluster around the distortion of reality, isolation, withdrawal and impaired self-agency. The lack of agency and traumatisation reflect primitive survival functions, and it is not until external and internal safety is restored that survivors can begin to gain control, plan and decide how they wish to progress. The fear of secondary victimisation through responses of friends, family, professionals and the community must also be addressed by counsellors, including their own capacity to retraumatise.

If the survivor has children, it may also be necessary to explore how DA can impact on children so that the survivor can make appropriate choices. Most survivors believe that as long as the children do not witness actual physical abuse they are left relatively unscathed. Yet research has shown that the complex dynamics and behaviours associated with DA can have a huge impact on children ranging from constant fear and anxiety, emotional abandonment, low self-esteem, behavioural difficulties, somatic symptoms such as headaches, sense of shame and isolation, and feeling powerless. To manage this, they are vulnerable to self-medication and self-harming behaviours as a way of restoring control. In addition, many children from DA families take on adult roles prematurely, are unable to set healthy boundaries or resolve conflicts, and are vulnerable to use of aggression and violence in their own relationships.

LONG-TERM EFFECTS OF DOMESTIC ABUSE

Long-term effects of prolonged DA include loss of control, both external and internal, and severe depletion of resources as all energy is mobilised towards survival. This impacts on emotional, physical, and cognitive functioning as well as interpersonal relationships (see Box 10.1). Counsellors need to assess which of the core clinical symptoms are of most concern to the survivor and ensure that the therapeutic focus incorporates the most pressing symptoms in order to restore better functioning.

Box 10.1 Core clinical symptoms of domestic abuse

- Constant fear, terror and anxiety – if left relationship, fear of reprisals; if still in relationship, concerns about leaving
- Helplessness, powerlessness, lack of agency
- Loss of external and internal control
- Numbness
- Depression
- Dissociation
- Hyper or hypovigilance
- Self-harm
- Substance abuse
- Feeling suicidal
- Self-blame
- Withdrawal, isolation
- Concerns about children

WORKING WITH SURVIVORS OF DOMESTIC ABUSE

The core goals when counselling survivors of DA are accurate assessment, re-establishing safety to work through the trauma and grieving the myriad losses, in order to restore control and make personally meaningful choices that minimise the risk of future abusive relationships. Counsellors need to focus on understanding presenting symptoms as normal responses to prolonged trauma, not individual pathology or personality disturbance, and validate existing survival strategies and internal resources to strengthen the sense of self and restore self-agency (see Box 10.2).

Box 10.2 Core therapeutic goals

- Accurate assessment
- Name and legitimise DA
- Establish a secure base
- Establish safety, internal and external
- Restore control and self-agency
- Identify and validate existing resources and survival strategies and build upon them
- Create coherence out of chaos
- Identify and restructure cognitive distortions
- Inform and facilitate access to other services
- Understand obstacles to leaving
- Safety planning
- Increase support network
- Grieve losses

Counsellors need to enable survivors to name the ineffable and legitimise the DA to reduce self-blame and apportion the responsibility for the abuse to the abuser. This is pivotal to challenging the distortion of reality and mind control inherent in DA.

It is critical that counsellors respect the survivor's autonomy in making choices and decisions, especially whether to stay or leave the abusive relationship. Counsellors need to support the survivor's decisions and work within what is realistic and manageable for the survivor. This is critical if the survivor is to restore a sense of control and self-agency. If the survivor decides to stay, the therapeutic focus needs to be on building existing resources and strategies to minimise harm and risk to self, and others such as children. If the survivor decides to leave, then counsellors need to support this through developing a concrete safety plan to ensure safety, given that it is when leaving that survivors are most at risk (Sanderson, 2008).

It is helpful to make a list of items to pack so that the survivor can begin to collect important documents and items over time rather than try to find these in an emergency. These items, especially the legal documents, are essential and will be necessary to re-establish life outside the relationship (see Box 10.4).

One of the core therapeutic goals is to grieve the many losses associated with DA. The grieving process can be complicated as the survivor often is not able to legitimise grieving or have the space to do so, especially if they are preoccupied

Box 10.3 Safety planning (Sanderson, 2008)

- Keep safe important emergency telephone numbers, such as the local Women's Aid project, or Refuge, and other DA services such as the police Community Safety Unit, GP, social worker, and social services emergency numbers. Also children's school, solicitor, freephone 24-hour National Domestic Violence Helpline run in partnership between Women's Aid and Refuge (0808 2000 247).
- In emergency dial 999: the police will attend the call, even if you are unable to speak. If possible leave phone off hook after dialling.
- Teach children, if appropriate and old enough, to call 999 in an emergency or when they feel in danger. It may help to establish a code word to convey that that is what they should do. Specify what information will be required such as name and address. Rehearsing the procedure with the child can make it easier to execute this in an emergency. However, survivors need to be cautious that the child does not become a target for physical attack and does not feel overly responsible for ensuring safety.
- Attend GP whenever injured to obtain medical notes and photographs of all injuries for later evidence.
- Archive abusive texts and voicemail messages as evidence.
- Keep a diary or log of abusive incidents and store in a safe place, preferably not in the home.
- If there are neighbours who can be trusted then it may help to inform them about the violence and abuse. Neighbours can afford an immediate place of safety in an emergency. It is helpful to discuss what you would like them to do if they hear sounds of abuse or violent attack such as calling the police.
- Choose a code word for a neighbour or friend that will trigger a particular action such as calling the police, or coming to the house to visit. Consideration needs to be given to their fears of safety, and only appropriate friends or neighbours should be co-opted.
- Shouting "fire" is more likely to attract attention than shouting "help".
- If in a public place it is helpful to attract the attention of a specific person, who looks most likely to extend help, and be clear what it is they need to do.
- Rehearse escape plan so it is easier to expedite in an emergency without having to think too much.
- If considering leaving or needing to leave in a hurry, it is crucial to have emergency numbers and money put aside, and easily accessible. It is also useful to have access to important documents pertaining to survivor and children such as passports, identification or naturalisation papers. If relevant benefit or rent books, birth certificates and credit cards may be necessary, along with utility bills.
- Try to keep a small amount of money available at all times, including change for phone or bus fares.

- It is important to know where the nearest public phone is located. If survivors have access to a mobile, keep it on them at all times.
- If survivors fear the partner is about to attack, they should endeavour to get to a lower-risk area of house or flat where there is a way out, or access to a phone or panic button.
- Survivors should avoid the kitchen or garage, where there are likely to be knives or other weapons. It is also crucial to avoid rooms where they could be trapped, such as a bathroom, or where they could be shut in, such as a cupboard or small space.
- Survivors must be prepared to leave the house in case of emergency.
- Consider bare essentials that might be needed in order to leave, such as documents, and any irreplaceable items of strong sentimental value, such as treasured photos or children's drawings, along with a favourite toy for each child.
- If possible survivors should store some items such as clothes, documents and mementoes with a trusted friend, neighbour, family member or women's project.
- Survivors should pack a small emergency bag of essentials and hide it somewhere safe so that it can be accessed in a hurry but does not arouse suspicion.

Box 10.4 List of items to pack (Sanderson, 2008)

- Some form of identification.
- Birth certificates for survivor and children.
- All necessary passports, visas, work permits or naturalisation documents.
- Money, bank books, cheque book, credit and debit cards.
- Keys for house, car and work. It is helpful to get an extra set of keys cut to be kept in the emergency bag.
- Cards or benefit books for child and welfare benefits.
- Driving licence and car registration documents, if applicable.
- Any prescribed medication.
- Copies of documents relating to housing tenure such as mortgage details, lease or rental agreement.
- Utilities bill which may be needed as additional identification, or for opening a separate bank account.
- Insurance documents, including national insurance number and child health numbers.

- Address book.
- Family photographs, diary, jewellery and small items of sentimental value.
- Clothing and toiletries for survivor and children.
- Small toy for each child.
- Also any documentation pertaining to abuse such as police reports, court orders such as injunctions and restraining orders, copies of medical records if available.

with practicalities of leaving and if children are upset. Many survivors believe that there is nothing to grieve as they should be relieved to have escaped DA. However, there are a number of very significant losses that do necessitate grieving for the survivor to readjust to life outside the DA (see Figure 10.4).

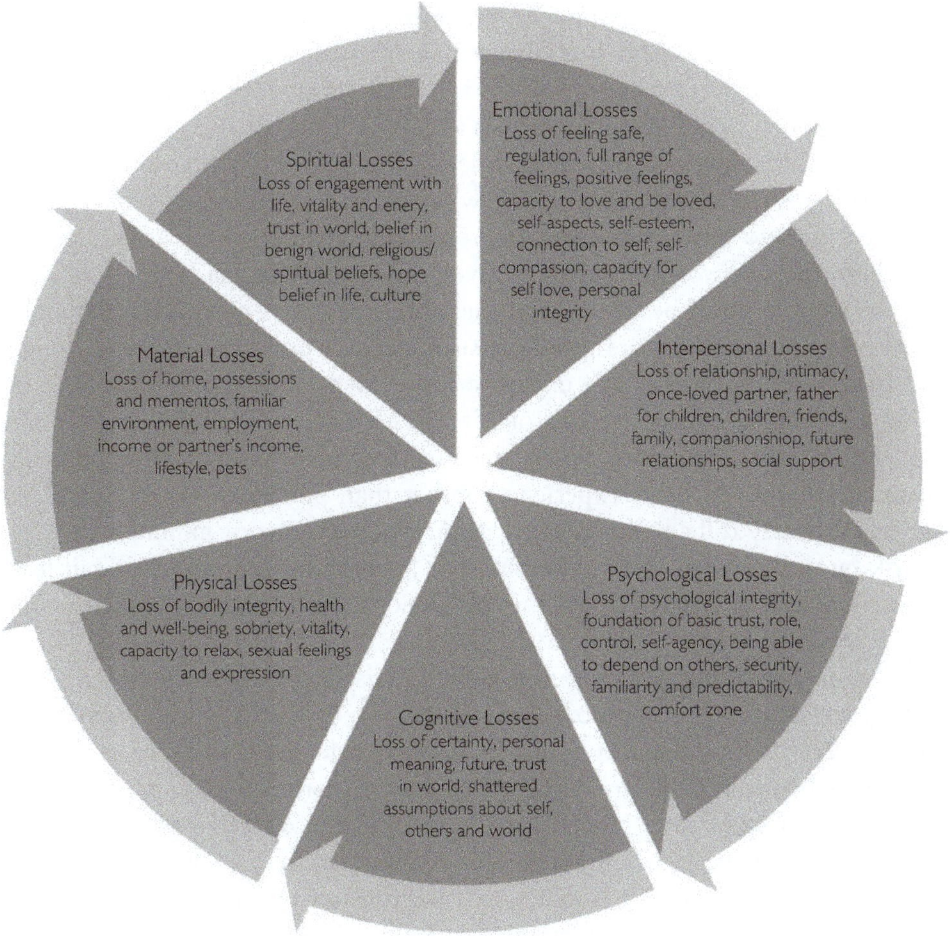

Figure 10.4 Spectrum of losses associated with domestic abuse (Sanderson, 2008)

In working through the losses the survivor can begin to access a sense of entitlement to respect, equality, trust, support and shared responsibility.

THERAPEUTIC CHALLENGES

Given the fluctuating levels of danger, either while in, or when leaving an abusive relationship, counsellors need to continuously assess survivors' external and internal safety, and be flexible in changing the therapeutic focus accordingly. One of the prominent therapeutic challenges is that the therapeutic process is not linear with regular diversions or distractions, especially when there is direct, or indirect contact with the abuser through court appearances, custody hearings, financial settlements, or contact visits with children. These can be extremely distressing and overwhelming as they reactivate fears, increase survivor vulnerability and risk to further abuse. This is compounded if the abuser uses these opportunities to intimidate, threaten or harass the survivor. Counsellors need to be able to tolerate these diversions and remain constant in their support rather than try to control the therapeutic process in the direction they believe it ought to take. This can be frustrating as it appears to prolong the recovery process, and yet is a necessary part of working through the danger of DA even after the survivor has left.

Counsellors must also be able to tolerate the degree of uncertainty associated with DA. This can sometimes manifest when the survivor describes harrowing experiences that go beyond human comprehension. Counsellors may be tempted to disbelieve the survivor, or find themselves colluding with the abuser's perception that the survivor must be "crazy" and therefore culpable. This can be compounded when other professionals are involved, such as child protection services, solicitors and barristers whose emphasis on gathering evidence and assessing veracity may undermine the survivor's account of the abuse. Counsellors need to be mindful that their role is to support the survivor in their perception of and concomitant meaning around the abuse experiences rather than pursue an evidence trail. This can be extremely difficult when other agencies undermine or minimise the degree of risk by not intervening or providing the appropriate support. This can lead to counsellors feeling isolated from other professionals and believing that they are the only true advocate of the client.

To minimise such isolation counsellors are advised to seek links with DA agencies and organisations and other professionals involved. Particularly useful is knowledge and contact with local domestic violence projects, including DA advocates and family solicitors who are experienced in DA. One concern for counsellors who work with DA is the reaction of other professionals to the role the counsellor plays in the survivor's process which can sometimes develop into (dis)courtesy stigmatisation (Mattley, 1998) whereby the counsellor's motivation and role in working with survivors of DA is brought into question, or undermined as lacking partiality. Counsellors may also need to consider to what degree they may need to become involved as an advocate for the client such as attending meetings, writing reports or attending court. It is imperative that counsellors consider their boundaries and are clear about what they can and cannot offer, and ensure that this is explicitly stated and understood by the survivor (Sanderson, 2008).

Finally counsellors can become overwhelmed by the sheer enormity of the inexorable issues associated with DA. To avoid burnout, disillusionment and secondary traumatic stress, counsellors must ensure that they seek appropriate professional support through supervision, or if necessary consultation with other professionals in the field. They also need to ensure that they have access to peer support. Alongside this it is critical that they look after themselves by balancing the trauma work with taking regular breaks and engaging in activities that are nurturing and restorative (see Chapter 14). With this in place, counsellors will be able to provide a safe and secure base in which survivors can work through their experiences, and regain the control and autonomy to make decisions about how to live their lives more authentically without fear of abuse.

Case vignette: Sophie

Sophie was in her mid-thirties when she met and married her partner. They both had successful careers and wanted to start a family as soon as possible. They had three children in quick succession, although there were some medical concerns with their last child due to birth complications. Sophie had happily decided to take a career break to look after the children and in many respects they were the epitome of a successful middle-class family. Sophie's husband was perceived as extremely charming and a doting father.

Upon the birth of the third child, a boy, Sophie's husband began to question the quality of Sophie's mothering and began to undermine her capacity to cope with the children, citing mental instability and history of childhood abuse making her an unfit mother. His concerns were voiced behind her back to the consultant paediatrician and the health visitor, neither of whom found any evidence to support these allegations. When these professionals failed to act Sophie's husband took out a High Court injunction preventing the children from being taken out of the country and started custody proceedings.

Throughout this process Sophie's husband presented himself as a loving caring father who had no choice but to remove the children from their unfit mother. To gather support for his position he sent endless emails to Sophie's friends, family and peers, telling them how worried he was for Sophie and the children. He also informed all the neighbours, thereby ensuring Sophie's isolation from all forms of support. Although he never used violence, the level of threat, intimidation and control was palpable to Sophie. Unfortunately both children's services and the police were not able to act upon her concerns as no actual crime, or act of violence had been committed. This served to elevate Sophie's terror and fear as she felt she was not believed or taken seriously in her concerns. This was reinforced by her solicitor who would not see the case as a DA case but rather as an acrimonious custody battle despite evidence of controlling and intrusive behaviour such as rearranging items in the house on contact visits, washing Sophie's clothes, insisting how the children were dressed, refusing to pay for the children's nursery and constantly delaying payment of agreed financial support for the children.

Sophie used the therapeutic process to validate her experience of DA as all those around her had been duped by her husband to the degree that she began to question her own sanity. It was clear that Sophie had little if any control over her husband's behaviour and very little support. In conjunction with the local domestic violence intervention project and a designated advocate, Sophie was gradually able to legitimise her experience and begin to restore trust and belief in her perceptions. In addition, the therapy setting became a sanctuary for Sophie to just "be" rather than having to be hypervigilant and put on a brave face for the children. The sheer process of contact visits three times a week, the harassment and intimidation, took a huge toll on Sophie's energy levels resulting in huge weight loss and chronic fatigue. The therapy session would often be a place of rest away from the terror of being controlled. It was critical to allow Sophie to use this space for whatever was predominant, which at times was just to rest. Much of the therapeutic work was to create a holding environment in which to support the client in whatever way necessary, and to help Sophie manage and restore control over the range of psychobiological symptoms through affect regulation and stress tolerance.

Sophie's biggest fear was losing her children as her husband seemed to be able to charm and dupe all the professionals involved, including Sophie's solicitor and barrister, and the judge in the early hearings. When the case finally came before the family court 18 months later, Sophie was lucky enough to be appointed a judge with many years of experience, who despite the absence of physical violence, could see beyond her husband's charm, deception and manipulation and identify the degree of control and coercion. Once custody was awarded to Sophie and the level of contact with her husband was reduced, Sophie was able to embark on the deeper therapeutic work including grieving the many losses in order to regain control and self-agency to make decisions and choices without the fear of abuse.

SUMMARY

- To work with survivors of DA counsellors need to be aware of the spectrum of DA behaviours, and understand that these are not confined to physical abuse but include sexual abuse, emotional and psychological abuse, neglect, financial abuse, and spiritual abuse.
- It is essential that counsellors contextualise DA within a trauma framework in which prolonged coercion and control give rise to a range of psychobiological symptoms that are normal responses to trauma rather than indices of pathology, or personality disturbance. To avoid pathologising survivors, counsellors also need to be mindful of the sociopolitical framework which gives rise to, and supports DA.

- While both males and females are at risk of DA, the most at risk are females with two women a week murdered by their partner or ex-partner. DA is also the highest killer of unborn children and can have adverse long-term consequences for children raised in DA environments. Other high-risk groups are young women, BME females, those with disabilities, trafficked women and refugees who fear deportation.
- Although perpetrators of DA are not homogenous there are a number of commonalities such as need to control and dominate through the use of coercion, threat and violence, in order to ensure total submission and compliance. Abusers also display pathological jealousy which is thought to reflect insecure attachment, fear of abandonment and rejection which promotes need to control the survivor, even if this is through fear and violence.
- The nature and dynamics of DA is a subtle and gradual escalation of coercion and control starting with loving care and attention, or "love bombing", to entrap the partner and escalating to increased use of threats, intimidation and violence which the abuser uses to dominate and ensure total submission. These dynamics are part of the cycle of abuse in which the tension-building phase is followed by the assault, which is followed by the conciliation, or honeymoon phase. The intermittent reinforcement in this cycle ultimately leads to traumatic bonding.
- The impact of prolonged DA must be contextualised within a trauma framework and the concomitant symptoms must be understood as normal responses to complex trauma rather than individual pathology.
- The core therapeutic goals are to provide a secure base in which to make accurate assessment and establish both external and internal safety. Counsellors need to act as advocates for the survivor and respect the need for autonomy and striving for control. Counsellors need to support survivors when leaving an abusive relationship through careful safety planning, and provide the space for the grieving of the many associated losses.
- There are a number of therapeutic challenges inherent in working with survivors of DA, not least the need for flexibility, tolerance of diversions and distraction, and the lack of certainty. To avoid being overwhelmed by the enormity of DA, counsellors need to ensure that they access professional and personal support so that they can enable survivors to move towards living life more authentically, with greater self-agency and equality, without the fear of further abuse.

SUGGESTED READING

Abrahams, H. (2007) *Supporting Women after Domestic Violence: Loss, Trauma and Recovery.* London: Jessica Kingsley Publishers.

British Medical Association (2007) *Domestic Abuse.* London: BMA.

Dutton, F.G. (2007) *The Abusive Personality: Violence and Control in Intimate Relationships.* Second edition. New York: Guilford Press.

Dutton, M.A. (1992) *Empowering and Healing Battered Women: A Model for Assessment and Intervention.* New York: Springer.

Herman, J.L. (1992) *Trauma and Recovery.* New York: Basic Books.

Hester, M., Pearson, C. and Harwin, N. (2007) *Making an Impact – Children and Domestic Violence: A Reader.* Second edition. London: Jessica Kingsley Publishers.

Hirigoyen, M.-F. (2004) *Stalking the Soul: Emotional Abuse and the Erosion of Identity.* New York: Helen Marx Books.

Horley, S. (1988) *Love and Pain: A Survival Handbook for Women.* London: Bedford Square Press.

Humphreys, C. and Thiara, R. (2003) 'Mental health and domestic violence: "I call it symptoms of abuse".' *British Journal of Social Work 33*, 2, 209–226.

Pearlman, L.A and Courtois, C.A. (2005) 'Clinical applications of the attachment framework: relational treatment of complex trauma.' *Journal of Traumatic Stress 18*, 449–459.

Sanderson, C. (2008) *Counselling Survivors of Domestic Abuse.* London: Jessica Kingsley Publishers.

Women's Aid Federation (2005) *The Survivor's Handbook.* Bristol: Women's Aid Federation.

CHAPTER 11

ELDER ABUSE AS INTERPERSONAL TRAUMA

There has been growing awareness over the last few years of the range of interpersonal abuse experienced by the elderly. These abuses occur in a variety of settings from the family home to institutional care. Elderly people may be abused in their own home by partners, family members such as adult children, or by carers, or institutional settings such as hospitals, prisons, sheltered housing, day care centres and elderly care homes. As in child abuse these abuses can happen either through active commission or through omission as in neglect.

In a culture obsessed with youth, elderly people are increasingly invisible and frequently objectified and infantilised making them vulnerable to a range of interpersonal abuses and mistreatment. This can range from inconsiderate slights such as being ignored or dismissed, removal of their right to have control over their lives, to active abuses and interpersonal trauma. This is compounded by increased social mobility and the erosion of the extended family in which elderly relatives become alien to younger generations as they rarely interact in a meaningful way. As a result elderly people are denied respect and appropriate care and attention, and as they deteriorate physically and psychologically, can be seen as a burden, and yet they are often the least protected members of society. With a rapidly increasing older population, elder abuse is a growing problem which must be taken seriously and seen within the context of interpersonal trauma.

This chapter will look at the range of interpersonal abuse committed against the elderly, assess the prevalence data and examine who is most at risk and who the perpetrators are. The nature and dynamics of elderly abuse will be explored alongside identifying the impact and long-term effects. Although there are a number of obstacles to working with the elderly due to deteriorating physical and psychological health, and counsellors' own existential fears around aging, loss of control and dependency, it is critical that they are given the same secure base from which to recover from the interpersonal trauma of elder abuse.

THE SPECTRUM OF ELDER ABUSE

Elder abuse is highly complex and must be appropriately understood rather than categorised as resentful staff preying on vulnerable adults, or evil family members wishing to dispose of elderly relatives to gain access to their inheritance. In an increasingly ageist society it is easy for individuals to view the elderly as dependent and burdensome, leading to objectification and infantilisation. Given the number of derogatory terms for the elderly one can see how these impact on perceptions that lend themselves to abusive behaviour and active mistreatment (Biggs, Phillipson and Kingston, 1995).

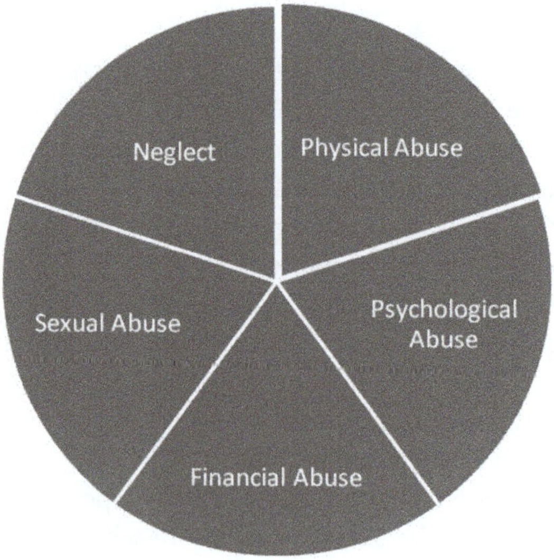

Figure 11.1 Spectrum of elder abuse

In many respects elder abuse is very similar to domestic abuse in that it is easily hidden behind closed doors and suffused with secrecy wherein the abuse is covert and subtle making it difficult to spot the signs. As in domestic abuse, there is a range of abuses that are generally agreed to constitute elder abuse. These are primarily physical abuse, psychological abuse, financial abuse, sexual abuse and neglect.

While elder abuse can occur anywhere, at home, in day care, in care homes (formerly known as residential or nursing homes), hospital or sheltered housing, there is evidence that financial and psychological abuse is primarily associated with abuse in the home, while physical abuse and neglect is primarily associated with abuse in institutional settings (AEA, 2004).

Physical abuse involves a range of physical violence and assaults such as hitting, slapping, pushing, kicking or burning, physical restraint, force feeding and misuse of medication. Physical abuse is most commonly seen in institutional settings such as hospitals (26%) or care homes (25%) but is also found in 18% of older people living at home, either by relatives or paid carers, and in sheltered housing (10%) (AEA, 2004).

Psychological abuse clusters around persistent insults and threats, and involves the infliction of anguish, pain or distress through verbal and non-verbal acts. It includes emotional abuse, threats of harm and abandonment, deprivation of contact, humiliation, blaming, controlling, intimidation, harassment, verbal abuse, and isolation from family, friends, services or support networks (BMA, 2007). Psychological abuse is primarily seen in older people in sheltered housing (46%) followed by 38% of those cared for at home, 27% in care homes and 25% in hospitals (AEA, 2004).

Financial, or material, abuse is the illegal or improper use of an older person's money, property or assets such as theft, fraud, exploitation, forging signatures, and misuse of power of attorney. It also includes pressurising or deceiving the older person to sign important documents such a will, contract or power of attorney (BMA, 2007). Financial abuse is greatest for older people at home (24%) or in sheltered housing (23%) with 14% taking place in care homes and 8% in hospital settings (AEA, 2004).

The sexual abuse of older people includes a range of behaviours ranging from verbal harassment, unwanted sexual touching, coerced nudity, sexually explicit photography and rape. The charity Action on Elder Abuse (AEA) are particularly concerned with what appears to be a genuine increase in the sexual abuse of the elderly possibly due to sexual abusers moving from child care settings where there are increased controls and vigilance to adult care environments that are less regulated (AEA, 2004). As Glendenning (1999) states, "Sexual offenders are attracted by the vulnerability and availability of their potential victims and those who suffer from physical and mental impairment may be especially at risk."

Arguably neglect underpins all other types of elder abuse as it consists of repeated failing of a designated carer to provide help with or give access to personal, medical or social care. It also includes failure to provide basic physiological needs such as food, water, clothing, personal hygiene and safety, or day-to-day activities. Abandonment is subsumed under neglect and is defined as desertion of an older person (BMA, 2007). Like sexual abuse there seems to be an increased reporting of neglect, with the majority seen in hospital settings (23%) and care homes (18%) with 6% among those cared for at home and 5% in sheltered housing. Research in America has found neglect to be the most common form of elder abuse accounting for 55% of cases in the US (National Center on Elder Abuse, 1997).

DEFINITION OF ELDER ABUSE

Elder abuse is as complex as all the other forms of interpersonal trauma and clinicians need to be mindful of making assumptions based on their own prejudices or ageist beliefs. There is no standard definition of elder abuse; however, AEA define elder abuse as: "A single or repeated act or lack of appropriate action occurring within any relationship where there is an expectation of trust, which causes harm or distress to an individual" (AEA, 2004).

While this definition is broad enough to include relationships of care such as a health care professional, if the abuse is perpetrated by a carer who is an intimate partner or family member, this would be defined as domestic elder abuse (Sanderson, 2008; BMA, 2007). Domestic elder abuse is estimated to account for two thirds of cases of elder abuse, with adult children the most frequent perpetrators (Sanderson, 2008).

Furthermore AEA categorise elder abuse as a hate crime and believe that it needs to be perceived as such in order to demand the attention of health, social and criminal justice professionals to implement appropriate policies. The physical, psychological, financial, and sexual abuse and neglect must be seen as crimes against adults as they include theft, fraud, assault and rape and not diminished just because they are perpetrated against older people. It is only with such policies in place that this most vulnerable population can be appropriately protected.

PREVALENCE AND INCIDENCE OF ELDER ABUSE

There is a distinct lack of research on the prevalence of elder abuse, and that which is available desperately needs to be updated. Government statistics (House of Commons Health Committee, 2004) based on research by Ogg and Bennet (1992) state that approximately half a million older people are abused in the UK at any one time. However this figure does not provide a full picture of elder abuse due to definitional and methodological problems, and significant under-reporting. It is imperative that more up-to-date, robust prevalence research is conducted in order to understand the sheer scale of this pernicious interpersonal abuse. Although elder abuse is more widely recognised, much remains hidden due to the "hidden voice" of the elderly (AEA, 2004) who dare not speak out for fear of further abuse. To ascertain whether elder abuse really is on the increase, or has reached epidemic proportions, can only be clarified through robust research.

The National Centre for Social Research in their *UK Study of Abuse and Neglect of Older People: Prevalence Survey Report* estimate that 2.6% of people over the age of 66 in private households are subjected to mistreatment by a family member, care worker or friend. The most common form of elder abuse is neglect at 1.1%, financial abuse 0.7%, physical and psychological abuse both at 0.4% and sexual abuse at 0.2% (National Centre for Social Research, 2007).

Incidence data based on calls to their National Elder Abuse Helpline published in 2004 by AEA found that the most frequently reported elder abuse to their National Helpline was psychological abuse at 34%, followed by financial abuse at 20%, physical abuse at 19%, with neglect at 12% and sexual abuse at 3%. By far the highest percentage of calls reported multiple abuse with 44% of calls reporting more than one type of abuse. In addition, AEA found that the majority (64%) of elder abuse occurs in the home while 23% occurs in care homes, 5% in hospital settings and 4% in sheltered housing. While these figures give an indication of the level of elder abuse, practitioners need to be mindful that these data may be the tip of the iceberg as many older people may be prevented from phoning a helpline as they are too frail or because they do not have access to a private, secure telephone line.

WHO IS AT RISK?

While all older people are vulnerable to interpersonal abuse, AEA have found that females are more at risk (67%) compared to males (22%), with 11% of males and females being abused simultaneously, usually in care homes. This finding may be due to several factors, not least that females on average live longer than males and are thus more likely to live alone thereby making them more vulnerable to elder abuse. In addition, women may be more likely to seek help if they have concerns, or report abuse, than males. This is attested to by the number of telephone calls to the National Elder Abuse Helpline which received three times (76%) more phone calls from women than men (24%).

O'Keefe *et al.* (2007) found that the risk of elder abuse appears to increase with declining physical health, depression and loneliness with 78% of abuse perpetrated against people over the age of 70, with the highest risk to those between the ages of 80 and 89 at 40% compared to 22% for the age group 70–79 and 16% for those over the age of 90. The lowest risk was to those between 55 and 64 at 4% while 18% of those in the 65–69 age group were found to be at risk. Women were found to be more at risk of interpersonal abuses such as physical, psychological and sexual abuse especially between the ages of 66 and 74, although this seemed to tail off after the age of 85 (O'Keefe *et al.*, 2007). In contrast males are more at risk of financial abuse and neglect, which seems to increase with age, and this is more prevalent in those living alone.

Older women who are divorced or separated, or lonely and in bad physical health, are also at considerable risk, especially if they are dependent on home care services. Research has consistently demonstrated that social isolation and a lack of actively engaged relatives or friends give rise to greater opportunities for abuse and make this a particularly vulnerable group (AEA, 2004). This finding highlights the importance of social networks as a protective factor in elder abuse, something that can be actively encouraged by clinicians.

THE PERPETRATORS OF ELDER ABUSE

By far the majority of elder abuse, 46%, is perpetrated by relatives of the older person in their own home, compared to 34% of paid carers in the home. In 41%

of cases the perpetrator is a male relative compared to 25% of female relatives, although more females are implicated in elder abuse by paid carers (33%). According to O'Keefe *et al.* (2007) the most common relative to engage in elder abuse is either a son or daughter as seen in 50% of cases, while partners or spouses are implicated in 23% of cases. This is followed by 9% being in-laws committing elder abuse, 3% siblings, 2% nieces or nephews, 1% parents and 11% other extended family members such as a grandchild who resents the attention demanded by the older person. To add to the betrayal, it is worth noting that in 23% of abuse perpetrated by relatives there is collusion between family members, with the abuse sometimes perpetrated by more than one person. Furthermore, in 5% of cases elder abuse is committed by friends of the older person.

According to AEA (2004) elder abuse by non-relative or paid carers is most likely to occur in care homes (53%) and 26% is by paid carers in the victim's own home. Other paid carers implicated in elder abuse consist of nursing staff in hospital settings, social workers and hospital doctors as well as other professionals who have a duty of care to the older person. In some instances abuse in residential setting is perpetrated by other residents increasing the lack of safety in such settings and the effects of institutional abuse.

Despite the majority of elder abuse being perpetrated by a relative, AEA (2004) proposes that there is little support for the hypothesis that elder abuse is caused by the stress of caring for an elderly family member, as they receive less than 1% of calls that fit that category. This finding leads AEA to suggest that elder abuse has less to do with the physical and mental condition of the older person such as immobility, incontinence or dementia, and more to do with family dynamics, interpersonal relationships, and living arrangements. This would support Amiel and Heath's (2003) suggestion that elder abuse must be seen within a domestic abuse perspective in which the pre-morbid relationship may be pertinent in understanding the dynamics of elder abuse. Finally practitioners must be mindful that there are a larger number of family members who care for elderly relatives, sometimes under difficult and stressful conditions, and yet do not commit abuse.

THE NATURE AND DYNAMICS OF ELDER ABUSE

Researchers have identified a variety of factors that may predispose to elder abuse (AEA, 2004) as shown in Figure 11.2. Although these factors have been identified practitioners must not be rigidly driven by these or seek to use them as a check list as it is the choreography of many complex dynamics that account for elder abuse.

Intra-individual dynamics as a risk factor in elder abuse refers to individual personality traits, of both the older person and the carer and the dynamics of their interaction. In many instances this could reflect the continuation of domestic abuse dynamics in which one member of the couple has always exerted power and control over the other. The only change is in terms of nomenclature wherein domestic

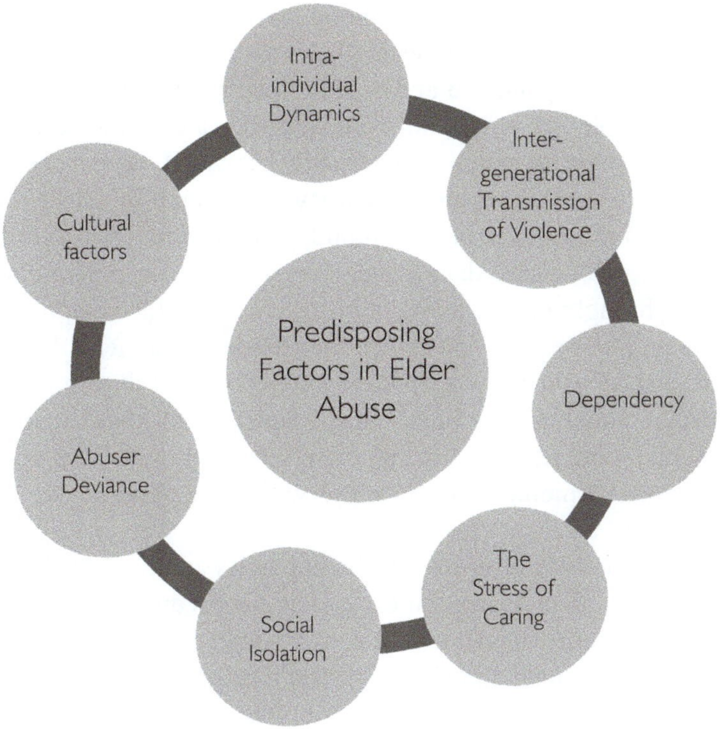

Figure 11.2 Factors identified that predispose to elder abuse (adapted from AEA, 2004)

abuse becomes elder abuse. Alternatively a spouse who has suffered systematic domestic abuse over many years, may exert power and control as the abuser becomes increasingly frail and dependent. Other factors that predispose to elder abuse in this category are mental health problems or alcohol dependency in either the older person or their carer. What needs to be assessed is whether these are pre-morbid or as a result of being dependent, or taking on the role of carer.

Research has also shown that attachment patterns are a potent factor in interactions between caregiver and the older person (Magai and Cohen, 1998) and can evoke the potential for elder abuse especially in those with insecure attachment styles (Magai and Cohen, 1998; Perren, Schmid *et al.*, 2007). Magai (2001) found that the attachment style of the older person and the caregiver has an effect on the relationship, and that carers of securely attached individuals saw the older person as less of a burden than those with an insecure-avoidant (dismissive) or insecure-ambivalent attachment style. Similarly, Perren, Schmid *et al.* (2007) found that the higher the degree of insecure-avoidant attachment style in the carer, the greater the level of agitation and aggression expressed by the older person leading to stubbornness and resistance to being helped.

It is not surprising that early childhood attachment patterns are activated in older people, especially those with dementia, as memories of early childhood events become increasingly consolidated and begin to overshadow more recent memories. In addition, as people get older and experience repeated losses through bereavements their attachment systems are repeatedly activated, or deactivated in those who have an insecure-avoidant attachment style. Research by Diehl *et al.* (1998) in comparing older and younger people, found a higher rate of insecure attachment styles, especially insecure-avoidant (dismissive) in the older generation. This could be due to being brought up in a different historical time which emphasised stoicism, independence and self-sufficiency rather than close attachments between parents and children, and in which many children were evacuated during the war, leading to more insecure attachments. Magai and Cohen (1998) found that older people with secure childhood attachments feel more secure in later years and are able to enjoy closer, more harmonious relationships with their current carer, and are thus easier to look after.

In contrast those with insecure-attachment styles are more likely to externalise their fears, rage and affect dysregulation, and as a consequence are more difficult to look after in being more demanding and dismissive, and perceived to be more of a burden or liability (Magai and Cohen, 1998). Furthermore, older people with an insecure-ambivalent attachment style are more likely to have a higher incidence of depression and anxiety than those with a secure or insecure-avoidant style, while those with an insecure-avoidant attachment style have a higher incidence of dementia, are more distrustful and paranoid, and have greater activity disturbance (Magai and Cohen, 1998), suggesting a deactivation of the attachment system.

The *intergenerational transmission of violence* as a factor in elder abuse is an extension of domestic abuse, or may reflect pathological family cultures (Eastman, 1984) in which alcohol or drug misuse, mental health problems and physical violence flourish. In such families adult children of previously physically abusive or cruel parents direct their anger and violence onto the now dependent mother or father as the only known way of dealing with dependency or conflicts, or as a form of retaliation. In contrast some adult children from violent families attempt to overcompensate by becoming the perfect carer that the parent(s) never was, and when conflicts arise, or frustration becomes overwhelming, may enact the violence they once experienced.

Dependency is a further risk factor in elder abuse and can impact on the relationship between the carer and older person. This is related to attachment style in which the carer may recoil from the dependency needs of the older person, or the older person fears dependency. This is associated with older people who have experienced abandonment in childhood, have been in care, or whose dependency has been exploited. The fear of dependency becomes so great that they become hostile or dismissive of the carer, or become distrustful. One client who had been brought up in care and had been both physically and sexually abused by staff in the care home, became so terrified of being dependent on her family that she contemplated suicide as a better alternative than taking the risk of being cared for. The frailty of the older person may necessitate a carer having to give up paid employment and in turn become trapped into relying on statutory benefits, which may activate uncomfortable feelings of dependency.

The *stress of caring* is a further predisposing factor in elder abuse. The role of carer is often stressful especially if juggling work and other family commitments, leading to strained family relationships, although this is not always supported by research (AEA, 2004). The impact of stress of caring will be influenced by a number of other factors such as socioeconomic status, amount of living space, time demands, multiple caring roles and the motivation of the carer. Carers who take on the role with reluctance, or out of a sense of duty rather than genuine affection may experience being a carer as much more stressful than one who takes on the role with love and compassion. The stress of caring is exacerbated in those who are sole carers, or those that receive no help from other siblings or family members. The absence of support and help from others to share the care, can breed resentment which may be directed at the older person. Arguably, the stress of caring is delicately balanced and dependent on level of support, including access to resources such as respite care, and individual family circumstances. A carer who has multiple caring roles such as young children and other family commitments may find it much harder to juggle competing demands than one who is subject to fewer demands.

Research has shown that *social isolation* can be a predisposing factor in elder abuse as this renders the older person more dependent on others such as paid carers and means that they are away from the scrutiny of caring relatives or friends. According to the Department of Health (2000) 36% of older people in care homes and 19% of older people living in private households are rarely visited by relatives or friends, with 6% of those in care homes and 2% living at home receiving no visits at all. In the absence of relatives or friends the older person often suffers in silence as there is no-one to tell, or no-one to monitor the level of care being administered. Social isolation is often a by-product of economic factors and the social and economic migration of adult children to other areas of country or world.

Pillemer and Finkelhor (1989) have postulated that "*abuser deviance*" is a potent predisposing factor in elder abuse in which "...elder abusers appear to be severely troubled individuals with histories of antisocial behaviour or instability". This may reflect the presence of an abusive personality (Dutton, 2007) which thrives on power and control over others. Such individuals need to dominate and specifically target the vulnerable and frail to shore up their own fragile sense of self (Sanderson, 2008). Such dynamics are more likely to be enacted when there is a clear imbalance of power (Whittaker, 1997) in which one person perceives himself and is perceived by the other as more powerful, while the other perceives himself and is perceived by the other as relatively powerless. While this is not necessarily conscious, it is derived and reinforced by patterns of interaction which confirm and reinforce such imbalance.

Cultural factors may also predispose to elder abuse especially in individualistic cultures which emphasise the pursuit of individual success rather than care and compassion for others. A danger of such cultural attitudes is that individual needs over-ride the needs of others, including elderly relatives. This is compounded by depictions of elderly people as frail, weak, dependent and a burden rather than deserving of respect. Cultures that emphasise youth and render older people invisible, seeing them as a "group" rather than individuals, and that emphasise control and deplore dependency, are less likely to respond compassionately to older members of society. In doing so they fail to give older people a voice and largely ignore their needs for care and protection. Furthermore, cultural variations based on rigid hierarchical family structures, including the use of physical force, may also predispose to elder abuse. Sanderson (2008) has highlighted this in families where physical punishment and sanctions are condoned, and transmitted through patriarchal power structures which permit the beating of women, and wherein adult sons go on to beat their own mothers.

Finally, abusive regimes that are allowed to flourish in institutional settings can give rise to systematic institutional abuse (see Chapter 12). Institutions which tolerate ageist and racist attitudes and fail to monitor abusive practices may be vulnerable to condoning, albeit at times unwittingly, abusive treatment of older people by both staff and other residents. While such abuse is often rationalised as a by-product of low pay, lack of training, poor staff retention, and poor supervision, it is imperative that institutions have clear policies and good practice guidelines and ensure these are implemented at all times. In addition, institutions need to monitor personality traits, interpersonal skills, attachment style and motivation of staff during the selection process to ensure they choose wisely in who will care for the elderly residents.

While the predisposing factors in elder abuse are a useful framework to understand the nature and dynamics of elder abuse, practitioners need to be mindful of the complex choreography that leads to elder abuse. What is critical is to avoid prejudices and making assumptions which prevent real engagement with the older person. It is only through giving the older person their voice and really hearing what is being communicated, both verbally and non-verbally, that a true understanding of their experience can be captured.

THE IMPACT OF ELDER ABUSE

The impact of elder abuse is not dissimilar to the impact found in survivors of domestic abuse (Sanderson, 2008). Commonly the older person is unable to see themselves as victims of abuse and as such cannot name their experiences as such. This is not due to lack of understanding or disorientation but due to heinous acts of betrayal from family members or those that are supposed to care for them. In addition, their frailty and dependency engenders fear of disclosure in case this leads to further abuse. The feeling of being trapped, with no escape can lead to further psychobiological trauma alongside the range of abuses perpetrated by their putative carers on whom they rely for protection.

Given the range of elder abuse the impact will vary depending on which abuse is committed. Each type of abuse will be highlighted in terms of indicators and impact.

Physical abuse

The physical abuse of older people includes a range of physical assaults such as slapping, hitting, burning, head butting, scalding, bruising, pushing, and restraining such as tying or binding to a bed or chair as well as the inappropriate administration of medication. While the impact of physical abuse is primarily on the body (see Box 11.1) it will exacerbate already fragile physical health and activate a cascade of neurobiological and psychological responses such as fear, anxiety, and shame. If physical assaults are repeated systematically with no means of escape the older person will develop post-traumatic stress responses. Over or under-medication can cause further medical complications and ultimately hasten the older person's death, as can injuries that are left untreated.

Box 11.1 Indicators and impact of physical abuse

- Cuts, lacerations, puncture wounds, open wounds, bruises, welts, discoloration, black eyes, bone fractures, broken bones, skull fractures
- Untreated injuries in various stages of healing, not properly treated
- Poor skin condition or poor skin hygiene
- Dehydration
- Malnourished without illness-related cause
- Loss of weight
- Soiled clothing or bed
- Broken eyeglasses/frames
- Welts on wrists and ankles as a result of being restrained
- Inappropriate use of medication, over/under-dosing
- An older person disclosing they have been hit, slapped, kicked or mistreated

Psychological abuse

The psychological abuse of older people includes shouting, swearing, blaming, threatening, intimidating, ignoring, humiliating and the use of a variety of threats. These verbal assaults can also be accompanied by threats of denying the person access to something such as a person, pet, object or activity that they enjoy, value or love. Psychological abuse while leaving no physical bruising or scars is nevertheless extremely terrifying for the older person and activates a range of responses such as feelings of helplessness and excruciating shame leading to withdrawal, non-responsiveness and failure in the will to live (see Box 11.2). Given the lack of physical signs, the impact of psychological abuse is often dismissed as confusion or disorientation, or derided as paranoid ramblings and signs of dementia.

Box 11.2 Indicators and impact of psychological abuse

- Helplessness
- Hesitation to talk openly
- Implausible stories of mental cruelty
- Confusion or disorientation
- Anger without apparent cause
- Sudden changes in behaviour
- Emotionally overwrought or agitated
- Unusual behaviour such as sucking, biting, rocking
- Unexplained fears
- Denial of the situation
- Extremely withdrawn
- Non-communicative
- Non-responsive
- Deep sense of shame
- Disclosure of verbal or psychological abuse

Financial abuse

The financial abuse of older people can range from relatives' expectation that they will inherit the bulk of the older person's estate to stealing or defrauding them of money, goods, pension book or property. AEA (2004) found that 24% of older people lost their home through it being sold or taken away without their consent, while 17% gave their houses away under pressure or without knowing what they were doing. Fraud and stealing is often conducted under the auspices of power of attorney contracts, although 10–15% of these are not registered and so are not legally binding. The older person may also be coerced or pressured to change their will in favour of the abuser. In addition, unscrupulous builders are known to prey on older people, especially those living alone who are socially isolated, by carrying out unnecessary repairs to the older person's home at vastly inflated prices (see Box 11.3). Financial abuse has a considerable impact on older people who often become anxious about their financial situation, and who worry about having sufficient funds for their funeral. These anxieties can cause considerable distress to the older person and have considerable impact on their sense of safety and security.

Box 11.3 Indicators and impact of financial abuse

- Cheques not signed by the older person
- Sudden changes in bank accounts such as unexplained withdrawals of large sums of money by someone accompanying older person
- Inclusion of additional names on older person's bank account
- Abrupt changes to or sudden establishment of will
- Sudden appearance of uninvolved relatives claiming rights to an older person's affairs or possessions
- Unexplained sudden transfer of assets to a family member or someone outside the family
- Numerous unpaid bills or overdue rent when someone is supposed to be paying bills
- Excessive amounts of money being spent on care of older person
- Lack of amenities, such as TV, personal grooming items
- Absence of appropriate clothing that person should be able to afford
- Unexplained disappearance of funds or valuable possessions such as art, silverware, or jewellery
- Deliberate isolation of older person from friends or family, giving the carer total control
- Unscrupulous builder insisting on unnecessary repairs to home

Sexual abuse

The sexual abuse of the elderly is often poorly understood by professionals especially as cultural norms do not deem them sexually attractive. Practitioners need to be mindful that like all sexual violence and rape, the sexual abuse of older people is an expression of power, control and violence. The range of sexually abusive behaviour seen in older people includes sexually suggestive language and behaviour, sexual touching and forcing the person to engage in sexual acts against their wishes, and rape (see Box 11.4). The sexual abuse of older people is undoubtedly the least reported of the abuses as older people are forced to suffer in silence. Most sexual abuse of older people is committed by carers either in the victim's home, or in care homes, although sometimes it can be a fellow resident. AEA (2004) have expressed concern that there may be a genuine increase of sexual abuse in the elderly population as sexual offenders move from the more closely monitored residential children's homes to care homes for the elderly.

Box 11.4 Indicators and impact of sexual abuse

- Bruises around the breasts or genital area
- Unexplained STIs or genital infections
- Unexplained vaginal or anal bleeding
- Torn, stained or bloody underclothes
- Shame
- Reluctance to undress or be naked
- An older person disclosing that they have been sexually assaulted or raped
- Emotional shock
- Disbelief and/or denial
- Embarrassment
- Shame
- Guilt
- Depression
- Powerlessness
- Disorientation
- Flashbacks
- Fear and anxiety
- Anger
- Physical stress

Sexual abuse has considerable impact on the older person as in all forms of sexual violence. Being forced to perform sexual acts that they would never have performed with their partner can be extremely humiliating and shaming. Many older people come from a generation that had very different attitudes to sex and sexuality and so will feel deeply embarrassed and uncomfortable talking about such experiences. In addition they may blame themselves which could be a further barrier to disclosure. As in child sexual abuse and rape the impact of sexual violation can lead to a range of psychobiological reactions (see Chapter 7 and Chapter 8). The most common responses centre around emotional shock, numbness, disbelief and denial that the sexual abuse has happened. This commonly elicits feelings of embarrassment, shame and guilt and engenders loss of control and a sense of powerlessness and disorientation.

Neglect

As in child abuse, neglect to some degree underpins all the other abuses in not providing safety and care to vulnerable individuals. Commonly neglect in older people includes failing to provide food, heat, clothing, appropriate medical attention or access to resources and basic needs that are essential to physical and mental well-being. A common indicator of neglect is pressure or bed sores which are seen in approximately 10% of elderly hospital inpatients. Neglect has significant impact on individuals as it fails to provide basic physiological and psychological needs necessary for security and safety. In the absence of feeling safe, older people will lose trust and faith in others that they will be cared for leading to a failure to thrive and willing themselves to die (see Box 11.5).

While the indicators of the range of abuse provide a framework of common warning signs that the older person is being abused they must be seen within the context of the sociopsychological world of the survivor, as well as current medical concerns. Furthermore the impact of elder abuse can vary enormously and clinicians must avoid using a rigid check list to assess degree of abuse. To make a full assessment it is critical to engage with the older person and explore their experiences, and understand barriers to disclosure such as denial or shame. In addition they must guard against dismissing some of the symptoms as a feature of the deteriorating mental capacities of the older person, or rely on reports by carers which may be attempts to undermine the veracity of the older person's experiences and cover up any abuse. To truly uncover elder abuse, practitioners need to build a respectful relationship with the older person in which their concerns are taken seriously and responded to appropriately.

Box 11.5 Indicators and impact of neglect

- Dirt, faecal or urine smell
- Health and safety hazards in older person's living environment
- Rashes
- Bed sores
- Lice
- Inadequately clothed
- Malnourished, dehydrated
- Untreated medical condition
- Poor personal hygiene
- Withholding medication, or over-medication
- Complication to other medical conditions
- Lack of assistance with eating or drinking
- Unsanitary and unclean conditions
- Helplessness and powerlessness
- Lack of security
- Impaired trust that they will be cared for appropriately
- Failure to thrive
- Willing themselves to die

LONG-TERM EFFECTS

The long-term effects of elder abuse are an undermined sense of safety and increased sense of powerlessness and autonomy. The trauma of systematic elder abuse can give rise to post-traumatic stress symptoms which may remain undiagnosed and untreated leading to further deficits in physical and psychological well-being. A danger associated with elder abuse is that symptoms that arise from interpersonal trauma may be attributed to declining cognitive capacities, and thus not addressed. An example of this is the disorientation seen in trauma being misdiagnosed as dementia, or psychosis. It is for this reason that accurate assessment is made to ascertain the relative contribution to symptoms of trauma and abuse, and those that are a result of a medical condition (see Box 11.6).

Box II.6 Core symptoms and long-term effects of elder abuse

- Loss of control, autonomy and self-agency
- Powerlessness and helplessness
- Fear of retaliation and consequences
- Betrayal and mistrust
- Deteriorating physical and mental health
- Reduced recovery from minor illnesses or surgery
- Impaired immune system functioning
- Failure to thrive, wishing to die
- Under or over-medicating
- Self-medicating through alcohol misuse
- Post-traumatic stress symptoms and PTSD
- Disorientation
- Flashbacks
- Hyper-reactivity, affect dysregulation and hypervigilance
- Memory impairment
- Suicidal ideation and covert suicide attempts
- Anxiety
- Depression
- Fear of increasing dependency or going into care home
- Helplessness
- Feeling trapped and unable to escape
- Shame
- Social isolation

While it is not uncommon for many older people to experience exaggerated anxiety and fear as well as depression in the absence of elder abuse, clinicians must be open to the possibility that some of these symptoms may be exacerbated by deliberate elder abuse. Fears such as not having enough money for their funeral, fear of abandonment or desertion and going into care may not be irrational but may be as a result of threats made by family members. This will impact on increased fear of dependency which over time can give rise to depression and a loss of will to live. While many older people do not necessarily have the energy to commit suicide they may become preoccupied with suicidal ideation, and may attempt covert suicide by refusing to eat or over or under-dosing prescribed medication. In addition, the loss of will to live may impact on difficulties in recovering from minor illnesses, or surgery.

Prolonged activation of stress reaction can put extra strain on already depleted physical energy and physiological functioning with a concomitant deterioration in health. There is evidence that prolonged stress and the cascade of biochemical and neurochemical changes in the body puts extra strain on internal organs and immune system functioning which can be fatal in elderly people who already have an array of medical problems.

Post-traumatic stress symptoms such as hyper-reactivity can lead to exaggerated irritability in the older person with pronounced affect dysregulation, making them difficult to calm or soothe. Some elderly people may resort to alcohol misuse as a form of affect regulation and psychic numbing. Protracted interpersonal trauma invariably evokes confusion, disorientation and memory impairment which further undermines the older person's ability to process and integrate the trauma.

Ultimately the older person feels trapped with no form of escape which reinforces their dependency. The fear of further abuse and shame inculcates silence which is compounded if there are no active relatives or friends in the older person's social support network. Furthermore, many older people come from an era that advocated stoicism and self-sufficiency, and discouraged talking about worries and concerns, a factor that many abusers capitalise on as it minimises the risk of disclosure and detection.

WORKING WITH ELDER ABUSE

The nature of elder abuse is such that many survivors will not necessarily seek counselling. This can be due to a variety of factors, not least lack of mobility or ill health. In addition, older people often come from an era in which they were taught to be stoical in the face of adversity, suffer in silence and not to make a fuss. This makes it not only difficult to disclose elder abuse but also to seek help. As a result many generic counsellors will have little or no experience of working with older people. Arguably, all counsellors would benefit from contextualising their work into a developmental lifespan perspective, including training and awareness of working with elderly clients. Generic counsellors may be more likely to see relatives or adult children of older people who are being abused and who are suffering from the vicarious traumatisation of seeing a loved one being abused and exploited. Such counsellors may find that the principles of working with a survivor of elder abuse may be helpful in working with adult children.

Those clinicians who do work with survivors may need to be more flexible in their work in terms of providing home or hospital visits especially if the survivor's medical condition is compromised. They also need to liaise much more regularly with other agencies to ensure all the needs of the survivor are supported and met. Most critically they need to be knowledgeable about the impact of aging on older people, and the range of physical and mental difficulties that they may encounter. Specialist training on working with the older people is invaluable, as is knowledge of the range of services that can be accessed. This is critical to accurate assessment and establishing a holistic care plan in which the range of needs can be addressed. This would also provide an opportunity to explore their attitudes and beliefs about older people and to confront their own existential fears around aging, invisibility, loss of control or potency, and dependency.

As in domestic abuse and most forms of interpersonal abuse, survivors of elder abuse invariably feel powerless and helpless and have difficulty identifying and naming their abuse. To this effect counsellors need to establish a secure base and ensure safety in order to explore the survivor's experiences. In many respects the core therapeutic goals resemble those of working with survivors of domestic abuse (see Box 11.7 and Chapter 10). It is imperative that the older person be given a voice to express their experiences and to explore their options. As in domestic abuse many survivors of elder abuse feel that they have no means of escape and that things will only get worse. Although there may not be immediate solutions or options it is important to work towards recognising and accepting any available options and develop and implement these over time. In the interim counsellors need to offer psychological support and focus on validating the survivor's commitment to seeking help, harm minimisation and restoring control to the survivor.

In order to establish the therapeutic relationship it is necessary to get to know the older person rather than allow any preconceived attitudes or beliefs to contaminate the therapeutic setting. Counsellors need to be aware of how they construct older people and ensure that they are not seen as dependent and a burden but as having a unique identity. It is worth remembering that older people come from an era in which respect and forms of address were highly prized. To facilitate engagement it may be helpful to check how the survivor would prefer to be addressed, as many prefer Mr or Mrs rather than first name terms, which they may experience as patronising or over-familiar.

It is also critical to contextualise the survivor within a lifespan perspective and to respect their history and identity, not just in the present but also in the past. To accord the older survivor respect, status and dignity for their rich life experiences enables them to relate with the core of their identity rather than just how they present now as an older person. This can restore visibility and potency and make them feel valued as an individual. It can be extremely helpful and restorative to revive and explore the dreams and hopes, achievements and successes that they had in their younger years to get a comprehensive view of who they are. This includes respect

Box 11.7 Core therapeutic goals

- Comprehensive and accurate assessment
- Establish secure base and safety
- Make the client visible
- Identify and encourage naming of abuse
- Restore control and autonomy
- Restore dignity and respect
- Harm minimisation
- Give choices
- Value and respect their unique identity within lifespan perspective
- Validate help seeking
- Identify needs
- Reduce anxiety and depression
- Build increased support network – family, befriending, activities
- Encourage access to range of services
- Multidisciplinary approach, co-ordination between agencies and sharing information
- Facilitate informed choices without pressure or coercion
- Grieve losses such as trust in others, especially family, and un-mourned bereavements

for their ethnicity, culture, religion and the historical time in which they lived. It is all too easy to only see the person at the age they are now rather than when they were younger, and in doing so filter out their essential self.

In seeing the client as primarily frail, dependent and in need of protection, the counsellor may infantilise the survivor and reinforce loss of control which can impede the restoration of control, choice and autonomy over their lives, and thereby collude with the abuser and reinforce dependency. Counsellors must restore dignity to the survivor and empower them as much as they would a younger person. This will enable the survivor to reconnect to the essential self and allow them to reconnect to others. As in other types of interpersonal abuse the presence of a support network is critical to healing. This can be difficult for elderly people as they may have lost friends, siblings and partners through bereavement which can be traumatic as they have faced myriad losses, making it hard to reattach. Counsellors need to be respectful of this and yet sensitively encourage establishing new friendships with supportive others. This can be done through engaging in local community clubs and the range of activities available to older people. In the case of mobility problems it may be possible to link to a befriending scheme whereby they are visited in their own home. While this may be hard to do initially due to impaired trust, it is a goal to work towards. In combination this will reduce social isolation and loneliness and could prevent further abuse.

The many losses elderly people face through loss of control, potency, and loss of agency as well as multiple bereavements, may make it hard to mourn each individual loss, making it crucial that the therapeutic process can provide the opportunity to grieve. Such grieving also needs to include loss of trust in people once held dear, especially if they are the abuser(s), loss of trust in others, and loss of faith in humanity (Sanderson, 2008). Other losses that may come to the fore are those related to failing health, mobility and psychological faculties as they grow older, and the restrictions these place on their lives. Loss invariably activates, or in some cases deactivates, the attachment system and can trigger insecure attachment patterns and style. In order to provide a truly secure base, counsellors need to identify the survivor's and their own attachment style in order to ensure that the interaction of the two styles does not interfere with the therapeutic relationship and that they are able to connect in a sensitively attuned way. It is through such connection that the survivor can learn to trust again, reconnect to others and the world.

THERAPEUTIC CHALLENGES

Working with elder abuse generates a number of therapeutic challenges, not least mobility issues, complex medical needs, reduced faculties and deteriorating physical and mental health. Impaired hearing or speech can make communication arduous or laboured, while confusion, disorientation and impaired memory can impede coherent narrative. Counsellors need to be patient and allow the survivor to pace the session and be attuned to a different rhythm so that they are in synchrony with the survivor. Due to the betrayal of trust, survivors may be highly suspicious and reluctant to engage in the therapeutic process. This needs to be understood within the context of interpersonal trauma rather than resistance or the survivor being curmudgeonly.

Age difference can sometimes be a barrier for older clients, in feeling that a young counsellor is ill equipped to really understand their experiences, especially how it feels to experience the many losses associated with aging. Many older people are not used to revealing private information to those younger than themselves which can make self-revelation awkward. Counsellors need to understand this concern and not dismiss it out of hand. Showing genuine interest in the survivor's past and present life can reduce awkwardness and facilitate deeper exploration.

Fierce self-sufficiency and need for control in the survivor also needs to be sensitively understood as a way to ward off fears of dependency which become increasingly manifest as the person ages or deteriorates physically or mentally. While truculent independence may be a defence against dependency it may also indicate an insecure-avoidant (dismissive) attachment style, or reflect feelings of shame at being abused. Counsellors must assess the origins of these dynamics to fully understand the survivor's fears or defences and respond appropriately. They may also need to be aware of their own attachment style and the interplay of this with the attachment style of the survivor. As such it helps to have an understanding of the survivor's pre-morbid personality as well as the current presentation. Alongside this any pre-existing abuse or vulnerability must be identified, processed and integrated. Working with elder abuse demands enormous amounts of patience and tolerance and counsellors must ensure they have these in abundance in order to remain compassionate. It is only with such compassion that survivors can find compassion for themselves and begin the healing process.

The sharing of information with others in a professional way which does not undermine the confidentiality necessary for the therapeutic process presents a further challenge. Counsellors will need to consider how comfortable they feel about sharing information and to what degree they wish to communicate with distressed family member(s), who may also be suffering, knowing that their relative has been abused. Relatives may wish to attend sessions, or need their own counselling, and counsellors may need to consider providing referrals so that they can be supported. It is important to assess the safety of family members and their motivation to ensure that the counsellor is not seduced into colluding with abusive relatives. Counsellors must be clear about their boundaries and what they can and cannot offer, and if information is shared or relatives are seen, that this is always done with the survivor's permission.

A final challenge to the counsellor is the impact of working with survivors of elder abuse as it may elicit fears around the inexorable reality of the aging process. If the counsellor has anxieties around growing old and concomitant losses, he may feel overwhelmed in the presence of older people whose frailties are all too palpable. Working with older people forces clinicians to confront their own existential fears around invisibility, loss of control, potency and dependency, which can feel overwhelming. Knowing the extent of elder abuse and the cruelty and brutality therein can shatter counsellor assumptions about the world, and raise questions and concerns about their own fears of dependency and vulnerability in old age. This is exacerbated if they themselves have had negative experiences of being cared for or have an insecure attachment style, and can evoke anxieties about how they might be cared for as they age. Such fears may lead some counsellors to recoil from working with survivors of elder abuse, to avoid confronting their own dread of growing old and anxieties about how they will manage their own aging process and dependency needs.

Working with elder abuse can be highly demanding and extremely rewarding. With appropriate training, supervision, and the courage to challenge any negative perceptions of older people, counsellors can facilitate post-traumatic growth. To be able to restore faith in humanity and renewed vigour in such a vulnerable client group can do much to restore belief and faith in the power of a genuine caring relationship.

Case vignette: Margaret

Margaret, a 77-year-old married woman, was referred to a counsellor who specialised in working with older people. As English was not her first language she presented with a thick strong accent despite being married to her English husband for 48 years. Margaret's husband was eight years her junior and they had two children together, plus a child from a previous relationship of Margaret's. Margaret had had a hard life and had started to deteriorate physically when she retired, when she had a minor stroke resulting in a variety of health problems. Margaret and her husband had never had a harmonious marriage, as he was demanding and controlling, and had been cruel and brutal with the children, especially his stepdaughter. Although not physically violent towards Margaret, he controlled the children through physical abuse, and consistently humiliated Margaret with verbal assaults and degrading treatment, often in front of the children. The husband's abusive personality and systematic domestic abuse had terrified Margaret, and rendered her mute and powerless, leading to her becoming increasingly withdrawn and isolated. Despite her becoming increasingly frail, Margaret's husband still insisted that she do all the traditional female chores such as shopping, cooking and cleaning, and be responsive to his daily sexual demands. If Margaret resisted his sexual advances he would rape her.

Margaret's husband also took her pin number and consistently used her debit card to buy gifts for others without telling her. As her health deteriorated and she was no longer able to prepare meals, he refused to cook anything more elaborate than a microwave meal. Margaret began to lose weight at an alarming rate and became so frail that she was too unwell to have necessary surgery. The children became alarmed at his neglect of her, leaving her in a bedroom riddled with damp all day, preferring to buy a new car rather than make essential repairs to the bedroom. He refused to help with Margaret's personal hygiene or encourage any daily activities, preferring to shut her into her bedroom night and day. Margaret received no nutritious food and sustained daily verbal assaults about her uselessness and what a burden she was.

As Margaret continued to lose weight with no medical explanation, it was clear that she was failing to thrive and that she had lost the will to live. Finally the children intervened and asked for a counsellor to visit. Luckily the counsellor spoke the same native language as Margaret and slowly she began to speak about the years of psychological and sexual abuse she had suffered and how this abuse was still being enacted. Although invited to live with one of her children, Margaret had always refused as she feared the consequences and reprisals. Through the warmth, compassion and empathy provided by the counsellor Margaret found a renewed will to live and as a result decided to move in with one of her children. Away from her abusive husband and fuelled by healthy, nutritious food Margaret was able to put on sufficient weight to have surgery which significantly improved her quality of life. To date she has never returned to her husband and takes pleasure in spending time with her children and grandchildren.

SUMMARY

- Elder abuse is a pernicious interpersonal trauma which, when perpetrated in the home, resembles domestic abuse in being largely hidden with the older person suffering in silence. Elder abuse incorporates five forms of interpersonal abuse: physical abuse, psychological abuse, financial abuse, sexual abuse, and neglect. Elder abuse is often minimised but is of growing concern as people live longer and society faces an increasing older population.
- There is insufficient up-to-date prevalence data but it is estimated that half a million people are subjected to some form of elder abuse, although this may represent the tip of the iceberg as older people are often too frail and frightened to report their abuse.
- Females are most at risk of elder abuse as they live longer and the age group most at risk is the 80 to 89-year-olds. Two thirds of perpetrators of elder abuse are family members, the most common being adult children, although partners and spouses are also implicated. Older people are also at risk of abuse in their own home by paid cares or in care homes.
- The impact and long-term effects of physical and psychological abuse is a compromised sense of security and safety, with financial abuse eliciting anxiety about financial security and having enough to pay for their funeral. Elder abuse is also characterised by fears of increasing dependency, and about what is going to happen to them and anxieties about having to go into a care home.
- The trauma of elder abuse can lead to post-traumatic stress symptoms that are often not diagnosed and left untreated, which can lead to deteriorating physical and mental health, depression and failure to thrive, and loss of will to live.
- Working with the elderly is predicated on the same principles as all other forms of interpersonal trauma but can give rise to additional considerations such as deteriorating physical and psychological health, immobility, impaired hearing or speech, and confusion and disorientation.
- Counsellors need to see the older person within a developmental lifespan perspective which respects their unique history and identity throughout their lifespan and not just as they are in the present. It is imperative that counsellors do not make assumptions about older people and that they make them visible and provide a secure base and voice from which to recover from the interpersonal trauma of elderly abuse.

- While there are a number of challenges and obstacles when working with elder abuse such as the survivor's deteriorating physical and psychological health, and myriad losses, counsellors need to work with these and ensure that they have faced their own existential fears of growing old, having to face inexorable losses, and increased dependency, to ensure that they remain empathic and compassionate. With this they will be able to work towards restoring faith in humanity and a renewed will to live.

SUGGESTED READING

Action on Elder Abuse (AEA) (2004) *Hidden Voices: People's Experience of Abuse.* London: Help The Aged.

British Medical Association (2007) *Domestic Abuse.* London: BMA.

Department of Health (2000) *No Secrets: The Protection of Vulnerable Adults: Guidance on the Development and Implementation of Multi Agency Policies and Procedures.* London: TSO.

Penhale, B., Parker, J. and Kingston, P. (2000) *Elder Abuse: Practitioners Guide.* London: Venture.

Pritchard, J. (2001) *Male Victims of Elder Abuse.* London: Jessica Kingsley Publishers.

Pritchard, J. (ed.) (2008) *Good Practice in Safeguarding Adults: Working Effectively in Adult Protection.* London: Jessica Kingsley Publisher.

Sanderson, C. (2008) *Counselling Survivors of Domestic Abuse.* London: Jessica Kingsley Publishers.

CHAPTER 12

INSTITUTIONAL ABUSE AS INTERPERSONAL TRAUMA

There has been an increasing number of scandals and inquiries into institutional abuse in recent years that have highlighted the scale and spectrum of abuses committed in residential settings. The hidden nature of institutional abuse, and the secrecy surrounding it, has made it difficult for researchers to obtain accurate incidence and prevalence data. It is clear that institutional abuse is a varied phenomenon involving individual risk factors as well as those that emanate from residing in institutional settings such as institutionalisation, the impact of brutal regimes, and abuse through care systems that fail to safeguard individuals. While institutionalisation results in de-individuation, depersonalisation, and lack of autonomy and self-agency which can be harmful, it is the vulnerability to direct abuse by both staff and peers that when enacted can have the most traumatising impact and long-term effects which compromise mental and psychical well-being.

Institutions and residential homes are commonly populated by vulnerable individuals who are rendered invisible and voiceless by being hidden away from the rest of the community. Many of those in institutional care feel abandoned, neglected or rejected which increases their need to be seen and heard, and yet they are often largely ignored until a scandal unfolds. It is only when inquiries are launched that the plight of many of those in institutional care is brought to society's attention and a recognition of the traumatising effects of institutional abuse emerge. Such investigations also illuminate how the vulnerability of those in residential care becomes a target for abuse not just by individuals but also by an inadequate care system.

While institutional abuse can occur in a variety of settings such as residential care for both adults and children, including boarding schools, general and psychiatric hospitals, nursing homes for the elderly, young offender institutions, prison, the armed forces and closed religious communities and cults, this chapter will focus primarily on the interpersonal trauma of institutional abuse in residential children's homes. Arguably some of the dynamics of institutional abuse highlighted in this chapter will have some validity in survivors from other institutional settings and clinicians may find that similar therapeutic considerations will apply.

This chapter will focus on the institutional abuse of children in residential homes and look at the spectrum of abuse committed by both staff and peers. While under-reporting makes it difficult to ascertain accurate incidence or prevalence rates, the chapter will examine which children are most at risk and who the perpetrators are. In exploring the nature and dynamics of abuse, risk factors such as previous abuse experience, especially physical and sexual abuse, will be identified, and the impact of traumatisation will be assessed. As in other forms of interpersonal trauma, survivors of institutional abuse commonly present with a range of mental health problems such as mood disorder, self-destructive behaviour, suicidal ideation and substance misuse. Working with such survivors generates innumerable challenges such as impaired trust, attachment and relational difficulties and fear of rejection and abandonment. It is only through a safe therapeutic relationship that survivors of institutional abuse can experience a secure base, perhaps for the first time, from which to connect to self and others.

SPECTRUM OF INSTITUTIONAL ABUSE

Institutional abuse is a varied phenomenon which cannot be explained by any individual factor but needs to be understood across three dimensions. According to Gil (1982) institutional abuse in children's homes operates on three discrete levels; overt and direct abuse, regime abuse and system abuse (see Table 12.1), although some argue that it is not institutions that abuse but individuals (Thomas, 1990). While this is true, institutions can render individuals vulnerable to abuse by turning a blind eye.

Table 12.1 Three levels of institutional abuse (adapted from Gil, 1982)

Overt and direct abuse	Regime/Programme abuse	System abuse
• Physical, emotional or sexual abuse • Committed by individual staff and peers	• Legitimised aspects of regime or treatment • Forms of discipline and control	• Not single individual • Aspects of the larger system of child care and child protection

Overt and direct abuse incorporates physical, emotional and sexual abuse and neglect and can be committed by carer to child or child to child. Direct abuse by staff is usually individually motivated and specifically directed at individual children rather than being part of an overall regime. Peer abuse is usually committed by other residents within a hierarchical power structure and incorporates peer bullying such as physical and psychological abuse, as well as sexual abuse. In addition, peers are known to coerce and entice other children into substance abuse, delinquency and crimes, and sexual exploitation (see Chapter 9).

A further form of institutional abuse comes from regimes employed in individual children's homes that aim to discipline or restrain residents. These are usually believed to be in the interests of all residents and staff, and are often implemented within a culture or ethos that believes that they are a necessary and appropriate form of ensuring safety. These regimes may include physical restraint which includes a degree of physical abuse, and psychological abuse such as humiliation and derogation which impacts on emotional well-being.

Much regime abuse is committed indirectly through poor staff ratios, making it difficult to provide individual care and whereby children are left to their own devices without adequate supervision. This is compounded by limited access to additional resources such as adequate training, high-quality supervision and access to psychological support for staff. This leads to a sense of powerlessness in staff who feel isolated, stigmatised, under-valued and under-paid. The lack of psychological support and supervision renders staff vulnerable to burnout, or secondary traumatic stress, high staff absenteeism and poor staff retention which impacts on the children in care, as they are deprived of much-needed continuity of care. Although lack of training is not a causal factor it can exacerbate institutional abuse due to a lack of knowledge and understanding of the dynamics that give rise to abuse, and how to manage these. In addition beleaguered staff act may be compelled to act out any concomitant frustrations on the children.

Inquiry reports have also highlighted that the management style and leadership is a further factor in abuse in individual institutions as is the institution's culture, ethos and practice in terms of clear policies, open communication, clear expectations of staff and holding children in high regard. Barter *et al.* (2004) found that an authoritarian regime and leadership style is a common feature in UK inquiry reports whereby rigid hierarchical structures promote similar hierarchical structures in residents. Furthermore, a management style which is unresponsive to staff needs can create an atmosphere which is unresponsive to the children's needs.

Systems abuse is not committed by any one individual or institution but reflects failures in the larger system of safeguarding children and the provision of child protection and care. Such abuse commonly manifests as neglect whereby children who have been abused, or neglected, and placed into care are not provided with any therapeutic intervention to manage the effects of such abuses or the impact of severed attachments and concomitant relational difficulties. Thus children who have been traumatised prior to their entry into care, suffering from trauma symptoms of hyper-reactivity, poor affect regulation or impulse control, self-harming behaviours, anxiety or depression, are left untreated and unsupported in how to manage their distress. This results in a large number of vulnerable and needy children being corralled in a highly charged atmosphere whose needs are not met due to the competing demands on the staff. A particularly insidious example of this is when children who have been sexually abused are placed with other children who are sexually harmful (Farmer and Pollock, 1998; Lindsay, 1997; O'Neil, 2001; Barter, 1997).

A corollary to this failure is lack of adequate resourcing for residential child care in terms of professional qualifications, staff training, supervision and pay structures that reflect the important role that child care professionals perform in safeguarding children. Making safeguarding children in care a priority by providing high-quality care may reduce the stigma of being in care in the UK and subvert the cultural legacy of shame and stigma associated with being in care. This in turn would minimise the negative assumption made about children in care who are often not believed when making allegations of abuse, or who experience revictimisation. All too often children who have been in care are seen as lacking in morals and as architects of their own downfall. This is aptly illustrated when such children are sexually exploited, or raped, and this is attributed to promiscuity or loose morals, rather than an increased vulnerability to abuse.

In combination the three levels of abuse can result in a range of abuses (see Figure 12.1) including physical, emotional or sexual abuse as well as neglect, com-

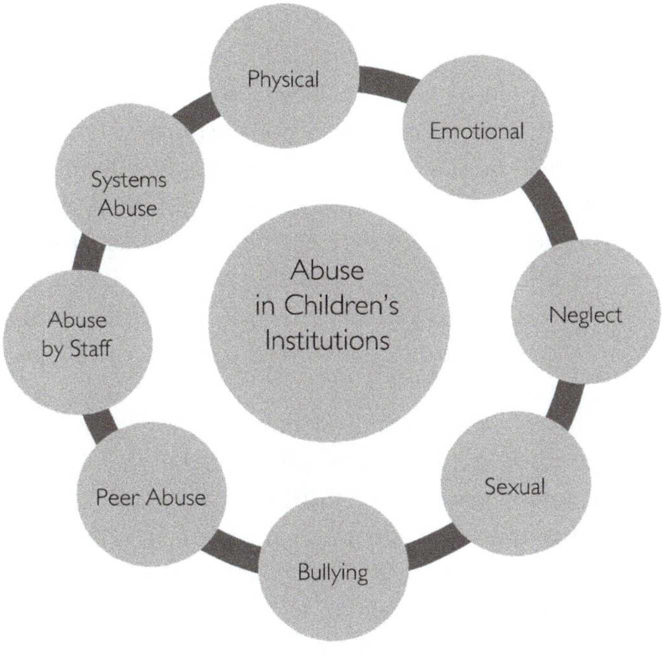

Figure 12.1 Spectrum of abuse in children's institutions

mitted either by staff or peers.

The most common form of institutional abuse in children's homes is physical abuse by both staff and peers, followed by verbal assaults, and sexual abuse. Inquiries have shown that staff and peers have been implicated in the full spectrum of abuse, though abuse by peers is driven by different dynamics and risk factors.

DEFINITION OF INSTITUTIONAL ABUSE

There is no universally agreed definition of institutional abuse of children, although Gil's 1982 proposed definition that "... any system, programme, policy, procedure or individual interaction with a child placement that abuses, neglects, or is detrimental to the child's health, safety, or emotional and physical well-being, or in any way exploits or violates the child's basic rights" (p.9) has been used by some researchers as a good starting point (Barter *et al.*, 2004). In the UK, the National Association of Young People in Care (NAYPIC, 1989) considers institutional abuse of children to be reflected in "...a system becoming increasingly more punitive in its failure to respond to their [children's] needs" (p.1). To really legitimise the institutional abuse of children, and give victims a voice, it is necessary to have an agreed definition that specifies more precisely what is meant and included under the term "institutional abuse".

INCIDENCE AND PREVALENCE OF INSTITUTIONAL ABUSE

Like most interpersonal trauma, institutional abuse is under-reported, and most data comes from high-profile scandals. This under-reporting is in part due to the closed nature of institutions, secrecy and fear of the consequences of disclosure, by either children or staff. Most incidence is collected when a whistle blower leaks information, or a tragedy occurs and a scandal erupts. While this is often illuminating it only provides information on what occurred in that individual home and may not reflect data in other homes. To date there is insufficient robust data as to the actual level of abuse, and that which is available may only be the tip of the iceberg. Some data is available through retrospective, or historical, accounts from adults who were in residential care who come forward years later to support current abuse allegations.

Available data suggests that the most common form of abuse in children's homes is physical abuse ranging between 35% (Blatt, 1992) and 55% (Rosenthal *et al.*, 1991), with sexual abuse between 17% (Blatt, 1992) and 24% (Rosenthal *et al.*, 1991). Although sexual abuse appears to be less frequent, this is likely to be due to under-reporting as the secret nature of such abuse means there is rarely any corroborating evidence. In addition, children may be reluctant to disclose sexual abuse due to shame and embarrassment, and the fear that they will not be believed.

WHO IS MOST AT RISK OF INSTITUTIONAL ABUSE?

All children in residential care are at risk of institutional abuse but those with disabilities and a previous history of abuse, especially sexual abuse, have an elevated risk. Research has also shown that male children are more at risk of physical abuse from both staff and peers, while females are three times more likely to face sexual abuse (Barter, 2006, Rosenthal *et al.*, 1991). Clinicians need to be mindful that the gender difference for sexual abuse may reflect a reporting bias whereby males may be reluctant to disclose such abuse. When assessing clients who have been in care it is important to consider that sexual abuse may have been a feature even if initially the client may be reluctant to disclose this.

Research further indicates that children in care are more vulnerable to sexual exploitation as they are lonely, isolated from their families, and feel unwanted and abandoned and will crave "special" attention. The risk of sexual abuse is further elevated if the child has a history of sexual abuse, or behavioural difficulties. Blatt and Brown (1986) also propose that there is an elevated risk of abuse in children who are perceived as more difficult, demanding or needy. Sadly, children labelled as difficult are more likely to be ignored, and less likely to be believed if they complain or make a disclosure due to negative assumptions about their character, behaviour and truthfulness. This increases the chance that the child's evidence will be discounted and rejected, reinforcing their sense of helplessness and voicelessness. Finally, research suggests that adolescents are more at risk of abuse by staff and peers, although this may reflect a reporting bias in young adults being more able to disclose than younger children, who are more likely to normalise their experiences, including institutional abuse.

PERPETRATORS OF INSTITUTIONAL ABUSE

According to the research literature, the majority of staff who commit abuse in children's homes are male. Rosenthal *et al.* (1991) found that males were implicated in 62% of physical abuse, 54% in neglects and 77% in sexual abuse, despite the fact that less than a third of all residential staff in children's homes are male. Penhale (1999) found that although female staff were less likely to use force, a proportion collaborated in physical abuse administered by males. While there is little empirical evidence to support the belief that potential child sexual abusers deliberately enter child care work to target and gain access to vulnerable children, anecdotal evidence from large scale inquiries suggests this is commonly the case. Inquiries have further indicated that sexual abusers in children's homes may also have links to paedophiles outside the residential home to whom they supply children for sexual purposes. An example of this was seen in the investigation in Islington Council's Children's homes in 1995 where all 12 homes were found to have been infiltrated by paedophiles who not only sexually abused children in the homes, but also acted as pimps for paedophile rings outside the homes (Fairweather, 2009), some of whom are allegedly linked to the sexual abuse of children at the Haut de la Garrene children's home in Jersey (Fairweather, 2008). These have included respected members of the community in a variety of professions, and even if they are not directly involved in sexual abuse, they nevertheless turn a blind eye to such sexual exploitation. A further risk is posed by sexual predators who target children from residential homes and entice them into sexual exploitation and prostitution.

In the case of peer abuse, research has shown that the most serious abuse occurred away from staff and was often premeditated and planned. Although staff tended to intervene in physical and sexual abuse when they were aware of it, some abuse was normalised by staff through hierarchical power dynamics (Barter *et al.*, 2004). The most serious sexual assaults by peers were generally not reported to staff and children tended to rely on each other for emotional support. The range of peer violence identified in the research includes direct physical assault, systematic physical abuse, and non-contact abuse such as threatening looks or gestures, written threats, and destruction of possessions or rooms. The range of unwelcome sexual behaviour includes sexual gestures and remarks, flashing of genitals, grabbing of breasts or genitals, inappropriate sexual touching, sexual assault and rape. Peers are also implicated in indirect abuses through the recruitment of other children into delinquency, substance abuse and sexual exploitation, often under threat of physical assaults.

NATURE AND DYNAMICS OF INSTITUTIONAL ABUSE

Institutionalisation as a result of confinement elicits a number of powerful dynamics such as depersonalisation and de-individuation (Goffman, 1968), as well as powerlessness and dependency which can render children in residential care highly vulnerable to further abuse. The nature of institutions means that individuals are forced into relinquishing control, autonomy and self-agency. Such loss is compounded by a number of other losses such as loss of family, friends, pets, home, and loss of continuity of identity. The trauma of depersonalisation, separation, loss and the rupture to affiliative bonds, activates a number of adaptive survival strategies. The sense of abandonment and desolation evokes either a desperate need to replace lost attachments by attaching to others, or to avoid any future attachments for fear of being abandoned again.

The basic human need to attach and form bonds renders children vulnerable to attaching to anyone who shows them any level of care, attention or affection, leading to indiscriminate attachments which could place them at risk. Such children will attach to staff in the hope that their dependency needs will be met, not realising that some staff may exploit these by emotionally or sexually abusing them. Alternatively they may attach to their peers to have their needs met, which, while in essence a positive solution, is fraught with difficulties as their peers are also hurting and thereby can only offer limited support due to their own dependency hunger. Some children, especially those previously abused by adults, may falsely believe that forming attachments with peers is safer, not realising that they are caught in a web of hierarchical power structures based on dominance and subordination which can put them at risk of further abuse.

Children who have been placed in residential care as a protection from abuse by parents and other adult caregivers may be suffering from trauma which has shaped their attachment patterns (Crittenden, 2000) which if left untreated may be re-enacted while in care. Abused children develop a variety of survival strategies which, while adaptive, may also increase vulnerability to abuse. As a protection from abuse some children will avoid any focus of attention by becoming invisible, by blending into the background and disavowing all emotional needs and feelings, which renders them vulnerable to neglect. In repudiating the need for attention, the self is sequestered into an inner fortress and becomes unreachable, to be replaced with a false self. This will manifest in appeasement behaviour in which the child will cover profound sadness or rage with a mask-like smile. This smile, which never reaches the eyes, is not predicated on real happiness or laughter but on despair and feelings that are too dangerous to express. Such children are often overly compliant and only experience themselves as extensions of other people, making it difficult to set boundaries, assert themselves or say "No". This unwittingly delivers them into the clutches of abusive adults or peers.

A compelling example of appeasement behaviour and compliance is seen in the child becoming extremely helpful to adults and staff in a form of traumatic bonding. Such children demonstrate a high degree of pseudomaturity which occludes their deeply buried dependency needs, turning them into "little helpers". Clinicians need to be mindful that this default position of submissiveness and compliance can persist into adulthood and lead to an increased risk of further victimisation and traumatisation such as domestic abuse. It can also manifest in the therapeutic setting in which the survivor will continue to cover up the full range of their feelings for fear of contaminating the counsellor. Such clients are often over-protective of the therapist and find it hard to relinquish their submissive and compliant stance.

An alternative survival strategy employed by children in care is distancing themselves from earlier abuse in order to minimise the traumatic impact by becoming hostile and avoidant of others. Here, through identification with the aggressor, the best form of defence becomes attack. Such children become hostile towards staff and peers by engaging in negative or aggressive behaviour which elicits hostility from others. This keeps people at bay and avoids further impingement from others. While this wards off boundary violations such as physical or sexual abuse, it nevertheless increases vulnerability to psychological abuse, brutalising physical restraint and punishment. It also reinforces the already negative self-image that they are "difficult" and deserving of abuse.

Whatever the reasons for a child entering care, the trauma of separation will heighten arousal and activate neurobiological reactions such as hyper-reactivity, poor impulse control and volatility. This makes for a highly combustible environment which is so highly charged that it further escalates traumatic responses. If these are left uncontained or untreated they can unleash primitive needs for control such as power and dominance hierarchies in which abuse is committed to avert feelings of helplessness and powerlessness. The competition for meagre resources to satisfy dependency needs for individual time, care and attention leads to further frustration and the sense of abandonment and rejection. To gain much-needed attention children may engage in liaisons with either staff or peers that are dangerous and coercive rather than cast themselves into an abyss of loneliness. The biological imperative to attach thus over-rides the quality of the attachment, even if it compromises physical or sexual safety. Counsellors need to be mindful that such attachment patterns persist into adulthood and are commonly enacted in the therapeutic relationship.

While in care all effort is directed into surviving, with little or no open protest, mourning, or grief. Bowlby (1973) found that when children were separated from their primary attachment figures three clear stages emerged: protest, despair and detachment. In the first stage the child would attempt some degree of protest through crying or negative behaviour, and this would soon be replaced with despair once the child recognised that their protest signals failed to elicit a return of the attachment figure. To conceal the intense inner feelings of despair and desolation, the child enters the stage of detachment in which they are forced to ignore what they feel or perceive. This detachment can lead to a pervasive depression and a wish to die which threatens to persist into adulthood. If the child has any disposable psychic energy, it may engage in fantasies of being rescued, preferably by the now idealised parent.

To offset the lack of power, children and young people in care may seek power through access to resources such as status, money, alcohol, drugs or association with other powerful individuals. This renders them vulnerable to other adults outside the institution who may encourage them to commit crime and become involved in drugs and sexual exploitation. While this is not performed within the institution, such individuals deliberately target vulnerable children in care as they are more malleable and easily coerced. In addition, once lured into criminal activities these children are often tasked to recruit other children in the home. This is done through enticement, coercion or threat, thus providing a constant supply of young people to predatory adults.

Inquiries have also shown that some individuals working with children in residential settings may have links with other predatory adults, including paedophile rings, outside the institution. This is often seen in sexual abuse and sexual exploitation, whereby a staff member may groom the child and once "broken in" will make the child available to other adults for sexual purposes. This can include systematic and regular sexual abuse, or being sold into sexual exploitation and prostitution. As many young people in care are invisible and abscond, or go missing for periods of time, the disappearance of a young person may not be assiduously investigated. The shame and humiliation associated with sexual exploitation or prostitution reduces detection and exposure of such abuses and prevents the young person from accessing appropriate protection.

THE IMPACT AND LONG-TERM EFFECTS OF INSTITUTIONAL ABUSE

The impact of the institutional abuse varies depending on the age of the child when entering residential care, with very young children at greater risk of institutionalisation due to normalisation and depersonalisation. Another crucial factor is the circumstances under which the child entered residential care and presence of pre-existing abuse prior to being taken into care. In terms of the impact of the abuse committed in the institution there are factors such as how long and how often the abuse occurred, the type of abuse experienced, the age of the victim when the abuse occurred, the relationship of the abuser to the victim and the reaction to the incident once it was reported.

One way to manage the trauma of separation when entering care is dissociation in which the child or young person compartmentalises their experience and organises attachment relationships around biases either toward cognition, thereby ignoring emotion, or vice versa (Crittenden, 2000). This dissociation can occur as a defence against shame which is manifest in a submissive stance, or narcissistic rage and revenge which is commonly reflected in a need to dominate and control. Dissociation also serves to sever contact with, or access to, the authentic self leading to depersonalisation. This is manifest in the child never showing how they feel and never saying what they think especially if it conflicts or disagrees with others who have power over them. The child must be hypervigilant and always remain attentive to adults, or those peers who hold power over them. In the absence of adequate protection or a secure base, the child has to search inside for safety and an inner secure base. To protect the vulnerable inner self the child builds a fortress to keep the authentic self safe by shutting others out, and locks the self away so it cannot be harmed or contaminated.

This fortress can sometimes be so impenetrable that it becomes virtually impossible to dismantle even in adulthood. As there are no external role models the child becomes reliant on inner resources and becomes disconnected from others as a form of protection. If on occasions the child does reach out, only to be rebuffed, or hurt, the more the child needs to retreat. As the child becomes more disconnected the more it is consumed with loneliness and despair. This is exacerbated in children who are frequently moved from one residential placement to another whereby every time the child moves she has to disconnect and reconnect. Such frequent dissociation will impede coherent memories as it becomes impossible to integrate these traumatic experiences. Although the inner secure base offers some solace, it cannot replace the biological imperative of connection to others which evokes a yearning for connection and a need to avoid closeness. To manage this, the child and later adult will oscillate between connect and disconnect, and approach and avoid. Counsellors need to be mindful that this oscillation will manifest in the counselling setting and in order to promote connection, internal as well as external safety must be addressed. Some may also disconnect due to fear of impingement or contamination by others and counsellors must be sensitive to such defences.

Dissociated children are often overlooked or ignored by carers because they do not present with challenging or confrontational behaviour, as they keep their inner distress invisible and provide an illusion of containment. As they do not generate any concerns, such children are also often deemed less interesting by researchers and may not be included in data on the impact of institutional abuse. And yet they may present as by far the most traumatised, as they are in a frozen watchfulness where they are highly sensitised to non-verbal cues that might predict danger, inconsistencies or abuse. To achieve this, the child will engage in mind reading to predict anticipated responses, which further takes them out of their own experience and sense of self, into that of the other.

If the range of survival strategies employed by children in residential care are not recognised as trauma symptoms the resulting behaviours may be labelled as oppositional, defiance, or antisocial disorders. As such behaviours are not tolerated in the care home some children will become malleable and chameleon-like, and become whoever others want them to be leading to "identity death" and the development of a false self, or selves. This is necessary to avoid a worse fate such as being sent to a more restrictive or controlling institution or secure unit. Being labelled rebellious, disturbed or obviously troubled will also reduce the chances of being fostered or adopted. This can lead to submit and comply, in effect to adapt to the system rather than fight it.

The false self is in essence an identity death in which an outer shell of politeness is accompanied with a quiet, smiling disposition and compliant behaviour designed to make others feel good and to elicit positive responses. In reality the exterior calm of the false self is a cover to conceal a tsunami-like inner rage, and sadness which can never be expressed. To keep this hidden the child needs to develop a body armour, or carapace that projects external control to belie the inner collapse. This false body (Orbach, 2002) can also be reflected in external displays of sexuality that are in stark contrast to the inner sexual frozenness which is devoid of feeling, sensuality or passion. Any external expressions of vitality become a masquerade for inner desolation, depletion and collapse.

As can be seen in Box 12.1, the impact of institutional abuse includes a range of physical and psychological symptoms including injury, broken bones, and potential brain damage, as well as difficulties with sleeping, including recurring nightmares, headaches and irritable bowel syndrome. It is also associated with a range of psychobiological symptoms such as PTSD, depression, suicidal ideation, impulsivity and aggression, as well as fragmented memory, depersonalisation, low self-esteem and negative coping strategies, in particular alcohol and drug misuse (Wolfe *et al.*, 2006; O'Riordan and Arensman, 2007).

Box 12.1 Impact and long-term effects of institutional abuse

- Injuries, broken bones, brain damage
- Sleep disturbance, nightmares
- PTSD, hyper-reactivity, hypervigilance, flashbacks, impulsivity
- Anxiety disorders, obsessive-compulsive disorder, fear of public spaces
- Fragmented memories
- Depersonalisation
- Self-destructive behaviours, self-harm, self-medication, eating disorders
- Elevated dependency fears, fear of being alone, fear of drawing attention to self
- Inability to trust
- Boundary issues
- Suppressed rage
- False self
- Learning disabilities
- Developmental disabilities
- Mood disorders, depression
- Suicidal ideation and suicide attempt
- Borderline personality features
- Shame
- Stigmatisation
- Isolation
- Low self-esteem, low self-worth and or self-image
- Loss of dignity, autonomy and agency
- Fear of intimacy and relational difficulties
- Sexual difficulties, sexual exploitation, risky sexual behaviour
- Fear of impaired parenting and intergenerational abuse
- Difficulty trusting authority figures
- Powerlessness and learned voicelessness
- Negative coping strategies

- Vulnerable to revictimisation
- Interrupted schooling, reduced employment opportunities, poverty
- Loss of family, siblings and significant others
- Poor adjustment to life outside institution
- Attributional errors
- Attachment and relational difficulties
- Dependency fears, fear of aging, needing care
- Revictimisation

The lack of worth, stigmatisation and lack of entitlement impacts on relational worth leading to relational apprehensiveness. Most survivors of institutional abuse feel compelled to disconnect or withdraw from relationships. Invariably they see relationships as fraught with ambivalence and paradoxes in which others are seen alternately as figures of hope and dread, or sources of protection and abuse. This often mirrors earlier relational experiences in which benign figures are also hostile. This creates a double-bind in which the survivor yearns for closeness, yet fears impingement and engulfment. To reconcile this double-bind the survivor engages in a persistent pattern of approach and avoid in all their relationships, including the therapeutic one. For some the expectation of abuse, and concomitant need for protection and concealment, is so great that they develop a phobic avoidance of all relationships thereby reducing availability of social support and reinforcing the chasm of loneliness.

Those that do risk entering a relationship commonly have no concept of nurturing and often falsely equate attention and care with love, making them susceptible to entrapment into abusive, or exploitative relationships. Their lack of value also makes it hard to accept healthy nurturing leading them to return to familiar non-nurturing relationships. This is often compounded by fear of being alone which leads them into accepting even the most tenuous or inappropriate relationships, as these are better than the sense of rejection and abandonment in being single. Relationships may also highlight sexual difficulties, especially if there is a history of sexual abuse and no concept of consensual sex, including risky sexual behaviour. The anxiety and tension associated with being in a relationship may activate negative coping strategies such as alcohol and substance misuse. In addition, the lack of nurturing in their early life evokes deeply embedded fears in the survivor that they lack even rudimentary parenting skills, which will impact negatively on their children resulting in intergenerational transmission of abuse. This becomes a powerful motivator to not enter long-term relationships and risk becoming a parent.

There are also a number of social effects associated with institutional abuse that clinicians need to be mindful of. One impact of institutional abuse on children is poor concentration, impaired information processing and poor academic achievement. This is compounded by interrupted schooling, either through exclusion or because of being moved while in care. When compounded by learning difficulties, these children will grow into young adults whose employment opportunities may be greatly reduced, which can increase the risk of poverty and associated social disadvantage. This is often further exacerbated by substance or alcohol abuse and vulnerability to delinquency, crime or sexual exploitation. Many adults who were institutionalised as children experience considerable problems adjusting to the outside world due to lack of routine and structure, stigmatisation and social isolation, and therefore seek refuge in institutional settings such as the armed forces, closed religious communities or cults, and even prison as this represents a return to the familiar.

Later on in adulthood many survivors of institutional abuse will fear becoming old and dependent on others, and be terrified of having to rely on a carer, or enter residential care in case they are abused again. This poses an increased risk of suicidal ideation and actual suicide attempts (O'Riordan and Arensman, 2009) which clinicians need to be mindful of and not dismiss as irrational fears. To be cared for in a nursing home will reactivate the terror felt during childhood, which threatens to overwhelm the survivor. In addition it will evoke all the losses associated with residential care such as loss of family, friends, and missed opportunities. To return to an institution setting not dissimilar to one in which they were abused as children will erode any hope of having escaped the legacy of abuse. The lack of control and anticipated abuse may compel the elderly survivors of institutional abuse to take their own life rather than risk betrayal again.

WORKING WITH SURVIVORS OF INSTITUTIONAL ABUSE

Many of the survival strategies learnt while in care are pragmatic responses as opposed to passive acceptance and counsellors need to validate these as such. It is these very resources that have aided survival and hope which has brought the survivor into therapy. During the assessment process, counsellors need to identify which coping strategies are still adaptive and which ones the survivor wishes to jettison or transform. The assessment also needs to identify the survivor's immediate concerns and how these might be addressed. Given the impact of institutional abuse on attachment and relational patterns, counsellors need to ascertain any difficulties that the survivor has and be aware of how these might impact on the therapeutic relationship.

Institutionalisation strips the individual of control, autonomy and self-agency and the restoration of these is one of the first therapeutic goals (see Box 12.2). This can only be established in a safe and secure setting which minimises external stimulation to avoid collision with the inner turmoil of the survivor and the threat of overload. Kalsched (1996) argues that such overload will act as a circuit breaker prompting disconnection through dissociation or withdrawal. This circuit breaker is bidirectional and can be activated if there is too much internal stimulation as the survivor explores the trauma narrative. Counsellors need to employ appropriate techniques to facilitate affect regulation and distress tolerance to restore control over turbulent physiological arousal. This will also stabilise PTSD symptoms and reduce the need for self-harm and self-medication. Through restoring control in a safe environment, the survivor will be able to develop the necessary trust in themselves and the counsellor to fully engage in the therapeutic relationship. Counsellors need to ensure that they do not impinge on the survivor as so many others have before, and focus on making the survivor visible so that they can find their own voice.

Box 12.2 Core therapeutic goals

- Assessment
- Safety – external and internal
- Restore control, dignity
- Psychoeducation on therapeutic process and to normalise responses
- Establish trust and therapeutic relationship
- Stabilise PTSD symptoms and work through trauma, integrate memories
- Affect regulation and modulation
- Make visible and give a voice
- Loss and mourning
- Restore compassion for self
- Educational attainment and acquisition of skills
- Reporting, compensation claims

The depersonalisation and dehumanisation associated with institutional abuse can be ameliorated by making the survivor visible in a warm, empathic and sensitively attuned therapeutic relationship which is genuinely human and is safe enough to permit the expression of the inner self. In making the survivor visible and giving her a voice, the counsellor will be able to explore the myriad fears associated with institutional abuse such as relational apprehensiveness, sexual difficulties, fears pertaining to parenting of own children, dependency fears in old age and fear of revictimisation. Exploration of these will also allow the survivor to work through the shame and stigmatisation of having been in residential care. Through this the survivor will be able to challenge the attributional errors that have held her in thrall to the institutional abuse such as self-blame for being in care and abused, not stopping abuse, and not managing or tolerating the abuse. In challenging these false beliefs, the survivor can transform negative self-perceptions, restore trust in self and access self-compassion.

An essential part of recovery from interpersonal trauma is the mourning of the myriad associated losses. Counsellors need to enable survivors to identify the range of losses such as loss of growing up in a family and all that entails, loss of continuity, loss of family attachments including siblings and concomitant lack of skills for effective parenting, and missed educational opportunities. In grieving these losses the survivor is able to acknowledge the impact of being in care, and the long-term effects of institutional abuse. Through the grief process the survivor can work through denial and minimisation of the abuse, allowing them to access and express the full range of emotions including anger and sadness. The grieving process allows for an acceptance of the survivor's experiences which permits self-compassion and post-traumatic growth. It also identifies missed opportunities that can be transformed. Survivors whose education was interrupted, or who suffered from poor academic attainment may feel able to return to educational studies and thereby enhance self-esteem and improve employment opportunities.

Some survivors may wish to establish contact with their family, or family members such as siblings, grandparents, uncles and aunts in order to re-establish a sense of continuity and connection. In contrast some may wish to trace some of the peers that they were close to while in care. While this can be an important aspect of healing, it can only ever be the survivor's choice and must never be imposed by the clinician. If the survivor wishes to reconnect, the counsellor must explore the motivation for this and consider the range of outcomes of such action. Most importantly counsellors need to be clear and explicit about the degree to which they are able to support the survivor's search.

Counsellors must also be clear about the degree of support that they would be able to provide if the survivor decides to report the institutional abuse to the relevant authorities. In such cases, it may be necessary to work through the potential for retraumatisation if a full investigation is launched, and the impact any compensation claims may have on the survivor's self-worth and value. Counsellors and survivors need to be mindful that investigations and inquiries into institutional abuse can be incredibly lengthy processes which can be physically and emotionally draining and reactivate trauma-related symptoms. It is critical that counsellors assess to what degree they can commit to a high level of support for a considerable period of time to avoid letting the survivor down during such a harrowing process. In addition, they need to be aware of the impact a paltry compensation offer can have on the survivor's sense of self-worth and value. While counsellors can be an integral part of the process of restoration and reparation, they must ensure that they do not give assurances that cannot be delivered.

THERAPEUTIC CHALLENGES IN WORKING WITH SURVIVORS OF INSTITUTIONAL ABUSE

An effect of institutionalisation and institutional abuse is a lack of trust in authority figures leading many survivors to enter therapy with fear and trepidation around risking connection and attachment again. This manifests in a variety of ways in the therapeutic process in which the survivor is hypervigilant, especially in tracking the counsellor's verbal and non-verbal communications. Survivors of institutional abuse will be highly sensitised to even imperceptible cues as to what they might be thinking or experiencing, and will attempt to "mind read" the counsellor at every opportunity. Counsellors need to be mindful that this represents a highly adaptive survival strategy that enabled the survivor to anticipate and predict the behaviour of others to avert danger. While these strategies need to be validated, they must also be evaluated in terms of adaptiveness in the present experiencing. Counsellors can usefully explore with the survivor that every time they mind read they come out of their own self-experiencing and enter the realm of the other, and thereby lose contact with the self. In disconnecting from the self the survivor is unable to track their own inner experiencing as they are consumed to track that of other (counsellor) and in effect become an extension of the other. In this the survivor is compelled to modulate her experiencing and behaviour to suit what she perceives the counsellor's desires or demands to be. To manage this, the false self is activated and the authentic self repudiated, as seen in over-compliance, and submissiveness. Mind reading the counsellor also leads to over-analysing to the detriment of emotional experiencing. Counsellors need to understand the function of this as it promotes a level of control and predictability, and yet sensitively encourage the survivor to stay embodied in their inner experiencing to allow a voice to the authentic self. This is most likely to occur the safer the survivor feels and the more secure the therapeutic relationship.

In contrast some survivors of institutional abuse will present as hostile in an attempt to block any opportunity for connection or attachment. Counsellors must not personalise this and stay sensitively attuned to the relational apprehensiveness of the survivor. It is only in acceptance and a full understanding of the terror associated with attachment and the concomitant fear of rejection and abandonment that the survivors can feel safe to trust and risk connection. Counsellors must be careful to not force trust and connection, but allow this to evolve through sensitive attunement and making the client visible and feel genuinely cared for. Although the many survivors of institutional abuse are mirror hungry (constantly searching for reflection from others to reassure them of their existence) and have a desperate need to feel special, counsellors must guard against being over-responsive to these needs as they could unwittingly be replicating the dynamics of the abuse experience. In addition, counsellors who try to over-compensate for lack of mirroring, and not being made to feel special, can be experienced by the survivor as intrusive in the same way the abuser was. Counsellors need to ensure that the survivor's nascent self is able to evolve without impingement and support the survivor's journey of discovery.

The nature of institutional care is such that many survivors become intensely private, making it hard to engage them. Counsellors need to be patient and not rush the survivor as to do so would be experienced as dangerous and lead to disconnection. Alongside this, the risk of connection will evoke powerful transference and counter-transference reactions. Many children in residential care are consumed with rescue fantasies that will be enacted in the therapeutic relationship in which the survivor sees the counsellor as the long-awaited "knight in shining armour" finally come to rescue her. Such rescue fantasies can be hard to resist and evoke powerful counter-transference reactions such as wanting to rescue the adult but also the abandoned child.

This is compounded by the survivor's omnipresent fear of abandonment and rejection. It is the fear of abandonment that enforces the survivor's compliance and malleability to ensure that they are not rejected. It is also this fear that underpins fear of therapeutic breaks such as holidays. Many survivors of institutional abuse will fear that during such breaks the counsellors will no longer have them in mind, making it easier to abandon them. Counsellors need to understand and validate such fears within the context of the survivor's experiences rather than dismiss these as histrionic or manipulative. As the cost of attachment is loss survivors will be preoccupied by abandonment throughout the therapeutic process. It is this anticipated loss that can impede attachment, and elevate fears of dependency. The therapeutic relationship must allow for dependency needs to be expressed and enacted without the counsellor recoiling from them. Furthermore once attachment has occurred, counsellors need to be mindful of the importance of encouraging and supporting the survivor's striving for individuation, much as a mother would with the developing child. To prolong dependency unnecessarily, no matter how much the survivor might desire this, is tantamount to abuse. While it is hard for some survivors to move towards independence, counsellors must support this and seek skilled supervision to manage what can often be a harrowing process.

Fear of abandonment and attachment can result in an oscillation between approach and avoid behaviours that resemble borderline personality features. Counsellors must refrain from making a putative diagnosis of borderline personality disorder or labelling the survivor, and view such oscillation within the context of an insecure and ambivalent attachment pattern. It may also be beneficial for counsellors to explore how the survivor's attachment style impacts on them, and how it interacts with their own attachment style. If counsellors feel uncomfortable in the presence of high dependency needs, they need to know what it evokes in them and how they might react. Some counsellors may be consumed with a desire to detach and disconnect, while others will feel compelled to succumb to such dependency needs and attempt to satisfy them rather than enable the survivor to learn to manage them through self-soothing. The intermingling of the survivor's and counsellor's attachment style can either enhance or subvert the therapeutic relationship and have significant impact on the outcome of the therapeutic process.

Counsellors must be able to be genuinely human in the therapeutic relationship without hiding behind a clinical professional mask. Survivors of institutional abuse will have met many professional figures who have purported to care for them, only to be betrayed. They will be highly sensitised to genuine warmth, care and concern and will find it difficult to fully engage in the absence of these. Rather than striving for professional distance and a clinical façade counsellors need to provide a secure base in which spontaneity and human qualities of humour and laughter can be expressed.

Working with survivors of institutional abuse is not a linear process as the survivor vacillates between current relational and psychological issues, past experiences of abandonment and rejection, and missed opportunities and fears of the future. This is especially the case with survivors who self-medicate through substance misuse, self-harm or who are suicidal. Counsellors must be patient and sensitive to detours and not ascribe these to avoidance or resistance. Ruptures in the therapeutic relationship must be embraced and worked through rather than catastrophising them. Survivors will fear that each rupture is a failure and counsellors must reassure them that ruptures in any relationship are opportunities for growth and enrichment rather than harbingers of abandonment and rejection. Working through such ruptures in the safety of a therapeutic relationship will provide the survivors with the skills to navigate and negotiate other relationships in a more effective way. Counsellors must also explore the function of disconnections in the therapeutic relationship and manage these accordingly. For instance the survivor may disconnect for fear of "malignant contagion" (Grand, 2000) in which they try to protect the counsellor from being contaminated by the abuser's brutality by not exploring the full extent and details of the abuse and traumatisation. This protection of the counsellor may replicate the survivor's protection of significant others, such as family or partners, by not disclosing the traumatising aspects of the abuse.

Such over-protection may also represent an adaption to interpersonal abuse in which the child and adult survivor take on the role of protector of others rather than the self. This is a way to ward off feelings of helplessness and powerlessness through helping others, thereby counteracting their own lack of protection. In becoming the eternal helper and protector the survivor can feel that some good has come out of the abuse, not realising that by focusing on others they may be ignoring their own needs. Such survivors often present as highly empathic and compassionate towards others, including the counsellor, and yet are impoverished when it comes to self-compassion. Counsellors must be careful not to collude with such dynamics as it subverts the survivor's healing process.

In listening to survivors' accounts of abuse committed by professionals who are employed to protect vulnerable children, counsellors may be shocked into disbelief that such abuse can occur. While this is a natural reaction, counsellors must be mindful of processing their reactions to such accounts to ensure that they do not silence the survivor, or contaminate the abuse narrative. Knowledge that professionals can and do commit abuse can raise questions about the clinician's own professional practice, leading to self-doubts and fears of unprofessional behaviour. In addition, exposure to survivors' narratives of brutalising, multiple abuses can be traumatising for the clinician, and lead to vicarious traumatisation, or secondary traumatic stress. To minimise this counsellors need to ensure that they seek appropriate professional and personal support, and make time to nurture themselves (see Chapter 14).

There is no doubt that the impact of institutional abuse can engender severe traumatising effects on children which can persist into adulthood. However, it can also give rise to remarkable resilience in children and opportunity for post-traumatic growth. Counsellors must guard against assuming that the traumatising impact of institutional abuse is so damaging as to subvert any opportunity for recovery or growth. Counsellors must be open to a wide range of impacts, including increased resilience, and be aware that these can be mobilised to allow for post-traumatic growth. In the presence of survivors of interpersonal trauma and institutional abuse, counsellors can witness the intricacies of the human spirit that can transform trauma and allow healing to occur. Such work is invariably transformational not only for the survivor but also for the practitioner.

Case vignette: Willow

Willow had been abandoned by her single mother at the age of two when her mother decided to leave her with her grandmother while she pursued employment opportunities in another country. Willow's grandmother was furious to be left with her illegitimate grandchild and projected and evacuated her rage onto Willow through frequent beatings and physical restraint by tying her to her bed and other pieces of furniture. As Willow failed to thrive her mother returned briefly to collect her and take her abroad with her. It soon became evident that Willow's mother could not work and look after her traumatised daughter and so she placed her in an orphanage run by nuns in the hope that they would be able to take better care of her until she was settled in a job that would allow her to care for her daughter more effectively.

Although the children's home was run by nuns it was clear that they disapproved of illegitimate children as they saw them as products of sin. During her time in the children's home Willow was sexually abused and although she reported this to the nuns she was not believed and vilified for making such wicked allegations. As Willow was unable to defend herself against the sexual abuse, and in the absence of any support from staff or peers, she began to adapt to her abuse by becoming overly compliant and submissive. She quickly learnt that if she smiled sweetly and made herself helpful to the staff she would at least get some positive responses. This extended to her looking after the younger children to protect them from some of the worst abuses. Willow felt that although she couldn't protect herself, at least she could protect the younger ones.

After four and a half years in the orphanage, Willow's mother came to collect her with a new husband and baby in tow. Willow was delighted to be reunited with her mother and vowed to be the best daughter she could be so that she would not be sent away again. This meant being extremely pliable and malleable to ensure her mother's approval and love. Willow's default position of taking care of others manifested in helping her mother in looking after her younger brother and her new husband. When the husband started to sexually abuse her, Willow felt that she could not disclose this partly to protect her mother and baby brother and to avoid being sent back to the home. Her fear of losing her mother's love and approval and being taken into care again meant that Willow was entrapped into daily sexual abuse until she left home at the age of 15.

Homeless and with no-one to look out for her, Willow became involved in a series of inappropriate relationships, usually with older men who initially appeared loving and caring, and yet ended up being abusive. Willow lived in constant terror of abandonment and rejection and would submit herself to whatever her current lover desired. She became chameleon-like in trying to satisfy their every desire with no regard for what she needed or wanted. To manage her fears, anxiety and shame, Willow started to drink. Unable to regulate her feelings other than through self-harm and self-destructive behaviours Willow soon became dependent on alcohol as an alternative form of soothing. Willow would drink to the point of blackout and would invariably end up in bed with increasingly dangerous men.

After a particularly long drinking session she blacked out and collapsed in a block of flats with no idea how she got there. One of the residents found her and persuaded her to seek help. Although reluctant to do so, Willow went to her GP and asked to be referred to an alcohol rehabilitation programme. This signalled the beginning of her healing and when Willow came out of rehab she entered therapy. This was extremely difficult for Willow as she feared becoming attached because she did not want to cope with the loss when therapy ended. Throughout the therapeutic process Willow would oscillate between wanting to be close and attached and avoiding any closeness. It took several years until Willow could trust the therapeutic relationship and learn to manage her fear of abandonment. Towards the end of her therapy Willow met her future husband who was able to provide the stability Willow had craved. This allowed her to resume her education and train to work with vulnerable children. In helping vulnerable children Willow feels that she can triumph over her own trauma by making such children visible and helping them to transform their lives. Willow's only outstanding concern is how she will manage in old age as she fears that her vulnerability and dependency needs could be exploited if she were to go into a nursing home. Willow knows that this is something she may need to explore as she becomes older and plans to return to therapy to work on this. For the moment she wants to enjoy her renewed connection to herself, her husband and children and honour the transformation that has taken place. For the first time in her life she feels alive and unencumbered by crippling fears of abandonment and rejection.

SUMMARY

- The institutional abuse of children in residential homes, while hidden and invisible, has pervasive and insidious effects on children that can persist into adulthood and throughout the lifespan into old age. Being abused by the very people who are tasked to provide care can be experienced as a double betrayal to children who already feel rejected and abandoned by their families.
- Institutional abuse can be committed directly by individuals such as staff and peers, or indirectly through abusive institutional regimes and systems that fail to safeguard children. A society that renders children invisible through a care system that stigmatises children who are in care promotes learned voicelessness and effectively colludes with the abuse of the most vulnerable members of society.
- Voicelessness leads to under-reporting which makes it difficult to ascertain accurate data on incidence or prevalence rates. While all children in care are at risk, research has shown that boys are more vulnerable to physical abuse and girls to sexual abuse. In addition children who have a pre-existing history of abuse, and children with disabilities, are also most at risk. Some research suggests that adolescents in care are more at risk, although this may reflect a reporting bias as younger children may normalise their abuse or may be more easily silenced through fear and the consequences of disclosure.
- The majority of perpetrators are male, although some females collude in physical abuse, and are represented in both staff and peers. The impact and dynamics of abuse will vary depending upon whether it is perpetrated by staff or peers, although the cumulative effect of both has the most traumatising effect as the child has no access to any support.
- The nature and dynamics of abuse, including risk factors such as previous abuse experience, especially physical and sexual abuse, can lead to both traumatisation and retraumatisation. Children feel helpless in the face of further abuse having already been abandoned and unsupported. The lack of control, betrayal of trust, isolation from families and fear of not being believed, compound the traumatising impact of institutional abuse.
- As in other forms of interpersonal trauma, survivors of institutional abuse commonly present with a range of mental health problems such as PTSD symptoms, mood disorders, self-destructive behaviour, suicidal ideation and substance misuse. In addition, the betrayal of trust in institutional abuse, dependency needs and impaired attachment leads to relational apprehensiveness and elevated fears of abandonment and rejection. These are enacted

in the therapeutic relationship in which the survivor is reluctant to engage as the cost of attachment is loss, and in which they might vacillate between approach and avoidance relational patterns.

- Working with such survivors generates innumerable challenges such as how to establish trust and allow for attachment without impingement, to allow the survivor to relinquish the false self and reclaim the authentic self. It is through a safe therapeutic relationship that survivors of institutional abuse can experience a secure base from which to reconnect to self and others, and access the resilience that allows for post-traumatic growth. Such work is invariably transformational for both the survivor and the practitioner.

SUGGESTED READING

Barter, C. (2006) *Abuse of Children in Residential Care.* London: NSPCC Inform.

Barter, C., Renold, E., Berridge, D. and Cawson, P. (2004) *Peer Violence in Children in Residential Care.* Basingstoke: Palgrave Macmillan.

Crittenden, P.M. (2000) 'A Dynamic-maturational Approach to Continuity and Change in Patterns of Attachment.' In P.M. Crittenden and A.H. Claussen (eds) *The Organisation of Attachment Relationships – Maturation, Culture and Context.* New York: Cambridge University Press.

Finkelhor, D. (2008) *Childhood Victimisation: Violence, Crime and Abuse in the Lives of Young People.* New York: Oxford University Press.

O'Riordan, M. and Arensman, E. (2007) *Institutional Child Sexual Abuse and Suicidal Behaviour: Outcomes of Literature Review, Consultation Meetings and Qualitative Studies.* Cork, Ireland: National Suicide Research Foundation.

Purnell, C. (2008) 'Surviving the Care System: A Story of Abandonment and Reconnection.' In S. Benamer and K. White (eds) *Trauma and Attachment.* London: The Centre for Attachment-based Psychoanalytic Psychotherapy and Karnac Books.

CHAPTER 13

PROFESSIONAL ABUSE AS INTERPERSONAL TRAUMA

A highly pernicious form of interpersonal abuse is that committed by professionals, especially mental health professionals. Commonly, clients who enter therapy are vulnerable and need a secure, safe therapeutic setting in which to explore the source of their suffering. For them to take the risk of entrusting a professional with their most archaic, deeply buried fears and dependency needs is something to be honoured and valued, not exploited. Interpersonal abuse by mental health professionals is in essence a double betrayal especially for those clients who enter therapy having already experienced a betrayal of trust, which could prevent them from risking trust or seeking help again.

Due to the power imbalance, dependency needs and transference inherent in professional relationships, it is imperative that they are bounded by clear ethical boundaries to which the professional adheres. Professionals have a duty of care to their clients to promote well-being (beneficence) and a commitment to avoid harm to the client (non-maleficence) and to have a full understanding of the importance of establishing and maintaining boundaries to keep both client and practitioner safe. In addition, professionals need to have a clear appreciation of the impact of boundary violations on the client and their own integrity. Counsellors need to be mindful that the imbalance of power, dependency needs and transference means that clients are unable to provide informed consent making any sexual advances by a therapist tantamount to sexual assault or rape.

While all professionals have the potential to abuse in a variety of settings, this chapter will focus specifically on abuse by mental health professionals, in particular counsellors and psychotherapists. The chapter will look at the nature and dynamics of professional abuse, with particular focus on the sexual abuse of clients by clinicians. It will look at what constitutes sexually exploitative practice and the prevalence of such abuse, and identify who is most at risk. The impact and long-term effects of sexual exploitation by the clinicians will be identified, along with core therapeutic goals to ensure effective, non-exploitative practice. The chapter will also examine the therapeutic challenges when working with survivors of professional abuse and how these might be overcome. Ultimately, sensitively attuned and thoughtful therapeutic work with survivors of professional abuse can facilitate better practice and illuminate the complex processes inherent in psychotherapeutic practice.

THE SPECTRUM OF INTERPERSONAL ABUSE BY PROFESSIONALS

The spectrum of interpersonal abuse committed by mental health professionals includes the abuse of power and a range of boundary violations (see Figure 13.1). These include a number of non-sexual boundary violations as well as sexual abuse. Some of these violations are subtle and may be hard to identify by clients who lack knowledge of the ethical framework in which all therapy must be conducted. While all clinicians should include statements about their ethical framework as part of the therapeutic contract, many do not, especially those who are most likely to exploit their clients.

Figure 13.1 Spectrum of interpersonal abuse by professionals

Boundary violations include terminating or extending sessions without prior agreement, breaking confidentiality without good cause, terminating therapy after several years with no warning, or entering into dual relationships including business relationships. The abuse of power can be to impose rigidly held theoretical beliefs or interpretations on the client, and to misuse knowledge of the client to manipulate them. Financial abuse consists of increasing charges without consultation, prolonging therapy beyond what is reasonable to ensure therapist income, or coercing clients to invest in therapist's interests. Emotional abuse can incorporate such tactics as encouraging dependency on the therapist, or not allowing clients to take significant decisions without the therapist's approval. It can also include shaming or humiliating the client, blaming them for their problems, or threatening to disclose personal information about them to other parties. The sexual abuse of clients includes any sexual act or acts such as sexually suggestive language, sexual touching, oral sex as well as sexual intercourse.

ABUSE OF POWER IN PROFESSIONAL RELATIONSHIPS

Fundamental to all therapeutic relationships, irrespective of which model or approach is practised, is an imbalance of power between client and clinician. This imbalance of power is manifest on three dimensions in which the therapist has access to, and is accorded with, *legitimate power, expert power* and *referent power.* Legitimate power is most evident in the counsellor's role as one of providing care and help to those who are vulnerable, while expert power is embedded in the counsellor's expertise in knowledge of mental health, and training and competency to provide care to those in need. Counsellors are also in possession of referent power which refers to power through "perceived" attractiveness, friendliness and personal qualities that enable them to be effective practitioners.

The imbalance of power is evident in the theoretical model applied to the client, the time and place in which therapy is conducted, the duration and cost of therapy. To support the power differential counsellors may rigidly adhere to their theoretical model and impose this on to the client through destructive and shaming interpretations (Clarkson, 1993). In addition, the practitioner has a lot of, often very personal and intimate, information about the client, whereas the client knows very little, if anything about the counsellor.

Power dynamics are also embedded in transference and counter-transference reactions. A potent aspect of transference is the capacity to distort perception and judgment even in otherwise "high powered" individuals (Schoener, 2008) in which clients perceive the therapist as the omnipotent and omniscient parent who will nurture and protect, or rescue them from their suffering. Transference also evokes primitive or previously unmet dependency needs which further bind the client to the therapist. Alongside this, transference elicits counter-transferential reactions (CTR) in the therapist such as the benign protector, or the narcissistic grandiosity of being the perfect therapist, or the hostile, rejecting and punitive parent. This can reinforce the power invested in the therapist and lead to an over-inflated sense of potency.

The power dynamics manifest in the counselling process can be both conscious and unconscious and counsellors must be committed to unravelling and reflecting on how these dynamics are enacted. This is initially facilitated through rigorous training, but needs to be consistently monitored through supervision, consultation, reflexivity and self-reflection. It is only with a robust understanding of the complex interplay of power dynamics and the effect of these on both client and therapist that practitioners can fully appreciate the role these play in interpersonal abuse by mental health professionals. Such knowledge and self-awareness will enable counsellors to be scrupulous in not misusing the power invested in them by their professional body and the clients who consult them. To keep both client and counsellor safe, counsellors must also be aware that the power imbalance is not unidirectional and that clients also have some power over the practitioner. Despite this counsellors need to be mindful that they are the professional in charge, and act accordingly to discuss the relative power dynamics to minimise the misuse of power by either party.

Counsellors need to be aware that the power invested in them makes it difficult for the client to challenge them, or indeed to say "No" or resist interpretations. The concomitant dependency and investment of trust make clients extremely vulnerable to suggestion without having the knowledge or power to challenge these, or make fully informed choices. This renders any sexual advances made by the therapist an act of sexual assault or rape. This is compounded in clients who have had a history of interpersonal abuse or have suffered boundary violation. In essence the sexual exploitation by professionals is akin to CSA and other forms of sexual violence in that the client is unable to give informed consent, or be confident in saying "No". This is reflected in other dynamics employed by exploitative therapists to entice and ensnare clients such as promoting dependency, making clients feel "special" through a complex grooming process, and heightening arousal through secrecy.

BOUNDARY VIOLATIONS BY PROFESSIONALS

One way to minimise the abuse of power in the therapeutic process is to ensure that the therapeutic encounter is well bounded. The role of boundaries is critical to keep both client and clinician safe and to provide a secure base. There are a number of boundaries that need to be observed, both sexual and non-sexual, such as financial boundaries, and boundaries around confidentiality. Counsellors must also ensure that they do not deliberately foster dependency in their clients which could lead to prolonging the therapeutic process unnecessarily.

The intimate nature of the therapeutic process makes it essential that there are clear boundaries around dual relationships, especially of a romantic or sexual nature. While much of interpersonal abuse by professionals consists of non-sexual boundary violations such as financial abuse and breaches of confidentially, a significant number are sexual. This is in part due to the intimacy of the therapeutic process and the concomitant erotic transference and counter-transference. Given the presence of such powerful erotic dynamics in the therapeutic process it is essential that all clinicians are adequately trained in understanding and managing these without acting upon them.

Unfortunately, most psychotherapy and counselling training is woefully inadequate in addressing erotic transference and counter-transference dynamics leading to shame, embarrassment and discomfort rendering practitioners all too vulnerable to sexual boundary violations. This is attested to in a recent report published by the Council for Healthcare Regulatory Excellence (CHRE, cited in Coe, 2008) which found that training on professional boundaries, including sexual boundaries, is frequently not provided either at graduate level or as part of continuous professional development (CPD). In the absence of mandatory training and a clear understanding of the dynamics of power, dependency, trust and boundary violations clinicians may be seduced into, or compelled to adopt unethical practices.

DEFINITION OF PROFESSIONAL ABUSE

The standard code of ethics for all mental health professionals, irrespective of their training and governing body, specifies that practitioners must not abuse their client's trust in order to gain sexual, emotional, financial, or any other kind of personal advantage (BACP, 2007; UKCP, 2005; BPS, 2008). While all of them prohibit sexual relations with a client, not all provide clear guidelines in terms of what is meant by "sexual" or under what circumstances clinicians may enter into romantic or sexual relations with former clients.

The British Association for Counselling and Psychotherapy states that:

> Sexual relations with clients are prohibited. Sexual relations include intercourse, any other type of sexual activity or sexualised behaviour. Practitioners should think carefully about, and exercise considerable caution before, entering into personal or business relationships with former clients and should expect to be professionally accountable if the relationship becomes detrimental to the client or the standing of the profession. (BACP, 2007, p.6)

To avoid any sexual involvement with clients, most professional guidelines urge practitioners to terminate the therapeutic relationship and refer the client on. Once the therapeutic relationship has ended, professional organisations vary in terms of when, or if, a romantic or sexual relationship can be pursued. Some organisations recommend no contact for a minimum of three months, while some specify at least two years. Some professional governing bodies such as the American Psychiatric Association state that romantic or sexual relationships between therapist and client are *never* acceptable, and that once the therapeutic relationship has ended no further contact should occur. The rationale for this is that the power imbalance and dependency needs characteristic of any therapeutic relationship is such that it will influence the texture and course of any future personal relationship.

Arguably, the lack of clarity and agreement between various governing bodies on sexual relations between clinicians and former clients can lead to confusion and uncertainty. As many practitioners are required to self-regulate their behaviour within the context of their organisation's ethical framework, such lack of clarity can lead to uncertainty and doubt, which in turn render the clinician vulnerable to potential boundary violations.

The level of sexual abuse by professionals is testament to the inadequacy of self-regulation. To this effect half the states in America and some European countries have made the sexual exploitation of clients by psychotherapists a crime whereby any sexual advance made by a professional is considered as sexual assault or rape. This is predicated on the proposition that (a) a client is unable to give consent because they do not have a full understanding of what is happening and its consequences, (b) that transference can distort perception and judgment and impede accurate perception of appropriate behaviour, and (c) there is an imbalance of power both in the role of the professional and the dependency of the client (Schoener, 2008).

Conceptualising the sexual exploitation by professionals as a crime and an act of sexual violence invests such abuse with a level of seriousness that is not reflected in current professional guidelines. Such reconceptualising would legitimise the client's experience and the concomitant symptoms, as well as provide clarity around reporting such abuse. Given that up to 90% of clients who have suffered abuse by professionals do not take formal action (Coe, 2008) knowing that it is a crime may validate their experience as abuse and facilitate formal reporting. It would also clarify the role of the reparative therapist in terms of action that can be taken. Finally it would provide more accurate terminology to name and describe sexual boundary violations by professionals, and prevent minimisation, by referring to such exploitation as an "affair" or sexual relationship which falsely implies a degree of consent.

PREVALENCE OF INTERPERSONAL ABUSE BY PROFESSIONALS

The most recent data on the prevalence and incidence of abuse by mental health professionals in the UK comes from the professional boundaries charity WITNESS (formerly POPAN) who collated data based on telephone calls to its helpline in 2005/2006, although these figures are by no means exhaustive and may represent the tip of the iceberg, as the secrecy and shame associated with sexual abuse by professionals prevents up to 90% of clients disclosing or taking any form of action (Coe, 2008). The data from WITNESS (Coe, 2008) categorises four main types of mental health professionals: psychotherapist, counsellor, psychologist and hypnotherapist. WITNESS found that two thirds of calls to the WITNESS helpline were of a non-sexual nature with 63.4% characterised by psychological abuse, 33.3% consisting of sexual abuse and 3.2% financial abuse. The most highly represented professionals in this data were psychotherapists with 48.8%, followed by counsellors with 32.1%, psychologist with 10.7%, and the least represented were hypnotherapists with 8.3%.

Earlier research conducted by Tanya Garrett in 1992 surveyed members of the British Psychological Society (BPS) Division of Clinical Psychology (DCP) to ascertain members' personal experiences, or second-hand knowledge of sexual contact between professionals and clients, and found that less than 4% reported sexual contact with their own patients while in therapy or with former patients. More significantly however, over 38% of clinical psychologists surveyed reported knowing someone who had been sexually involved with their patients, only half (54.6%) of which were reported. Garrett (1998) also found that 22.7% of clinical psychologists had treated patients who had been sexually involved with a previous therapist, with the most commonly cited group being psychiatrists and private sector psychotherapists. That the risk is greatest in the private sector was replicated in the WITNESS data which found that almost three quarters (71.8%) of abuse by professionals occurred in private practice compared to 28.2% in the National Health Service.

The high level of sexual abuse found in the data may in part be due to the presence of sexual attraction in the therapeutic relationship. Pope *et al.* (1986) found that sexual attraction towards clients among 575 registered psychologists in private practice in the US was almost ubiquitous with 95% of male therapists and 76% of female therapists reporting being sexually attracted to their clients. Significantly though, despite the sexual attraction only 9.4% of male and 2.5% of female therapists acted upon this attraction. This would indicate that sexual attraction is common in the therapeutic relationship, and not something to be ashamed of but something to be worked through in supervision and with the client, rather than acted upon.

WHO IS AT RISK OF ABUSE BY PROFESSIONALS?

Research (Coe, 2008) has shown that those most at risk of sexual abuse by mental health professionals are female clients, especially those who have a history of boundary violations, in particular sexual abuse. Such clients are often ill equipped, or afraid to say "No", and are most vulnerable to being groomed and violated. This is particularly the case when the therapist makes the client feel "special" and emphasises the reparative nature of the therapeutic relationship in which "healthy" touch can repair the damage of the sexual abuse. Unbeknownst to the client, such statements are invariably an entry point for sexual touch and sexual boundary violations (see the case vignette at the end of this chapter). In such cases the professional is replicating the dynamics inherent in CSA in which the client is enticed and coerced into a sexually abusive relationship through being made to feel "special", and to which she cannot give informed consent. In addition, the legacy of CSA is not being able to resist boundary violations and difficulties around saying "No".

PERPETRATORS OF PROFESSIONAL ABUSE

According to WITNESS (Coe, 2008) the majority of abuse by mental health professionals is perpetrated by males with 62.8% compared to 37.2% of females. The perpetrators most commonly reported among health and mental health professionals include doctors, general practitioners, psychiatrists, psychotherapists, psychologists, counsellors, hypnotherapists, psychiatric nurses and staff in institutional settings. Other workers in health care that have been identified include social workers and general nursing staff, although trainers, supervisors and mentors may also be implicated in boundary violations. WITNESS reports that psychotherapists are most highly represented with 48.8% implicated in professional abuse, followed by counsellors with 32.1%, psychologists with 10.7%, and hypnotherapists with 8.3% (Coe, 2008).

When this is broken down by category of abuse it becomes clear that the most common form of professional abuse by psychotherapists is financial abuse at 66.7%, followed by psychological abuse at 50.8% and sexual abuse at 38.7%. The percentage of counsellors implicated in financial abuse and psychological abuse is considerably lower with 33.3% and 28.8% respectively, although the percentage for sexual abuse is the same at 38.7%. Abuse by psychologists is lower still with 13.6% implicated in psychological abuse and 12.9% committing sexual abuse, and none reported as having committed financial abuse. The lowest amount of reported abuse is among hypnotherapists with 9.7% committing sexual abuse and 6.8% implicated in psychological abuse, and no reported financial abuse.

NATURE AND DYNAMICS OF INTERPERSONAL ABUSE BY PROFESSIONALS

Interpersonal abuse by professionals can be committed in a variety of professional relationships in which there is a power imbalance and heightened dependency. These include a range of clinicians including doctors, psychiatrists, psychologists, psychotherapists and counsellors, as well as tutors, trainers and supervisors. All of these professionals must ensure that they do not exploit the power invested in them and ensure that they conduct their work within well-bounded parameters to avoid any sexual, emotional or financial boundary violations. To minimise such abuse clinicians need to be aware of power dynamics in professional relationships and the impact of boundary violations. They also need to be aware of their own reactions and responses to power and recognise that power can be very seductive and compelling and that even they can succumb. The more self-awareness counsellors have the less likely it is that they will misuse the power invested in them.

It is also useful to acknowledge that sexual attraction between therapist and client is not uncommon and should be understood within the context of the dynamics of the therapeutic relationship. Given the omnipresent nature of sexual attraction, counsellors must not feel ashamed or embarrassed in the presence of such attraction.

If they are able to accept that this is not uncommon, it will make it easier to talk to colleagues and supervisors to ensure that the sexual attraction is not acted upon. Research has shown that when clinicians are ashamed of acknowledging such feelings they are less likely to discuss these with others, which increases the potential for not processing them and acting upon them (Pope, 1994). This is why training is so critical in developing understanding of sexual attraction in the therapeutic setting in terms of meaning and function, as well as being able to discuss it openly without discomfort. The more comfortable the practitioner is in the presence of such dynamics the more willing they will be to discuss them with others and the less likely they will be to act upon them.

It is also essential that clinicians know how to manage sexual attraction in a professional way. This is not just their own sexual attraction, but also the sexual attraction that clients have for the clinician. Some clients enter therapy expecting to fall in love with the therapist and as a result may present as highly seductive, or make sexual advances. It is crucial that counsellors do not respond to this and that they are clear and explicit about what is on offer and what is not. It is always the responsibility of the clinician to boundary sexual advances from clients, no matter how attractive or seductive these might be, and it is never acceptable to act upon these. Clients who make sexual advances need to be well bounded, and assured that this is something that can and must be worked through rather than acted upon, and that this is not negotiable.

This is especially the case with clients who have a history of boundary violations, or who have been sexually abused. Such clients commonly relate to others, including authority figures, in a sexually seductive way as a conditioned response. Counsellors need to understand such conditioned responses and explore these with the client to ensure that they are understood within the context of their abuse experience. If acted upon, the client's belief that they have no other value than as a sexual object will be reinforced and that they deserve to be sexually abused. Counsellors need to be mindful that survivors of sexual abuse and sexual violence are particularly vulnerable to further sexual exploitation given that their central organising principle is constructed around sex, and that this is the only way they know how to relate to others.

If counsellors respond to the survivor's sexual way of relating, or act upon the client's sexual seduction, they are in essence replicating previous sexual abuse experiences, especially as such clients are ill equipped to say "no" and lack the assertions skills to boundary sexual advances. Counsellors must remember that the power imbalance in the therapeutic relationship means that clients are unable to give informed consent due to transference and counter-transference reactions, as well as lack of knowledge, or naïvety. Most importantly counsellors need to contain their own narcissistic grandiosity by resisting sexual flattery and not personalising sexual advances by contextualising them within the dynamics of the therapeutic relationship.

A potent dynamic in enticing or entrapping individuals into sexually exploitative relationships is the manipulation of transference and making the client feel "special". The human need to matter, be special or mean something to someone is a powerful motivator for people to attach to others. This is heightened in those individuals who have a history of insecure attachments, been abandoned, rejected or abused in some way: the very people who most frequently seek therapeutic help. Many individuals who have suffered ruptured attachments often mistake being made to feel "special", or being given attention, for love and caring and as such are most vulnerable to exploitation and boundary violations. Unscrupulous clinicians may deliberately prey on and exploit clients who have high attachment needs by paying them extra attention, showering them with compliments and flattery.

This resembles the "love bombing" or grooming seen in other forms of sexual and interpersonal abuse, and is designed to render the client more pliable and dependent on the therapist. It is also a way of gaining trust and to feel safe. As the client becomes enthralled by the therapist she may come to believe that he really cares for her, and will do anything to make him feel good, including sleep with him. Alternatively the client may come to believe that they are genuinely in love and will see any sexual contact as a way of expressing this. The secrecy that has to surround such encounters merely serves to heighten the "specialness" of the relationship making it even more exciting. The illicitness of the relationship enhances already heightened arousal and intensifies the client's feelings. This can be so powerful that the client feels she is head over heels in love and that any sexual contact is consensual and entirely reciprocal.

Counsellors need to be aware of the power of compliments and their tendency to evoke a desire in the client to please the therapist, and how this can impact on the client's perception of intimacy. While it is essential that practitioners value the unique aspects of each client, they must guard against inculcating a "false" sense of specialness or intimacy. Moreover, while intimacy is an important facet of the therapeutic relationships it must be well bounded and not be a cover for ulterior motives. Similarly, while some dependency is part of the therapeutic process, counsellors must be mindful that encouraging dependency can make clients more vulnerable and is disempowering rather than empowering, and is more likely to render the client in thrall to the therapist. Furthermore the complex interplay of power imbalance and dependency needs can lead to *traumatic bonding* as seen in CSA and domestic abuse in which the victim succumbs to the more powerful figure with no hope for escape.

The dynamics of sexual boundary violations are predicated on the collapse of other therapeutic boundaries. There has been considerable research that indicates that prior to sexual abuse clinicians may also violate other, non-sexual boundaries (Simon, 1995; Coe, 2008). As in CSA, sexual abuse by professionals rarely starts with an act of rape but progresses over time. Simon (1995) has suggested a common "slippery slope" to boundary violation by therapists which can ultimately lead to sexual exploitation. This process is reminiscent of the "grooming" process seen in CSA in which the clinician exploits the client's dependency needs and manipulates the transference. The collapse of boundaries may start with the erosion of the therapist's neutrality with sessions becoming increasingly less clinical and more social. In this the client is treated as "special" or as a confidant(e) with the therapist engaging in lengthy self-disclosure of personal details and problems, as well as sexual fantasies about the client.

Once the client feels "special" the therapist may begin touching the client and progress to hugs and embraces. In addition the therapist may extend sessions without prior arrangement, waive the fee, and begin scheduling sessions at the end of the working day. These may be extended to meeting outside the therapy setting with client and therapist having drinks or dinner. From this it is easy to make the transition into having sex with the client. While this scenario is not true for all sexual exploitation of clients by therapists it is an all too common progression of boundary violations. As can be seen in the case vignette at the end of this chapter, some clinicians do not necessarily conduct a personal relationship outside of the therapy setting, preferring to have sex in the consulting room. Counsellors working with survivors of sexual abuse by professionals may wish to explore the meaning behind where the sexual violation takes place and how this relates to power dynamics both for client and clinician.

In line with Simon's (1995) findings, Coe (2008) confirms the range of non-sexual boundaries violations that frequently precede sexual contact, including excessive self-disclosure, special fee arrangements by lowering or waiving fees, extending length of sessions, dual relationships and socialising with clients, relating to the client as a friend or confidant(e) and touching or frequent hugs.

THE IMPACT AND LONG-TERM EFFECTS OF SEXUAL EXPLOITATION BY PROFESSIONALS

Research has shown that the sexual abuse of clients by therapists can cause significant harm and lead to what one leading researcher in the field has called *therapist–patient sex syndrome* (Pope, 1989; see Box 13.1). Sexual advances made by professionals are an act of sexual violence and can have the same traumatising effects as CSA and rape which can give rise to a range of trauma-type symptoms including PTSD. Along with the betrayal of trust, the client will experience a range of ambivalent feelings including anger, sadness and loss as well as affection and love for the abusive clinician. Clients may also blame themselves and feel they are not entitled to express the rage or anger they might feel and internalise their feelings. This can lead to self-harm, depression and suicidal ideation and suicide attempts.

Following on from Pope's therapist–patient sex syndrome, other researchers have identified a range of impacts and long-term effects (Russell, 1993; Coe, 2008). However there has not been sufficient research on actual client experiences in terms

Box 13.1 Therapist–patient sex syndrome (adapted from Pope, 1989)

- Ambivalent feelings towards therapist, including investing the therapist with parental or god-like authority, idealisation which can compromise disclosure
- Guilt and mistaken feelings that the sexual violation was the client's fault
- Emptiness and isolation
- Sexual confusion as a result of the therapist sexualising issues that were non-sexual such as responding to the need for physical comfort with a sexual intervention
- Impaired ability to trust, as once trust has been betrayed the client will be fearful of investing again
- Identity and role reversal in that the client may feel responsible for the therapist's feelings and actions, and become the therapist's therapist
- Emotional lability or dyscontrol, and the tendency to feel strong and varied emotions in inappropriate unsupportive situations
- Suppressed rage
- Increased suicide risk
- Range of cognitive dysfunctions including inability to concentrate, preoccupation with what has happened, flashbacks

of impact which means that the range of impacts are primarily based on effects reported by clinicians. It is hoped that future research will concentrate on giving more voice to survivors' experiences rather than clinician check lists.

As can be seen from Box 13.2 the impact and long-term effects give rise to a number of core symptoms that reflect the traumatising effect of sexual boundary violations by therapists. Like other types of sexual violence, especially within an interpersonal context, the sexual abuse by therapists can elicit trauma-type symptoms such as post-traumatic stress symptoms including affect dysregulation, hypervigilance and hyper-reactivity and concomitant cognitive disturbances. The nature of such abuse in which abuse and exploitation masquerades as therapeutic and caring behaviour, evokes a range of ambivalent feelings ranging from love and affection, to sadness, anger and rage. Such ambivalence makes it difficult for survivors to trust self or others, especially mental health professionals. It also makes it difficult to disclose the abuse as the client may not wish to lose the therapeutic relationship, or feel responsible for the consequences of such disclosure.

The shame and humiliation associated with sexual violation will make it difficult for clients to report the therapist or to seek help. This is compounded by cynicism and disillusionment about therapy and therapists which is particularly

Box 13.2 Core symptoms associated with survivors of professional abuse

- Traumatisation
- Post-traumatic stress symptoms such as flashbacks, intrusive memories, affect dysregulation
- Poor self-concept – low self-esteem, sense of worthlessness, degradation, self-disgust
- Ambivalent feelings ranging from affection and love to rage
- Not being able to name it as abuse
- Shame
- Distorted perceptions of self, other, and the abuse experience
- Fear of retraumatisation
- Increased dependency, fear of independence, fear of being alone, traumatic bonding
- Depression
- Suicidal ideation and suicide attempts
- Self-destructive behaviours such as self-harm, self-medication
- Sexual confusion in which affection and care is sexualised and sexuality is seen as site of blame, ambivalence around sexual abuse
- Negative sexual behaviour used to restore illusory sense of power
- Isolation and secrecy
- Impaired trust of self, others and professionals, especially therapists, leading to avoidance of seeking professional help
- Fear of reinvesting in therapy
- Cynicism about therapy and therapists
- Feeling of disloyalty and fear of betraying therapist
- Ambivalence around taking formal action or reporting therapist
- Fear of retraumatisation or stigmatisation through reporting
- Remorse
- Loss, especially of the therapeutic relationship, or the "good" therapist, loss of special relationships, or feeling "special"
- Personal losses such as partners, spouses, children, family or friends, loss of self-respect, self-esteem and integrity

disturbing as the client is unable to access therapeutic help for either the original problem(s) or the traumatisation of the sexual abuse. In the absence of therapeutic help the client's original presenting problems and symptoms may deteriorate further compromising their physical and psychological well-being. Ultimately this can lead to deepening depression, self-harm, suicidal ideation and suicide attempts. Clients who have been sexually abused by their therapist may also find that their sexuality is compromised leading to negative sexual behaviours putting them at risk of further retraumatisation.

As in all interpersonal trauma, survivors of professional abuse will experience a range of losses, not least loss of the therapeutic relationship and the "good" therapist as well as loss of feeling "special" and loved. Given the ambivalence associated with sexual abuse by therapists survivors may not feel entitled to grieve such losses, making it even harder to process and integrate the experience. The survivor may also experience a range of losses in their personal life such as loss of spouse or partner who feel betrayed, loss of connection with children as they are consumed and distracted by sexual exploitation, and loss of support from family and friends. This is often accompanied by a loss of self-respect, self-esteem and integrity all of which need to be mourned.

Given the impact and long-term effects of sexual abuse by therapists, it is a wonder that survivors of such abuse risk investing again by seeking therapeutic help. In essence this is an indication that hope has not been extinguished despite betrayal and that the client is willing to entrust herself again to a professional. Clinicians need to be mindful of the courage it takes to risk entering therapy again and must honour and respect this, and ensure that they are scrupulous in setting and maintaining the full range of therapeutic boundaries.

WORKING WITH SURVIVORS OF ABUSE BY PROFESSIONALS

Given the impact and long-term effects of sexual abuse by therapists, clinicians need to be mindful of the challenges of working with survivors of such abuse. Survivors will enter therapy with myriad ambivalent feelings ranging from rage, sadness, love and affection for their previous therapist. They will also be suffused with fears around being able to trust again, fear of being believed and understood, and fears of retraumatisation. It is critical that counsellors create a safe and secure therapeutic setting in which the survivor is validated and believed, so that she can work through the range of ambivalent feelings and integrate the abuse experience. This can only be achieved in the presence of clear, explicitly stated boundaries which are scrupulously upheld to avoid ambiguity and unpredictability.

When survivors of professional abuse enter therapy it is essential that they are validated in their willingness to risk investing their trust again. A good starting point is to explore how the survivor feels about re-entering therapy and what they hope to achieve (Schoener *et al.*, 1989). Survivors may feel angry about having to invest in a new therapist both emotionally and financially and may initially be hard to engage. Counsellors must be mindful of not trying too hard to engage the survivor as this may replicate the abuse. It is more productive to remain well bounded and professional in setting goals and being explicit in what they can offer the survivor. Counsellors need to clarify the survivor's current concerns and needs, and assess how these can best be met. It may be that initially the focus is on crisis intervention and establishing internal and external safety.

With this in mind counsellors will need to ascertain the current status of the relationship between the survivor and the abusive therapist, identify if there is continuing contact, and what needs to be resolved. Counsellors must avoid making any assumptions, especially around the nature, or degree of the sexual contact, the gender of therapist or sexual orientation of either the therapist or client, or how the sexual advances have affected the client. These need to be explored at the survivor's pace and clearly articulated. Once these have been clarified it is essential to put the abuse experience into context with any other problems that the survivor may be facing. This might centre around the impact the abuse has had on their personal life as well as an exacerbation of the original presenting issues that prompted their entry into therapy with the abusive practitioner.

Counsellors are advised to focus their assessment of the survivor not just on the sexual exploitation but also include an assessment of the original presenting problem, and take into consideration any deterioration in symptoms. To this effect the assessment needs to include an evaluation of pre-existing problems, the impact of the abuse, and those that have resulted from the abuse. This might include other crises such as the breakup of the survivor's relationship as a result of the sexual exploitation, or alienation from friends or family, pregnancy, STIs or suicidal ideation, or attempts. Counsellors must also evaluate how the sexual abuse has contributed to any deterioration in original presenting symptoms.

Such work will not be linear as the survivor may oscillate between the sexual exploitation, pre-existing problems and current crisis. Counsellors need to be able to tolerate such oscillation and be able to allow the survivor to pace the therapeutic work in a way that is most manageable. This is especially the case in not directing the survivor to make any decisions with regard to reporting the exploitative therapist or making a complaint. While this will need to be explored it is critical that the survivor does this at their own pace and that they are able to make informed decisions without pressure from the therapist. This needs to be balanced with the clinician's professional responsibility with regard to reporting of professional misconduct as specified by their professional body. If the survivor decides to make a complaint counsellors need to be clear to what degree they will be able to support the survivor in this. They need to consider to what extent they can act as the survivor's advocate, or if they need to refer them to someone who can provide such advocacy. It is imperative that the counsellor does not make promises or assurances that they cannot deliver.

It may also be helpful to put the survivor in contact with advocacy groups, or direct the survivor to support groups comprised of other survivors of sexual exploitation by professionals. These can often be invaluable as it gives the survivor the opportunity to share their experience with others and talk with other survivors to reduce stigmatisation.

Counsellors need to be aware of their own feelings about taking on survivors of professional abuse and how this impacts on their own boundary issues. If the counsellor is too flexible around boundaries they may need to abstain from working with survivors of professional abuse as they need clear and explicitly stated boundaries. This is necessary to reduce any ambiguity or confusion and also to offer the survivor safe enough boundaries in which to check perceptions in the knowledge that the counsellor will respond with honesty and authenticity. To facilitate this counsellors must be able to clearly state what therapy should be, what the therapist can do and cannot offer, and what is expected of the client. To this effect counsellors need to provide a level of psychoeducation to make the therapeutic process comprehensible, and be prepared to reiterate and restate these throughout the therapeutic process. This needs to be supported by clear contracting which leaves no room for misunderstanding, and which stipulates and articulates the limitations of the therapeutic relationship. It is often helpful to put such a contract in writing and give the survivor a copy so that they can refer to it when necessary. Such a contract needs to include a clear statement about sexual boundaries to ensure client safety.

Restoring trust is one of the core therapeutic goals (see Box 13.3) as issues of trust will be exaggerated. Counsellors will need to be aware of impaired trust but need to guard against making this the sole focus of the work and concentrating too heavily on trying to gain the survivor's trust, as this will put extra pressure on the survivor. It is more productive to acknowledge lack of trust and emphasise that this is entirely valid as it represents a good "reality test", as there is no evidence that they should trust the counsellor as they are a stranger, and from the same profession as their previous abuser (Schoener, 1993). Counsellors need to remember that trust needs to be earned and in providing a safe, secure therapeutic setting in which the focus is on what the survivor needs help with, they will enable the survivor to judge the quality of the relationship and begin to trust. This needs to be left in the survivor's control rather than imposed to avoid replicating any abusive practices.

As in CSA survivors of sexual exploitation by professionals will present with tremendous ambivalence, not only a range of ambivalent feelings about the abuse and their previous therapist, but also around reporting the abuse and working with a new therapist. This ambivalence needs to be acknowledged and explored in order to reduce ambiguity, confusion and uncertainty. Survivors will need to be encouraged to express the full range of feelings such as sadness, affection, anger and rage without feeling ashamed. As this is necessary to fully integrate the abuse experience counsellors need to guard against contaminating the expression of the survivor's feelings by only permitting anger, outrage and rage. The practitioner

Box 13.3 Core therapeutic goals

- Assessment – pre-existing issues that are on hold, impact of sexual exploitation
- Set and maintain clear boundaries and foster predictability
- Crisis intervention
- Restore safety, establish safe, secure therapeutic relationship
- Restore control, internal and external
- Focus on clarity to minimise ambiguity
- Psychoeducation on therapeutic process, boundaries, impact of abuse by professionals
- Name the abuse and attribute responsibility to therapist
- Explore and accept ambivalence – rage and affection, feeling special, illicitness, work with full range of feelings
- Tolerate uncertainty and oscillation
- Identify impact of abuse
- Identify outstanding work on original presenting problem
- Reduce guilt, responsibility, shame, self-disgust
- Facilitate expression of full range of emotions, including anger if genuinely present
- Process and integrate experience
- Explore options with regard to reporting, making a complaint or confronting abuser and be facilitative, not directive
- Explore function and consequences of reporting
- Resume the therapeutic work that was interrupted
- Work through compromised sexuality
- Identify losses and facilitate mourning

must also ensure that any anger and rage expressed is genuine and not an artefact of the therapist. Often survivors need to work through the sadness and loss before they can access rage and counsellors need to be tolerant of this by supporting the survivor in whatever feelings are present and permit their expression.

Most survivors will have a false belief that the sexual exploitation was their fault, and feel guilty about the sexual contact, while others will believe that the relationship was consensual and a representation of the love between survivor and therapist. If the survivor ended the relationship the client may feel guilty for ending the relationship, or fear that they are betraying the therapist. They may feel very protective towards the therapist and wish them no harm, and be reluctant to file a complaint. Counsellors must guard against indulging in assumptions about how the survivor will feel and which emotions will dominate, or how they will experience the ending of the relationship.

The ending of a sexually abusive relationship with a once trusted therapist will generate a number of losses which need to be acknowledged and mourned before the survivor can fully integrate the abuse experience. Counsellors need to enable the survivor to identify these losses and acknowledge the impact these have. The losses will vary for each survivor but commonly include the loss of the "special" relationship, the loss of a once trusted and "good" therapist, the loss of love, and the loss of the therapist's regard. To understand these losses counsellors need to explore the circumstances around the ending of the relationship and the impact this had, as this will evoke different reactions depending on whether the survivor ended it, or if they were rejected or replaced by the therapist, or if someone else made a disclosure. This will be further complicated in those clients who want to marry or have a long-term partnership with their former therapist. Other losses such as partners, family or friends must also be identified. Once the myriad losses are identified counsellors need to facilitate the grieving process and allow for integration, so that the survivor can truly reconnect to self, others and the world.

To achieve these therapeutic goals WITNESS propose a good practice model using the acronym **RISC** (Coe, 2008) which stands for **R**ole (as in the role of the professional), **I**mpact (as in the impact of the abuse on the client), **S**etting (as in the context of the work) and **C**lient's needs (as in the relevant needs of the client). This needs to be supported by counsellor reflexivity and self-monitoring through Socratic questioning to ascertain the reasons behind therapeutic interventions and actions. This can be further developed through high-quality supervision and appropriate consultation. Counsellors need to remember that such questioning and reflexivity will enable them to gain greater insight into the survivor's relational style and provide a deeper understanding of their own relational style in the therapeutic relationship.

THERAPEUTIC CHALLENGES

While the therapeutic setting offered by the clinician can provide the opportunity for reparative work this is not always easily achieved as it is beset with a number of significant therapeutic challenges. Given the impaired trust, survivors of sexual abuse by therapists may enter therapy feeling hostile, defensive or ashamed and for this reason may be difficult to engage. The combination of traumatisation and risking trust again with another therapist can make them hyper-reactive and hypervigilant to all verbal and non-verbal communications emanating from the counsellor.

Counsellors need to ensure careful and sensitive use of language, and be aware of their non-verbal responses to ensure that they appear neutral and professional.

Counsellors must also be able to tolerate any hostility or anger projected onto them and refrain from personalising these but see them as normal reactions within the context of the survivor's abuse and exploitation. It is completely natural that the survivor would feel cynical about therapy and distrust or disbelieve the new therapist. Counsellors need to be mindful that it will take time for the survivor to trust the new therapist and until they do they may test boundaries to ensure they really are safe and containing. Thus survivors may present as rejecting, or resentful at having to pay more money, invest more energy to undertake yet more therapy to undo the "bad" therapy, and having to interrupt the original therapeutic work. This can manifest as silence and brooding resentment making it extremely difficult to engage the survivor.

The survivor may test boundaries through hostility, rejection and by making constant comparisons with the previous therapist which can feel disempowering, making the counsellor feel helpless and hopeless, leading them to try too hard to be the perfect, or ideal counsellor. In order to prove that they are better, more trustworthy and more caring than the previous therapist, the counsellor may confer special privileges on to the survivor (Schoener, 1993) not realising that this might replicate the "special" relationship dynamics of the abuse relationship. Counsellors may be tempted to give more latitude, offer extra support through phone calls, extend the length of sessions, schedule extra appointments or make home visits, or arrange special payment such as reduced, or waived fees. All of these constitute a collapse of therapeutic boundaries not dissimilar to the boundary breakdown and violations preceding the original abuse. Some counsellors may also offer touch or hugs as comfort and unwittingly intensify feelings of confusion and ambivalence. Ironically some counsellors working with survivors of sexual abuse by professionals have ended up becoming romantically or sexually involved with previously abused clients (Schoener, 1993), including female therapists who often think that they can offer touch and hugs safely, only to find that they may also be susceptible to boundary violations.

In many respects the clinician's genuine desire to undo the harm perpetrated by a colleague is the ultimate counter-transference trap whereby the counsellor tries to be the perfect therapist to undo harm of the imperfect or exploitative therapist. In trying to compensate for the deficits in the previous therapeutic process, the reparative therapist may feel compelled to loosen boundaries rather than provide the clear and firm boundaries that do not collapse. Counsellors also need to ensure that the therapeutic boundaries are strong enough to resist any erotic transference on the part of the survivor. As the survivor's experience of therapy has been sexualised, the survivor may believe that this is the only way to gain attention and be made to feel "special" and will behave accordingly. Such clients may present as highly seductive and unconsciously test the therapeutic boundaries. Counsellors must ensure that the therapeutic boundaries are impervious to such seduction and remain steadfast and professional. This may be difficult as the survivor may continually test the counsellor hoping for some response, and feel rejected when this is not provided. It is at this point that the counsellor needs to explore the meaning behind such transference and ensure that the survivor feels she has appropriate attention without responding to any sexual acting out.

A further challenge is for the counsellor to tolerate not just the survivor's ambivalent feelings but also their own. Many clinicians working with survivors of professional abuse are shocked into disbelief, and may question the veracity of the survivor's account, wondering if they have misconstrued the physical contact. While this is a natural reaction, in not wanting to acknowledge that colleagues can and do sexually abuse clients, counsellors must not lose sight of the survivor's experience. Any doubts or fears that are evoked must be explored outside the therapeutic session through supervision and self-supervision. Counsellors must be comfortable in exploring the full range of the survivor's feelings including the positive as well as the more negative ones.

It is critical that counsellors do not encourage survivors to focus purely on anger and rage but to explore the positive feelings of love and affection, and the good aspects of the relationship. The survivor may feel a degree of gratitude towards the previous therapist for the helpful therapeutic work that was undertaken and if this is reality based, it must be honoured and valued. To avoid exploration of the survivor's positive feelings will contaminate the survivor's process and is tantamount to abuse. Moreover, it is often the positive aspects that require the most expression as friends, family or partners are less likely to be able to listen or accept these. Counsellors need to acknowledge and accept expressions of warmth for the abuser as genuine and real and avoid interpreting these as denial, co-dependency, or identification with the aggressor.

Those survivors who have formed a really strong bond, albeit a traumatic one, may be so in thrall to the previous therapist, that they resent having to see another therapist. They may be so in love with the previous therapist that they will be highly resistant to having that image of love destroyed and not be able to name their experience as abuse. This is exacerbated in those survivors who went on to have a long-term relationship, marriage or civil partnership with a former therapist that subsequently became abusive. Counsellors will need to be patient and use psychoeducation to enhance awareness of the inappropriateness of such a relationship, and allow the survivor to draw her own conclusions rather than impose the counsellor's own views and beliefs. This can be a lengthy process and will necessitate a considerable amount of grieving for the loss of what was a highly significant and intense relationship. Survivors may also fear naming the relationship as abuse as they fear being seen as a victim, or being in contact with vulnerability, helplessness and exploitation preferring to idolise the previous therapist as a defence against fragmentation of the self.

In contrast some survivors may enter therapy so full of suppressed anger and rage for being exploited that they may project this on to the new therapist and see him as the abuser. Through this process of splitting, the survivor can continue to idealise the previous counsellor and see the current counsellor as the abuser for not satisfying her dependency needs and desperate yearning to feel special. Conversely, some survivors may begin to idealise, or fall in love with, the new therapist and see them as the ultimate rescuer and protector and the previous therapist as all bad. Such transferential issues must be addressed and explored in order for the new counsellor to avoid colluding or reinforcing such splitting.

It is imperative that counsellors are aware of their counter-transferential reaction either as a response to the transference, or as an evocation of own unresolved dynamics. To avoid a collapse of boundaries counsellors need to ensure that they do not over-compensate by taking on the role of rescuer, protector or ideal therapist in order to make-up for the previous "bad" one. Being ensnared into such competition is counterproductive as it fails to address the importance of working through the ambivalence and allowing integration to take place. Finally, counsellors need to guard against being drawn into the erotic transference by looking for what the previous therapist found attractive about the survivor, and being aroused by the sexual attributes of the survivor. Such arousal may also emerge while exploring the sexual aspect of the survivor's narrative and while this is a normal response, counsellors must contain this to ensure that it does not contaminate the therapeutic process or relationship.

Alongside this, counsellors may fear working with survivors of sexual abuse by therapists for fear of being seduced, over-identifying with the abuser in finding the survivor sexually attractive, or the collapse of their own boundaries. Knowing that a therapist has sexually abused can evoke fears of own potential to abuse, leading to a variety of defences such as disbelief, need to protect a fellow practitioner and the conscious or unconscious closing of ranks. It may also evoke ambivalent feelings about the allegation which may be difficult to reconcile. It is such challenges that necessitate high-quality supervision or consultation in order to separate the counsellor's own fears and ambivalent feelings from those of the survivor in order to not pollute the survivor's experience or add to her burden. While there is considerable value in counsellors sharing their well-modulated feelings of dismay and anger about the abuse it should not become the whole focus of the therapeutic work.

Counsellor ambivalence around alleged abuse by a fellow therapist is exacerbated if the therapist is a colleague or is highly respected. This can have a considerable impact on whether to report the abuse or not. Not all governing bodies specify whether colleagues should report misconduct by other colleagues to their professional body, or whether this is up to the individual client. Arguably this needs to be standardised in order to ensure clarity across the many professional training institutes and also to provide clarity for the client. In some states of America counsellors must report the sexual abuse of clients or patients whether the individual client wishes to or not. While this has considerable advantages in terms of ensuring safe practice for future clients, it may be detrimental to the client who may not wish to report or endure the retraumatisation of an investigation.

In the absence of clear guidelines counsellors must balance the needs and concerns of the client with the seriousness of the allegation and the likelihood that the therapist may be abusing other clients, not just in the present but also in the future. If there are no guidelines around counsellor responsibility to report colleagues' misconduct, then the decision to report or not must remain with the client and the counsellor must support the client's decision irrespective of whether it fits their own beliefs. Regulatory bodies may need to address this issue and develop a unified approach in their Code of Practice specifying clinicians' duty of care to their clients and duty to report professional misconduct. Until these are clarified practitioners must ensure they discuss their dilemmas and ambivalence around reporting in supervision or seek appropriate consultation.

It is clear that counsellors working with survivors of sexual abuse by a mental health professional face a number of significant challenges. The necessary reparative work can be impeded by fears around the collapse of boundaries, uncertainty and ambivalence. The nature of abuse by care professionals is multifaceted, and consists of choreography of complex dynamics. It is only with clarity and firm boundaries that these dynamics can be unravelled. While working with survivors can be extremely difficult and raise all sorts of issues around practice, professionalism and abuse it can also be illuminating and instructive. Working with survivors of abuse by mental health professionals can provide invaluable insights about the nature of power dynamics in interpersonal relationships, complex therapeutic processes, and the centrality of boundaries, all of which can facilitate becoming a better practitioner.

Case vignette: Amber

Amber entered therapy at the age of 42 as she was experiencing relationship problems with her husband. As a mother of four children she felt beleaguered by trying to care for them, work and run a largely chaotic household with no real support from her husband. Amber knew nothing about therapy and was happy to entrust herself to this professional who had come highly recommended. In the early sessions Amber's therapist was courteous and scrupulous in maintaining boundaries. In fact as Amber engaged in the therapeutic process she began to wish that her therapist would give her reassurance and comfort through a judicious hug. Initially when she requested these, her therapist rejected her request although he did allow Amber to sit closer to him and hold his hand. Amber enjoyed this close contact and felt very special that he had made an exception for her in breaking the "no touch" boundary. She also felt that no-one understood her as well as her therapist did, and for the first time in her life she felt understood and valued for being her. She eagerly awaited each session and asked if she could increase her session to two hours a week.

Several months after permitting close contact, Amber's therapist began to explain some of the difficulties heterosexual women had in their relationship with males. He presented a corrupted form of Kleinian theory which, he claimed, was necessary to resolve her relational difficulties, and which would entail a return to her mother's breast. As this was not possible she would need to replace the desire for her mother's nipple with a desire to suckle a penis. This notion was presented with such conviction and made to sound so plausible that Amber believed that this could prove to be the beginning of her healing. Given her difficult relationship with her husband, Amber felt that she would not wish to do this with her husband, at which point the therapist suggested that she could do this with him. Although surprised at first, Amber was not repulsed by this suggestion and felt that it was something that would bind her even closer to her therapist. At the next session her therapist suggested that she lay her head in his lap next to his exposed penis and suckle this as a baby would suckle on a nipple, while he rhythmically stroked her hair. Amber found the stroking comforting and was happy to suckle the penis, especially as she saw how much her therapist enjoyed this contact.

This would become the pattern of her twice-weekly sessions in which some therapeutic work would be followed by laying her head in his lap and providing oral sex. As Amber enjoyed this contact she wanted to develop it further into sexual intercourse although her therapist always refused this as he felt this would be violating his professional boundaries. While frustrated by this, Amber found herself in love with her therapist and was happy that she was as close to him as she was. She became so consumed with her relationship with the therapist that she left her husband and children in the hope that one day when her therapy was complete she and her therapist would set up home as he promised.

For ten years Amber continued to see her therapist twice a week repeating the same pattern until one day her therapist abruptly terminated her therapy with no reason or explanation. Amber hoped that this signified that she was finally "cured" and that they would now set up home together. When it became evident that this was not the case, Amber took a massive overdose. During her three-month hospitalisation the therapist visited her to inform her that she had taken the wrong combination of tablets to make the suicide attempt a success, and proceeded to tell her which tablets would ensure success in any future attempt. Amber was so devastated by the betrayal by her therapist that she was sectioned.

Towards the end of her hospitalisation Amber was assigned a female psychologist who she was able to engage with and who would support her as an outpatient. Although Amber still believed herself to be in love with her therapist, gradually through psychoeducation and painstaking psychological work Amber began to see how she had been enticed and coerced into a sexually exploitative relationship with her therapist. Once Amber recognised this she was able to unleash some of her sadness and anger, although she continued to be protective of her former therapist in not revealing his name, or wanting to take any formal action against him. To date she still has highly ambivalent feelings for her former therapist, although she can acknowledge what harm has been done to her. As she says, it was the most significant relationship in her life as he embodied her mother, father, lover and therapist – a potent cocktail which was impossible to resist.

SUMMARY

- Interpersonal abuse by professionals consists of a range of boundary violations including financial, psychological and sexual exploitation. The sexual exploitation of clients is conceptualised as an act of sexual violence and rape.
- The ubiquitous imbalance of power, dependency needs and transference in the therapeutic relationship render sexual exploitation a pernicious form of interpersonal trauma as it involves a number of complex dynamics such as traumatic bonding, boundary violations, and the betrayal of trust, to ensnare a vulnerable individual into sexual contact(s) to which they cannot give informed consent, and as such resembles CSA and domestic abuse.
- To minimise sexual exploitation clinicians need to receive robust training around power dynamics, the importance of professional boundaries and knowledge of the traumatising effects of such abuse. Clarity and explicit articulation of the importance of boundaries and how to work through erotic transference and counter-transference need to feature in all training courses and professional codes of practice.
- There is no clear definition of what constitutes sexual abuse by therapists or acknowledgment in the UK that this is a crime or act of rape. This makes it difficult for clients to legitimise their experience and causes dilemmas around taking formal action. It also impedes collection of prevalence data as up to 90% of survivors do not report such abuse.
- The majority of sexual abuse appears to be committed against females by males, although female therapists are also known to sexually abuse clients. Research indicates that psychotherapists and counsellors in private practice are most highly represented in the reported abuse by professionals.
- The impact and long-term effects of abuse by therapists resemble those of interpersonal trauma which give rise to a range of psychobiological symptoms including fear, anxiety, PTSD, depression, self-destructive behaviour and suicidal ideation. It also impairs trust in self and others, especially other professionals making it difficult to seek therapeutic help.
- Working with survivors of professional abuse can provide the opportunity for reparative works and yet presents innumerable challenges. It is imperative that the reparative therapist sets and maintains scrupulous boundaries to restore safety and establish a safe, secure therapeutic base. Counsellors will need to ensure that both pre-existing problems as well as the sexual

exploitation is worked through, including the myriad losses associated with sexual abuse.

- To manage the therapeutic challenges counsellors need to have a high level of awareness of the role of transference and counter-transference, power and dependency in the therapeutic process and how this is enacted in the reparative work in order to prevent a collapse of boundaries which can lead to further boundary violations and retraumatisation.
- Despite these challenges, working with survivors of professional abuse can provide invaluable insight into the therapeutic process and enhance practice.

SUGGESTED READING

Alexander, R. (1995) *Folie à Deux: An Experience of One-to-One Therapy.* London: Free Association Press.

Bates, C.M. and Brodsky, A.M. (1993) *Sex in the Therapy Hour: A Case of Professional Incest.* New York: The Guilford Press.

Bates, Y. (2006) (ed.) *Shouldn't I be Feeling Better by Now? Client Views of Therapy.* Basingstoke: Palgrave Macmillan.

Coe, J. (2008) 'Being clear about boundaries.' *The Independent Practitioner,* Spring 2008, 9–12.

Garrett, T. (1998) 'Sexual contact between patients and psychologists.' *The Psychologist,* May 1998, 227–229.

Pope, K. (1989) 'Therapist–Patient Sex Syndrome: A Guide for Attorneys and Subsequent Therapists to Assessing Damage.' In G. Gabbard (ed.) *Sexual Exploitation in Professional Relationships.* Washington, DC: American Psychiatric Press.

Pope, K. (1994) *Sexual Involvement with Therapist: Patient Assessment, Subsequent Therapy, Forensics.* Washington, DC: American Psychiatric Association.

Richardson, S. and Cunningham, M. (2008) *Broken Boundaries: Stories of Betrayal in Relationships of Care.* London: WITNESS.

Russell, J. (1993) *Out of Bounds: Sexual Exploitation in Counselling and Therapy.* London: Sage.

Rutter, P. (1991) *Sex in the Forbidden Zone.* New York: Ballantine Books.

Sands, A. (2000) *Falling for Therapy: Psychotherapy from a Client's Point of View.* Basingstoke: Macmillan Press.

Schoener, G.P. (1993) 'Common errors in treatment of victims/survivors of sexual misconduct by professionals.' *Dulwich Centre Newsletter 3 and 4,* pp.55–61.

Schoener, G.P. (2008) 'Foreword.' In S. Richardson and M. Cunningham *Broken Boundaries: Stories of Betrayal in Relationships of Care.* London: WITNESS.

Schoener, G.P., Milgrom, J., Gonsiorek, J., Luepker, E. and Conroe, R. (1989) *Psychotherapists' Sexual Involvement with Clients: Intervention and Prevention.* Minneapolis, MN: Walk In Counselling Center.

PART III

PROFESSIONAL ISSUES

CHAPTER 14

PROFESSIONAL CHALLENGES AND IMPACT OF COUNSELLING SURVIVORS OF INTERPERSONAL TRAUMA

There are a number of professional challenges when working with survivors of interpersonal trauma. While some of these challenges will vary depending upon the type of interpersonal trauma, there are a number that are generic to all trauma work. It is imperative that counsellors develop a level of awareness of the array of professional issues and challenges ubiquitous in working with survivors of interpersonal trauma. In order to provide the most effective therapeutic practice counsellors need to have a good knowledge and understanding of interpersonal trauma and its psychological impact as well as being able to see it within a sociopolitical context. To facilitate this, practitioners need to ensure that they have sufficient training in the nature and dynamics of interpersonal trauma and access to the range of agencies and services specialising in specific types of interpersonal abuse.

Counsellors also need to have substantial self-awareness of their own experiences of interpersonal abuse, their feelings and reactions to such abuse, as well as how this has impacted on them, to avoid contaminating the survivor's experience. Working with trauma and abuse can have considerable impact on clinicians and elicit a range of emotional and cognitive reactions, which, if left unattended, can lead to vicarious traumatisation, or secondary traumatic stress. To manage the impact of such traumatisation, counsellors are urged to prioritise self-care to ensure that they are able to fully engage with clients without feeling overwhelmed.

This chapter will identify the range of professional issues and challenges inherent in working with survivors of interpersonal trauma. Through this counsellors will be able to ensure that they are more equipped to avoid any pitfalls which can impede good practice. In addition, the chapter will also look at the impact of working with interpersonal trauma on professional and personal functioning, and emphasise the importance of practitioners' self-care to minimise secondary traumatic stress.

PROFESSIONAL ISSUES

When working with survivors of interpersonal trauma, clinicians may face a number of professional issues that need to be addressed before commencing such work (see Box 14.1). To fully engage with survivors of interpersonal trauma and prevent distancing and disconnection, counsellors need to ensure that they have a full understanding of the nature and dynamics of interpersonal trauma and how it impacts on both client and professional. Working with this client group requires specific training in trauma and the development of additional skills to integrate into the existing therapeutic repertoire. Listening to and really engaging in traumatic experiences in which heinous abuses are committed can feel overwhelming and traumatising, and counsellors need to be aware of the psychobiological impact of prolonged coercive control. Alongside this, counsellors need to be able to contextualise symptoms within a trauma framework to avoid pathologising survivors. To provide an optimal therapeutic relationship, counsellors need to be sensitive to the specific needs of survivors and respond to these within a well-bounded therapeutic process.

Given that the majority of interpersonal abuse is committed by males, counsellors need to be sensitive to client preferences for gender of the counsellor. Female survivors of CSA, rape or sexual exploitation by males may find a male therapist terrifying and prefer a female counsellor. Such preferences need to be understood within the context of the abuse rather than be perceived as controlling. Ideally such preferences need to be honoured as they will facilitate therapeutic engagement and ensure safety. It is worth noting that when the interpersonal trauma has been worked through and integration has taken place some survivors may request and benefit from working with a male counsellor. This can help the survivor to experience a positive, non-sexual and non-abusive relationship with a male which can restore trust in men.

Counsellors also need to be culturally sensitive and be able to understand the survivor within a cultural framework. This entails knowledge of a range of cultural attitudes and beliefs with may differ from their own. Survivors who come from collectivist cultures which are predicated on honour will find it hard to report, or to talk about, their experiences, and be fearful of re-establishing contact with their families. Counsellors need to respect this and explore the options that are most beneficial to the survivor rather than impose their own cultural view. What is critical is to empower the survivor to make informed choices which enable them to reconcile their experiences without creating further disconnection and alienation.

As working with interpersonal trauma can reactivate the counsellor's own experiences of interpersonal abuse, it is imperative that they have a good understanding of how this impacted on them and that they have worked through such experiences. Even if counsellors have not been abused, they need to have a high level of self-awareness around their own experiences of power and control, shame, and their own patterns of relating, including attachment style. Such knowledge will enable

Box 14.1 Core professional issues in working with survivors of interpersonal trauma

- Adequate training in interpersonal trauma and its impact
- Full understanding of nature and dynamics of interpersonal trauma
- Awareness of power and control dynamics
- Acquisition of additional therapeutic skills
- Gender preferences in matching client and counsellor
- Cultural sensitivity
- High degree of self-awareness, especially own abuse experiences
- Attachment style
- Clarity and explicitness
- Boundaries
- Tolerating uncertainty
- Flexibility of approach
- Understanding and preventing secondary traumatic stress
- Role of practitioner self-care

the practitioner to recognise how this might manifest in the therapeutic relationship and ensure that their own issues do not contaminate or impede the therapeutic process (Sanderson, 2008). Alongside this, counsellors may need to revisit their own motivation in choosing to enter the mental health profession and their choice of clinical work to minimise negative counter-transference reactions.

Self-awareness around counsellors' own needs for power and control is critical to minimise re-enactment of unhealthy power dynamics. Counsellors need to be mindful of the power imbalance inherent in the therapeutic relationship and how this can be manipulated by either client or clinician. Survivors of interpersonal abuse will be highly sensitised to power dynamics and may see the clinician as an authority figure who they fear will abuse their power as others have done. To counteract anticipatory exploitation or abuse, counsellors need to ensure that clear and explicitly stated boundaries are in place at all times to reduce misunderstanding and misinterpretation, to provide the safe and secure base necessary to work through interpersonal trauma.

Counsellors must be aware of their own need for control and feel comfortable about relinquishing control in order to fully restore control to the survivor. To this effect counsellors must minimise dependency and respect the survivor's striving for mastery, autonomy and self-agency. This includes not imposing rigid therapeutic models and practices to enable the survivor to derive her own meaning from her abuse experience and the impact it has had. To facilitate this, counsellors may need to acquire additional therapeutic skills and techniques to integrate into their already existing therapeutic repertoire, to allow for flexibility of approach that can address the individual needs of each survivor. Such flexibility however needs to be conducted within clear explicitly stated boundaries, to maintain a safe and secure base, and prevent a collapse of the therapeutic alliance. Counsellors will also need to be aware of the array of therapeutic challenges that they face when working with survivors of interpersonal trauma, and the impact these can have on their own psychobiological well-being.

CHALLENGES FOR PROFESSIONALS WORKING WITH SURVIVORS OF INTERPERSONAL TRAUMA

Clinicians may be drawn to trauma work because of their own traumatic experiences and must be aware of not becoming trapped by the "three most common narcissistic snares...to heal all, know all and love all" (Maltsberger and Buie, 1974, p.627). Not only can working with trauma reawaken old wounds, it can also erode the sense of well-being, trust in the world and relationships, and faith and humanity. Many counsellors fear how the work will impact on them and will feel tempted to approach a rigid and structured approach that allows them to be in control of the process. However, they must guard against this as it may dismiss more traditional tools, such as being with the client rather than "doing" or "fixing" the client. If the counsellor loses touch with the human aspects of trauma, then she is in danger of disconnecting from the client and thereby undermining the therapeutic process. What is paramount is listening, noticing, intuiting and being present in the therapeutic relationship. To counteract the inexorable dehumanisation in interpersonal abuse, counsellors must restore the survivor's connection to self and others through the safety of the therapeutic relationship.

There are a number of challenges associated with working with survivors of interpersonal trauma that can disempower counsellors and lead to feelings of inadequacy and frustration. Counsellors need to be apprised of these so that they can face such challenges with confidence rather than dread. Many counsellors fear that they may not be able to help the survivor cope with the enormity of the trauma, or that they may make things worse by opening Pandora's Box. This can lead to feeling deskilled and to concomitant defensive strategies such as disconnection from the client and distancing from the traumatic material. This is compounded by a compromised sense of safety, both in the presence of the material and in the world, which can be so overwhelming to the point of paralysis and frozen watchfulness. If left unattended, this can develop into vicarious traumatisation, or secondary traumatic stress (Sanderson, 2006; 2008).

One danger when working with people who have experienced interpersonal trauma is that it can evoke similar psychobiological changes leading to PTSD symptoms not unlike those seen in the survivor. These can activate a range of symptoms in the clinician including dissociation, flashbacks and intrusive imagery of the survivor's abuse, leading to withdrawal, numbness or uncontrollable anger and rage, as well as shame and guilt (Sanderson, 2008). To manage these some counsellors resort to defensive coping mechanisms such as self-medication through food, alcohol or drug misuse, or detachment and disconnection from self and survivor. Such problems need to be closely monitored and contained either through supervision, affect regulation, taking a break or if necessary returning to personal therapy.

Box 14.2 Impact of working with survivors of interpersonal trauma

- Compromised safety
- Dissociation
- Post-traumatic stress symptoms
- Collapse or constriction of boundaries
- Compromised ability to tolerate uncertainty
- Powerlessness, sense of inadequacy
- Need to be in control and feel safe
- Lack of resources
- Anger and rage
- Shame and guilt
- Disconnection from client
- Shattered assumptions about the world
- Transference and counter-transference reactions
- Secondary traumatic stress

Working with survivors of interpersonal trauma can also feel overwhelming due to the lack of resources and inadequate sociopolitical investment to reduce interpersonal abuse. Many survivors of interpersonal abuse face multiple challenges such as access to employment or adequate housing, or financial difficulties as well as potential retraumatisation through court proceedings. While it is helpful for counsellors to have links with other agencies that can offer support in these areas, the pressures on such agencies are often such that they can only offer limited support which can at times appear insufficient to the survivor's complex needs. As a result counsellors can feel beleaguered and come to believe that they are the only ones who are willing and able to really support the survivor. This is often a reaction to a profound sense of helplessness which activates compensatory strategies such as trying to be the "perfect" therapist and the only one who can "rescue" the client from a hostile world. Such grandiosity can create tremendous pressure on both client and counsellor which is counterproductive as it impedes the therapeutic process.

Such responses are also indicative of transference and counter-transference reactions (CTR). The survivor will transfer a range of feelings onto the counsellor along with hopes and expectations. In turn the counsellor will experience a range of emotional and cognitive CTR. Emotional CTR such as rage can threaten to engulf counsellors as they become in touch with their vulnerability, risk of abuse, and anxieties about their professional abilities., or experience guilt for having been protected from interpersonal abuse. Counsellors must differentiate between CTR that are elicited through transference, and those that derive from the counsellor's own subjective experience, biases and attitudes. A high level of self-awareness of dynamics of interpersonal abuse, and how these intrude consciously and unconsciously in the therapeutic space, is essential, as is self-knowledge of own narcissistic needs for omnipotence and omniscience (Sanderson, 2006; 2008).

Traumatic counter-transference can evoke helplessness, rage, grief, identification with the perpetrator, witness guilt and dissociative responses (Herman, 1992a), all of which activate primitive needs for affiliation, safety, trust, esteem, and control. As these needs emerge the counsellor may try to defend against them by adopting cognitive strategies such as avoidance of trauma narrative, distancing and therapeutic blankness. Alternatively, the counsellor may over-identify with the survivor and become over-invested in rescuing her and develop an inflated sense of responsibility, or narcissistic grandiosity whereby the survivor is relegated to the role of weak victim and the counsellor is the saviour. In contrast, some counsellors may retreat to pathologising or blaming the survivor for the abuse in order to alleviate the affective intensity and retain control (Sanderson, 2008). Counsellors need to be mindful that emotional responses are an integral part of the therapeutic work and make for more sentient counsellors as they are an opportunity for reflection and mentalising. Moreover, CTR are a powerful resource for expanding insight into the realities of the impact of interpersonal trauma which enhances understanding of survivors as well as increasing self-knowledge.

One challenge that can be difficult to master is uncertainty. Working with interpersonal abuse is suffused with uncertainty which can lead to disorientation, loss of control, self-doubt and destabilisation. To manage this, counsellors need to be able to tolerate uncertainty, and contain their anxieties and doubts, so that the survivor feels contained and held in their exploration of the interpersonal trauma. The complex nature of interpersonal trauma means that there will always be an element of uncertainty in terms of coherent narrative, reasons for the abuse and prognosis. Counsellors may need to accept that they may never be able to gain full certainty, and be satisfied with a "good enough" percentage of clarity and knowledge.

IMPACT OF COUNSELLING SURVIVORS OF INTERPERSONAL TRAUMA

Working with survivors of interpersonal trauma can evoke myriad responses, many of which mirror the experiences of survivors. Counsellors need to understand the impact working with interpersonal trauma has on professional and personal functioning in order to identify individual risk factors and to monitor their coping and self-care strategies. The impact can be exacerbated in those professionals who are in private practice (Sanderson, 2008) due to professional isolation, and can also manifest in organisations and agencies especially if they expect staff to be impervious to trauma and demand robotic responses (Yassen, 1995; Wastell, 2005; Sanderson, 2008). Systemic indicators of secondary traumatic stress (STS) include widespread cynicism in staff, high levels of illness, low recruitment and retention rates, decreased motivation and productivity, and ethical or boundary violations. When the personal impact of STS is denied, it is projected on to the organization with staff being overly critical of management structure, procedures and systems. Organisations need to be aware of the impact working with trauma has on staff and how this might be projected. To minimise this requires awareness of STS, regular debriefing, psychological support and open communication between staff and the organisation.

Considerable research has shown that professionals working with trauma can become affected by their work (McCann and Pearlman, 1989; Pearlman and Saakvitne, 1995b; Figley, 1982), and that such exposure is associated with strong reactions of disbelief, anger, and an erosion of the counsellor's sense of well-being as manifested in feelings of helplessness, powerlessness, and loss of faith in humanity (Herman, 1992a). In the words of Nietzsche (1886) "If you gaze into an abyss, the abyss gazes also into you." The impact of working with trauma has also been variously referred to as "burnout" (Figley, 1982), "compassion fatigue" (Figley, 1995), and "vicarious traumatisation" (McCann and Pearlman, 1990), as well as STS (Figley and Kleber, 1995) which is characterised by the evocation of behaviours and emotions that are not dissimilar to the trauma responses of the survivor. The difference is that counsellors will be exposed to many accounts of trauma on a daily basis, which has a cumulative impact. Not only does this reinforce the darker side of human nature, it threatens the health and well-being of the therapist. Counsellors have to be containers not only of clients' material but also of the emotional impact of such material.

The impact of working with interpersonal trauma commonly mirrors the reactions seen in survivors (see Table 14.1) and affects clinicians across several dimensions: emotional, cognitive, physical, behavioural and spiritual. If counsellors are not aware of the impact trauma work has on them they may fail to see how their well-being is compromised, which can undermine their professional functioning leading to "burnout".

Table 14.1 Impact on personal functioning

Emotional	Cognitive	Physical	Behavioural	Spiritual
• Anger and rage • Sadness • Depression • Hyperarousal • Hypervigilance • Anxiety • Apathy • Numbness • Terror • Frustration	• Impaired concentration • Confusion and disorientation • Dissociation • Forgetfulness • Rumination and preoccupation • Guilt • Impaired trust • Disbelief	• Somatic reactions • Impaired immune functioning • Changes in cortisol levels • Self-medication • Changes in appetitive behaviours – sleep, rest, eating, sex, activity	• Withdrawal • Isolation • Avoidance • Irritability • Impatience • Increased neediness	• Loss of meaning/ purpose • Hopelessness • Disconnection from others • Loss of vitality • Loss of spirituality • Loss of faith in humanity • Loss of joy

Pines and Aronson (1988, p.9) describe burnout as

> [A] state of physical, emotional and mental exhaustion caused by long-term involvement in emotionally demanding situations. It is marked by physical depletion and chronic fatigue, by feelings of hopelessness, and by the development of negative self-concept and negative attitudes toward work, life and other people. The negative self-concept is expressed in feelings of guilt, inadequacy, incompetence and failure. Such emotional exhaustion can lead to depression, sense of hopelessness, depersonalization, desensitization, habituation and normalization, in which the counsellor becomes emotionally hardened to trauma work. In turn, this can lead to mental exhaustion, a sense of disillusionment and of reduced personal accomplishment, a feeling of being deskilled and resentment of others.

Burnout is a process that progresses from disillusionment to a reduction of energy levels and unrealistic expectations. To manage this a counsellor may over-extend herself and over-identify with the survivor. Disillusionment is usually followed by stagnation, in which the counsellor no longer finds the work thrilling or satisfying. This invariably leads to frustration and erosion of idealism, in which the counsellor questions the value and effectiveness of work, and yet feels trapped in the work with no way to escape. If burnout is not identified, or is ignored, the process continues, leading to an erosion of self, loss of meaning, and powerlessness which ultimately leads to STS.

STS is akin to PTSD as counsellors experience PTSD-like symptoms, such as avoidance, numbing and depersonalisation. This leads to an avoidance of trauma material, withdrawal, diminished interest in activities, and a sense of detachment and estrangement from others. Counsellors may experience either hyper-reactivity or diminished affect (desensitisation), and difficulties with attention and concentration. This can lead to changes in appetitive behaviours such as eating, drinking, smoking, sleeping and libido. Exposure to trauma can also lead to desensitisation in which the professional habituates to trauma experiences and becomes inoculated, making it hard to accurately assess the degree of trauma and suffering. This can be seen in child protection professionals who become so accustomed to seeing child abuse that they can fail to make accurate risk assessments.

STS in turn leads to shattered assumptions about the self, others and the world as a meaningful place (Janoff-Bulman, 1985) which evokes pervasive uncertainty, increased levels of anxiety and hypervigilance. The world which was once perceived as benign becomes a hostile one, in which control is eroded and danger is palpable. As a result the counsellor may feel paralysed and helpless (just as the client does) which further impacts on professional functioning (see Table 14.2).

Table 14.2 Impact on professional functioning

Emotional	Cognitive	Behavioural
• Burnout • Exhaustion • Dissatisfaction • Feeling overwhelmed • Lack of motivation • Desensitisation and habituation	• Negative attitude to work • Poor concentration • Inattentiveness • Inoculation to trauma and abuse • Impaired risk assessment • Impaired decision making • Increased mistakes	• Impaired communication • Increased mistakes • Increased absences • Avoidance of co-workers • Avoidance of supervision • Irresponsibility • Adversarial stance • Increasing work load • Taking on more clients • Not taking regular breaks

Impaired professional functioning manifests in the therapeutic setting in which the counsellor may distance herself from the survivor, leading to a reduction in empathy and a rupture in the therapeutic relationship. Counsellors may habituate to trauma and become inoculated to the pain and suffering which can impair accurate risk assessment and compassion fatigue. STS can also result in a loss of self-efficacy and resourcefulness, loss of autonomy and feelings of helplessness. Despite this the counsellor may avoid seeking professional support or supervision due to shame or embarrassment, or to deny her own vulnerability. To support and retain a sense of invulnerability, or to challenge herself, the counsellor may take on more and more trauma work in order to test her ability to cope (Sanderson, 2006; 2008).

THE PREVENTION OF SECONDARY TRAUMATIC STRESS

To prevent or minimise the STS, counsellors need to ensure that they have a strong personal and professional support network and understand the importance of self-care. Counsellors need to engage in regular and adequate supervision, preferably with a supervisor who is experienced in trauma work. In addition to individual supervision, and to reduce isolation, counsellors may also benefit from peer or group supervision in which they can receive and give support. In complex cases clinicians may benefit from consulting with a specialist in interpersonal trauma or in the particular type of abuse experienced. To extend knowledge and develop greater awareness of trauma counsellors must ensure they access continuous professional development and forge links with statutory and voluntary agencies. Creating a comfortable and nurturing work environment predicated on mutual support and respect from others can ameliorate the impact of working with trauma and susceptibility to STS.

Reflexivity, or self-supervision (Casement, 1990) is another important preventive strategy that allows the counsellor to mentalise their experience of working with survivors of interpersonal abuse and to connect to their responses. The use of self-reflection can also facilitate the growth of the therapist as a sentient practitioner. In combination, these can reduce the evocation of negative counter-transferential reactions, erosion of empathy and compassion fatigue.

To prevent or minimise the impact of STS on personal functioning, counsellors need to remain connected to the self, ensure their needs are responded to, and maintain a balance between personally meaningful life activities and work. Yassen (1995) proposes that counsellors balance client work with other activities that support the prevention of trauma, as well as extending their support network beyond their immediate work. Counsellors must also develop their capacity for self-support both professionally and personally. Essential to this is the ability for self-compassion and opportunities to be fully expressive of all their emotions, including doubts and uncertainties as well as joy and happiness. Most importantly, the counsellor must be authentic and honest in acknowledging and recognising her vulnerabilities as well as strengths (Sanderson, 2008).

It is also essential to balance the trauma work with regular breaks in which the counsellor can pursue personal pleasures that provide "avocational avenues for creative and relaxing self-expression in order to regenerate" (Danieli, 1994), and have fun. Some clinicians argue that "feeling free to have fun and joy is not frivolity in this field but a necessity without which one cannot fulfil one's professional obligations..." (Danieli, 1994). Counsellors must incorporate physical and creative activities that induce relaxation and spiritual well-being. Embodiment can be enhanced by engaging in physical activities such as martial arts, tai chi, yoga and meditation which stimulate the right hemisphere activity in the brain (van der Kolk, 2004). These need to be accompanied by regular sleep patterns and a healthy diet to ensure self-nurturing and capacity to enjoy and take pleasure in life through play, humour and love. Humour has a powerful restorative value in connecting the clinician with others and to life (Sanderson, 2008) and is a powerful indicator of well-being and connection to life. To counterbalance loss of meaning, or loss of faith in humanity, the counsellor is urged to pursue a range of personally meaningful activities that inspire and allow for passion and joy to predominate, such as time with family and friends and engaging in activities unconnected to work, to ensure a more grounded and balanced lifestyle.

THE IMPORTANCE OF SELF-CARE

Counsellors need to ensure self-care to minimise STS. This needs to take place on several dimensions, in particular work, body, mind, emotion and spirit and creativity (see Figure 14.1).

Figure 14.1 Self-care when working with survivors of interpersonal trauma

Counsellors must find whatever brings them peace or contentment whether it be love, friendship, their children, play or laughter, or being in contact with nature, writing or visiting museums or galleries (Sinason, 2008). While this will vary from counsellor to counsellor, it is critical to implement these regularly and to engage in activities that inspire passion, and facilitate creativity and connection to spirituality. Self-nurturing must also incorporate an ability to allow others to care and to be able to accept companionable support (Sinason, 2008; de Zulueta, 2008). It is critical that counsellors can permit the expression of their own vulnerabilities and dependency needs to avoid defensive feelings of invincibility or self-sufficiency. With appropriate support counsellors can minimise STS and remain empathically attuned to the client. This allows them to focus on the therapeutic relationship as a vehicle to enable survivors to restore trust and reconnection to self, others and the world. Counsellors who have remained connected throughout the counselling process will have contributed to the survivor's post-traumatic growth and will have been transformed in their own personal and professional growth in becoming more sentient practitioners with a greater appreciation of being alive.

SUMMARY

- Knowledge of the impact of trauma on personal and professional functioning is critical in understanding secondary traumatic stress (STS). Counsellors, managers and organisations need to know the warning signs of STS as these symptoms serve to alert them to burnout, compassion fatigue or STS.
- Working with trauma can also impact on organisations and agencies. To counteract this necessitates knowledge of STS, provision of training, psychological support, regular supervision and regular breaks to ensure staff cohesion and satisfaction.
- There are a number of professional and personal strategies that can minimise STS which counsellors need to implement. To avoid professional isolation, counsellors need to build professional support networks through supervision, specialist consultations and collaboration with other agencies. Such multidisciplinary support will enhance knowledge and enable practitioners to provide a holistic approach to treatment.
- Counsellors also need to ensure self-care through balancing trauma work with more general client work, taking regular breaks, and making time to relax. To counteract working with trauma, counsellors need to stay connected to ordinary, everyday activities outside of trauma, such as time with family and friends and activities that are grounding or inspiring.

- It is critical that they pursue valued activities and passions that allow them to take pleasure and delight in other areas of their lives. Physical activities that stimulate right brain hemisphere activation such as tai chi, yoga and meditation are found to be particularly useful. A life–work balance is crucial to avert burnout and counsellors must prioritise this so that they can remain embodied and emotionally connected to survivors.
- With appropriate strategies in place, counsellors can embrace the therapeutic work without fear of being engulfed or threatened by STS. This allows them to be open to their client's experiences and remain sensitively attuned to them. With this in place they can enable the survivor to move from merely surviving to being alive, and begin to rebuild their lives outside the shadow of abuse.
- In this survivor and counsellor can experience post-traumatic growth, making the counsellor a more sentient practitioner with a greater appreciation of what it means to be human and being alive.

RESOURCES

FOR CHILDREN

UK

Childline
Tel: 0800 1111
Website: www.childline.org.uk
Confidential counselling service for children. The website has a weblink for children and young people to use.

The Hideout
Website: www.thehideout.org.uk
Link from Women's Aid for children or young people.

NSPCC Child Protection Helpline
Tel: 0808 800 5000
Website: www.nspcc.org.uk
Advice and information on parenting-related issues. The website has a weblink for children to use.

Ireland

Childline Ireland
Tel: 1800 666 666
Website: www.childline.ie

Australia

Australian Childhood Foundation
Tel: 1800 176 453 (national helpline)
Tel: (03) 9874 3922
Website: www.childhood.org.au
Offers information, help, support, education, counselling and advocacy.

Kids Helpline
Tel: 1800 551 800

Kidscount
Website: www.kidscount.com.au
For help in relation to child abuse and protection.

Lifeline Australia
Tel: 13 11 14
Website: www.lifeline.org.au

Stop Child Abuse
Website: www.stopchildabuse.com.au
Offers a services directory across all states.

Canada

Child Abuse Prevention
Tel: 310 1234 (Helpline British Columbia)
Website: www.safekidsbc.ca
Provides child protection services, information, links and resources across all states.

National Helpline
Tel: 1 866 660 0505

US

National Child Abuse Hotline
Tel: 1 877 723 2445
Website: www.childhelp.org
Provides information, links and resources on child abuse.

FOR ELDERLY PEOPLE

UK and Ireland

Action on Elder Abuse
Tel: 0808 808 8141 (UK)
1800 940 010 (Republic of Ireland)
Website: www.elderabuse.org.uk
Confidential helpline providing information and emotional support to elderly people and their carers and to professionals on all aspects of elder abuse.

Help the Aged
Tel: 020 7278 1114 (England)
0131 551 6331 (Scotland)
02920 346 550 (Wales)
02890 230 666 (Northern Ireland)
Website: www.helptheaged.org.uk
Email: info@helptheaged.org.uk
Help the Aged is committed to ending elder abuse and offers advice and support to victims and their carers.

Worldwide

International Network for the Prevention of Elder Abuse
Tel: 01482 465 716
Website: www.inpea.net
Aim is to increase society's ability, through international collaboration, to recognise and respond

to mistreatment of older people in whatever setting. Has chapters in Europe, North America, Latin America, Asia, Africa and Australia/ Oceania.

Australia

Aged Care Crisis
Website: www.agedcarecrisis.com
Provides information on elder abuse.

Elder Abuse Prevention Line
Tel: 02 6205 3535

Elder Abuse Prevention Unit (Queensland)
Tel: 1300 651 192 or 07 3250 1955
Website: www.eapu.com.au

Seniors
Website: www.seniors.gov.au
Provides information on elder abuse.

Canada

Ontario Network for the Prevention of Elder Abuse
Tel: (416) 978 1716 or Toll free: 1 888 579 2888
Website: www.onpea.org

US

National Center on Elder Abuse
Tel: 1 800 677 1116
Website: www.ncea.aoa.gov

FOR LESBIAN, GAY, BISEXUAL AND TRANSGENDER PEOPLE

UK

Broken Rainbow
Tel: 0845 260 4460
Website: www.broken-rainbow.org.uk
Service for lesbians, gay men, bisexual or transgender people.

London Lesbian and Gay Switchboard
Tel: 020 7837 7324
Website: www.llgs.org.uk
Offers 24-hour information and support for lesbians and gay men.

Survivors of Lesbian Partner Abuse (SOLA)
Tel: 020 7328 7389
Supports women who have experienced domestic abuse within a lesbian relationship.

Australia

Gay and Lesbian Counselling Service of NSW
PO Box 334, Darlinghurst NSW 2010
Tel: (02) 9207 - 2800
Email: glcs@bigpond.com
Telephone counselling and info service, open 4:00 PM till midnight.

PFLAG NSW Inc
PO Box 1488, Darlinghurst NSW 2010
Tel: (02) 9249 - 1002, Fax: (02) 9439 - 5024
Email: pflagnswnews@primus.com.au
PFlag meet monthly to offer support to parents, family and friends of GLBT's as well as advice to GLBT's who wish to come out to parents and friends.

Canada

The Centre
Updated: 4/23/2009
Website: www.lgtbcentrevancouver.com
A community centre serving and supporting lesbian, gay, transgender, bisexual people and their allies in Vancouver, British Columbia.

USA

LGBT Community Centers listing of 174 Community Centers across the USA
Website: www.resources.lgbtcenters.org/Directory
This is a directory of Centers across the USA providing support to the LGBT communities.

FOR VICTIMS OF DOMESTIC ABUSE

UK

Black Association of Women Step Out (BAWSO)
Tel: 029 2043 7390
Offers advice and support to black women who have experienced or are experiencing domestic abuse.

Chinese Information and Advice Centre (CIAC)
Tel: 020 7692 3697
Website: www.ciac.co.uk
Offers information and support on family issues, domestic abuse and immigration.

Domestic Violence National 24-hour Helpline
Tel: 0808 2000 247 (minicom available)
Websites: www.refuge.org.uk
www.womensaid.org.uk

English Women's Aid
Tel: 0808 2000 247
Website: www.womensaid.org.uk

Families Without Fear Project
Tel: 020 7644 6255
Website: www.familieswithoutfear.org.uk
A charity providing a programme of individual counselling and group work for men and women dealing with domestic abuse in North West London.

Hidden Hurt
Tel: 0808 2000 247
Website: www.hiddenhurt.co.uk
A domestic abuse website with list of information and support.

Jewish Women's Aid (JWA)
Tel: 0800 59 12 03
Website: www.jwa.org.uk
Offers domestic abuse awareness-raising programmes and help.

Kiran – Asian Women's Aid
Tel: 020 8558 1986
Provides safe, temporary accommodation for Asian women and their children escaping domestic abuse.

ManKind Initiative
Tel: 0870 794 4121
Website: www.mankind.org.uk
Advice, information and support for male victims.

Men's Advice Line (MALE)
Tel: 0845 064 6800
Website: www.mensadviceline.org.uk
Email: info@mensadviceline.org.uk
Offers advice and support for men in abusive relationships.

Men's Aid
Tel: 0871 223 9986
Helpline available 8 am to 8 pm seven days a week.
Website: www.mensaid.com
Free practical advice and support to men who have been abused.

Northern Ireland Women's Aid Helpline
Tel: 0800 917 1414
Website: www.niwaf.org

Refuge: Combined Women's Aid and Refuge Helpline
Tel: 0808 2000 247
Website: www.refuge.org.uk
Email: info@refuge.org.uk

Scottish Women's Aid
Tel: 0800 027 1234
Website: www.scottishwomensaid.org.uk

Southall Black Sisters
Tel: 020 8571 9595
Website: www.southallblacksisters.org.uk
Specialist advice and support for Asian and African Caribbean women suffering violence and abuse.

Supportline
Tel: 01708 765 200
Website: www.supportline.org.uk
Email: info@supportline.org.uk
A telephone helpline providing emotional support to children, young people and adults on any issue including domestic abuse. It keeps details of other agencies, support groups and counsellors throughout the UK.

Victim Support Male Helpline
Tel: 0800 328 3623
For male victims of domestic abuse or sexual abuse.

Welsh Women's Aid
Tel: 0800 8010 800
Website: www.welshwomensaid.org
Resources 249

Ireland

Amen Ireland
Tel: (046) 902 3718
Website: www.amen.ie
Confidential helpline, support service and information for male victims of domestic violence and their children.

Irish Women's Aid Domestic Abuse
Tel: 1800 341 900
Website: www.womensaid.ie

Worldwide

Andrew Vachss
Website: www.vachss.com
Offers information, links and international resources on domestic violence and child abuse.

Hot Peach Pages
Website: www.hotpeachpages.net
Global directory of domestic abuse agencies, hotlines, shelters, refuges, crisis centres and women's organisations searchable by country, plus index of domestic abuse resources in over 75 languages.

Australia

Domestic Violence Resource Centre
Tel: (03) 9486 9866
Website: www.dvirc.org.au
Provides information and referrals to local services for domestic violence victims and children of domestic violence throughout Australia.

Men's Domestic Violence Helpline
Tel: 08 9242 9218

Canada

Assaulted Women's Helpline
Tel: (416) 863 0511; Toll free 1 866 863 0511; TTY Toll free 1 866 863 7868
Website: www.awhl.org

Canadian National Clearinghouse for Family Violence
Tel: 613 957 2838; Toll free 1 800 267 1291; TTY Toll free 1 800 561 5643
Website: www.hc-sc.gc.ca

Family of Men Support Society
Tel: 403 242 4077
Website: www.familyofmen.com
Information and help for abused males. Offers crisis support, information, links and list of resources such as shelters for abused men.

Men's Alternative Safe House: MASH Project
Website: www.4077.ca
Information and help, including shelters for abused males.

National Domestic Violence Hotline (Canada)
Tel: Toll free 1 800 363 9010
Covers all provinces and is bilingual (English and French).

SafeCanada
Website: www.safecanada.ca
Provides information and services on domestic violence.

Shelternet
Website: www.shelternet.ca
Connects abused women to local shelters.

US

Battered Men
Website: www.batteredmen.com
List of helplines for abused males across all states.

Domestic Rights Coalition
Tel: 651 774 7010
Provides help for males who have experienced domestic abuse along with advocacy and finding shelters for abused males.

National Center for Victims of Crime
Tel: 1 800 394 2255
Website: www.endabuse.org
Information on domestic violence.

National Domestic Violence Hotline
Tel: 1 800 799 7233 or 1 800 787 3224
Hotline has 24-hour access from all 50 states. There are translators available.
Website: www.ndvh.org
List of help and information on domestic violence in each state.

Safe Horizon
Tel: 1 800 621 4673
Website: www.safehorizon.org
Provides hotline, counselling centre and information on domestic violence.

Stop Abuse For Everyone (SAFE)
Website: www.safe4all.org
Serves those who typically fall between the cracks of domestic violence services. Lists helplines and numerous international organisations and agencies that provide services for people suffering from abuse across all states.

FOR PERPETRATORS OF DOMESTIC ABUSE

UK

Everyman Project
Tel: 020 7263 8884
Website: www.everymanproject.co.uk
Service providing counselling and anger management services to men wishing to end abusive behaviour.

Freedom Programme
Tel: 0151 630 0651
Website: www.freedomprogramme.co.uk
Email: atcraven@aol.com
Offers a 12-week programme for any man who wishes to stop abusing women and children.

ManKind Initiative
Tel: 0870 794 4124
Website: www.mankind.org.uk

The Men's Centre
West Hill House
6 Swains Lane
London N6 6QS
Tel: 020 7267 8713
Website: www.themenscentre.co.uk
Counselling and psychotherapy for angry/abusive or violent men and for men and women with emotional, relationship and sexual problems.

Respect
Tel: 0845 122 8609
Website: www.respect.uk.net
Helpline providing information and advice for perpetrators of domestic abuse, and domestic abuser support programme.

Ireland

MOVE – Men Overcoming Violence
Website: www.moveireland.ie
Facilitates men in a weekly group process that involves them taking responsibility for their violence and changing their attitude and behaviour.

FOR VICTIMS OF RAPE AND SEXUAL ABUSE

UK

Rape Crisis
See local telephone numbers in phone directories
Website: www.rapecrisis.org.uk

The Sexual Violence Action and Awareness Network (SVAAN)
Website: www.eaves4women.co.uk/Lilith_Project/Support_and_networking/SVAAN.php
A network coordinated by the Lilith Project for voluntary and statutory agencies which provide support services to women who have been raped or sexually assaulted.

Survivors
Tel: 020 7357 8299
Helpline for male victims of sexual abuse.

Women Against Rape
Tel: 020 7482 2496
Fax: 020 7209 4761
Website: www.womenagainstrape.net
A grassroots multi-racial women's organisation offering counselling, support, legal advocacy and information to women and girls surviving rape, sexual assault including racist sexual assault, rape in marriage and other domestic violence.

Ireland

Rape Crisis Network – Ireland
The Halls, Quay Street, Galway, Ireland
Tel: 091 563676
Fax: 091 563677
Website: www.rcni.ie
A network provoding links to various support organisations.

Australia

Abused Empowered Survive Thrive
www.aest.org.uk
An online directory of Australian and New Zealand survivor helplines and support groups.

CASA Forum Victorian Centres Against Sexual Assault
Website: www.casa.org.au
Provides counselling and other emotional support across 15 centres in the State of Victoria.

Canada

Website: www.aswaterspassingby.org
Online directory of sexual abuse and rape survivior links to Canadian organisations

USA

Website: www.vaonline.org
Online directory of sexual assault and abuse resources both in USA and internationally.

FOR ADULT SURVIVORS OF CHILD ABUSE

UK

Family Matters UK
Helpline: 01474 537 392
Website: www.familymattersuk.org
The largest provider of specialist counselling services for children and adult survivors of sexual abuse and rape in the UK

One in Four UK
Tel: 020 8697 2112
Website: www.oneinfour.org.uk
Email admin@oneinfour.org.uk
An organisation run for and by people who have experienced sexual abuse which provides a unique service to individuals through individual therapy and helpline support. Also actively involved in campaigning, policy making, in-house research, training, and consultancy work with statutory and non statutory agencies.

Survivors Swindon
Helpline: 0845 430 9371
Tel: 0870 950 3567
Website: www.survivorsswindon.com
Counselling service for adult male survivors of child sexual assault and adult male sexual assault/rape through telephone helpline, group therapy, one to one counselling.

The Survivors Trust
Tel: 01788 550554
Website: www.thesurvivorstrust.org
A national umbrella agency for over 120 specialist voluntary sector agencies providing a range of counselling, therapeutic and support services working with women, men and children who are victims/survivors of rape, sexual violence and childhood sexual abuse.

Ireland

One in Four Ireland
Website: www.oneinfour.org
Tel: 01 662 4070
Fax: 01 611 4650
Email info@oneinfour.org

US

ASCA (Adult Survivors of Child Abuse)
Website: www.ascasupport.org
An innovative recovery program for adult survivors of childhood abuse.

Worldwide

The Broken Spirits Network
Website: www.brokenspirits.com
An online community and support group that focuses on aiding both current and past victims of child abuse, sexual abuse, and domestic violence. Provides a comprehensive International Directory of shelters, hotlines and organizations that can provide help for potential victims.

FOR VICTIMS OF PROSTITUTION

UK

Eaves
Tel: 020 7735 2062
Fax: 020 7820 8907
Website: www.eaves4womenco.uk
Email: post@eaveshousing.co.uk
A London-based charity that provides high quality housing and support to vulnerable women.

Kalabash Forum
Website: www.eaves4women.co.uk/Lilith_Project/Support_and_networking/Kalabash.php
A networking initiative of around 55 organisations that have a remit to support Black Minority Ethnic (BME) women and girls who have experienced any form of gendered violence. Members include therapeutic counselling services, supported housing providers and advocacy services.

Lilith Project
Website: www.eaves4women.co.uk/Lilith_Project/Lilith_Project.php
A London-based organisation which works to eliminate all aspects of violence against women.

The Poppy Project
Tel: 020 7735 2062.
Website: http://www.eaves4women.co.uk/POPPY_Project/POPPY_Project.php
Funded by the Office for Criminal Justice (reporting to the Ministry for Justice) to provide support and accommodation to women who have been trafficked into prostitution.

Rape Crisis Centre: SWAP (Supporting Women Abused in Prostitution)
Tel: 0141 552 3201 (Office); 0141 552 3520 (Support/Textphone)
Fax: 0141 552 3204
A project to support women in prostitution who have experienced rape and sexual assault.

Ireland

Ruhama (Hebrew for "renewed" life)
Tel: 01 836 0292
Fax: 01 836 0268
Email: admin@ruhama.ie
Website: www.ruhama.ie
Dublin-based support organisation providing advocacy and counselling for victims of prostitution and trafficking.

FOR VICTIMS OF HUMAN TRAFFICKING

UK

CEOP (Child Exploitation and Online Protection)
Tel: 0870 000 3344
Website: www.ceop.gov.uk
Part of UK policing – track and bring offenders to account either directly or in partnership with local and international forces.

The Helen Bamber Foundation
Tel: 020 7631 4492
Fax: 020 7631 4493
Website: www.helenbamber.org
Email: info@helenbamber.org
Works with survivors of cruelty to help rebuild lives and inspire a new self-esteem in survivors of gross human rights violations such as those who have been trafficked.

NSPCC National Child Trafficking Advice and Information Line (CTAIL)
Helpline: 0800 107 7057
Website: www.nspcc.org.uk
A new service for anyone with concerns about human trafficking.

International

Website: www.humantrafficking.org
An international resource to combat human trafficking.

Australia

Project Respect
Website: www.projectrespect.org.au
Provides outreach services to women working in the Australian sex industry.

Canada

Department of Justice
Website: www.justice.gc.ca
Defines policy on protection of victims of human trafficking.

PACT – Persons Against the Crime of Trafficking in Humans
Website: www.pact-ottawa.org
Link to Canadian Agencies providing support to victims of human trafficking.

USA

See under USA on the following website: www.humantrafficking.org
Approximately 40 organisations across the USA providing support for victims of human trafficking.

OTHER USEFUL RESOURCES

UK

Beverly Lewis House
Tel: 020 8522 2000
Email: info@east-living.co.uk
A haven for women with learning disabilities who have suffered from abuse or who are at risk of abuse.

Crown Prosecution Service Victims and Witnesses
www.cps.gov.uk/victims_witnesses

Mind
Tel: 0845 766 0163
Website: www.mind.org.uk
A mental health charity that supports people in distress.

Tulip Group
Tel: 0151 637 6363
Support for parents experiencing abuse from their children.

Victim Support
Tel: 0845 303 0900
Website: www.victimsupport.org.uk
Service for the victims of crime, and those who are acting as witnesses in court.

WITNESS
Helpline: 08454 500 300
Website: www.popan.org.uk
Email: info@professionalboundaries.org.uk
Offers a helpline and professional support and advocacy services for the victims and survivors of professional abuse; campaigns for improvements in policy law and practice; conducts research; and provides education and training.

Australia

Men's Health Network Helpline
Tel: 02 9743 4434

Men's Line Australia
Tel: 1300 789 978 (24-hour helpline)
Website: www.menslineaus.org.au
A dedicated service for men with relationship and family concerns.

National Confidential Helpline
Tel: 1800 200 526
24-hour helplines by state:
ACT: (02) 6280 0900
NSW: 1800 656 463
NT: 1800 019 116
QLD: 1800 811 811
SA: 1800 800 098
TAS: 1800 608 122 or 6233 2529
VIC: 1800 015 188 or 9373 0123
WA: 1800 007 339 or 9223 1188

Women's Resource Information and Support Centre
Tel: (03) 53 333 666
Website: wrisc.ballarat.net.au
Provides help and support and local referrals throughout Australia.

BIBLIOGRAPHY

Abrahams, H. (2007) *Supporting Women after Domestic Violence: Loss, Trauma and Recovery.* London: Jessica Kingsley Publishers.

Action on Elder Abuse (AEA) (2004) *Hidden Voices: People's Experience of Abuse.* London: Help The Aged.

Ainsworth, M.D.S., Blehar, M.C., Waters, E. and Wall, S. (1978) *Patterns of Attachment: A Psychological Study of the Strange Situation.* Hillsdale, NJ: Lawrence Erlbaum.

Alexander, P.C. and Anderson, C.L. (1994) 'An attachment approach to psychotherapy with the incest survivor.' *Psychotherapy 31,* 665–673.

Allen, J.G. (1997) *Sexual Harassment from the Trauma Perspective.* Topeka, KS: Menninger Clinic and Office of Army Chief of Chaplains.

Allen, J.G. (2001) *Traumatic Relationships and Serious Mental Disorders.* Chichester, UK: Wiley.

Allen, J.G. (2006a) *Coping with Trauma: Hope through Understanding.* Second edition. Washington, DC: American Psychiatric Publishing.

Allen, J.G. (2006b) *Coping with Depression: From Catch 22 to Hope.* Washington, DC: American Psychiatric Publishing.

Allen, J.G. and Fonagy, P. (eds) (2006) *Handbook of Mentalization Based Treatment.* Chichester, UK: Wiley.

Allen, J.G., Bleiberg, E. and Haslam-Hopwood, T. (2003) *Mentalizing as a Compass for Treatment.* Houston, TX: Menninger Clinic.

Allen, J.G., Fonagy, P. and Bateman, A.W. (2008) *Mentalizing in Clinical Practice.* Arlington, VA: American Psychiatric Publishing.

American Psychiatric Association (2000) *Diagnostic and Statistical Manual of Mental Disorders (DSM) IV-TR.* Washington, DC: American Psychiatric Association.

Amiel, A. and Heath, I. (2003) *Family Violence in Primary Care.* Oxford: Oxford University Press.

Anderson, C.L. and Alexander, P.C. (1996) 'The relationships between attachment and dissociation in adult survivors of incest.' *Psychiatry 59,* 240–254.

Arnsten, A.F. (1998) 'The biology of being frazzled.' *Science 280,* 1711–1721.

Aurelius, M. (2002) *Meditations.* New York: Modern Library.

BACP (British Association for Counselling and Psychotherapy) (2007) *Ethical Framework of Good Practice in Counselling and Psychotherapy.* Lutterworth, Leicestershire: BACP.

Bales, K. (2004) *Disposable People: New Slavery in the Global Economy.* Berkeley, CA: University of California Press.

Bandura, A. (1979) 'The Social Learning Perspective: Mechanisms of Aggression.' In A. Toch (ed.) *Psychology of Crime and Criminal Justice.* New York: Holt, Rinehart & Winston.

Barnardo's (2002) *Stolen Childhood: Barnardo's Work with Children Abused Through Prostitution.* London: Barnardo's.

Barter, C. (1997) 'Who's to blame: Conceptualising institutional abuse by children.' *Early Child Development and Care 133,* 101–104.

Barter, C., Renold, E., Berridge, D. and Cawson, P. (2004) *Peer Violence in Children in Residential Care.* Basingstoke: Palgrave Macmillan.

Barter, C. (2006) *Abuse of Children in Residential Care.* London: NSPCC Inform.

Bartholomew, K. (1990) 'Avoidance of intimacy: An attachment perspective.' *Journal of Social and Personal Relationships 7,* 147–148.

Bashir, J. and Bashir, C. (2001) *Attempted Suicide and Self Harm: South Asian Women.* Manchester: Women's Studies Research Centre, Manchester Metropolitan University.

Batsleer, J. *et al.* (2002) *Domestic Violence and Minoritisation: Supporting Women to Independence.* Manchester: Manchester Metropolitan University.

Baumeister, R.F. (1990) 'Suicide as escape from self.' *Psychological Review 97,* 90–113.

Beck, A.T. (1976) *Cognitive Therapy and Emotional Disorders.* New York: New American Library.

Berger, H. (2001) 'Trauma and the Therapist.' In T. Spiers (ed.) *Trauma: A Practitioner's Guide to Counselling.* Hove, UK: Brunner-Routledge.

Bergin, A.E. and Garfield, S.C. (eds) (1994) *Handbook of Psychotherapy and Behaviour Change.* Fourth edition. Chichester, UK: Wiley.

Bevan, S. (2008) 'Sexual Abuse and Rape Against Men.' Paper presented at Tackling Sexual Violence Conference: Investigation, Prosecution and Victim Support, 12 December, London.

Bifulco, A. and Moran, P. (1998) *Wednesday's Child: Research into Women's Experiences of Neglect and Abuse in Childhood and Adult Depression.* London: Routledge.

Biggs, S., Phillipson, C. and Kingston, P. (1995) *Elder Abuse in Perspective.* Buckingham: Open University Press.

Blackman, J. (1989) *Intimate Violence: A Study in Injustice.* New York: Columbia University Press.

Blake-White, J. and Klein, C.M. (1985) 'Treating the dissociative process in adult victims of childhood incest.' *Social Casework 66,* 394–402.

Blatt, E. (1992) 'Factors associated with child abuse and neglect in residential care settings.' *Children and Youth Services Review 14,* 493–517.

Blatt, E. and Brown, S. (1986) 'Environmental influences on incidents of alleged child abuse and neglect in New York state psychiatric facilities: Toward an ecology of institutional child maltreatement.' *Child Abuse and Neglect 10,* 171–180.

Blizzard, R.A. (2003) 'Disorganised attachment, development of dissociated self states and a relational approach to treatment.' *Journal of Trauma and Dissociation 4,* 3, 27–50.

Bond, S. and Bond, M.H. (2004) 'Attachment styles and violence within couples.' *Journal of Nervous and Mental Disease 192,* 12, 851–863.

Boseley, S. (2008) 'One in 10 children suffers abuse, say experts.' *The Guardian,* 3 March.

Bowlby, J. (1969) *Attachment and Loss: Attachment.* London: Penguin.

Bowlby, J. (1973) *Attachment and Loss: Separation.* London: Penguin.

Bowlby, J. (1977) 'The making and breaking of affectional bonds.' *British Journal of Psychiatry 130,* 201–210.

Bowlby, J. (1980) *Attachment and Loss: Loss, Sadness and Depression, Vol. III.* New York: Basic Books.

Bowlby, J. (1988) *A Secure Base.* London: Routledge.

BPS (British Psychological Society) (2008) *Generic Professional Practice Guidelines,* Second edition. Leicester: BPS.

Brand, P.A. and Kidd, A.H. (1986) 'Frequency of physical aggression in heterosexual and female homosexual dyads.' *Psychological Reports 59,* 1307–1313.

Brandon, M (2007) 'Confident Workers, Confident Families: Exploring Sensitive Outcomes in Family Centre Work in England.' In M. Berry *Identifying Essential Elements of Change: Lessons from International Research in Community Based Family Centres.* Leuven: ACCO.

Brandon, M., Belderson, J., Warren, C., Howe, D., Gardner, R., Dodsworth, J. and Black, J. (2008) *Analysing Child Deaths and Serious Injury through Abuse and Neglect: What Can we Learn?'* London: DCSF and DBIS.

Braun, M.D. (1988) 'The BASK Model of Dissociation.' *Dissociation 1,* 1, 416–423.

Brett, E.A. (1996) 'The Classification of Posttraumatic Stress Disorder.' In B.A. van der Kolk, A.C. McFarlane and L. Weisaeth (eds) *Traumatic Stress: The Effects of Overwhelming Experience on Mind, Body, and Society.* New York: Guilford Press.

Briere, J. and Scott, C. (2006) *Principles of Trauma Therapy: A Guide to Symptoms, Evaluation and Treatment.* Thousand Oaks, CA: Sage.

Briere, J. and Spinazzola, J. (2005) 'Phenomenology and psychological assessment of complex post-traumatic states.' *Journal of Traumatic Stress 18*, 401–412.

British Medical Association (BMA) (2007) *Domestic Abuse.* London: BMA.

Broken Rainbow (2005) *Annual Report 2004/2005.* Available at www.broken-rainbow.org.uk/2004-05.pdf accessed 10 July 2007.

Bromberg, P. (1993) 'Shadow and substance: A relational perspective on clinical process.' *Psychoanalytic Psychology 10*, 147–168.

Bromberg, P M. (1994) '"Speak! that I may see you": Some reflections on dissociation, reality, and psychoanalytic listening.' In Bromberg, P.M. (1998) *Standing in the Spaces: Essays on Clinical Process, Trauma, and Dissociation.* Hillsdale, NJ: The Analytic Press.

Bromberg, P. (1998) *Standing in the Spaces: Essays on Clinical Process, Trauma and Dissociation.* Hillsdale, NJ: Analytic Press.

Brown, R. and Stobart, K. (2008) *Understanding Boundaries and Containment in Clinical Practice.* Sterling, VA: Stylus Publishing.

Browne, A. (1987) *When Battered Women Kill.* New York: Free Press.

Buber, M. (1987) *I and Thou.* Edinburgh: T. and T. Clarke.

Burgess, A.W. and Holmstrom, L.L. (1974) 'The rape trauma syndrome.' *American Journal of Psychiatry 131*, 981–986.

Calder, M.C., Harold, G.T. and Howarth, E.L. (2006) *Children Living with Domestic Violence.* Lyme Regis, UK: Russell House.

Calof, D.L. (1995) 'Dissociation: nature's tincture of numbing and forgetting.' *Treating Abuse Today 5*, 3, 5–8.

Cantor, C. (2005) *Evolution and Posttraumatic Stress: Disorders of Vigilance and Defence.* Hove: Routledge.

Carlson, B.E. (1991) 'Domestic Violence.' In A. Gitterman (ed.) *Handbook of Social Work Practice with Vulnerable Populations.* New York: Columbia University Press.

Casement, P. (1990) *On Further Learning from the Patient.* London: Tavistock.

Cashdan, S. (1988) *Object Relations Therapy: Using the Relationship.* New York: Norton.

CEMACH (Confidential Enquiry into Maternal Child Health for England and Wales) (2004) *Why Mothers Die 2000–2002.* London: RCOG (Royal College of Obstetricians and Gynaecologists) Press.

Chantler, K., Burman, E., Batsleer, J. and Bashoir, C. (2001) *Attempted Suicide and Self Harm (South Asian Women).* Manchester: Women's Studies Research Centre, Manchester Metropolitan University.

Chefetz, A.A. and Bromberg, P.M. (2004) 'Talking with "Me" and "Not me".' *Contemporary Psychoanalysis 40*, 409–464.

ChildLine (2003) *Annual Report.* London: ChildLine.

Chu, J.A. (1991) 'The repetition compulsion revisited: Reliving dissociated trauma.' *Psychotherapy 28*, 327–332.

Chu, J.A. (1998) *Rebuilding Shattered Lives: The Responsible Treatment of Complex Post-traumatic and Dissociative Disorders.* New York: Wiley.

Clarkson, P. (1993) *On Psychotherapy.* London: Whurr.

Clarkson, P. (2003) *The Therapeutic Relationship.* Second edition. London: Whurr.

Coalition for the Removal of Pimping (CROP) (2005) *Parents, Children and Pimps: Families Speak Out About Sexual Exploitation.* Leeds: Coalition for the Removal of Pimping.

Coe, J. (2008) 'Being clear about boundaries.' *The Independent Practitioner,* Spring 2008, 9–12.

Cohen, D. (2009) 'Generation of teenage girls growing up in fear of rape.' *The Evening Standard,* 9 January.

Cohen, J.A., Mannarino, A.P. and Deblinger, E. (2006) *Treating Trauma and Traumatic Grief in Children and Adolescents.* New York: Guilford Press.

Coleman, K., Jansson, K. and Kaisa, P. (2007) *Homicides, Firearm Offences and Intimate Violence 2005/2006. Home Office Statistical Bulletin, January.* London: Home Office.

Colson, E (1991) 'Coping in adversity.' Paper given at 'African and Refugees', Carter Symposium, University of Florida, Gainesville.

Cook, P.W. (1997) *Abused Men: The Hidden Side of Domestic Violence.* Westport, CT: Praeger.

Courtois, C.A. (1988) *Healing the Incest Wound: Adult Survivors in Therapy.* New York: Norton.

Courtois, C.A. (1999) *Recollections of Sexual Abuse: Treatment Principles and Guidelines.* New York: Norton.

Coxell, A.W., King, M.B., Mezey, G.C. and Kell, P. (2000) 'Sexual molestation of men: Interviews with 224 men attending a genitourinary medicine service.' *International Journal of STD and AIDS 11,* 9, 574–578.

Crawford, M. and Gartner, R. (1992) *Women Killing: Intimate Femicide in Ontario 1974–1980.* Toronto: Women We Honour Action Committee.

Crittenden, P.M. (2000) 'A dynamic-maturational approach to continuity and change in patterns of attachment.' In P.M. Crittenden and A.H. Claussen (eds) *The Organisation of Attachment Relationships – Maturation, Culture and Context.* New York: Cambridge University Press.

Csaky, C. (2008) *No One to Turn To: The Under Reporting of Child Sexual Exploitation and Abuse by Aid Workers and Peace Keepers.* London: Save the Children UK.

Curran, D. (1996) *Tyranny of the Spirit: Domination and Submission in Adolescent Relationships.* Northvale, NJ: Jason Aronson.

Dale, P. (1999) *Adults Abused as Children: Experiences in Counselling and Psychotherapy.* London: Sage.

Dalenberg, C.J. (2000) *Counter-transference and the Treatment of Trauma.* Washington, DC: American Psychological Association.

Danieli, Y. (1994) 'Countertransference, Trauma and Training.' In J.P. Wilson and J.D. Lindy (eds) *Countertransference in the Treatment of PTSD.* New York: Guilford Press.

Davies, J.M. and Frawley, M.G. (1994) *Treating the Adult Survivor of Childhood Sexual Abuse: A Psychoanalytic Perspective.* New York: Basic Books.

Department for Children, Schools and Families (2008a) *Referrals, Assessments, and Children and Young People who are the Subject of a Child Protection Plan, England.* London: Department for Children, Schools and Families.

Department for Children, Schools and Families (2008b) *Safeguarding Children and Young People from Sexual Exploitation.* Draft Consultation Document. (Launched: Friday 18 July 2008. Closed: Friday 10 October 2008.) London: Department for Children, Schools and Families.

Department of Health (2000) *No Secrets: The Protection of Vulnerable Adults: Guidance on the Development and Implementation of Multi Agency Policies and Procedures.* London: TSO.

Department of Health (2005) *Interventions to Reduce Violence and Promote the Physical and Psychosocial Well-being of Women who Experience Partner Violence: A Systematic Review of Controlled Evaluations.* London: Department of Health.

Department of Health (2006) *Working Together to Safeguard Children.* London: Department of Health.

de Zulueta, F. (2006) 'The treatment of psychological trauma from the perspective of attachment research.' *Journal of Family Therapy 2,* 4, 334–351.

de Zulueta, F. (2008) 'Developmental Trauma in Adults: A Response to Bessel van der Kolk.' In S. Benamer and K. White (eds) *Trauma and Attachment.* London: Karnac Books.

Diehl, M., Elnick, A.B., Bourbeau, L.S. and Labouvie-Vief, G. (1998) 'Adult attachment styles: Their relation to family context and personality.' *Journal of Personality and Social Psychology 74,* 6, 1656–1669.

Dobash, R.E. and Dobash, R.P. (1979) *Violence against Wives: A Case against the Patriarchy.* New York: Free Press.

Dobash, R.E. and Dobash, R.P. (1988) 'Research as Social Action: The Struggle for Battered Women.' In K. Yllö and M. Bogard (eds) *Feminist Perspectives on Wife Abuse.* Thousand Oaks, CA: Sage.

Dobie, D.J., Kivlahan, D.R., Maynard, C., Bush, K.R., Davis, T.M. and Bradley, K.A. (2004) 'Post-traumatic Stress Disorder in female veterans: Association with self reported health problems and functional impairment.' *Archive of International Medicine 164,* 4, 394–400.

Dozier, M. and Tyrrell, C. (1998) 'The Role of Attachment in Therapeutic Relationships.' In J. Simpson and W. Rholes (eds) *Attachment Theory and Close Relationships.* New York: Guilford Press.

Dutton, D.G. (1985) 'An ecologically nested theory of male violence towards intimates.' *International Journal of Women's Studies 8*, 4, 404–413.

Dutton, D.G. (2007) *The Abusive Personality: Violence and Control in Intimate Relationships.* Second edition. New York: Guilford Press.

Dutton, D.G. and Painter, S.L. (1981) 'Traumatic bonding: The development of emotional attachment in battered women and other relationships of intermittent abuse.' *Victimology: An International Journal 6*, 139–155.

Dutton, D.G. and Painter, S.L. (1993) 'Emotional attachment in abusive relationships: A test of traumatic bonding theory.' *Violence and Victims 8*, 105–120.

Dutton, M.A. (1992) *Empowering and Healing the Battered Woman: A Model for Assessment and Intervention.* New York: Springer.

Eastman, M. (1984) *Old Age Abuse.* London: Age Concern.

Ehrensaft, M.K., Moffit, T.E. and Caspi, A. (2004) 'Clinically abusive relationships in an unselected birth cohort: Men's and women's participation and developmental antecedents.' *Journal of Abnormal Psychology 113*, 2, 258–270.

Engel, G.L. and Schmale, A.H. (1972) 'Conservation-Withdrawal: A Primary Regulatory Process for Organismic Homeostasis.' In Ciba Foundation Symposium *Physiology, Emotion and Psychosomatic Illness.* New York: Elsevier.

Ettore, E. (1997) *Women and Alcohol: A Private Pleasure or Public Problem.* London: Women's Press.

Fairbairn, W. R. D. (1952) *Psychoanalytic Studies of the Personality.* London: Routledge & Kegan Paul.

Fairweather, E. (2008) 'I have known about Jersey paedophiles for 15 years.' *The Daily Mail,* 2 March.

Fairweather, E. (2009) 'I raised the alarm about the family 15 years ago. I still want answers.' *The Evening Standard,* 22 May.

Farmer, E. and Pollock, S. (1998) *Sexually Abused and Sexually Abusing Children in Substitute Care.* Chichester: Wiley.

Field, N. (1989) 'Listening with the body: An exploration in the countertransference.' *British Journal of Psychotherapy 5*, 4, 512–522.

Field, T. (1985) 'Attachment as Psychobiological Attunement: Being on the Same Wavelength.' In M. Reite and T. Field (eds) *The Psychobiology of Attachment and Separation.* New York: Academic Press.

Figley, C.R. (1982) 'Traumatization and comfort: Close relationships may be hazardous to your health.' Keynote presentation. Families and close relationships: Individuals in social interaction. Conference held at the Texas Tech University, Lubbock, March.

Figley, C.R. (1995) 'Compassion Fatigue as Secondary Traumatic Stress Disorder: An Overview.' In C.R. Figley (ed.) *Compassion Fatigue: Coping with Secondary Stress Disorder in Those who Treat the Traumatized.* New York: Brunner/Mazel.

Figley, C.R. (2002) *Treating Compassion Fatigue.* New York: Brunner/Mazel.

Figley, C.R. (2004) 'Foreword.' In J.P. Wilson and R.B. Thomas (eds) *Empathy in the Treatment of Trauma and PTSD.* New York: Brunner-Routledge.

Figley, C.R. and Kleber, R.J. (1995) 'Beyond the "Victim": Secondary Traumatic Stress.' In R.J. Kleber, C.R. Figley and B.P.R. Gersons (eds) *Beyond Trauma: Cultural and Societal Dynamics.* New York: Plenum.

Flood-Page, C. and Taylor, J. (eds) (2003) *Crime in England and Wales 2001/2002: Supplementary Volume.* London: Home Office.

Foa, E. B. and Rothbaum, B.O. (1998) *Treating the Trauma of Rape: Cognitive Behavioral Therapy for PTSD.* New York: Guilford Press.

Foa, E. B., Rothbaum, B. O., Riggs, D. S. and Murdock, T. (1991) 'Treatment of posttraumatic stress disorder in rape victims: A comparison between cognitive behavioural procedures and counselling.' *Journal of Consulting and Clinical Psychology 59*, 715–723.

Foa, F.B., Zinbarg, R. and Rothbaum, B.O. (1992) 'Uncontrollability and unpredictability in posttraumatic stress disorder: An animal model.' *Psychological Bulletin 112*, 218–238.

Fonagy, P. (1999) 'Pathological Attachments and Therapeutic Action.' Paper presented at the Annual Meeting of the California Branch of the American Academy of Child and Adolescent Psychiatry, Yosemite Valley, CA, January.

Fonagy, P. (2001) *Attachment Theory and Psychoanalysis.* New York: Other Press.

Fonagy, P. (2002) 'Multiple Voices versus Metacognition: An Attachment Theory Perspective.' In V. Sinason (ed.) *Trauma and Multiplicity: Working with Dissociative Identity Disorder.* London: Routledge.

Fonagy, P. and Target, M. (1997) 'Perspectives on Recovered Memories Debate.' In J. Sandler and P. Fonagy (eds) *Recovered Memories of Abuse: True or False.* Madison, CT: International Universities Press.

Fonagy, P., Target, M. and Gergely, G. (2003) 'Attachment and borderline personality disorder.' *Psychiatric Clinics of North America 23*, 91, 103–123.

Fonagy, P., Gergely, G., Jurist, E.L. and Target, M. (2002) *Affect Regulation, Mentalization and the Development of the Self.* New York: Other Press.

Fonagy, P. *et al.* (1995) 'Attachment, the Reflective Self, and Borderline States.' In S. Goldberg, R. Muir and J. Kerr (eds) *Attachment Theory: Social, Developmental and Clinical Perspectives.* Hillsdale, NJ: Analytic Press.

Ford, J.D. and Kidd, P. (1998) 'Early childhood trauma and disorders of extreme stress to predictors of treatment outcome with chronic PTSD.' *Journal of Traumatic Stress 11*, 743–761.

Ford, J.D., Courtois, C.A., Steele, K., Van der Hart, O. and Nijenhuis, E.R.S. (2005) 'Treatment of complex posttraumatic self regulation.' *Journal of Traumatic Stress 18*, 437–447.

Frankl, V. (1946) *Man's Search for Meaning.* London: Hodder & Stoughton.

Frayne, S.M., Seaver, M.R., Loveland, S., Christiansen, C.L., Spiro, A. and Parker, V.A. (2004) 'Burden of medical illness in women with depression and post traumatic stress.' *Archive of International Medicine 164*, 1306–1312.

Frayne, S.M., Skinner, K.M., Sullivan, L.M., Tripp, T.J., Hankin, C.S., Kressin, N.R. and Miller, D.R. (1999) 'Medical profile of women veterans administration outpatients who report a history of sexual assault occurring while in the military.' *Journal of Women's Health & Gender-Based Medicine 8*, 6, 835–845.

Freud, A. (1936) *The Ego and the Mechanism of Defence.* New York: International Universities Press.

Freud, S. (1914/1958) 'Remembering, Repeating, and Working Through.' In Strachey, J (ed.) *Standard Edition of the Complete Psychological Works of Sigmund Freud, Vol. 12.* London: Hogarth Press.

Freyd, P. (1996) *Betrayal Trauma.* Cambridge, MA: Harvard University Press.

Fromm, E. (1973) *The Anatomy of Human Destructiveness.* New York: Holt Paperbacks.

Gabbard, G. and Wilkinson, S. (1994) *Management of Counter-transference with Borderline Patients.* Washington, DC: American Psychiatric Press.

Garrett, I. (1998) 'Sexual contact between patients and psychologists.' *The Psychologist,* May 1998, 227–229.

Gerbode, F. (1989) *Beyond Psychology: An Introduction to Meta Psychology.* Second edition. Palo Alto, CA: IRM Press.

Gil, E. (1982) 'Institutional abuse of children in out-of-home care.' In R. Hanson (ed.) *Institutional Abuse of Children and Youth.* New York: The Haworth Press.

Gilbert, R., Kemp, A., Thoburn, J., Sidebotham, P., Radford, L., Glaser, D. and MacMillan, H.L. (2009a) 'Recognising and responding to child maltreatment.' *The Lancet 373*, 9658, 167–180.

Gilbert, R., Widon, C.S., Browne, K., Ferguson, D., Webb, E. and Janson, S. (2009b) 'Burden and consequences of child maltreatment in high income countries.' *The Lancet 373*, 9657, 68–81.

Glendenning, F. (1999) 'The Abuse of Older People in Institutional Settings.' In N. Stanley, J. Manthorpe and B. Penhale (eds) *Institutional Abuse: Perspectives across the Life Course.* London: Routledge.

Glenny, M. (2008) *McMafia: Crime without Frontiers.* London: The Bodley Head Ltd.

Goffman, E. (1968) *Stigma: Notes on the Management of Spoiled Identity.* Harmondsworth: Penguin Books.

Goldberg, H. (1982) 'Dynamics of Rage between the Sexes in a Bonded Relationship.' In L.R. Barnhill (ed.) *Clinical Approach to Family Violence.* Rockville, MD: Aspen Systems.

Golding, J.M. (1999) 'Intimate partner violence as a risk factor for mental disorders: A meta-analysis.' *Journal of Family Violence 14,* 2, 19–132.

Goodwin, J. (1993) *Rediscovering Childhood Trauma: Historical Casebook and Clinical Applications.* Washington, DC: American Psychiatric Press.

Grand, S (2000) *The Reproduction of Evil: A Clinical and Cultural Perspective.* Hillsdale, NJ: The Analytic Press.

Groth, A.N. and Birnbaum, H.J. (1979) *Men Who Rape: The Psychology of the Offender.* Cambridge, MA: Perseus Publishing.

Gunderson, J.G. (1984) *Borderline Personality Disorder.* Washington, DC: American Psychiatric Press.

The Guardian (2003) 'Child abuse victims become perpetrators, survey reveals.' *The Guardian,* 7 February.

Halperin, D.A. (1983) 'Group Processes in Cult Affiliation and Recruitment.' In D.A. Halperin (ed.) *Psychodynamic Perspectives on Religion, Sect and Cult.* Boston, MA: John Wright.

Harlow, H.F. and Harlow, M. (1971) 'Psychopathology in Monkeys.' In H.D. Kinnel (ed.) *Experimental Psychopathology.* New York: Academic Press.

Harper, Z. and Scott, S. (2005) *Meeting the Needs of Sexually Exploited People in London.* London: Barnardo's.

Harter, S. (1999) *The Construction of the Self: A Developmental Perspective.* New York: Guilford Press.

Heard, D. and Lake, B. (1997) *The Challenge of Attachment for Caregiving.* London: Routledge.

Henderson, A.J.Z., Bartholomew, K. and Dutton, D.G. (1997) 'He loves me; he loves me not: Attachment and separation resolution of abused women.' *Journal of Family Violence 12,* 169–191.

Henderson, L. (2003) *Prevalence of Domestic Violence among Lesbians and Gay Men.* London: Sigma.

Henwood, M. (2000) *Domestic Violence: A Resource Manual for Health Care Professionals.* London: Department of Health.

Herman, J.L. (1988) 'Father–Daughter Incest.' In F.M. Ochberg (ed.) *Post Traumatic Therapy and Victims of Violence.* New York: Brunner/Mazel.

Herman, J.L. (1992a) *Trauma and Recovery.* New York: Basic Books.

Herman, J.L. (1992b) 'Complex PTSD: A syndrome in survivors of prolonged and repeated trauma.' *Journal of Traumatic Stress 5,* 377–392.

Herman, J.L. (2001) *Trauma and Recovery.* Second edition. London: Pandora.

Herman, J.L. (2002) 'Evolution of Trauma Therapy.' Paper presented at Trauma Conference. Psychological Trauma: Maturational Processes and Therapeutic Interventions. Boston University School of Medicine and Trauma Center, Boston, MA, 31 May – 1 June 2002.

Herman, J.L. (2005) 'Justice from the victim's perspective.' *Violence Against Women 11,* 571–602.

Herman, J.L. (2006) 'My Life and Work.' In C.R. Figley (ed.) *Mapping Trauma and its Wake: Autobiographical Essays by Pioneer Trauma Scholars.* New York: Routledge.

Herman, J.L. (2007) 'Shattered States and their Repair: An Exploration of Trauma and Shame.' The John Bowlby Memorial Lecture presented at the Centenary John Bowlby Memorial Conference 1907–2007. Shattered States: Disorganised Attachment and its Repair. London, 9–10 March 2007.

Herve, H.F.M. (2002) 'The Masks of Sanity and Psychopathy: A Cluster Analytical Investigation of Subtypes of Criminal Psychopathy.' Doctoral dissertation, Department of Psychology, University of British Columbia.

Hester, M., Pearson, C. and Harwin, N. (2007) *Making an Impact: Children and Domestic Violence – A Reader.* Second edition. London: Jessica Kingsley Publishers.

Hirigoyen, M-F. (2004) *Stalking the Soul: Emotional Abuse and the Erosion of Identity.* New York: Helen Marx Books.

Holmes, E.A., Brown, R.J., Mansell, W., Fearon, R.P., Hunter, E.C.M., Frasquilhoe, F. and Oakley, D.A. (2001) 'Are there two qualitatively distinct forms of dissociation? A review and some clinical implications.' *Clinical Psychology Review 25*, 1, 1–23.

Home Office (2003) *Sexual Offences Act 2003*. London: HMSO.

Home Office (2004) *Paying the Price: A Consultation Paper on Prostitution*. London: Home Office.

Home Office (2006) *National Report for Domestic Violence – Progress Report*. London: Home Office.

Home Office (2003) *Sexual Offences Act 2003*. London: HMSO.

Horley, S. (1988) *Love and Pain: A Survival Handbook for Women*. London: Bedford Square Press.

House of Commons Health Committee (2004) *Second Report on Elder Abuse*. London: House of Commons.

Humphreys, C. and Thiara, R. (2002) *Routes to Safety: Protection Issues Facing Abused Women and Children and the Role of Outreach Services*. Bristol: Women's Aid Federation of England.

Humphreys, C. and Thiara, R. (2003) 'Mental health and domestic violence: "I call it symptoms of abuse".' *British Journal of Social Work 33*, 2, 209–226.

Island, D. and Letellier, P. (1991) *Men who Beat the Men who Love Them*. Binghamton, NY: Harrington Park Press.

Jacobson, N. and Gottman, J. (1998) *Breaking the Cycle: New Insights into Violent Relationships*. London: Bloomsbury.

James, K. (1999) 'Truth or Fiction: Men as Victims of Domestic Violence.' In J. Breckenridge and L. Laing (eds) *Challenging Silence: Innovative Responses to Sexual and Domestic Violence*. Sydney: Allen & Unwin.

Janoff-Bulman, R. (1985) 'The Aftermath of Victimisation: Rebuilding Shattered Assumptions.' In C.R. Figley (ed.) *Trauma and its Wake: The Study and Treatment of Post Traumatic Stress Disorder*. New York: Brunner/Mazel.

Janoff-Bulman, R. (1992) *Shattered Assumptions: Towards a New Psychology of Trauma*. New York: Free Press.

Jones, L., Hughes, M. and Unterstaller, U. (2001) 'Post-traumatic stress disorder (PTSD) in victims of domestic violence.' *Trauma Violence Abuse 2*, 99–119.

Jukes, A. (1993) *Why Men Hate Women*. London: Free Association Books.

Jukes, A. (1999) *Men Who Batter Women*. London: Routledge.

Kahn, M. (1997) *Between Therapist and Client: The New Relationship*. New York: W. H. Freeman and Company.

Kahn, M. (2000) 'Domestic violence against women and girls.' *Innocenti Digest 6*, 1–22.

Kahn, M.E., Ubaidur, R. and Hossain, S.M.I. (2001) 'Violence against women and the impact on women's lives: Some observations from Bangladesh.' *Journal of Family Welfare 46*, 2, 12–24.

Kalsched, D. (1996) *The Inner World of Trauma: Archetypal Defences of the Personal Spirit*. London: Routledge.

Kaschak, E. (ed.) (2001) *Intimate Betrayal: Domestic Violence in Same Sex Relationships*. Binghamton, NY: Haworth Press.

Kelly, A. (2009) 'Raped and killed for being a lesbian: South Africa ignores "corrective attacks".' *The Guardian*, 12 March.

Kelly, L., Lovett, J., and Regan, L. (2005) 'A gap or a chasm? Attrition in reported rape cases'. Child and Women Abuse Studies Unit. Home Office Research Study 293. London: Home Office.

Kelly, L. and Regan, L. (2000) *Stopping Traffic: Exploring the Extent of, and Responses to, Trafficking of Women for Sexual Exploitation in the UK*. London: Home Office.

Kershaw, C., Chivite-Mathews, N., Thomas, C. and Aust, R. (2001) *The 2001 British Crime Survey*. London: Home Office Research, Development and Statistics Directorate.

Kilpatrick, D., Amstadter, A., Resnick, H. and Ruggiero, K. (2007) 'Rape-related PTSD: Issues and interventions.' *Psychiatric Times 7*, 24.

Kinnell, H. (2006) 'Murder made easy: The final solution to prostitution?' In R. Campbell and M.O'Neill (eds.) *Sex Work Now*. Cullompton, Devon: Willan Publishing.

Kinnell, H. (2008) *Violence and Sex Work in Britain.* Collumpton, Devon: Willan Publishing.

Klein, M. (1946) 'Notes on Some Schizoid Mechanisms.' In M. Klein (ed.) (1980) *Envy and Gratitude and Other Works 1946–1963.* London: Hogarth Press.

Kluft, R.P. (1992) 'Dissociative disorders in childhood and adolescence: new frontiers.' *Dissociation 5,* 1, 2–3.

Kohut, H. (1971) *The Analysis of the Self.* New York: International Universities Press.

Kohut, H. (1972) 'Thoughts on Narcissism and Narcissistic Rage.' In P. Ornstein (ed.) *The Search for Self: Selected Writings of Heinz Kohut, Vol. 2.* New York: International Universities Press.

Kohut, H. (1977) *The Restoration of the Self.* New York: International Universities Press.

Krause, E.D., Kaltman, S., Goodman, L.A. and Dutton, M.A. (2006) 'Role of distinct post traumatic stress disorder symptoms in intimate partner violence re-abuse: A prospective study.' *Journal of Traumatic Stress 19,* 4, 507–516.

Kreiter, S. R., Krowchuk, D. P., Woods, C. R., Sinal, S. H., Lawless, M. R. and DuRant, R. H. (1999) 'Gender differences in risk behaviors among adolescents who experience date fighting.' *Pediatrics 104,* 6, 1286–1292.

Kritsberg, W. (1988) *The Adult Children of Alcoholics Syndrome: From Discovery to Recovery.* Toronto: Bantam.

Krystal, J.H. (1988) *Integration and Self Healing: Affect, Trauma and Alexithymia.* Hillsdale, NJ: Analytic Press.

Kübler-Ross, E. (1969) *On Death and Dying.* New York: Macmillan.

Lachkar, J. (2004) *The Narcissistic/Borderline Couple: A Psychoanalytic Perspective on Marital Treatment.* Second edition. Hove, UK: Brunner-Routledge.

Laing, R.D. (1967) *The Politics of Experience and the Bird of Paradise.* Harmondsworth: Penguin.

Lambert, M.J. (ed.) (2003) *Handbook of Psychotherapy and Behavior Change.* Fifth edition. New York: John Wiley and Sons.

Langer, L.L. (1995) *Admitting the Holocaust: Collected Essays.* New York: Oxford University Press.

Lattanzi, M. and Hale, M.E. (1984) 'Giving grief words: Writing during bereavement.' *Omega 15,* 45–52.

LeDoux, J.E. (1996) *The Emotional Brain: The Mysterious Underpinnings of Emotional Life.* New York: Simon & Schuster.

Lenihan, T. and Dean, P. (2000) 'Child Prostitution in England.' In D. Barrett, E. Barrett and N. Mullenger (eds) *Youth Prostitution in the New Europe: The Growth in Sex Work.* Cullompton, Devon: Russell House Publishing.

Lewinsohn, P.M. (1975) 'The Behavioural Study and Treatment of Depression.' In M. Hersen, R. Eisler and P. Miller (eds) *Progress in Behaviour Modification.* New York: Academic Press.

Lewis, D.O. (1998) *Guilty by Reason of Insanity.* New York: Ballantine.

Lichtenberg, J.D. (1989) *Psychoanalysis and Motivation.* Hillsdale, NJ: Analytic Press.

Lindsay, M. (1997) *The Tip of the Iceberg: Sexual Abuse in the Context of Residential Child Care.* Strathclyde: Centre for Residential Child Care, University of Strathclyde.

Linehan, M. (1993) *Cognitive-Behavioral Treatment of Borderline Personality Disorder.* New York: Guilford Press.

Liotti, G. (1992) 'Disorganised/disoriented attachment in the etiology of the dissociative disorders.' *Dissociation 5,* 196–204.

Lockley, P. (1999) *Counselling Women in Violent Relationships.* London: Free Association Books.

Loftus, E.F., Polonsky, S. and Fullilove, M.T. (1994) 'Memories of childhood sexual abuse: Remembering and repressing.' *Psychology of Women Quarterly 18,* 67–84.

Lomas, P. (1987) *The Limits of Interpretation:What's Wrong with Psychoanalysis.* London: Penguin.

Lomas, P. (1994) *Cultivating Intuition: An Introduction to Psychotherapy.* London: Penguin.

MacLean, P.D. (1990) *The Triune Brain in Evolution: Role in Paleocerebral Functions.* New York: Plenum.

Magai, C. (2001) 'Emotion over the Lifecourse.' In J. Birren and K.W. Schaie (eds) *Handbook of the Psychology of Aging.* San Diego, CA: Academic Press.

Magai, C. and Cohen, C. (1998) 'Attachment style and emotional regulation in dementia patients and their relation to caregiver burden.' *Journal of Gerontology Series B. Psychological Sciences and Social Sciences 53,* 3, 147–154.

Magdol, L., Moffit, T.E., Caspi, A., Newman, D.L., Fagan, J. and Silva, P.A. (1997) 'Gender differences in partner violence in a birth cohort of 21 year olds: Bridging the gap between clinical and epidemiological approaches.' *Journal of Counselling and Clinical Psychology 65,* 1, 68–78.

Magnavita, J.J. (1999) *Relational Therapy for Personality Disorders.* New York: Wiley.

Main, M. (1999) 'Attachment Theory: Eighteen Points with Suggestions for Future Studies.' In J. Cassidy and P.R. Shaver (eds) *Handbook of Attachment: Theory, Research and Clinical Applications.* New York: Guilford Press.

Mair, M. (1989) *Between Psychology and Psychotherapy: A Poetics of Experience.* London: Routledge.

Maltsberger, J.T. and Buie, O.H. (1974) 'Countertransference: Hate in the treatment of suicidal patients.' *Archives of General Psychiatry 30,* 625–633.

Mattley, C. (1998) 'Field Research with Phone Fantasy Workers: Managing the Researcher's Emotions.' In M.D. Schwartz (ed.) *Researching Sexual Violence Against Women: Methodological and Personal Considerations.* Thousand Oaks, CA: Sage Publications.

McCann, I.L. and Pearlman, L.A. (1989) 'Vicarious traumatisation: A framework for understanding the psychological effects of working with victims.' *Traumatic Stress 3,* 131–149.

McCann, I.L. and Pearlman, L.A. (1990) *Psychological Trauma and the Adult Survivor: Theory, Therapy and Transformation.* New York: Brunner/Mazel.

McCann, I.L., Sakheim, D.K. and Abrahamson, D.J. (1988) 'Trauma and victimisation: A model of psychological adaptation.' *Counselling Psychologist 16,* 4, 531–594.

McDougall, J. (1989) *Theatres of the Body: A Psychoanalytical Approach to Psychosomatic Illness.* London: Free Association Books.

Meins, E. (1997) *Security of Attachment and the Social Development of Cognition.* Hove, UK: Psychology Press.

Meloy, J.R. (1992) *Violent Attachments.* Northvale, NJ: Jason Aronson.

Melrose, M., Barrett, D. and Brodie, I. (1999) *One Way Street.* London: The Children's Society.

Melzack, R. (1990) 'The tragedy of needless pain.' *Science 362,* 27–88.

Merleau-Ponty, M. (1962) *The Phenomenology of Perception.* London: Routledge & Kegan Paul.

Merrill, G. (1996) 'Ruling the Exceptions: Same-sex Battering and Domestic Violence Theory.' In C.M. Renzetti and C.H. Miley (eds) *Violence in Gay and Lesbian Domestic Partnerships.* Binghamton, NY: Haworth Press.

Miller, B.D. (1992) 'Wife Beating in India: Variations on a Theme.' In D.A. Counts, J.K. Brown and J.C. Campbell (eds) *Sanctions and Sanctuary: Cultural Perspectives on the Beatings of Wives.* Boulder, CO: Westview.

Miller, D.T. and Porter, C.A. (1993) 'Self-blame in victims of violence.' *Journal of Social Issues 39,* 2, 139–152.

Millon, T. (1977) *Millon Clinical Multiaxial Inventory Manual.* Minneapolis, MN: National Computer Inventory and Computer Systems.

Millon, T. (1996) *Disorders of Personality: DSM IV and Beyond.* Second edition. New York: Wiley.

Millon, T. and Grossman, S. (2007) *Moderating Severe Personality Disorders: A Personalised Psychotherapy Approach.* New York: Wiley.

Mitchell, E. and Gilchrist, E. (2004) 'Can Knowledge of Panic Attack Help to Explain Some Domestic Violence Offending?' Paper presented at the British Psychological Society Division of Forensic Psychology, Leicester, UK, 22–24 March 2004.

Moffit, T.E., Caspi, R., Rutter, M. and Silva, P.A. (2001) *Sex Differences in Antisocial Behaviour.* Cambridge: Cambridge University Press.

Mollica, R.F. (1988) 'The Trauma Story: The Psychiatric Care of Refugee Survivors of Violence and Torture.' In F.M. Ochberg (ed.) *Post Traumatic Therapy and the Victims of Violence.* New York: Brunner/Mazel.

Mollon, P. (2000) 'Is Human Nature Intrinsically Evil?' In U. McCluskey and C. Hooper (eds) *Psychodynamic Perspectives on Abuse: The Cost of Fear.* London: Jessica Kingsley Publishers.

Mollon, P. (2002a) 'Dark Dimensions of Multiple Personality.' In V. Sinason (ed.) *Attachment, Trauma and Multiplicity: Working with Dissociative Identity Disorder.* London: Brunner-Routledge.

Mollon, P. (2002b) *Remembering Trauma: A Psychotherapist's Guide to Memory and Illusion.* Second edition. London: Whurr.

Mollon, P (2005) *EMDR and the Energy Therapies: Psychoanalytic Perspective.* London: Karnac Books.

Moorhead, C. (2007) 'Women and children for sale.' *New York Review of Books 54,* 15.

Morgan, D.R. (1998) *Domestic Violence: A Health Care Issue.* London: British Medical Association.

Motz, A.P. (2000) *The Psychology of Female Violence: Crimes against the Body.* New York: Brunner-Routledge.

Nachmani, G. (1995) 'Trauma and ignorance.' *Contemporary Psychoanalysis 31,* 423–450.

Nair, P.M. (2004) *A Report on Trafficking in Women and Children in India 2002–2003.* New Delhi: National Human Rights Commission, Institute of Social Science and UNIFEM.

National Center for Victims of Crime (1992) 'Rape-related posttraumatic stress disorder.' *Infolink 1,*38. Arlington, VA: National Center for Victims of Crime.

National Center for Victims of Crime and Crime Victims Research and Treatment Center (1992) *Rape in America: A Report to the Nation.* Arlington, VA: National Center for Victims of Crime.

National Center on Elder Abuse (1997) *Trends in Elder Abuse in Domestic Settings.* Washington, DC: National Center on Elderly Abuse.

National Centre for Social Research (2007) *UK Study of Abuse and Neglect of Older People: Prevalence Survey Report.* London: Department of Health.

NAYPIC (National Association of Young People in Care) (1989) *Report on Violations of the Basic Human Rights of Young People in Care of London Borough of Greenwich and Other Local Authorities.* London: NAYPIC.

Newham Asian Women's Project (1998) *Young Asian Women and Self Harm: A Mental Health Needs Assessment of Young Asian Women in East London.* London: Newham Inner City Multifund and Newham Asian Women's Project.

Nietzsche, F. (2002) (first published 1886) *Beyond Good and Evil.* Translated by Judith Norman and edited by Rolf-Peter Horstmann. Cambridge: Cambridge University Press.

Nijenhuis, E.R.S., Spinhoven, P., and Vanderlinden, J. (1998) 'Animal defensive reactions as a model for dissociative reactions.' *Journal of Traumatic Stress 11,* 243–260.

Nord, D. (1996) 'Issues and implications in the counselling services of multiple AIDS-related loss.' *Death Studies 20,* 389–413.

Ochberg, F.M. (1988) *Post Traumatic Therapy with Victims of Violence.* New York: Brunner/Mazel.

Ogg, J. and Bennet, G. (1992) 'Elder abuse in Britain.' *British Medical Journal 305,* 998–999.

O'Keefe, M., Hills, A., Doyle, M., McCreadie, C., Scholes, S., Constantine, R., Tinker, A., Manthorpe, J., Biggs, S. and Erens, B. (2007) *UK Study of Abuse and Neglect of Older People; Prevalence Survey Report.* London: National Centre for Social Research and Kings College London.

Olio, K. and Cornell, W. (1993) 'The therapeutic relationship as the foundation for treatment with adult survivors of sexual abuse.' *Psychotherapy 30,* 512–523.

O'Neil, T. (2001) *Children in Secure Accommodation: A Gendered Exploration of Locked Institutional Care for Children in Trouble.* London: Jessica Kingsley Publishers.

Orbach, S. (2002) 'Revisiting the False Self.' In B. Kahr (ed.) *The Legacy of Winnicott.* London: Karnac Press.

O'Riordan, M. and Arensman, E. (2007) *Institutional Child Sexual Abuse and Suicidal Behaviour: Outcomes of Literature Review, Consultation Meetings and Qualitative Studies.* Cork, Ireland: National Suicide Research Foundation.

Orwell, G. (1949) *Nineteen Eighty-Four.* London: Penguin, 1990.

Parkes, C.M. (1986) 'Orienteering the care giver's grief.' *Journal of Palliative Care 1*, 5–7.

Parkes, C.M. (2001) *Bereavement: Studies of Grief in Adult Life.* Third edition. Philadelphia, PA: Taylor & Francis.

Parkes, C.M., Relf, M. and Couldrick, A. (1996) *Counselling in Terminal Care and Bereavement.* Baltimore, MD: BPS Books.

Pearlman, L.A. (1998) 'Trauma and the self: A theoretical and clinical perspective.' *Journal of Emotional Abuse 1*, 7–25.

Pearlman, L.A. (2001) 'The Treatment of Persons with Complex PTSD and other Trauma-related Disruptions to the Self.' In M.F. Friedman, J.P. Wilson and J.D. Lindy (eds) *Treating Psychological Trauma and PTSD.* NewYork: Guilford Press.

Pearlman, L.A. (2003) *Trauma Attachment Belief Scale (TABS) Manual.* Los Angeles, CA: Western Psychological Services.

Pearlman, L.A. and Courtois, C.A. (2005) 'Clinical applications of the attachment framework: Relational treatment of complex trauma.' *Journal of Traumatic Stress 18*, 449–459.

Pearlman, L.A. and Saakvitne, K.W. (1995a) *Trauma and the Therapist: Counter-transference and Vicarious Traumatization in Psychotherapy with Incest Survivors.* New York: Norton.

Pearlman, L.A. and Saakvitne, K.W. (1995b) 'Treating Therapists with Vicarious Traumatization and Secondary Traumatic Stress Disorders.' In C.R. Figley (ed.) *Compassion Fatigue: Coping with Secondary Traumatic Stress Disorder in Those who Treat the Traumatized.* New York: Brunner/Mazel.

Penhale, J. (1999) 'Introduction.' In N. Stanley, J. Manthorpe, and J. Penhale (eds) *Institutional Abuse: Perspectives Across the Life Course.* London: Routledge.

Perren, S., Schmid, R., Hermann, S. and Wettstein, A. (2007) 'The impact of attachment on dementia-related problem behaviour and spousal caregivers' well being.' *Attachment and Human Development 9*, 2, 163–178.

Perry, B.D. (2000) *Violence in Childhood: How Persisting Fear can Alter the Developing Child's Brain.* Available at www.childtrauma.org/ctamaterials/vio_child.asp, accessed 3 September 2009.

Piaget, J. (1952) *The Origins of Intelligence in Children.* Madison, VT: International Universities Press.

Pillemer, K. and Finkehor, D. (1989) Causes of elder abuse: Caregiver stress versus problem relatives.' *American Journal of Orthopsychiatry 59*, 179–87.

Pines, M. and Aronson, E. (1988) *Career Burnout: Causes and Cures.* New York: Free Press.

Pistole, C.M. and Tarrant, N. (1993) 'Attachment style and aggression in male batterers.' *Family Therapy 20*, 3, 165–174.

Pope, K. (1989) 'Therapist–Patient Sex Syndrome: A Guide for Attorneys and Subsequent Therapists to Assessing Damage.' In G. Gabbard (ed.) *Sexual Exploitation in Professional Relationships.* Washington, DC: American Psychiatric Press.

Pope, K. (1994) *Sexual Involvement with Therapist: Patient Assessment, Subsequent Therapy, Forensics.* Washington, DC: American Psychiatric Association.

Pope, K.S., Keith-Spiegel, P. and Tabachnick, B.G. (1986) 'Sexual attraction to clients: the human therapist and the (sometimes) inhuman training system.' *American Psychologist 41*, 147–158.

Porter, S. (1996) 'Without conscience or without active conscience? The etiology of psychopathy revisited.' *Aggression and Violent Behaviour 1*, 2, 179–189.

Powell, G.F. and Bette, B.A. (1992) 'Infantile depression, non-organic failure to thrive and DSM-III-R: A different perspective.' *Child Psychiatry and Human Development 22*, 3, 185–198.

Pryke, J. and Thomas, M. (1998) *Domestic Violence and Social Work.* Ashgate, UK: Arena.

Putnam, F.W. (1989) *Diagnosis and Treatment of Multiple Personality Disorder.* New York: Guilford Press.

Rape Crisis England and Wales (2008) Information available at www.rapecrisis.org.uk/rape.html, acceded 3 September 2009.

Read, J., Hammersley, P. and Mullen, P.E. (2005) 'Child sexual abuse and schizophrenia: Author's reply.' *The British Journal of Psychiatry, 186*, 76–76.

Renzetti, C. (1992) *Violent Betrayal Partner Abuse in Lesbian Relationships.* Newbury Park, CA: Sage.

Resick, P.A., Nishith, P., Weaver, T.L., Astin, M.C. and Feuer, C.A. (2002) 'A comparison of cognitive-processing therapy with prolonged exposure and a waiting condition for the treatment of chronic posttraumatic stress disorder in female rape victims.' *Journal of Consulting and Clinical Psychology 70,* 867–879.

Resick, P.A., and Schnicke, M.K. (1992) 'Cognitive processing therapy for sexual assault victims'. *Journal of Consulting and Clinical Psychology 60,* 748-756.

Respect (2004) *Statement of Principles and Minimum Standards of Practice for Domestic Violence Perpetrator Programmes and Associated Women's Services.* London: Respect.

Revitch, E. and Schlesinger, L.B. (1981) *Psychopathology of Homicide.* Springfield, IL: Charles C. Thomas.

Roe, C. M., and Schwartz, M. F. (1996) 'Characteristics of previously forgotten memories of sexual abuse: A descriptive study.' *Journal of Psychiatry and Law 24,* 2, 189–206.

Rosenthal, J., Motz, J., Edmonson, D. and Groze, V. (1991) 'A descriptive study of abuse and neglect in and out of home placement.' *Child Abuse and Neglect: The International Journal 15,* 249–260.

Ross, C.A. (1997) *Dissociative Identity Disorder: Diagnosis, Clinical Features and Treatment of Multiple Personality.* New York: Wiley.

Rothschild, B. (2000) *The Body Remembers.* New York: Norton.

Rothschild, L. (2003) 'A taxometric study of personality disorder.' *Journal of Abnormal Psychology 112,* 4, 657–666.

Roy, M. (1988) *Children in the Crossfire: Violence in the Home – How Does it Affect our Children?* Deerfield Beach, FL: Health Communications.

Russell, J. (1993) *Out of Bounds: Sexual Exploitation in Counselling and Therapy.* London: Sage.

Saakvitne, K.W. and Pearlman, L.A. (1996) *Transforming the Pain: A Workbook on Vicarious Traumatization.* New York: Norton.

Saakvitne, K.W., Gamble, S.G., Pearlman, L.A. and Lev, B. (2000) *Risking Connection: A Training Curriculum for Working with Survivors of Childhood Abuse.* Lutherville, MD: Sidran Foundation Press.

Sale, A.U. (2001) 'Nowhere to go.' *Community Care,* 19–25 July, 22–23.

Salter, A.C. (1995) *Transforming Trauma: A Guide to Understanding and Treating Adult Survivors of Child Sexual Abuse.* Thousand Oaks, CA: Sage.

Salter, A.C. (2003) *Predators, Paedophiles, Rapists and Other Sex Offenders: Who They Are, How They Operate, and How We Can Protect Ourselves and Our Children.* New York: Basic Books.

Samuels, A. (1985) 'Countertransference: The "mundus imaginalis" and a research project.' *Journal of Analytical Psychology 30,* 47–71.

Sanderson, C. (2004) *The Seduction of Children: Empowering Parents and Teachers to Protect Children from Child Sexual Abuse.* London: Jessica Kingsley Publishers.

Sanderson, C. (2006) *Counselling Adult Survivors of Child Sexual Abuse.* Third edition. London: Jessica Kingsley Publishers.

Sanderson, C. (2008) *Counselling Survivors of Domestic Abuse.* London: Jessica Kingsley Publishers.

Sapolsky, R.M. (2004) *Why Zebras Don't Get Ulcers.* Third edition. New York: Henry Holt.

Save the Children UK (2008) *The Small Hands of Slavery: Modern Day Child Slavery: A Report by Save the Children UK.* London: Save the Children UK.

Scarf, M. (2005) *Secrets, Lies, Betrayals.* New York: Ballantine.

Scheflin, A.A. and Brown, D. (1996) 'Repressed memory or dissociative amnesia: What the science says.' *Journal of Psychiatry and Law 24,* 143–188.

Schoener, G.P. (1993) 'Common errors in treatment of victims/survivors of sexual misconduct by professionals.' *Dulwich Centre Newsletter 3 and 4,* pp.55–61.

Schoener, G.P. (2008) 'Foreword.' In S. Richardson and M. Cunningham *Broken Boundaries: Stories of Betrayal in Relationships of Care.* London: WITNESS.

Schoener, G.P., Milgram, J., Gonsiorek, J., Luepker, E. and Conroe, R. (1989) *Psychotherapists' Sexual Involvement with Clients: Intervention and Prevention.* Minneapolis, MN: Walk In Counselling Center.

Schore, A.N. (2001) 'The effects of early relational trauma on right brain development, affect regulation and infant mental health.' *Infant Mental Health Journal 22,* 201–269.

Schore, A.N. (2003a) *Affect Dysregulation and Disorders of the Self.* New York: Norton.

Schore, A.N. (2003b) *Affect Dysregulation and the Repair of the Self.* New York: Norton.

Schuchter, S.R. and Zisook, S. (1993) 'The Course of Normal Grief.' In M.S. Stroebe, W. Stroebe and R.O. Hansson (eds) *Handbook of Bereavement: Theory, Research and Intervention.* New York: Cambridge University Press.

Schwartz, H.L. (2000) *Dialogues with Forgotten Voices: Relational Perspectives on Child Abuse Trauma and Treatment of Dissociative Disorders.* New York: Basic Books.

Scott, J.P. (1987) 'The Emotional Basis of Attachment and Separation.' In J.L. Sacksteder,D.P. Schwartz and Y. Akabane (eds) *Attachment and the Therapeutic Process: Essays in Honor of Otto Allen Will Jr., MD.* Madison, CT: International Universities Press.

Secretary of State for the Home Department (2003) *Safety and Justice: The Government's Proposals on Domestic Violence.* London: The Stationery Office.

Seligman, M.E.P. (1975) *Helplessness: On Depression, Development and Death.* San Francisco, CA: W.H. Freeman.

Shapiro, F. (1995) *Eye Movement Desensitisation and Reprocessing: Principles, Protocolsand Procedures.* New York: Guilford Press.

Shaver, P., Hazan, C. and Bradshaw, D. (1988) 'Love as Attachment: The Integration of Three Behavioural Systems.' In R.J. Sternberg and M. Barnes (eds) *The Psychology of Love.* New Haven, CT: Yale University Press.

Shaw, R. (2003) *The Embodied Therapist: The Therapist's Body Story.* Hove, UK: Brunner-Routledge.

Shaw, R. (2004) 'The embodied psychotherapist: An exploration of the therapist's somatic phenomena within the therapeutic encounter.' *Psychotherapy Research 14,* 3, 271–288.

Shengold, L. (1989) *Soul Murder: The Effects of Childhood Abuse and Deprivation.* New Haven, CT: Yale University Press.

Shepherd, J. (1990) 'Victims of personal violence: The relevance of Symond's model of psychological response and loss theory.' *British Journal of Social Work 20,* 309–332.

Siddiqui, H. (2003) 'Asian and Ethnic Minority Women's Groups.' In S. Amiel and J. Heath (eds) *Family Violence in Primary Care.* Oxford: Oxford University Press.

Siegel, D. (1999) *The Developing Mind.* New York: Guilford Press.

Simon, R. (1995) 'The natural history of therapist sexual misconduct: identification and prevention.' *Psychiatric Annals 25,* 90–94.

Sinason, V. (2008) 'How do we help ourselves?' In S. Benamer and K. White (eds) *Trauma and Attachment.* London: Karnac Books.

Skuse, D., Bentovim, A., Hodges, J., Stevenson, J., Andreou, C., Lanvado, M., New, M., Williams, B. and McMillan, D. (2003) 'Risk factors for development of sexually abusive behaviour in sexually victimised adolescent boys: cross sectional study.' *The Lancet 361,* 9356, 471–476.

Solomon, R.C. (2002) *Spirituality for the Skeptic: The Thoughtful Love of Life.* New York: Oxford University Press.

Spinelli, E. (1994) *Demystifying Therapy.* London: Constable.

St Just, A. (1999) 'Lecture Notes for a Workshop on Trauma.' University of Surrey, Guildford, UK.

Stark, E. and Flitcraft, A.H. (1988) 'Women and children at risk: A feminist perspective on child abuse.' *International Journal of Health Studies 18,* 1, 97–119.

Stark, E. and Flitcraft, A.H. (1996) *Women at Risk: Domestic Violence and Women's Health.* London: Sage.

Steele, K.S., van der Hart, O. and Nijenhuis, E.R.R. (2001) 'Dependency in the treatment of complex posttraumatic stress and dissociative disorders.' *Journal of Trauma and Dissociation 2,* 4, 79–116.

Stein, H., Allen, J.G. and Hill, J. (2003) 'Roles and relationships: A psychoeducational approach to reviewing strengths and difficulties in adulthood functioning.' *Bulletin of the Menninger Clinic 67,* 281–313.

Stern, D.N. (1985) *The Interpersonal World of the Infant: A View from Psychoanalysis and Developmental Psychology.* New York: Basic Books.

Stien, P.T. and Kendall, J. (2004) *Psychological Trauma and the Developing Brain: Neurologically Based Interventions for Troubled Children.* New York: Haworth Maltreatment and Trauma Press.

Stosny, S. (1995) *Treating Attachment Abuse: A Compassionate Approach.* New York: Springer.

Streeck-Fischer, A. and van der Kolk, B.A. (2000) 'Down will come baby, cradle and all: Diagnostic and therapeutic implications of chronic trauma in child development.' *Australian and New Zealand Journal of Psychiatry 34,* 903–918.

Stroebe, W. and Stroebe, M.S. (1987) *The Psychological and Physical Consequences of Partner Loss.* Cambridge: Cambridge University Press.

The Survivors Trust (2008) Information available at www.thesurvivorstrust.org/info/media.aspx, accessed 30 September 2009.

Sutton, J (2004) 'Understanding dissociation and its relationship to self injury and childhood trauma.' *Counselling and Psychotherapy Journal,* April 24–27.

Sutton, J (2005) *Healing the Hurt Within: Understand Self-injury and Self-harm, and Heal the Emotional Wounds.* Oxford: How To Books.

Szinovacz, M.E. (1983) 'Using couple data as a methodological tool: The case of marital violence.' *Journal of Marriage and the Family 45,* 633–644.

Tedeschi, R.G. (1999) 'Violence transformed: Posttraumatic growth in survivors and their societies.' *Aggression and Violent Behaviour 4,* 319–341.

Teicher, M.H. (2000) 'Wounds that time won't heal: the neurobiology of child abuse.' *Cerebrum 2,* 4, 50–67.

Terr, L.C. (1991) 'Childhood traumas: An outline and overview.' *American Journal of Psychiatry 148,* 1, 10–20.

Terr, L.C. (1994) *Unchained Memories.* New York: Basic Books.

Thomas, G. (1990) 'Institutional child abuse, the making and prevention of an un-problem.' *Journal of Child and Youth Care 4,* 6, 1–22.

Thornhill, R. and Palmer, C.T. (2000) *A Natural History of Rape: Biological Basis of Sexual Coercion.* Cambridge, MA: MIT Press.

UKCP (UK Council for Psychotherapy) (2005) *Code of Ethics.* London: UKCP.

United Nations (2004) *The UN Research Development and Statistics Directorate Convention Against Transnational Organized Crime and its Protocols.* New York: United Nations.

Valenti-Heim, D. and Schwartz, L. (1995) *The Sexual Abuse Interview for Those with Developmental Disabilities.* Santa Barbara, CA: James Stanfield Company.

van der Kolk, B.A. (1987) *Psychological Trauma.* Washington, DC: American Psychiatric Press.

van der Kolk, B.A. (1989) 'The compulsion to repeat the trauma: Re-enactment, revictimisation, and masochism.' *Psychiatric Clinics of North America 12,* 2, 389–411.

van der Kolk, B.A. (1994) 'The body keeps the score: Memory and evolving psychobiology of post-traumatic stress.' *Harvard Review of Psychiatry 1,* 253–265.

van der Kolk, B.A. (1997) 'Trauma, Memory and Self Regulation: Clinical Applications of Current Research.' Paper presented at Harvard Medical School Summer Seminars, Nantucket, MA, September 1997.

van der Kolk, B.A. (2004) 'The future of trauma work.' *Counselling and Psychotherapy Journal 15,* 4, 10–13.

van der Kolk, B.A. (2005) 'Developmental trauma disorder.' *Psychiatric Annals 35,* 401–408.

van der Kolk, B.A. (2008) 'The John Bowlby Lecture 2006: Developmental Trauma Disorder: A New Rational Diagnosis for Children with Complex Trauma Histories.' In S. Benamer and K. White (eds) *Trauma and Attachment.* London: Karnac Books.

van der Kolk, B.A. and Fisler, R.E. (1995) 'Dissociation and the fragmentary nature of traumatic memories: Overview and exploratory study.' *Journal of Traumatic Stress 8,* 505–525.

van der Kolk, B.A., McFarlane, A.C. and Weisaeth, L (eds) (1996) *Traumatic Stress: The Effects of Overwhelming Experiences on Mind, Body and Society.* New York: Guilford Press.

van der Kolk, B.A., Roth, S., Pelcovitz, D., Sunday, S. and Spinazzola, J. (2005) 'Disorders of extreme stress: The empirical foundation of complex adaptation to trauma.' *Journal of Traumatic Stress 18*, 5, 389–399.

van Deurzen-Smith, E. (1988) *Existential Counselling in Action.* London: Sage.

Vaughan, G. (2000) 'Violence, Sexuality and Gay Male Domestic Violence.' In K. Buckley and P. Head (eds) *Myths, Risks and Sexuality.* Lyme Regis, UK: Russell House.

Walby, S. (2004) *The Cost of Domestic Violence.* London: Women and Equality Unit.

Walby, S. and Allen, J. (2004) *Domestic Violence, Sexual Assault and Stalking: Findings from the British Crime Survey.* Home Office Research Study no. 276. London: Home Office.

Walker, E.A., Katon, W., Russo, J., Ciechanowski, P., Newman, E. and Wagner, A.W. (2003) 'Health care costs associated with posttraumatic stress disorder symptoms in women.' *Archives of General Psychiatry 60*, 369–374.

Walker, L.E. (1979) *The Battered Woman.* New York: Harper & Row.

Walker, L.E. (1984) *The Battered Woman Syndrome.* New York: Springer.

Walker, R., Logan, T.K. and Jordan, C.E. (2004) 'An integrative review of separation in the context of victimisation: Consequences and implications for women.' *Trauma Violence Abuse 5*, 2, 143–193.

Wastell, C. (2005) *Understanding Trauma and Emotion: Dealing with Trauma – An Emotion Focussed Approach.* Maidenhead: Open University Press.

Wellard, S. (2003) 'Victims on the margins.' *Community Care,* 6–12 March, 32.

Welldon, E.V. (2004) *Mother, Madonna, Whore: The Idealisation and Denigration of Motherhood.* London: Karnac Books.

Whittaker, T. (1997) 'Rethinking Elder Abuse: Towards an Age and Gender Integrated Theory of Elder Abuse.' In P. Decalmer and F. Glendenning (eds) *The Mistreatment of Elderly People.* Second edition. London: Sage.

Williams, L.M. (1995) 'Recovered memories of abuse in women with documented child sexual victimisation histories.' *Journal of Traumatic Stress 8*, 649–673.

Williamson, E. (2006) *Women's Aid Federation of England 2005 Survey of Domestic Violence Services Findings.* London: Women's Aid Federation.

Wilson, J.P. (2002) 'The Abyss Experience and Catastrophic Stress.' Paper presented at St Joseph's University, Philadelphia, PA, 11 October 2002.

Wilson, J.P. (2003) *Empathic Strain and Posttraumatic Therapy.* New York: Guilford Press.

Wilson, J.P. (2004) 'Broken Spirits.' In J.P. Wilson and B. Drozdek (eds) *Broken Spirits: The Treatment of Traumatized Asylum Seekers, Refugees, and War and Torture Victims.* New York: Brunner-Routledge.

Wilson, J.P. (2006) 'The Posttraumatic Self.' In J.P. Wilson (ed.) *The Posttraumatic Self: Restoring Meaning and Wholeness to Personality.* New York: Routledge.

Wilson, J.P. and Lindy, J.D. (eds) (1994) *Countertransference in the Treatment of PTSD.* New York: Guilford.

Wilson, J. P. and Thomas, R.B. (2004) *Empathy in the Treatment of Trauma and PTSD.* New York: Brunner Routledge.

Wilson, J.P., Friedman, M.J. and Lindy, J.D. (2001) *Treating Psychological Trauma and PTSD.* New York: Guilford Press.

Winchester, R. (2002) 'Common assault.' *Community Care,* 14–20 November, 24–26.

Winnicott, D.W. (1958) *Collected Papers: Through Paediatrics to Psychoanalysis.* London: Tavistock.

Winnicott, D.W. (1960) 'Ego Distortion in Terms of True and False Self.' In J.D. Sutherland (ed.) *The Maturational Processes and the Facilitating Environment.* London: Hogarth Press.

Winnicott, D.W. (1965) *The Maturational Process and the Facilitating Environment: Studies in the Theory of Emotional Development.* New York: International Universities Press.

Wolfe, D.A., Francis, K.J. and Straatman, A.L. (2006) 'Child abuse in religiously-affiliated institutions: long-term impact on men's mental health.' *Child Abuse & Neglect 30*, 205–212.

Women's Aid Federation (2005) *The Survivor's Handbook.* Bristol: Women's Aid Federation.

Worden, J.W. (2003) *Grief Counselling and Grief Therapy: A Handbook for the Mental Health Practitioner.* Third edition. London: Brunner-Routledge.

World Health Organisation (2000) *Factsheet no. 239.* Quoted in Women's Aid Federation (2005) *Domestic Violence: Frequently Asked Questions Factsheet 2004/2005.* London:

Women's Aid Federation.

World Health Organisation (2002) *Abuse of the Elderly – Facts.* Geneva: WHO.

World Health Organisation (2006) *Intimate Partner Violence and Alcohol.* Geneva: WHO.

World Health Organisation (2007) *The ICD-10 Classification of Mental and Behavioural Disorders: Clinical Descriptions and Diagnostic Guidelines.* Geneva: WHO.

Wortman, C.B., Battle, E. and Lemkau, J.P. (1997) 'Coming to Terms with the Sudden Death of a Spouse or Child.' In A.J. Lurigio, W.G. Skogan and R.C. Davis (eds) *Victims of Crime: Problems, Policies and Programs.* Second edition. Newbury Park, CA: Sage.

Woskett, V. (1999) *The Therapeutic Use of Self.* London: Routledge.

Wyre, R (2002) 'Our little secret.' In B. Long and B. McLachlan (eds) *The Hunt for Britain's Paedophiles.* London: Hodder and Stoughton.

Yalom, I. (1980) *Existential Psychotherapy.* New York: Basic Books.

Yalom, I. (2008) *Staring at the Sun: Overcoming the Dread of Death.* London: Piatkus.

Yassen, J. (1995) 'Preventing Secondary Traumatic Stress Disorder.' In C.R. Figley (ed.) *Compassion Fatigue: Coping with Secondary Stress Disorder in Those who Treat the Traumatized.* New York: Brunner/Mazel.

Zimbardo, P. (1969) *The Human Choice: Individuation, Reason and Order versus Deindividuation, Impulse and Chaos.* Lincoln, NE: University of Nebraska.

Zimmerman, C., Hossain, M., Yun, K., Roche, B., Morison, L. and Watts, C. (2006) 'Stolen smiles: The physical and psychological health consequences of women and adolescents trafficked in Europe.' Presentation on health consequences among women who have been trafficked and the implications for services and policy. London School of Hygiene and Tropical Medicine. Full report available at www.lshtm.ac.uk/genderviolence/recent.htm, accessed 3 September 2009.

SUBJECT INDEX

AUTHOR INDEX